PERFECTLY LEGAL
400 Foolproof Methods for Paying Less Taxes
1985 Edition

PERFECTLY LEGAL
400 Foolproof Methods for Paying Less Taxes
1985 Edition

BARRY R. STEINER, CPA

and

DAVID W. KENNEDY, MBA, JD

JOHN WILEY & SONS, New York Chichester Brisbane Toronto Singapore

ISBN 0-471-81639-6
ISBN 0-471-81638-8 (pbk.)

Printed in the United States of America

10 9 8 7 6 5 4 3 2 1

To Shauna, Miriam, and Marcie
and all other tax-deductible children,
wherever they may be

Preface

This is the fourth edition of a highly popular book. For this edition we have added more than 50 new questions and one new chapter. Among the topics newly covered are the Alternative Minimum Tax and a chapter on tax strategies that were not covered in previous editions.

The question and answer format in this book is unique among volumes on taxes, and readers find it an excellent way to learn about this normally complex subject. As with earlier editions, brevity, clarity, and accuracy are our major objectives.

Once again, we include the *Audit Technique Handbook for Internal Revenue Agents*. It has proved invaluable to readers and their advisors, giving them an idea of what to expect if they should be audited.

Our main goal is to help you save as much in taxes as you are legally entitled to. We sincerely hope that we succeed in that task.

Tax laws and regulations are continuously being reinterpreted and changed by Congress, by the courts, and by the Internal Revenue Service. For that reason it is always wise to seek competent tax advice from a specialist before making final tax-oriented decisions.

Barry R. Steiner
David W. Kennedy

Coral Springs, Florida
New York, New York
October 1984

> The forms included in this volume are for identification and information purposes only. The newest forms applicable to the latest tax year may differ slightly in content. You should of course obtain the most up to date forms from your local IRS office.

Contents

PERFECTLY LEGAL
400 Foolproof Methods for Paying Less Taxes
1985 Edition

1. Audits, Refunds, and Bookkeeping

Although an audit of your tax return normally occurs months or years after you have completed and filed it, if you are a typical taxpayer you worry more about an audit than any other tax matter. The answers to the questions in this chapter will indicate that an audit of your tax return need not be a fear-provoking experience.

One key to avoiding an audit is more important than all others. If you can substantiate a deduction with proper documentation, such as a receipt or cancelled check, and you attach an explanatory note to your return when you file it, your chances of being audited will probably be considerably lessened.

One other thing about an audit: if you must appear in person, take a professional into the audit with you. Unless you are a tax expert, the Internal Revenue Service offices can be an intimidating place.

The questions and answers that follow offer advice on what to expect during an audit and how to appeal an audit if you are dissatisfied with its results.

The chapter includes information about deductions that may invite an audit of your tax return, how returns are audited, common tax return errors, and average refunds.

Hows and Whys of Being Audited

Q I am afraid of being audited. Is there a best time of the year between January 1 and April 15 to file?

A Wait until April 14 to file. Returns are selected for audit on a first-come–first-served basis. Agents are under great pressure to clear up previous years' audits and get started on the new batch of returns. Filing at the last minute gives your return a better chance of passing through the computers—but this method is not foolproof.

Q A friend had his taxes audited for his return filed two years ago. Can the Internal Revenue Service (IRS) really do that?

A It sure can. The law permits the IRS to go back three years to audit a return. However, if the return reflects an understatement of 25% or more of gross income, the limitation period is six years. And, if the return is entirely fraudulent there is no limitation period at all.

Q Is it a fact that if you claim the home office deduction, you are marking your own return for audit?

A Not necessarily. If you use a room at home *exclusively and regularly* as an office for meeting clients, patients, or customers. Even the partial use of a room qualifies if the furniture is arranged in such a way as to give the appearance of a separated work area and you have no other office space. You have every legal right to claim the deduction. (See Chapter 17.)

Q Is it true that if you are audited by more than one agent you are in big trouble?

A It sure is. The second agent may be a special agent, one who is called in only when the IRS thinks you may be a candidate for criminal prosecution. If you are audited by a second agent, you had better call an attorney quickly.

Q Does the IRS have a method for selecting tax returns for audit? What are the chances of my particular return being chosen?

A Tax returns to be audited are chosen by computer, and the chances of an average return being selected is 1 in 50. Of course certain professionals such as doctors, dentists, and airline pilots are selected for audit much more frequently than the average person; if you are a member of one of those professions, you should go out of your way to keep good records.

Q If I am audited, what kind of evidence should I bring to back up my deductions?

A Bring all the original documents you can find. Receipts, cancelled checks, and the like are the best evidence, but any evidence that can back up your claim may give you a shot at taking at least part of the deduction. The moral of the story here is document everything and, whenever possible, pay by check or get receipts for cash transactions.

Q Once I get my refund from the IRS, am I off the hook for that year as far as audits are concerned?

A No. As soon as your return is received, it is keypunched and checked for mathematical accuracy. If the math checks out and a refund is called for, it is mailed out in short order. The IRS still has three years from the due date of your return to call you in for an examination. Long after your refund is spent, the keypunched figures are fed into a computer and compared against a complex set of standards; if your return deviates from the norm by too much, the computer rejects it. The rejected return is reviewed by agents who then decide whether the IRS should try to add a little excitement to your life.

Q My medical expense deduction was large last year. Will that be more likely than not to provoke an audit? If not, which deductions will?

A The IRS is much more interested in claims for business travel and entertainment expenses as well as large, nonreimbursed business expenses than anything else. Those items are much more likely to provoke an audit than any other deductions.

Q Are there any deductions that the average individual should be aware of as possibly provoking audits?

A Yes. Seven.

1 Noncash contributions–for example, food, clothing or automobiles–that total over $200.
2 Casualty losses over $500.
3 Tax shelters with losses in excess of $25,000 per year.
4 Gift lease-back arrangements.
5 Excessive travel and entertainment expenses.
6 Family trusts.
7 Interest paid to family members.

Q After all the computer processing is over and an agent reviews my tax return, are there any questions that he might ask himself to determine whether my return is worth going after?

A The agent will ask the following five questions:

1 Does the refund look high in relation to income and exemptions?
2 Could the taxpayer be in a business where payment is made in cash?
3 If a business return, is gross profit ratio in line?
4 Can the taxpayer support his family on reported income?
5 Was the zero bracket (standard deduction) used with a large gross income and low net income? (The incidence of fraud is high in this category.)

Q I guess I am lucky–I have never been audited. What I want to know is how will I be notified of an audit?

A If your return is selected, you will most probably be notified by a letter that will give you an appointment at the local IRS office. The letter will also tell you what items are being questioned and exactly what verification to bring along. If for any reason you can't keep the appointment, you can request a change of location or you can ask for a postponement to get your records in order.

Q What are the odds that my return will be audited?

A According to the Internal Revenue Service the odds for any return's being audited for the 1982 tax year were 1 in 55 or 1.55 percent. But if your gross income was over $50,000 your odds rise significantly to 4.93 percent.

Q Is there a list of the most common errors found on tax returns? I am interested because I want to get my refund as speedily as possible; I have plans for the money.

A The most common errors include the following:

1 Mathematical mistakes.
2 Failure to attach W-2 forms.
3 Failure to enclose a check for the amount due.
4 Incorrect computation of the zero bracket amount.
5 Failure to claim earned income credit.
6 Use of the wrong social security number.
7 Failure to have both spouses sign a joint return.
8 Forgetting to attach necessary schedules.
9 Placing entries on wrong lines.

Q What is the procedure for obtaining an extension of time to file my tax return?

A You must file Form 4868 before April 15. This gives you an automatic four-month extension, but you should be aware that you will be assessed a fine for late payment of your taxes.

Q I have been called for an audit. My question is, should I have my accountant present when I go to the audit?

A If your accountant prepared your return, he should certainly go with you to the audit. Remember, your accountant and the IRS agent speak the same language. Even though your accountant will charge you a fee to go to the audit, it will be money well spent.

Q I am in business and I can't take time off to go to an IRS office. I have been notified that my last year's return is being audited. Can the agent come to my home?

A Yes. A field agent will come to your home on a mutually agreeable date. You have an advantage when the agent comes to you: away from the intimidating atmosphere of the IRS office, you may be able to talk more freely. One disadvantage, however, is that field agents are better trained than office auditors, and they may find many more errors in your return.

Q If I am called in for an examination and I go without my accountant or attorney, what should I say during the examination?

A Nothing, if at all possible. Smile a lot. Don't volunteer anything. Let the agent set the pace of the audit. If you feel strongly about a particular point, make it obvious and chances are the agent will back off. This approach works particularly well if the agent should challenge you about charitable contributions.

Q I want to file an amended 1982 return. Is there anything I should know about before I file the amended return?

A Yes. You should be aware that the IRS will probably audit your return. Amended returns are almost always audited. So make sure that everything is correct on the return and don't take anything for granted.

Q After I have been audited and I agree with the agent's findings that I owe additional taxes, what should I do?

A If all the taxes are agreed on, the agent will tell you how much is owed and will try to get you to sign an agreement form. Once you've signed, you will have lost all rights of appeal, so try to delay signing unless the amount in question is under, say, $50. Never sign a blank agreement form where the agent says the numbers will be filled in later. If you agree to the change, you'll get a written report and a bill for the amount due plus interest. You can either pay the deficiency at that point or you can set up an installment payment plan. But you must ask to pay on the installment plan, because the IRS won't volunteer that such a payment plan exists.

Q What in the world is a TCMP audit, and why is it so dreaded?

A This is the most comprehensive, tedious audit you could imagine. The initials stand for Taxpayer Compliance Measurement Program. The auditor will ask you to prove absolutely everything on your tax return, even asking you for your children's birth certificates. Under no circumstances should you go into a TCMP audit without calling a tax accountant or attorney to go with you.

Q A neighbor had a disagreement with the IRS to the tune of $3000. He said he went to Small Claims Court to settle it. You can't go to small claims on a tax matter, can you?

A You can when it is the new small claims division of Tax Court and the amount in disagreement is under $10,000. These courts are scattered throughout the country. You don't need a lawyer to represent you–you can do it yourself. The paper work necessary is relatively simple and straightforward, but you must know that there is no appeal from the court's decision no matter what it is.

Q I walked out of an audit a few hours ago. I want to appeal just about all the changes that were made. How can I do that?

A You can request a meeting with the agent's supervisor. If that is unsatisfactory, you will receive a transmittal letter notifying you of the right to appeal within thirty days. You do this by simply addressing a letter to the district director with your request for an appeal. An appeals officer will hear your case. If you want to appeal further you go to the Tax Court or District Court, depending on your case. If you have not paid the taxes the IRS claims are due, you can only appeal to the tax court. In order to file an appeal in a U.S. District Court, the taxes must be paid in full.

Q I feel that the IRS is harrassing me. For three years in a row it has audited me, and identical issues are raised each time. What can I do?

A Although the IRS has the right to audit you each year, it can't audit you on the same problem year by year. If you were audited for one of the last three years and you received a No Change Report, mail a copy of that form letter to the agent in charge of your case. That should take care of it. When you do next year's taxes, be ultraconservative by only taking deductions where you have receipts. In case of an audit, you'll have your No Change letter.

Q I am a member of a partnership and we must file a partnership tax return. What are the chances of the return being audited?

A The IRS is paying particular attention to partnership returns. If you report a loss of $25,000 or more, you are almost certain to be audited.

Q A friend of mine was audited last year and he said it was because he had a bank account in Bermuda. I have an account in Nassau in the Bahamas. Will I be subject to audit as a result of it?

A Quite possibly. The IRS doesn't like to see "offshore" banking activities. In their view it means you are trying to hide some income, and if they find out that you have an account in the Bahamas, you will probably be audited.

On Schedule B, Part III you are asked whether or not you have a bank account in a foreign country. You should, of course, answer the question honestly. (See page xx for Schedule B, Part III.)

Q Do you have any general advice for someone facing an audit for the first time?

A First of all, don't panic. Spend as much time as possible reviewing your return and accumulating verification, that is, receipts and canceled checks. If you go into your first audit well prepared, you can't help but impress the agent that you know what you are doing. This way if there is an occasional item you can't locate, you'll usually get the benefit of the doubt—just so the case can be closed. By the way, if there is an item of proof you can't find, don't concede the point. Frequently the agent will accept some secondary form of verification, and in many cases your word will suffice.

Getting That Refund

Q Most taxpayers work for a salary and have taxes withheld from their paychecks. Has anybody ever figured out what the average refund for all taxpayers is?

A Yes. The average refund is $748. The reason for this rather high figure is that most taxpayers have too much taken out of their pay each year.

Q I want to maximize my tax refund. My employer told me that I can file a new W-4 form claiming that I am single when in fact I am married. Can I actually do that?

A Yes, you can. Single individuals are taxed at a higher rate than marrieds, and you can adjust your W-4 so that more tax is withheld. You can claim fewer exemptions than you are entitled to, but not more. (See Form W-4 at the end of the chapter.)

Q Do you have any reading on how long it will take after I file my return for a refund to be sent to me? I am expecting a large refund and it would sure help to pay some large bills.

A Normally, according to the IRS, you can expect your refund eight to ten weeks after you file your return. If you file by January 15 you should have the money in your hands by about March 30.

Proper Bookkeeping Procedures

Q I know I should keep my records organized to be prepared for an audit, but every year I have trouble putting my records together. When is the best time to assemble my records? Is there a preferred method of assembling them?

A You should put your records together at the same time you prepare your tax returns. The best way to do it is this: Put all receipts and canceled checks into envelopes by category and write the category on each envelope; make a copy of your tax return, put a rubber band around everything and put the entire package in a tax-deductible safe-deposit box.

Q I pride myself on being prepared for all contingencies. What documentation should I bring to an audit if I should be called for one?

A Bring documentation only for the items that are being questioned. Leave other returns and supporting data at home. But the information you bring along should be very well organized, preferably with adding machine tapes attached.

In General

Q I have heard that I can make some money by being an IRS informant. I know of some people who cheated on their taxes. Should I tell the IRS about them?

A If you are looking for money, you won't get rich by informing on people. In 1983, out of 5062 informants, only 1172 received any IRS rewards and these averaged only $534.23 apiece—hardly enough to make it worth losing a friend.

Q My taxes were done two years ago by a young certified public accountant who was a friend of my son. Unfortunately the young man made a mistake on my return, and a penalty was assessed against me. Because the tax preparer made the mistake, he paid the penalty for me. But the IRS came back and said that the penalty paid by the young man on my behalf is income to me. Can the IRS do that?

A Yes. The IRS has ruled that in such cases the penalty paid by a tax preparer is taxable income to the taxpayer whose return was penalized. Sorry about that.

Q The IRS touts the fact that it gives free tax advice during the tax season. But I have heard that the people who give the advice don't know what they are talking about. Can I depend on their advice?

A If you ask the IRS about some point and are given an answer, don't expect that to be a defense during an audit. Usually the people answering those toll-free numbers have limited training, and you can't realistically expect them to give you an answer that will cut your taxes.

Q Almost everything I read tells me I should have an accountant help me prepare my taxes. Fine, but how do I choose one?

A Pick one that is recommended by a co-worker, family member, or friend. The best accountant would be one who specializes in taxes for those in your profession or job. There is a big difference, by the way, between a tax preparer who disappears after April 15 and a tax advisor who is available all year round for tax advice.

Q I hear rumors all the time that there is a quota system at the IRS. What do you know about it?

A There is an unofficial quota system. Production in IRS terms is measured in money--your money, to be exact. Although IRS headquarters frowns on any quota system, there is no better way for a supervisor to evaluate an agent's performance than by the dollars generated through audits.

Q I filed my taxes late last year and I incurred a tax penalty. I know that some taxes such as state income and sales taxes are deductible, but are penalties deductible also?

A If you are hit with a tax penalty such as a late filing fee, you cannot deduct that on the following year's return. However, interest charged by the IRS on any deficiency is deductible.

Q I know that the top tax rate is 50 percent. When the tax rates are lowered, will the 50 percent bracket be reduced?

A No. It is true that some of the top limits have been reduced, but the highest rate is still 50 percent. If you are single and your taxable income is over $55,300, you will be taxed at the 50 percent rate; for joint filers taxable income must be $109,400 before the 50 percent rate applies.

Q I know I should file a new W-4 form if the number of exemptions I claim increases. How about if the number decreases? My daughter was recently married.

A Just as you should file a new W-4 on an increase you must do the same for a decrease. As a matter of fact there is a legal requirement that you inform your employer within 10 days of the decrease so that the proper adjustment can be made in your tax withholding.

Q My company's payroll department circulated a memo to all employees telling them that they should update their W-4 forms in light of some new tax rules. I understood that the only thing you could put on your W-4 was the number of family exemptions you have. For instance, I always declare four exemptions for my spouse, my two children, and myself. Am I wrong?

A Yes. You have always been allowed to take all your family exemptions as well as a number of "withholding allowances" such as your itemized deductions and some tax credits. Now you can add six new items: the marriage penalty deduction, employee business expenses, contributions to an IRA, any tax decrease due to income averaging, moving expenses, and net losses from various business or investment operations. This means that you can claim up to 13 exemptions and allowances without your employer having to submit a copy of your W-4 to the IRS. The back of the W-4 Form that follows this chapter shows the proper worksheet. If you make $30,000 or more a year, the additional exemptions can mean at least $100 more in your pocket each pay period.

Form **W-4** (Rev. January 1984)

Department of the Treasury—Internal Revenue Service

Employee's Withholding Allowance Certificate

OMB No. 1545-0010

1 Type or print your full name	2 Your social security number
Home address (number and street or rural route)	3 Marital Status: ☐ Single ☐ Married ☐ Married, but withhold at higher Single rate **Note:** If married, but legally separated, or spouse is a nonresident alien, check the Single box.
City or town, State, and ZIP code	

4 Total number of allowances you are claiming (from line F of the worksheet on page 2) . . . .

5 Additional amount, if any, you want deducted from each pay . . . . $

6 I claim exemption from withholding because (see instructions and check boxes below that apply):

a ☐ Last year I did not owe any Federal income tax and had a right to a full refund of **ALL** income tax withheld, **AND**

b ☐ This year I do not expect to owe any Federal income tax and expect to have a right to a full refund of **ALL** income tax withheld. If both a and b apply, enter the year effective and "EXEMPT" here . . . ▶ Year

c If you entered "EXEMPT" on line 6b, are you a full-time student? . . . . ☐ **Yes** ☐ **No**

Under penalties of perjury, I certify that I am entitled to the number of withholding allowances claimed on this certificate, or if claiming exemption from withholding, that I am entitled to claim the exempt status.

Employee's signature ▶ Date ▶ , 19

7 Employer's name and address **(Employer: Complete 7, 8, and 9 only if sending to IRS)**	8 Office code	9 Employer identification number

SAMPLE

Detach along this line. Give the top part of this form to employer; keep the lower part for your records.

Privacy Act and Paperwork Reduction Act Notice.—If you do not give your employer a certificate, you will be treated as a single person with no withholding allowances as required by law. We ask for this information to carry out the Internal Revenue laws of the United States. We may give the information to the Dept. of Justice for civil or criminal litigation and to the States and the District of Columbia for use in administering their tax laws.

Purpose.—The law requires that you complete Form W-4 so that your employer can withhold Federal income tax from your pay. Your Form W-4 remains in effect until you change it or, if you entered "EXEMPT" on line 6b above, until February 15 of next year. By correctly completing this form, you can fit the amount of tax withheld from your wages to your tax liability.

If you got a large refund last year, you may be having too much tax withheld. If so, you may want to increase the number of your allowances on line 4 by claiming any other allowances you are entitled to. The kinds of allowances, and how to figure them, are explained in detail below.

If you owed a large amount of tax last year, you may not be having enough tax withheld. If so, you can claim fewer allowances on line 4, or ask that an additional amount be withheld on line 5, or both.

If the number of withholding allowances you are entitled to claim decreases to less than you are now claiming, you must file a new W-4 with your employer within 10 days.

The instructions below explain how to fill in Form W-4. **Publication 505,** Tax Withholding and Estimated Tax, contains more information on withholding. You can get it from most IRS offices.

For more information about who qualifies as your dependent, what deductions you can take, and what tax credits you qualify for, see the Form 1040 Instructions.

You may be fined $500 if you file, with no reasonable basis, a W-4 that results in less tax being withheld than is properly allowable. In addition, criminal penalties apply for willfully supplying false or fraudulent information or failing to supply information requiring an increase in withholding.

Line-By-Line Instructions

Fill in the identifying information in Boxes 1 and 2. If you are married and want tax withheld at the regular rate for married persons, check "Married" in Box 3. If you are married and want tax withheld at the higher Single rate (because both you and your spouse work, for example), check "Married, but withhold at higher Single rate" in Box 3.

Line 4 of Form W-4

Total number of allowances.—Use the worksheet on page 2 to figure your allowances. Add the number of allowances for each category explained below. Enter the total on line 4.

If you are single and hold more than one job, you may not claim the same allowances with more than one employer at the same time. If you are married and both you and your spouse are employed, you may not both claim the same allowances with both of your employers at the same time. To have the highest amount of tax withheld, claim "0" allowances on line 4.

A. Personal allowances.—You can claim the following personal allowances:

1 for yourself, 1 if you are 65 or older, and 1 if you are blind.

If you are married and your spouse either does not work or is not claiming his or her allowances on a separate W-4, you may also claim the following allowances: 1 for your spouse, 1 if your spouse is 65 or older, and 1 if your spouse is blind.

B. Special withholding allowance.—Claim the special withholding allowance if you are single and have one job or you are married, have one job, and your spouse does not work. You may still claim this allowance so long as the total wages earned on other jobs by you or your spouse (or both) is 10% or less of the combined total wages. Use this special withholding allowance only to figure your withholding. Do not claim it when you file your return.

C. Allowances for dependents.—You may claim one allowance for each dependent you will be able to claim on your Federal income tax return.

Note: *If you are not claiming any deductions or credits, skip D and E, add lines A, B, and C, enter the total on line F and carry the total over to line 4 of W-4.*

Before you claim allowances under D and E, total your non-wage taxable income (interest, dividends, self-employment income, etc.) and subtract this amount from estimated deductions you would otherwise enter in D1. If your non-wage income is greater than the amount of estimated deductions, you cannot claim any allowances under D. Moreover, you should take one-third of the excess (non-wage income over estimated deductions) and add this to the appropriate "A" value in Table 1 if determining allowances under E.

D. Allowances for estimated deductions.—If you expect to itemize deductions, you can claim additional withholding allowances. See Schedule A (Form 1040) for deductions you can itemize.

You can also count deductible amounts you pay for (1) alimony (2) qualified retirement contributions including IRA and Keogh (H.R. 10) plans (3) moving expenses (4) employee business expenses (Part I of Form 2106) (5) the deduction for a married couple when both work (6) net losses shown on Schedules C, D, E, and F (Form 1040), the last line of Part II of Form 4797, and the net operating loss carryover (7) penalty on early withdrawal of savings and (8) charitable contributions for nonitemizers. **Note:** Check with your employer to see if any tax is being withheld on moving expenses or IRA contributions. Do not include these amounts if tax is not being withheld; otherwise, you may be underwithheld. For details, see **Publication 505.**

The deduction allowed a married couple when both work is 10% of the lesser of $30,000 or the qualified earned income of the spouse with the lower income.

Once you have determined these deductions, enter the total on line D1 of the worksheet on page 2 and figure the number of withholding allowances for them.

E. Allowances for tax credits.—If you expect to take credits like those shown on lines 41 through 48 on the 1983 Form 1040 (child care, residential energy, etc.), use the table on the top of page 2 to figure the number of additional allowances you can claim. You may estimate these credits. Include the earned income credit if you are not receiving advance payment of it, and any excess social security tax withheld. Also, if you expect to income average, include the amount of the reduction in tax because of averaging when using the table.

Line 5 of Form W-4

Additional amount, if any, you want deducted from each pay.—If you are not having enough tax withheld from your pay, you may ask your employer to withhold more by filling in an additional amount on line 5. Often, married couples, both of whom are working, and persons with two or more jobs need to have additional tax withheld. You may also need to have additional tax withheld because you have income other than wages, such as interest and dividends, capital gains, rents, alimony received, taxable social security benefits, etc. Estimate the amount you will be underwithheld and divide that amount by the number of pay periods in the year. Enter the additional amount you want withheld each pay period on line 5.

Line 6 of Form W-4

Exemption from withholding.—You can claim exemption from withholding only if last year you did not owe any Federal income tax and had a right to a refund of all income tax withheld, **and** this year you do not expect to owe any Federal income tax and expect to have a right to a refund of all income tax withheld. If you qualify, check Boxes 6a and b, write the year exempt status is effective and "EXEMPT" on line 6b, and answer Yes or No to the question on line 6c.

If you want to claim exemption from withholding next year, you must file a new W-4 with your employer on or before February 15 of next year. If you are not having Federal income tax withheld this year, but expect to have a tax liability next year, the law requires you to give your employer a new W-4 by December 1 of this year. If you are covered by social security, your employer must withhold social security tax.

Your employer must send to IRS any W-4 claiming more than 14 withholding allowances or claiming exemption from withholding if the wages are expected to usually exceed $200 a week. The employer is to complete Boxes 7, 8, and 9 only on copies of the W-4 sent to IRS.

Table 1—For Figuring Your Withholding Allowances For Estimated Tax Credits and Income Averaging (Line E)

Estimated Salaries and Wages from All sources	Single Employees (A)	Single Employees (B)	Head of Household Employees (A)	Head of Household Employees (B)	Married Employees (When Spouse not Employed) (A)	Married Employees (When Spouse not Employed) (B)	Married Employees (When Both Spouses are Employed) (A)	Married Employees (When Both Spouses are Employed) (B)
Under $15,000	$ 90	$150	$ 30	$150	$ 50	$120	$ 0	$120
15,000-25,000	120	250	0	250	70	170	310	170
25,001-35,000	190	300	0	300	130	250	800	220
35,001-45,000	250	370	0	370	170	320	1,500	250
45,001-55,000	690	370	0	370	230	340	2,210	330
55,001-65,000	1,470	370	220	370	310	370	3,020	330
Over 65,000	2,460	370	920	370	680	370	3,400	370

Worksheet to Figure Your Withholding Allowances to be Entered on Line 4 of Form W-4

A Personal allowances . . . . ▶ **A** ____

B Special withholding allowance (not to exceed 1 allowance—see instructions on page 1) . . . ▶ **B** ____

C Allowances for dependents . . . . ▶ **C** ____

If you are not claiming any deductions or credits, skip lines D and E.

D Allowances for estimated deductions:

1 Enter the total amount of your estimated itemized deductions, alimony payments, qualified retirement contributions including IRA and Keogh (H.R. 10) plans, deduction for a married couple when both work, business losses including net operating loss carryovers, moving expenses, employee business expenses, penalty on early withdrawal of savings, and charitable contributions for nonitemizers for the year . . . . ▶ **1** $

2 If you do not plan to itemize deductions, enter [illegible] on line D2. If you plan to itemize, find your total estimated salaries and wages amount in the left column of the table below. (Include salaries and wages of both spouses.) Read across to the right and find the amount from the column that applies to you. Enter that amount on line D2. . . . . ▶ **2** $

Estimated salaries and wages from all sources:	Single and Head of Household Employees (only one job)	Married Employees (one spouse working and one job only)	Employees with more than one job or Married Employees with both spouses working [1]
Under $15,000	$2,800	$3,900	40% of estimated salaries and wages
15,000-35,000	2,800	3,900	23% of estimated salaries and wages
35,001-50,000	8% of estimated salaries and wages	3,900	20% of estimated salaries and wages
Over $50,000	10% of estimated salaries and wages	7% of estimated salaries and wages	18% of estimated salaries and wages

3 Subtract line D2 from line D1 (But not less than zero) . . . . ▶ **3** $

4 Divide the amount on line D3 by $1,000 (increase any fraction to the next whole number). Enter here . . . ▶ **D** ____

E Allowances for tax credits and income averaging: use Table 1 above for figuring withholding allowances

1 Enter tax credits, excess social security tax withheld, and tax reduction from income averaging $

2 Enter the column (A) amount from Table 1 for your salary range and filing status (single, etc.). However, enter 0 if you claim 1 or more allowances on line D4 . . . . $

3 Subtract line 2 from line 1 (If zero or less, do not complete lines 4 and 5) . . . . $

4 Find the column (B) amount from Table 1 for your salary range and filing status . . . . $

5 Divide line 3 by line 4. Increase any fraction to the next whole number. This is the maximum number of withholding allowances for tax credits and income averaging. Enter here . . . . ▶ **E** ____

Example: A taxpayer who expects to file a Federal income tax return as a single person estimates annual wages of $12,000 and tax credits of $650. The $12,000 falls in the wage bracket of under $15,000. The value in column (A) is 90. Subtracting this from the estimated credits of 650 leaves 560. The value in column (B) is 150. Dividing 560 by 150 gives 3.7. Since any fraction is increased to the next whole number, show 4 on line E.

F Total (add lines A through E). Enter total here and on line 4 of Form W-4 . . . . ▶ **F** ____

[1] If you earn 10% or less of your total wages from other jobs or one spouse earns 10% or less of the couple's combined total wages, you can use the "Single and Head of Household Employees (only one job)" or "Married Employees (one spouse working and one job only)" table, whichever is appropriate.

☆ U.S.G.P.O.: 1983 - 390-044/6098

2. Charitable Giving

Like many Americans, you probably give money or property to various charities on a regular basis. Did you know that you should, whenever possible, donate *appreciated* property as a charitable gift? For example, if you own stocks or bonds that have increased in value since you purchased them and you donate the securities to a charity, you will not have to pay any capital gains tax on any profit earned.

Another tip: Try to donate unwanted clothes, books, furniture, and other household items to charitable organizations whenever possible. Request the organizations to give you a receipt for the value of the goods and add that value to your other annual charitable gifts when you figure the deduction.

This chapter tells you how to take a noncash deduction or how to put a value on gifts to charity, what to do about out-of-pocket expenses that you incur when traveling to and from charitable work, and where to get information about legitimate charitable organizations.

Taking the Deduction

Q I bought two tickets to the local policeman's ball last year, but because of pressing business commitments I could not attend the dance. Am I still allowed a charitable deduction for the purchase price of the tickets?

A Yes. You do not have to attend a charitable affair if you have bought tickets. You may still take the deduction.

Q I know that there is a 5 percent of adjusted gross income limitation on medical expenses. Is there any limitation on charitable contributions?

A Generally, your charitable deductions are limited to 50 percent of your adjusted gross income. But if you contribute capital gains property of certain types, your limitation drops to 30 percent of your adjusted gross income.

Q My wife volunteers as a nurse's aide at a nearby hospital. She is required to have a uniform for this purpose. Since she works at the hospital three days a week, she had to purchase two uniforms. Can we deduct the cost of the uniforms as well as dry cleaning expenses?

A Yes. The general rule is that costs of uniforms and their upkeep are deductible if the uniforms have no other use and there is a requirement that they be worn while performing donated services. Obviously your wife cannot reasonably be expected to wear her nurse's aide uniform when she is not working as an aide.

Q Our area was hit particularly hard by a hurricane last year. Fortunately our home escaped undamaged. But we were asked by the Red Cross to put up a family of five whose house was fully destroyed. The family stayed with us for about a week, and we fed and provided clothing for them. Can I take a deduction for the out-of-pocket expenses we incurred in taking care of that family?

A Yes. But be sure to obtain a letter from the Red Cross that confirms your story. The IRS is notoriously cynical about these things.

Q My brother-in-law keeps chuckling and saying that he put one over on the IRS. He says that he couldn't sell his gas-guzzling Cadillac to anybody, but he gave it to a charity and is now getting a hefty tax break. Can he legally do that?

A Smart man, your brother-in-law. Obviously he realized that if he sold the Cadillac he wouldn't get anywhere near its book value, so he donated it to a charity. By doing that he is allowed to deduct its full book value even though the charity may get much less for the car if it sells it. This is a perfectly legal tactic virtually unknown to taxpayers. Just make sure that the car is not in need of heavy repairs, because then it would not be worth its full book value.

Q Twice a week I work in a prison literacy program as a volunteer. The prison is located some twenty-five miles from my home, and I drive to and from the prison. The volunteer supervisor told me that I can get a tax deduction for my driving, but I don't know how much I am allowed. Can you tell me?

A You are entitled to a charitable deduction to the extent of 12 cents per mile. So since you travel 100 miles per week you can deduct $12 a week. Add that $12 per week to your other charitable deductions for your total charitable deduction figure.

Q I want to donate some stock to my college. For charitable deduction purposes, how do I determine its value?

A Its value depends on how long you have held the stock and whether it has appreciated in value since you acquired it. If it has appreciated and you have held the stock for more than twelve months, you can deduct its fair market value on the date of contribution. If you have held the stock less than a year, you must subtract the appreciation from its fair market value to determine the deduction. For example, if you bought stock for $4000 and it has appreciated $1000 since acquisition, you can take a deduction for only $4000 if you have held the stock less than a year.

Q Last year I went to the Elks Club national convention, which was held across the country from where I live. I spent over $1000 on air fare, hotels, and food while attending the convention. Can I deduct the $1000 as a charitable gift?

A You failed to indicate whether you were an elected delegate to the convention. That distinction is important to the IRS. If you were an elected delegate, you can deduct unreimbursed expenses; if, however, you were just attending as an Elks Club member, you can't.

Q I keep reading that I should contribute appreciated property to charity. What is appreciated property and why should I contribute it to a charitable organization?

A Appreciated property is simply property–works of art, stocks and bonds, stamp and coin collections or real estate–that has significantly grown in value since you acquired it. For instance, if you bought a painting 15 years ago for $500 and now it is worth $5000, that is tenfold appreciation.

You should donate appreciated property because you can take a charitable deduction for the full current value at the time of making the gift. Here, for example, you could take a $5000 deduction if you donated the painting to a museum. If, on the other hand, you sold the painting, after deducting tax payments you would not clear as much.

Q Is it true that I have to name on my tax return all organizations I gave to last year?

A No. If you make a cash contribution of more than $3000, you must name the organization on Schedule A. Formerly, it was not necessary to name any organization to which you donated.

Q What's this I hear about the fact that if I give a painting I own to a charity I must have it appraised first?

A The Tax Reform Act of 1984 has a requirement that if you claim a property donation of $5,000 or more on your tax return, you must attach an appraisal of that property directly to the return.

Of course, the appraisal must have been conducted by an art expert in the case of a painting or other artwork–or by experts who are familiar with other areas of property that might be donated.

Q What is the new rule with regard to charitable contributions and the standard deduction?

A For 1984 you can take a deduction of up to 25% of your first $300 in charitable contributions for a maximum deduction of $75 even if you use the zero bracket amount. Formerly, taxpayers could take a charitable deduction only if they itemized their returns. If you are married and filing separately the figure is 25% of the first $150.00.

Q I have heard that the video disc recorder and the video discs that I purchased two years ago can become a tax deduction for me. Since the company that made the machine and the discs has gotten out of the business, I want to get rid of the machine. How can I get the deduction that I heard about?

A You can make a gift of the recorder and the discs to a school, library, or the like and take a charitable contribution for the full value of the items. Your best bet for coming up with their value would be to contact the company who made the machine and the discs or the dealer who sold them to you.

Q My church held a raffle last year and I bought $50 worth of tickets. I read in the church program later that I can't deduct that money as a charitable contribution. Why not?

A If by purchasing the tickets you had a chance to win a prize of any value whatsoever then the money you laid out is not considered a charitable contribution but rather a gambling loss. The only way that you can write off a gambling loss is by offsetting your losses against winnings if any.

Q I made a pledge to a charity that I would donate a certain amount to their fund drive next year. Can I take the deduction this year?

A No. You are not allowed to take the deduction until the contribution is actually made to the charity. Since you will not be sending a check until next year, you cannot take the deduction until then even though you have committed yourself this year.

Noncash Deductions

Q I am on the board of directors of a local charity. Last year I threw open my house for a fund-raising event for the charity. I hosted a cocktail party and buffet dinner for seventy-five people. Can I deduct the cost of food and liquor as a charitable deduction?

A You sure can. Charitable contributions don't have to be in the form of hard cash. They can also be the cost of food and liquor donated on behalf of a fund-raising effort of a recognized charity.

Q Last year my husband and I gave a great deal of used clothing to the Salvation Army. How do we determine the fair market value of the clothing for charitable deduction purposes?

A Property such as clothing, antiques, art objects, or used furniture that is given to a recognized charitable organization should be appraised by a professional appraiser. That person will determine its fair market value and that figure is what you should use. If you value the property at more than about 15 cents on the dollar, the IRS might fight you unless you have a valid appraisal that shows otherwise. By the way, the fee the appraiser charges can also be claimed as an itemized miscellaneous deduction.

Approved and Disapproved Charities

Q There are so many charities soliciting funds that it's hard to know which ones are legitimate and which aren't. Does the IRS know?

A It definitely does. The IRS maintains a list of approved charities that you can contribute to without being questioned about their legitimacy as charitable organizations. All you need do is call the IRS and ask whether a particular organization is on the list; if it is not, you cannot take a charitable deduction.

Q I have been informed that my $250 contribution to the local chamber of commerce is nondeductible. Is that right?

A It sure is. Contributions to chambers of commerce and other business-oriented organizations are specifically denied deductibility, as are contributions to social clubs or civic leagues. But they would be deductible as a business expense.

3. Automobiles

Anyone who uses his or her car for any business or charitable purpose can take a tax deduction for the expenses incurred. Many circumstances that you may never have thought of constitute deductible uses. For example, if you regularly drive to a nearby town to do business research in a library on Saturdays, the costs of those trips are deductible. So are the expenses involved in traveling to and from a destination for the purpose of performing charitable work.

This chapter discusses some of those deductions and offers some tips on the tax aspects of car pooling and leasing a car. The very fine line between using a car for business or for pleasure is also explained.

The Mileage Deduction

Q We used our family car when we moved 600 miles away last year. I understand that on our tax return we can deduct the cost of using the car. How much can we deduct?

A The cost of using a personal automobile for moving and for traveling back and forth to medical appointments, is deductible to the extent of 9 cents per mile. In your case you can deduct $54.

Q Since I use my car for business about half the time, I was wondering whether I have any alternative other than deducting just 20 cents per mile?

A For unreimbursed taxpayers who use their automobiles for business, there is a choice. You can use the flat mileage calculation of 20.5 cents per mile for the first 15,000 miles and 11 cents for every mile thereafter, or you can deduct actual operating expenses including depreciation. The best idea is to calculate the expense both ways and use the more favorable figure.

Q My husband and I both drive "business cars" but we work in different jobs at different locations. Do we have to combine our business mileage deduction if we file a joint return?

A Certainly not. If you both drive 15,000 miles a year, each of you can take the full 20.5 cents per mile for your business driving. Two separate cars are involved and two distinct jobs; therefore each of you is entitled to your own deduction.

Automobile Expenses

Q Because I live in the same area as a number of my co-workers, I used my car last year for a car pool to and from work. Do I have to report as income money regularly given to me by the car pool members?

A No. The money you receive is considered reimbursement for incurred auto expenses, such as gasoline, depreciation, and so on. And it makes no difference that you would be driving to work anyway and you use a car pool as a service to your fellow workers.

Q I leased a car last year. Are any or all of the lease payments for the year deductible?

A It depends on how much you used the car for business. If you used the car entirely for personal use or nonbusiness commuting, then none of the lease payments are deductible. However, if you used the car 50 percent of the time for business, you could deduct 50 percent of the lease payments. Business use, however, has to be firmly established by documentation, such as gas receipts and credit card receipts.

Q Admittedly they don't amount to much, but aren't my auto registration and driver's license fees deductible on my federal tax return?

A No. This seems to be one of the common misconceptions about deductions. You cannot deduct automobile license or registration fees unless the fee is based to some extent on the automobile's value. The answer would be different if you use your car in business or if you are an outside salesman where driving a car is a necessity.

Q I think I goofed. I used my personal car last year for business purposes a number of times. I was supposed to receive reimbursement by my company, but I forgot to send in the vouchers. Now it is too late to get my company to reimburse me. Can I take the expenses off my tax return?

A You sure did goof. Because you had a claim of right to reimbursement that you didn't exercise, you also lose any applicable tax deduction you might have had.

Q I purchased an automobile last year during a period when the manufacturer was offering a $700 rebate to customers who purchased that particular model. Is that $700 that I received taxable income to me?

A No it isn't. So long as any retail customer could have received the identical rebate, it is not considered taxable income to you.

Q I am a self-employed business consultant. I do a lot of traveling by car and I want to deduct my car expenses. Where on the federal tax form do I take the deduction?

A As a self-employed individual you take your auto expense deductions on Schedule C where you report the profit or loss from your self-employment business. By the way, you write off depreciation for the auto on Form 4562. (See Form 4562 at end of chapter.)

Q I do a lot of driving and I look for every deduction I can take. However, my tax preparer told me that I can't deduct gasoline taxes. I used to deduct them and there was never any problem. What's the story?

A Your tax preparer is right. Gasoline taxes used to be deductible but can no longer be deducted.

Q I have an older car that I use for business commuting and for business trips. I have been told by my auto club that there is a limit on the number of years that I can take the auto expense deduction. Is that so?

A It is a little known fact that you can only deduct up to 60,000 miles at the top 20.5 cents a mile rate. Once you have reached that 60,000 limit all business miles can only be deducted at 11 cents a mile.

You would be wiser to adopt the actual cost method of computing your deduction. Under that method you deduct all expenses incurred operating your auto for business purposes.

Q I am a traveling salesman and I use my car to travel from client to client. To protect myself on the road I joined an automobile club. Are those dues that I pay for the club deductible?

A Yes. Just as gasoline, oil, tires, and repairs are deductible by an individual who uses his or her car for work, so are auto club dues.

Form **4562**

Department of the Treasury
Internal Revenue Service (0)

Depreciation and Amortization

▶ See separate instructions.

▶ Attach this form to your return.

OMB No. 1545-0172

1983

67

Name(s) as shown on return

Identifying number

Business or activity to which this form relates

PART I.—Depreciation

Section A.—Election to expense recovery property (Section 179)

A. Class of property	B. Cost	C. Expense deduction
1 Total (not more than $5,000). Enter here and on page 2, line 8 (Partnerships or S corporations—see the Schedule K and Schedule K-1 Instructions of Form 1065 or 1120S)		

Section B.—Depreciation of recovery property

A. Class of property	B. Date placed in service	C. Cost or other basis	D. Recovery period	E. Method of figuring depreciation	F. Percentage	G. Deduction for this year
2 Accelerated Cost Recovery System (ACRS) (See instructions):						
(a) 3-year property						
(b) 5-year property						
(c) 10-year property						
(d) 15-year public utility property						
(e) 15-year real property—low-income housing						
(f) 15-year real property other than low-income housing						
3 Property subject to section 168(e)(2) election (See instructions):						
4 Total column G. Enter here and on page 2, line 9						

SAMPLE

See Paperwork Reduction Act Notice on page 1 of the separate instructions.

Form **4562** (1983)

Section C.—Depreciation of nonrecovery property

A. Description of property	**B.** Date acquired	**C.** Cost or other basis	**D.** Depreciation allowed or allowable in earlier years	**E.** Method of figuring depreciation	**F.** Life or rate	**G.** Deduction for this year
5 Class Life Asset Depreciation Range (CLADR) System Depreciation . . . . ▶						
6 Other depreciation (See instructions):						
7 Total column G, Section C						
8 Enter amount from Section A, line 1 (Partnerships and S corporations enter zero)						
9 Enter amount from Section B, line 4						
10 Total—Add lines 7, 8, and 9. Enter here and on the Depreciation line of your return						

PART II.—Amortization of Property

A. Description of property	**B.** Date acquired	**C.** Cost or other basis	**D.** Amortization allowed or allowable in earlier years	**E.** Code section	**F.** Amortization period or percentage	**G.** Amortization for this year
1 Total column G. Enter here and on Other Deductions or Other Expenses line of your return						

☆ U.S. Government Printing Office: 1983—390-235 23-0916750

4. Income Averaging

Income averaging is available to any taxpayer whose income in one year suddenly and dramatically increases over the income in the immediately prior taxable year. Few taxpayers take advantage of this wonderful tax-saving technique because they simply don't know about it.

Income averaging is a complicated matter, especially if you have changed residences or have gotten a divorce during the past three years. A taxpayer who wants to take advantage of income averaging under these situations should seek professional assistance before filling out the form, especially since the law with regard to income averaging has changed in 1984.

What income averaging is, how it works, and the appropriate tax forms are included in this chapter.

What Is Income Averaging?

Q I have heard of income averaging, but I don't know what it is. Can you help me?

A If you have a big jump in income you may be able to soften the tax bite by income averaging. It is especially useful if you have jumped several tax brackets in one year. Income averaging spreads your increased income for the present year over the three preceding years so that each year's income is burdened with only a portion of the increase. (See Schedule G at the end of the chapter.)

Q My income increased $5000 last year over the previous year. Am I eligible for income averaging?

A Probably. For income averaging to apply, your income must have increased substantially in the taxable year over the previous year. In general, your taxable income in the taxable year must be more than 30 percent of the total taxable income for the previous three years.

Using Income Averaging

Q If I income average this year, could I income average next year if I am eligible?

A Even if your income dips next year, you still might be able to income average next year, and you can do it again and again. If in doubt, compute it mathematically with an accountant or by yourself, since your qualification to income average is determined at the end of each year.

Q Can you give me some typical situations in which tax averaging might be considered by the average taxpayer?

A Here are a few examples. If you are married and you file a joint return and both of you received raises of more than 10% last year. Also, if one or both of you had been unemployed for a long period of time the previous year and fully employed this year. Similarly, if you or your spouse or both of you received large bonuses during the year, you should investigate income averaging.

Schedule G (Form 1040)
Department of the Treasury
Internal Revenue Service (0)

Income Averaging

▶ See instructions on back. ▶ Attach to Form 1040.

OMB No. 1545-0074
1983
17

Name(s) as shown on Form 1040 | Your social security number

Step 1 Figure your income for 1979—1982

1979	1	Fill in the amount from your 1979 Form 1040 (line 34) or Form 1040A (line 11)	1		
	2	Multiply your total exemptions in 1979 by $1,000	2		
	3	Subtract line 2 from line 1. If less than zero, enter zero		3	
1980	4	Fill in the amount from your 1980 Form 1040 (line 34) or Form 1040A (line 11)	4		
	5	Multiply your total exemptions in 1980 by $1,000	5		
	6	Subtract line 5 from line 4. If less than zero, enter zero		6	
1981	7	Fill in the amount from your 1981 Form 1040 (line 34) or Form 1040A (line 12). If less than zero, enter zero		7	
1982	8	Fill in the amount from your 1982 Form 1040 (line 37), Form 1040A (line 16), or Form 1040EZ (line 7). If less than zero, enter zero		8	
Total	9	Fill in all income less deductions earned outside of the U.S. or within U.S. possessions and excluded for 1979 through 1982 (include housing exclusion in 1982)		9	
	10	Add lines 3, 6, 7, 8 and 9		10	

Step 2 Figure your averageable income

	Multiply the amount on line 10 by 30% (.30)		x .30
11	Write in the answer	11	
12	Fill in your taxable income for 1983 from Form 1040, line 37	12	
13	If you received a premature or excessive distribution subject to a penalty under section 72, see instructions	13	
14	Subtract line 13 from line 12	14	
15	If you live in a community property state and are filing a separate return, see instructions	15	
16	Subtract line 15 from line 14. If less than zero, enter zero	16	
17	Write in the amount from line 11 above	17	
18	Subtract line 17 from line 16. This is your averageable income	18	

SAMPLE

If line 18 is $3,000 or less, do not complete the rest of this form. You do not qualify for income averaging.

Step 3 Figure your tax

	Multiply the amount on line 18 by 20% (.20)				x .20
19	Write in the answer			19	
20	Write in the amount from line 11 above			20	
21	Add lines 19 and 20			21	
22	Write in the amount from line 15 above			22	
23	Add lines 21 and 22			23	
24	Tax on amount on line 23 (from Tax Rate Schedule X, Y, or Z)			24	
25	Tax on amount on line 21 (from Tax Rate Schedule X, Y, or Z)	25			
26	Tax on amount on line 20 (from Tax Rate Schedule X, Y, or Z)	26			
27	Subtract line 26 from line 25	27			
	Multiply the amount on line 27 by 4		x 4		
28	Write in the answer			28	
	If you have no entry on line 13, skip lines 29 through 31 and go to line 32.				
29	Tax on amount on line 12 (from Tax Rate Schedule X, Y, or Z)	29			
30	Tax on amount on line 14 (from Tax Rate Schedule X, Y, or Z)	30			
31	Subtract line 30 from line 29			31	
32	Add lines 24, 28, and 31. Write the result here and on Form 1040, line 38. Be sure to check the Schedule G box on that line			32	

For Paperwork Reduction Act Notice, see Form 1040 instructions. **Schedule G (Form 1040) 1983**

Instructions

If your income this year is much greater than the average of your income for the past 4 base period years (1979–1982), you may be able to pay less tax by income averaging. To see if you qualify, complete lines 1–18 of this schedule. If line 18 is more than $3,000, fill in the rest of this schedule to see if you will save by income averaging.

If you are eligible, and line 32 of this schedule is less than your tax using other methods, you may choose the income averaging method. You must attach this schedule to your Form 1040 to choose the benefits of income averaging. Generally, you may make or change this choice anytime within 3 years from the date you filed your return.

For more information and a filled-in sample Schedule G, please get **Publication 506,** Income Averaging.

Who Can Income Average?

To be eligible to file Schedule G with Form 1040, you (and your spouse, if you are filing a joint return) must meet the following requirements:

(1) Citizenship or residence.—You must have been a U.S. citizen or resident for all of 1983. You are not eligible if you were a nonresident alien at any time during the 5 tax years ending with 1983.

(2) Support.—You must have furnished at least 50% of your own support for each of the years 1979 through 1982. In a year in which you were married, you and your spouse must have provided at least 50% of the support of both of you. For the definition of support, see Form 1040 Instructions, page 7.

Exceptions: Disregard the support requirement if any one of the three following situations applies to you:

(1) You were 25 or older before the end of 1983 and were not a full-time student during 4 or more of your tax years which began after you reached 21; or

(2) More than 50% of your 1983 taxable income (line 12) is from work you performed in substantial part during 2 or more of the 4 tax years before 1983; or

(3) You file a joint return for 1983 and your income for 1983 is not more than 25% of the total combined adjusted gross income (line 33, Form 1040).

For the definition of full-time student, see Form 1040 Instructions, page 7.

Caution: In the same year you file Schedule G you may not claim the benefits of sections 911 or 931 through 934 (I.R. Code).

Figure Your Income for 1979–1982.

(1) Use your separate income and deductions for all years if you were unmarried in 1979 through 1983.

(2) Use the combined income and deductions of you and your spouse for a base period year:

- if in 1983 you are married and file a joint return, or are a qualifying widow(er), and
- you were not married to any other spouse in that base period year.

(3) If (1) and (2) do not apply, your separate base period income is the largest of the following amounts:

(a) Your separate income and deductions for the base period year;

(b) Half of the base period income from adding your separate income and deductions to the separate income and deductions of your spouse for that base period year; or

(c) Half of the base period income from adding your separate income and deductions to your 1983 spouse's separate income and deductions for that base period year.

Note: *If you were married to one spouse in a base period year and are married and file a joint return with a different spouse in 1983, your separate base period income is the larger of (3)(a) or (b) above. Combine that amount with your 1983 spouse's separate base period income for that base period year.*

Figuring Your Separate Income and Deductions.

The amount of your separate income and deductions for a base period year is your gross income for that year minus your allowable deductions.

If you filed a joint return for a base period year, your separate deductions are:

(1) For deductions allowable in figuring your adjusted gross income, the sum of those deductions attributable to your gross income; and

(2) For deductions allowable in figuring taxable income (exemptions and itemized deductions), the amount from multiplying the deductions allowable on the joint return by a fraction whose numerator is your adjusted gross income and whose denominator is the combined adjusted gross income on the joint return. However, if 85% or more of the combined adjusted gross income of you and your spouse is attributable to one spouse, all deductions allowable in figuring taxable income are allowable to that spouse.

Community property laws.—In figuring your separate taxable income when community property laws apply, you must take into account:

- all of your earned income without regard to the community property laws, or
- your share of the community earned income under community property laws, whichever is more.

If you must figure your separate taxable income for any of the base period years, attach a statement showing the computation and the names under which the returns were filed.

Line-by-Line Instructions

Lines 1–8.—If you did not file a return for any year from 1979 through 1982, enter the amounts that would otherwise be reportable on the appropriate lines. If the amount reported on your return for any of the years was changed by an amended return or by the Internal Revenue Service, enter the corrected amount.

Line 9.—If you excluded any income in any year from 1979 through 1982 because the income was earned from sources outside the United States or within U.S. possessions, fill in the total amount of income (less deductions) that you excluded during that period. Otherwise, leave line 9 blank.

Line 13.—If you are or were an owner-employee, and you received income in 1983 from a premature or excessive distribution from a Keogh (H.R. 10) plan or trust that was subject to a penalty under section 72(m)(5), fill in the amount of that income on this line. Or, if you were an employee in a qualified plan and made deductible voluntary contributions, and received a premature distribution of those contributions subject to a penalty under section 72(o), include that amount on line 13. If you received a premature distribution under an annuity contract subject to a penalty under section 72(q), that amount must also be included on line 13. Otherwise, leave line 13 blank.

Line 15.—You must make this adjustment if you are married, a resident of a community property State, and file a separate return for 1983. Enter the community earned income you reported minus that part of the income which is attributable to your services. Skip this line if the earned income attributable to your services is more than 50% of your combined community earned income.

Example:

	Attributable to Service of		
Community Earned Income	**John**	**Carol**	**Both**
	$40,000	$20,000	$60,000

- **John,** filing a separate return, has no adjustment since the amount of earned income attributable to the services of John ($40,000) is more than 50% of the combined community earned income ($30,000).
- **Carol,** filing a separate return, must include $10,000 in the total for line 15. This is the excess of the 50% of the community earned income reportable by Carol ($30,000) over the amount of community earned income attributable to Carol's services ($20,000).

Line 32.—If the tax on this line is less than the tax figured in any other way, enter the amount from this line on Form 1040, line 38, and check the Schedule G box on that line.

☆U.S. GOVERNMENT PRINTING OFFICE: 1983-390-096

23-188-5979

5. Credits

Credits and deductions often confuse the average taxpayer, but there is a big and profitable difference between the two terms. A credit is much better than a deduction because when you take a credit you are actually subtracting from the total tax you would have to pay if you did not have the credit. A deduction is simply a subtraction from your total income and does not necessarily reduce the amount of tax due. The more credits you can legally take, the lower your tax will be.

The federal government often uses tax credit legislation to implement a program that furthers some national purpose. For example, to support a policy of conserving energy, the government came up with the energy tax credit to induce people to save on home fuel.

To encourage working mothers the child care credit was instituted; to get a broader group of individuals to contribute to political campaigns, the political contribution credit was established. A tax credit is the government's way of paying you back for helping to further national goals.

In this chapter all of the major tax credits that are available to taxpayers are discussed.

Energy Tax Credit

Q We recently moved into a twenty-year-old house that was very poorly insulated. How large a tax credit can I claim if I insulate the house?

A So long as the home is your principal residence and it was built prior to April 20, 1977, you can claim a credit of up to $300 or 15 percent of the first $2000 you spend for the insulation.

Q I recently bought a wood-burning stove to heat my home. Does that qualify for the energy tax credit that I have been hearing so much about?

A Sorry about that. Wood-burning stoves, as well as new exterior siding, heat pumps, carpeting, drapes, and interior wood paneling, do not qualify. But if you install storm windows, insulation, or weatherstripping, the credit does apply.

Q Is the energy tax credit just limited to residences or can my business take the credit as well if work is done on my plant building?

A The credit is not limited solely to residences. Your plant qualifies and, what's more, you may also be able to take an investment tax credit for the equipment you install. That would give you a double tax break.

Q Since I live in the sunny southwest, I am considering installing a solar collection system for my new house. What kind of tax credit can I get, if any?

A You are definitely eligible for an energy credit. The credit amounts to 40 percent of the first $10,000 you spend. The maximum credit you can take then is $4000. The system must have a useful life of five years or more to qualify. You can install the system in a new or existing residence.

Q We rent our home, and I want to install storm windows. Can I take the energy tax credit?

A Definitely. You do not have to own a home to take the energy tax credit, but the home does have to be your principal residence, located in the United States, and it has to have been substantially completed before April 20, 1977.

Child Care Credit

Q My wife and I recently had a baby, but because inflation is so high she would like to go back to work to supplement our income. Can we get a tax break if we hire somebody to look after the child on a full-time basis?

A Yes. The credit ranges from $480 to $1,440 depending on the number of the children being cared for and your adjusted gross income. The child or children must be under 15 years old for the credit to apply. Make sure, however, that you pay the babysitter by check so that you have a record of the expenses. (See Form 2441 at the end of this chapter.)

Q I know we are eligible for the child care credit, but if my mother, who lives down the street, is the babysitter do we still qualify for the credit?

A Yes. You can hire your mother or any other mature relative as a babysitter as long as you do not claim that relative as a dependent. Do not pay your mother in cash for the babysitting; pay by check, and note on the check that the money was spent for child care expenses.

Q Since my separation I have been living with my child for two years. Can I file as head of household, which provides for lower rates, and can I take the child care credit as well?

A Yes you can. But you must meet the following three tests to qualify. First, you must file a separate return and not a joint one. Second, you must furnish more than half the cost of maintaining the household during the year. Finally, your husband cannot have been a member of the household at any time during the year. The requirements are different if you are single or unmarried (i.e., divorced), so investigate it carefully.

Q A friend sent her child to summer camp and took the child care credit for the cost of the camp. Can that be done?

A Yes. Also, if you send a child to a nursery school or kindergarten that charges a fee, those qualify for the child care credit as well.

Other Credits

Q If I make a contribution to a political party, do I get a tax break? If so, in what amount?

A If you are filing as an individual and not jointly you can get a maximum $50 tax credit, but you must contribute $100 to take the full credit. The credit is based on one-half the money you contribute. If you are filing jointly, the credit maximum is $100. So if as a couple you and your spouse contribute $500 to a political campaign, you can take only a $100 tax credit on your federal tax return.

Q I worked for two employers last year and I paid Social Security taxes in both jobs. Do I get a credit for an overpayment? What is the limit on how much Social Security I should have paid?

A You do get a credit. If you paid more than $2532.60 in Social Security (probably labeled FICA on your paychecks), you get a credit on your tax return for the excess.

Q I just turned 65 and I went to a commercial tax preparer who told me I was not eligible for the senior citizen tax credit because I receive social security benefits. Is he right?

A It depends how much you receive in social security benefits each year. That's because the maximum amount of the credit cannot exceed 15% of $2500 if you are single or $3750 if you are married and filing jointly and both you and your spouse are over 65. The maximum amount of your income must be reduced dollar for dollar by your social security income. So if you received social security payments of $1500 during the year and $2500 is the maximum amount available for the credit, you can take a credit of $1000.

Q I have a restaurant and for many years I have hired college students to work in it in the summer. In an industry newsletter there was an item that said I could get a tax credit if I hired disadvantaged teenagers for the summer. Can you confirm?

A The item was absolutely correct. The 1982 tax act added a provision giving employers who hire disadvantaged teenagers between the ages of 16 and 18 a credit for the wages paid of up to 85% of those wages to a limit of $3000 per employee.

Defining a disadvantaged youth may be difficult, but if you contact your industry association or your state labor department they may have guidelines they can offer.

1983

Department of the Treasury—Internal Revenue Service

Form 1040A US Individual Income Tax Return (0)

OMB No. 1545-0085

Step 1 Name and address

Use the IRS mailing label. If you don't have a label, print or type:

Your first name and initial (if joint return, also give spouse's name and initial) | Last name | Your social security no.

Present home address (number and street) | Spouse's social security no.

City, town or post office, State, and ZIP code

Presidential Election Campaign Fund

Do you want $1 to go to this fund? .... ☐ Yes ☐ No

If joint return, does your spouse want $1 to go to this fund? ☐ Yes ☐ No

Step 2 Filing status

(Check only one)

1 ☐ Single (See if you can use Form 1040EZ.)

2 ☐ Married filing joint return (even if only one had income)

3 ☐ Married filing separate return. Enter spouse's social security number above and spouse's full name here. ____

4 ☐ Head of household (with qualifying person). If the qualifying person is your unmarried child but not your dependent, write this child's name here. ____

Exemptions

Always check the exemption box labeled Yourself. Check other boxes if they apply.

5a ☐ Yourself ☐ 65 or over ☐ Blind

b ☐ Spouse ☐ 65 or over ☐ Blind — Write number of boxes checked on 5a and b

c First names of your dependent children who lived with you — Write number of children listed on 5c +

Attach Copy B of Form(s) W-2 here

d Other dependents:

1. Name	2. Relationship	3. Number of months lived in your home.	4. Did dependent have income of $1,000 or more?	5. Did you provide more than one-half of dependent's support?

Write number of other dependents listed on 5d +

e Total number of exemptions claimed. — Add numbers entered on lines above =

Step 3 Total income

6 Wages, salaries, tips, etc. (Attach Form(s) W-2.) 6

7 Interest income. (If line 7 is over $400, also complete Schedule 1, Part I.) 7

Attach check or money order here

8a Dividends. (If line 8a is over $400, also complete Schedule 1, Part II.) 8a

b Exclusion. See the instructions on page 14. ..... 8b

c Subtract line 8b from line 8a. Write the result. 8c

9a Unemployment compensation (insurance), from Form(s) 1099-G. 9a

b Taxable amount, if any, from the worksheet on page 15 of the instructions. 9b

10 Add lines 6, 7, 8c, and 9b. Write the total. This is your total income. 10

Step 4 Adjusted gross income

11a IRA deduction, from the worksheet on page 17. ..... 11a

b Write IRA payments made in 1984 that you included on line 11a: ($.)

12 Deduction for a married couple when both work. Complete Schedule 1, Part III. 12

13 Add lines 11a and 12. Write the total. These are your total adjustments. 13

14 Subtract line 13 from line 10. Write the result. This is your adjusted gross income. 14

1983 Form 1040A

Step 5 Taxable income

15	Write the amount from line 14.	15	.
16	Allowable part of your charitable contributions, from the worksheet on page 19 of the instructions.	16	.
17	Subtract line 16 from line 15. Write the result.	17	.
18	Multiply $1,000 by the total number of exemptions claimed on line 5e.	18	.
19	Subtract line 18 from line 17. Write the result. This is your taxable income.	19	.

Step 6 Tax, credits, and payments

If You Want IRS to Figure Your Tax, See Page 19 of the Instructions.

20	Find the tax on the amount on line 19. Use the tax table, pages 29–34.			20	.
21a	Partial credit for political contributions. See page 20 of the instructions.	21a	.		
b	Credit for child and dependent care expenses. Complete Schedule 1, Part IV.	21b	.		
22	Add lines 21a and 21b. Write the total. These are your total credits.			22	.
23	Subtract line 22 from line 20. Write the result. This is your total tax.			23	.
24a	Total Federal income tax withheld. This should be shown in Box 9 of your W-2 form(s). (If line 6 is more than $35,700, see page 23 of the instructions.)	24a	.		
b	Earned income credit, from the worksheet on page 24 of the instructions. See page 23 of the instructions.	24b	.		
25	Add lines 24a and 24b. Write the total. These are your total payments.			25	.

SAMPLE

Step 7 Refund or amount you owe

26	If line 25 is larger than line 23, subtract line 23 from line 25. Write the result. This is the **amount of your refund.**	26	.
27	If line 23 is larger than line 25, subtract line 25 from line 23. Write the result. This is the **amount you owe.** Attach check or money order for full amount payable to "Internal Revenue Service." Write your social security number and "1983 Form 1040A" on it.	27	.

Step 8 Sign your return

Under penalties of perjury, I declare that I have examined this return and accompanying schedules and statements, and to the best of my knowledge and belief, they are true, correct, and complete. Declaration of preparer (other than the taxpayer) is based on all information of which the preparer has any knowledge.

Your signature X	Date	Your occupation
Spouse's signature (if joint return both must sign) X	Date	Spouse's occupation
Paid preparer's signature X	Date	Preparer's social security no.
Firm's name (or yours, if self-employed)		Employer identification no.
Address and Zip code		Check if self-employed ☐

For **Privacy Act and Paperwork Reduction Act Notice,** see page 38.

1983

Schedule 1 (Form 1040A)

Part I—Interest Income
Part II—Dividend Income
Part III—Deduction for a Married Couple When Both Work

OMB No. 1545-0085

Name(s) as shown on Form 1040A. | Your social security number

Test to see when you MUST complete and attach Schedule 1 to Form 1040A

If you—	Complete the following part of Schedule 1—
• Have over $400 of interest income	• Part I, Interest income
• Have over $400 of dividend income	• Part II, Dividend income
• Claim the deduction for a working married couple	• Part III, Deduction for a married couple when both work
• Claim the credit for child and dependent care expenses	• Part IV, Credit for child and dependent care expenses

Part I

Interest income (See page 13)

Complete this part and attach Schedule 1 to Form 1040A if you received over $400 in interest income. If you received any interest from an All-Savers Certificate (ASC), use Form 1040 instead of Form 1040A.

1 List names of payers | Amount

List names of payers	Amount
	$.
	$.
	$.
	$.
	$.
	$.
	$.
	$.

SAMPLE

2 Add amounts on line 1. Write the total here and on line 7 of Form 1040A. 2 .

Part II

Dividend income (See page 14)

Complete this part and attach Schedule 1 to Form 1040A if you received over $400 in dividends.

1 List names of payers | Amount

List names of payers	Amount
	$.
	$.
	$.
	$.
	$.
	$.
	$.
	$.

2 Add amounts on line 1. Write the total here and on line 8a of Form 1040A. 2

Part III

Deduction for a married couple when both work (See page 18) 21

Complete this part to figure the amount you can deduct on line 12 of Form 1040A. Attach Schedule 1 to Form 1040A.

			(a) You	(b) Your spouse
1	Wages, salaries, tips, etc., from line 6 of Form 1040A.	1	.	.
2	IRA deduction, from line 11a of Form 1040A.	2	– .	– .
3	Subtract line 2 from line 1. Write the result.	3	= .	= .

4	Write the amount from line 3, column (a) or (b) above, whichever is smaller.	4	.
5	Multiply the amount on line 4 above by 10% (.10).	5	× .10
6	Write your answer here and on line 12 of Form 1040A.	6	=

1983 **Schedule 1 (Form 1040A)** OMB No. 1545-0085

Part IV—Credit for Child and Dependent Care Expenses

Name(s) as shown on Form 1040A. (Do not complete if name and SSN are shown on other side) | Your social security number

Part IV

Credit for child and dependent care expenses (See pages 20–22) 24
Complete this part to figure the amount of credit you can take on line 21b of Form 1040A. Attach Schedule 1 to Form 1040A.

1 Write the number of qualifying persons who were cared for in 1983. (See the instructions for the definition of a qualifying person.) 1

2 Write the amount of expenses you incurred and actually paid in 1983, but DO NOT write more than $2,400 ($4,800 if you paid for the care of two or more qualifying persons). 2 .

3 • If **unmarried** at the end of 1983, write your earned income on line 3, OR
• If **married,** filing a joint return for 1983,
a. Write your earned income $ ______ . ______, and
b. Write your spouse's earned income $ ______ . ______, and
c. Compare amounts on lines 3a and 3b, and write the **smaller** of the two amounts on line 3. 3 .

4 Compare amounts on lines 2 and 3. Write the smaller of the two amounts here. 4 .

SAMPLE

5 Write the percentage from the table below that applies to the amount on Form 1040A, line 15.

If line 15 is: Over—	But not over—	Percentage is:	If line 15 is: Over—	But not over—	Percentage is:
0—	$10,000	30% (.30)	$20,000—	22,000	24% (.24)
$10,000—	12,000	29% (.29)	22,000—	24,000	23% (.23)
12,000—	14,000	28% (.28)	24,000—	26,000	22% (.22)
14,000—	16,000	27% (.27)	26,000—	28,000	21% (.21)
16,000—	18,000	26% (.26)	28,000		20% (.20)
18,000—	20,000	25% (.25)			

5 × .

6 Multiply the amount on line 4 by the percentage on line 5. Write the result. 6 = .

7 Write the tax shown on Form 1040A, line 20, minus the amount of any partial credit for political contributions shown on line 21a. (If the result is zero or less, write zero.) 7 .

8 Compare amounts on lines 6 and 7. Write the **smaller** of the two amounts here. Also write this amount on Form 1040A, line 21b. 8 .

☆ U.S. GOVERNMENT PRINTING OFFICE: 1983—0.390-116 EI 13-2687299

Form **1040** Department of the Treasury—Internal Revenue Service
U.S. Individual Income Tax Return **1983** (0)

For the year January 1-December 31, 1983, or other tax year beginning , 1983, ending , 19 . OMB No. 1545-0074

Use IRS label. Otherwise, please print or type.	Your first name and initial (if joint return, also give spouse's name and initial) — Last name	**Your social security number**
	Present home address (Number and street, including apartment number, or rural route)	**Spouse's social security number**
	City, town or post office, State, and ZIP code	Your occupation / Spouse's occupation

Presidential Election Campaign ▶ Do you want $1 to go to this fund? . . . . . Yes / No
If joint return, does your spouse want $1 to go to this fund? Yes / No
Note: *Checking "Yes" will not increase your tax or reduce your refund.*

For Privacy Act and Paperwork Reduction Act Notice, see Instructions.

Filing Status

Check only one box.

1 ☐ Single
2 ☐ Married filing joint return (even if only one had income)
3 ☐ Married filing separate return. Enter spouse's social security no. above and full name here.
4 ☐ Head of household (with qualifying person). (See page 6 of Instructions.) If the qualifying person is your unmarried child but not your dependent, write child's name here.
5 ☐ Qualifying widow(er) with dependent child (Year spouse died ▶ 19). (See page 6 of Instructions.)

Exemptions

Always check the box labeled Yourself. Check other boxes if they apply.

6a ☐ Yourself ☐ 65 or over ☐ Blind
b ☐ Spouse ☐ 65 or over ☐ Blind
Enter number of boxes checked on 6a and b ▶

c First names of your dependent children who lived with you
Enter number of children listed on 6c ▶

d Other dependents: (1) Name	(2) Relationship	(3) Number of months lived in your home	(4) Did dependent have income of $1,000 or more?	(5) Did you provide more than one-half of dependent's support?

Enter number of other dependents ▶

e Total number of exemptions claimed . . . . . Add numbers entered in boxes above ▶

Income

Please attach Copy B of your Forms W-2, W-2G, and W-2P here.

If you do not have a W-2, see page 5 of Instructions.

Please attach check or money order here.

7 Wages, salaries, tips, etc. 7
8 Interest income *(also attach Schedule B if over $400 or you have any All-Savers interest)* . . . 8
9a Dividends *(also attach Schedule B if over $400)* 9b Exclusion
c Subtract line 9b from line 9a and enter the result . . . 9c
10 Refunds of State and local income taxes, from worksheet on page 10 of Instructions *(do not enter an amount unless you deducted those taxes in an earlier year—see page 10 of Instructions)* . . . 10
11 Alimony received 11
12 Business income or (loss) *(attach Schedule C)* . . . ▶ 12
13 Capital gain or (loss) *(attach Schedule D)* . . . 13
14 40% capital gain distributions not reported on line 13 (See page 10 of Instructions) . . . 14
15 Supplemental gains or (losses) *(attach Form 4797)* . . . 15
16 Fully taxable pensions, IRA distributions, and annuities not reported on line 17 . . . 16
17a Other pensions and annuities, including rollovers. Total received 17a
b Taxable amount, if any, from worksheet on page 10 of Instructions . . . 17b
18 Rents, royalties, partnerships, estates, trusts, etc. *(attach Schedule E)* . . . 18
19 Farm income or (loss) *(attach Schedule F)* . . . ▶ 19
20a Unemployment compensation (insurance). Total received . . . 20a
b Taxable amount, if any, from worksheet on page 11 of Instructions . . . 20b
21 Other income (state nature and source—see page 11 of Instructions) 21
22 **Total income.** Add amounts in column for lines 7 through 21 . . . ▶ 22

SAMPLE

Adjustments to Income

(See Instructions on page 11)

23 Moving expense *(attach Form 3903 or 3903F)* . . . 23
24 Employee business expenses *(attach Form 2106)* . . . 24
25a IRA deduction, from the worksheet on page 12 . . . 25a
b Enter here IRA payments you made in 1984 that are included in line 25a above ▶
26 Payments to a Keogh *(H.R. 10)* retirement plan . . . 26
27 Penalty on early withdrawal of savings . . . 27
28 Alimony paid . . . 28
29 Deduction for a married couple when both work *(attach Schedule W)* 29
30 Disability income exclusion *(attach Form 2440)* . . . 30
31 **Total adjustments.** Add lines 23 through 30 . . . ▶ 31

Adjusted Gross Income

32 **Adjusted gross income.** Subtract line 31 from line 22. *If this line is less than $10,000, see "Earned Income Credit" (line 59) on page 16 of Instructions. If you want IRS to figure your tax, see page 3 of Instructions* . . . ▶ 32

Form 1040 (1983) Page **2**

Tax Computation

(See Instructions on page 13)

Line	Description	Box	Amount
33	Amount from line 32 (adjusted gross income)	33	
34a	If you itemize, complete Schedule A (Form 1040) and enter the amount from Schedule A, line 28	34a	
	Caution: If you have unearned income and can be claimed as a dependent on your parent's return, check here ▶ ☐ and see page 13 of the Instructions. Also see page 13 of the Instructions if: • You are married filing a separate return and your spouse itemizes deductions, OR • You file Form 4563, OR • You are a dual-status alien.		
34b	If you do not itemize deductions on Schedule A (Form 1040), complete the worksheet on page 14. Then enter the allowable part of your charitable contributions here	34b	
35	Subtract line 34a or 34b, whichever applies, from line 33	35	
36	Multiply $1,000 by the total number of exemptions claimed on Form 1040, line 6e	36	
37	Taxable Income. Subtract line 36 from line 35	37	
38	Tax. Enter tax here and check if from ☐ Tax Table, ☐ Tax Rate Schedule X, Y, or Z, or ☐ Schedule G	38	
39	Additional Taxes. (See page 14 of Instructions.) Enter here and check if from ☐ Form 4970, ☐ Form 4972, ☐ Form 5544, or ☐ section 72 penalty taxes	39	
40	**Total.** Add lines 38 and 39 ▶	40	

Credits

(See Instructions on page 14)

Line	Description	Box	Amount
41	Credit for the elderly *(attach Schedules R&RP)*	41	
42	Foreign tax credit *(attach Form 1116)*	42	
43	Investment credit *(attach Form 3468)*	43	
44	Partial credit for political contributions	44	
45	Credit for child and dependent care expenses *(attach Form 2441)*	45	
46	Jobs credit *(attach Form 5884)*	46	
47	Residential energy credit *(attach Form 5695)*	47	
48	**Total credits.** Add lines 41 through 47	48	
49	**Balance.** Subtract line 48 from line 40 and enter difference (but not less than zero) ▶	49	

Other Taxes

(Including Advance EIC Payments)

Line	Description	Box	Amount
50	Self-employment tax *(attach Schedule SE)*	50	
51	Alternative minimum tax *(attach Form 6251)*	51	
52	Tax from recapture of investment credit *(attach Form 4255)*	52	
53	Social security tax on tip income not reported to employer *(attach Form 4137)*	53	
54	Uncollected employee social security tax and RRTA tax on tips *(from Form W-2)*	54	
55	Tax on an IRA *(attach Form 5329)*	55	
56	**Total tax.** Add lines 49 through 55 ▶	56	

SAMPLE

06

Payments

Attach Forms W-2, W-2G, and W-2P to front.

Line	Description	Box	Amount
57	Federal income tax withheld	57	
58	1983 estimated tax payments and amount applied from 1982 return	58	
59	Earned income credit. If line 33 is under $10,000, see page 16	59	
60	Amount paid with Form 4868	60	
61	Excess social security tax and RRTA tax withheld (two or more employers)	61	
62	Credit for Federal tax on special fuels and oils *(attach Form 4136)*	62	
63	Regulated Investment Company credit *(attach Form 2439)*	63	
64	**Total payments.** Add lines 57 through 63 ▶	64	

Refund or Amount You Owe

Line	Description	Box	Amount
65	If line 64 is larger than line 56, enter amount **OVERPAID** ▶	65	
66	Amount of line 65 to be **REFUNDED TO YOU** ▶	66	
67	Amount of line 65 to be applied to your 1984 estimated tax ▶	67	
68	If line 56 is larger than line 64, enter **AMOUNT YOU OWE.** Attach check or money order for full amount payable to "Internal Revenue Service." Write your social security number and "1983 Form 1040" on it ▶ (Check ▶ ☐ if Form 2210 (2210F) is attached. See page 17 of Instructions.) $	68	

Please Sign Here

Under penalties of perjury, I declare that I have examined this return and accompanying schedules and statements, and to the best of my knowledge and belief, they are true, correct, and complete. Declaration of preparer (other than taxpayer) is based on all information of which preparer has any knowledge.

▶ Your signature | Date | ▶ Spouse's signature (if filing jointly, BOTH must sign)

Paid Preparer's Use Only

Preparer's signature ▶	Date	Check if self-employed ☐	Preparer's social security no.
Firm's name (or yours, if self-employed) and address ▶		E.I. No.	
		ZIP code	

SCHEDULES A&B (Form 1040)
Department of the Treasury
Internal Revenue Service (0)

Schedule A—Itemized Deductions

(Schedule B is on back)

▶ Attach to Form 1040. ▶ See Instructions for Schedules A and B (Form 1040).

OMB No. 1545-0074
1983
07

Name(s) as shown on Form 1040 | **Your social security number**

Section	Line	Description		
Medical and Dental Expenses (Do not include expenses reimbursed or paid by others.) *(See page 18 of Instructions.)*	1	Medicines and drugs	1	
	2	Write 1% of Form 1040, line 33	2	
	3	Subtract line 2 from line 1. If line 2 is more than line 1, write zero	3	
	4	Other medical and dental expenses:		
	a	Doctors, dentists, nurses, hospitals, insurance premiums you paid for medical and dental care, etc.	4a	
	b	Transportation	4b	
	c	Other (list—include hearing aids, dentures, eyeglasses, etc.) ▶	4c	
	5	Add lines 3 through 4c	5	
	6	Multiply amount on Form 1040, line 33, by 5% (.05)	6	
	7	Subtract line 6 from line 5. If line 6 is more than line 5, write zero ▶		7
Taxes *(See page 19 of Instructions.)*	8	State and local income	8	
	9	Real estate	9	
	10 a	General sales (see sales tax tables)	10a	
	b	General sales on motor vehicles	10b	
	11	Other (list—include personal property) ▶	11	
	12	Add lines 8 through 11. Write your answer here ▶		12
Interest Expense *(See page 20 of Instructions.)*	13 a	Home mortgage interest paid to financial institutions	13a	
	b	Home mortgage interest paid to individuals (show that person's name and address) ▶	13b	
	14	Credit cards and charge accounts	14	
	15	Other (list) ▶	15	
	16	Add lines 13a through 15. Write your answer here ▶		16
Contributions *(See page 20 of Instructions.)*	17 a	Cash contributions. (If you gave $3,000 or more to any one organization, report those contributions on line 17b.)	17a	
	b	Cash contributions totaling $3,000 or more to any one organization. (Show to whom you gave and how much you gave.) ▶	17b	
	18	Other than cash (attach required statement)	18	
	19	Carryover from prior year	19	
	20	Add lines 17a through 19. Write your answer here ▶		20
Casualty and Theft Losses	21	Total casualty or theft loss(es) (attach Form 4684) (see page 20 of Instructions) ▶		21
Miscellaneous Deductions *(See page 21 of Instructions.)*	22	Union and professional dues	22	
	23	Tax return preparation fee	23	
	24	Other (list) ▶	24	
	25	Add lines 22 through 24. Write your answer here ▶		25
Summary of Itemized Deductions *(See page 21 of Instructions.)*	26	Add lines 7, 12, 16, 20, 21, and 25		26
	27	If you checked Form 1040 { Filing Status box 2 or 5, write $3,400; Filing Status box 1 or 4, write $2,300; Filing Status box 3, write $1,700 }		27
	28	Subtract line 27 from line 26. Write your answer here and on Form 1040, line 34a. (If line 27 is more than line 26, see the Instructions for line 28 on page 21.) ▶		28

SAMPLE

For Paperwork Reduction Act Notice, see Form 1040 Instructions. **Schedule A (Form 1040) 1983**

Schedule B—Interest and Dividend Income

08 OMB No. 1545-0074

Name(s) as shown on Form 1040 (Do not enter name and social security number if shown on other side) | Your social security number

Part I Interest Income

(See pages 9 and 21 of Instructions.)

Also complete Part III.

If you received more than $400 in interest or you received any interest from an All-Savers Certificate, you must complete Part I and list ALL interest received. If you received interest as a nominee for another, or you received or paid accrued interest on securities transferred between interest payment dates, see page 22.

Interest income other than interest from All-Savers Certificates		Amount
1 Interest income from seller-financed mortgages. (See Instructions and show name of payer.) ▶	1	
2 Other interest income (list name of payer) ▶	2	
3 Add lines 1 and 2	3	
Interest from All-Savers Certificates (ASCs). (See page 22.)		Amount
4	4	
5 Add amounts on line 4	5	
6 Write the amount of your ASC exclusion from the worksheet on page 22 of Instructions	6	
7 Subtract line 6 from line 5	7	
8 Add lines 3 and 7. Write your answer here and on Form 1040, line 8 ▶	8	

Part II Dividend Income

(See pages 9 and 22 of Instructions.)

Also complete Part III.

If you received more than $400 in gross dividends (including capital gain distributions) and other distributions on stock, or you are electing to exclude qualified reinvested dividends from a public utility, complete Part II. If you received dividends as a nominee for another, see page 22.

SAMPLE

Name of payer				Amount
9			9	
10 Add amounts on line 9			10	
11 Capital gain distributions. Enter here and on line 15, Schedule D.*	11			
12 Nontaxable distributions. (See Instructions for adjustment to basis.)	12			
13 Exclusion of qualified reinvested dividends from a public utility. (See page 22 of Instructions.)	13			
14 Add lines 11, 12, and 13			14	
15 Subtract line 14 from line 10. Write your answer here and on Form 1040, line 9a ▶			15	

**If you received capital gain distributions for the year and you do not need Schedule D to report any other gains or losses, do not file that schedule. Instead, enter 40% of your capital gain distributions on Form 1040, line 14.*

Part III Foreign Accounts and Foreign Trusts

(See page 22 of Instructions.)

If you received more than $400 of interest or dividends, OR if you had a foreign account or were a grantor of, or a transferor to, a foreign trust, you must answer both questions in Part III.	Yes	No
16 At any time during the tax year, did you have an interest in or a signature or other authority over a bank account, securities account, or other financial account in a foreign country? (See page 23 of the instructions for exceptions and filing requirements for Form 90-22.1.)		
If "Yes," write the name of the foreign country ▶		
17 Were you the grantor of, or transferor to, a foreign trust which existed during the current tax year, whether or not you have any beneficial interest in it? If "Yes," you may have to file Forms 3520, 3520-A, or 926		

For Paperwork Reduction Act Notice, see Form 1040 Instructions. **Schedule B (Form 1040) 1983**

☆ U.S. GOVERNMENT PRINTING OFFICE: 1984-423-338

Form **2441**

Department of the Treasury
Internal Revenue Service (0)

Credit for Child and Dependent Care Expenses

▶ Attach to Form 1040.
▶ See Instructions below.

OMB No. 1545-0063

1983

24

Name(s) as shown on Form 1040 | Your social security number

1 Write the number of qualifying persons who were cared for in 1983. (See the instructions below for the definition of qualifying persons.) . . . . . ▶

2 If payments listed on line 3 were made to an individual, complete the following: Yes | No

a If you paid $50 or more in a calendar quarter to an individual, were the services performed in your home? . . . . . .

b If "Yes," have you filed appropriate wage tax returns on wages for services in your home (see instructions for line 2)?

c If the answer to **b** is "Yes," write your employer identification number. . . . . . ▶

3 Write the amount of expenses you incurred and actually paid in 1983, but **do not** write more than $2,400 ($4,800 if you paid for the care of two or more persons) **3**

4 You **must** write your earned income on line 4. See the instructions for line 4 for the definition of earned income.

- If you were **unmarried** at the end of 1983, write your earned income on line 4, **OR**
- If you are **married,** filing a joint return for 1983,
  - **a** write your earned income $ ________________, and
  - **b** write your spouse's earned income $ ________________, and
  - **c** compare amounts on lines 4a and 4b, and write the **smaller** of the two amounts on line 4. . . . **4**

5 Compare amounts on lines 3 and 4, and write the **smaller** of the two amounts on line 5 . . . **5**

6 Write the percentage from the table below that applies to the adjusted gross income on Form 1040, line 33. . . . . **6**

If line 33 is: *Over— But not over—*	Percentage is:	If line 33 is: *Over— But not over—*	Percentage is:
0–$10,000	30% (.30)	$20,000–22,000	24% (.24)
$10,000–12,000	29% (.29)	22,000–24,000	23% (.23)
12,000–14,000	28% (.28)	24,000–26,000	22% (.22)
14,000–16,000	27% (.27)	26,000–28,000	21% (.21)
16,000–18,000	26% (.26)	28,000	20% (.20)
18,000–20,000	25% (.25)		

7 Multiply the amount on line 5 by the percentage shown on line 6 and write the result. **7**

8 Multiply any child and dependent care expenses for 1982 that you paid in 1983 by the percentage that applies to the adjusted gross income on Form 1040, line 33, for 1982. Write the result. (See line 8 instructions for the required statement.) **8**

9 Add amounts on lines 7 and 8, and write the total **9**

10 a Write the tax shown on Form 1040, line 40 . . . . . **10a**

b Add lines 41 through 44 of Form 1040, and write total. (See line 10 instructions.) **10b**

c Subtract line 10b from line 10a, and write the result. (If line 10b is more than line 10a, write zero.) **10c**

11 Compare amounts on lines 9 and 10c, and write the **smaller** of the two amounts on line 11. Also, write this amount on Form 1040, line 45 . . . . . **11**

General Instructions

Paperwork Reduction Act Notice.—We ask for this information to carry out the Internal Revenue laws of the United States. We need it to ensure that taxpayers are complying with these laws and to allow us to figure and collect the right amount of tax. You are required to give us this information.

What Is the Child and Dependent Care Expenses Credit?

You may be able to take a tax credit for amounts you paid someone to care for your child or other qualifying person so you could work or look for work in 1983. The credit will lower the amount of your tax. The credit is based on a percentage of the amount you paid during the year. The most you can take as a credit is $720 if you paid for the care of one qualifying person, or $1440 if you paid for the care of two or more qualifying persons.

Who is a qualifying person.— A qualifying person is any one of the following persons:

- Any person under age 15 whom you claim as a dependent (but see the special rule below for **Children of divorced or separated parents**).
- Your disabled spouse who is mentally or physically unable to care for himself or herself.
- Any disabled person who is mentally or physically unable to care for himself or herself and whom you claim as a dependent, or could claim as a dependent except that he or she had income of $1,000 or more.

Children of divorced or separated parents.—If you were divorced, legally separated, or separated under a written agreement, you may be able to claim the credit even if your child is not your dependent. Your child is a qualifying person if **all four** of the following apply:

1. You had custody for the longer period during the year, and

2. The child received over half of his or her support from one or both of the parents, and

3. The child was in the custody of one or both of the parents over half of the year, and

4. The child was under age 15, or was physically or mentally unable to care for himself or herself.

(Continued on back)

Who Can Take the Credit?

To claim the credit **all five** of the following must apply:

1. You paid for the care so you (and your spouse if you were married) could work or look for work (but see the rules at the line 4 instructions for **Spouse who is a full-time student or is disabled**).

2. One or more qualifying persons lived in your home.

3. You (and your spouse if you were married) paid over half the cost of keeping up your home. The cost includes: rent; mortgage interest; property taxes; utilities; home repairs; and food eaten at home.

4. The person you paid to provide the care was not your spouse or a person you could claim as a dependent.

Note: *If the person you paid for the care was your child, he or she must have been 19 or over by the end of 1983.*

5. If you were married at the end of 1983, generally, you must file a joint tax return. However, there are two exceptions to this rule. You will be treated as unmarried and can file a separate return and still be eligible to take the credit if:

a. You were legally separated; or

b. You were living apart, and:

- The qualifying person lived in your home over 6 months, and
- You provided over half the cost of keeping up your home, and
- Your spouse did not live in your home during the last 6 months of the tax year.

What Are Qualified Expenses?

Qualified expenses include amounts paid for household services and care of the qualifying person.

Household services.—These services must be needed to care for the qualifying person as well as to run the home. They include, for example, the services of a cook, maid, babysitter, housekeeper, governess, or cleaning person if the services were at least partly for the benefit of the qualifying person.

Care of the qualifying person.—Care includes the cost of services for the qualifying person's well-being and protection.

Generally, care does not include food, clothing, or schooling expenses; but if you paid for care that included these items, and you cannot separate their cost from the total payment, you can count the total payment. However, you cannot count the cost of schooling for a child in the first grade or above.

Care outside the home.—You can count care provided outside your home if the care was for:

a. Your dependent under age 15; or

b. Any other qualifying person who regularly spends at least 8 hours each day in your home.

Care that is provided by a dependent care center may be counted if the center complies with all applicable state and local laws and regulations. A dependent care center is a place that provides care for at least seven persons (other than persons who live there), and receives a fee, payment, or grant for providing the services for any of those persons, regardless of whether the center is run for profit.

Medical expenses.—Some dependent care expenses may qualify as medical expenses. If you itemize deductions, you may want to take all or part of these medical expenses on Schedule A (Form 1040). If you cannot use all the medical expenses on Form 2441 because of the dollar limit or earned income limit (explained later), you can take the rest of these expenses on Schedule A. But if you deduct the medical expenses first on Schedule A, you cannot use any part of these expenses on Form 2441.

For more information, get **Publication 503,** Child and Disabled Dependent Care.

Specific Instructions

We have provided specific instructions for most of the lines on the form. Those lines that do not appear in the instructions are self-explanatory.

Line 2.—In general, if you paid cash wages of $50 or more in a calendar quarter for household services provided by a person such as a housekeeper, maid, babysitter, or cook, you must file an employment tax return. If you are not sure whether you should file an employment tax return, get **Form 942,** Employer's Quarterly Tax Return for Household Employees.

Note: *You should file a* ***Form 940,*** *Employer's Annual Federal Unemployment Tax Return, for 1983 by January 31, 1984, if you paid cash wages of $1,000 or more for household services in any calendar quarter in 1982 or 1983.*

Line 3. Dollar limit.—On line 3 write the amount of qualified child and dependent care expenses you incurred and actually paid in 1983. However, the most you can figure the credit on is $2,400 a year for one qualifying person, or $4,800 a year for two or more qualifying persons.

Note: *Do not include on line 3 qualified expenses that you incurred in 1983 but did not pay until 1984. Instead, you may be entitled to increase the amount of your 1984 credit when you pay the 1983 expenses in 1984.*

Line 4. Earned income limit.—Figure your earned income on line 4. The amount of your qualified expenses **cannot** be more than your earned income.

In general, earned income is wages, salaries, tips, and other employee compensation. It also includes net earnings from self-employment. For more information on what is earned income for purposes of the credit, see Publication 503.

Unmarried taxpayers.—If you were unmarried at the end of 1983 or are treated as being unmarried at the end of the year, write your earned income on line 4.

Married taxpayers.—If you are married, filing a joint return, figure each spouse's earned income separately and disregard community property laws. Write your earned income on line 4a and your spouse's earned income on line 4b. Then, write the **smaller** of your earned income or your spouse's earned income on line 4.

Spouse who is a full-time student or is disabled.—If your spouse was a full-time student or was mentally or physically unable to care for himself or herself, figure your spouse's earned income on a monthly basis to determine your spouse's earned income for the year. For each month that your spouse was disabled or a full-time student, your spouse is considered to have earned income of not less than $200 a month ($400 a month if more than one qualifying person was cared for in 1983).

If, in the same month, both you and your spouse were full-time students and did not work, you cannot use any amount paid that month to figure the credit. The same applies to a couple who did not work because neither was capable of self-care.

A full-time student is one who was enrolled in a school for the number of hours or classes that is considered full time. The student must have been enrolled at least 5 months during 1983.

Self-employment income.—You must reduce your earned income by any loss from self-employment. If your net earnings from self-employment are less than $1,600, and you use the optional method to figure your self-employment tax, you may be able to increase your net earnings to $1,600. See **Publication 533,** Self-Employment Tax, for details. If you only have a loss from self-employment, or your loss is more than your other earned income and you do not use the optional method, you cannot take the credit.

Line 8.—If you had qualified expenses for 1982 that you did not pay until 1983, you may be able to increase the amount of credit you can take in 1983. To do this, multiply the 1982 expenses you paid in 1983 by the percentage from the table on line 6 that applies to the adjusted gross income shown on your 1982 Form 1040, line 33. Your 1982 expenses must be within the 1982 limits. Attach a computation showing how you figured the increase. (Use the example in Publication 503 as a guide.)

Line 10.—Your credit cannot be more than your tax after subtracting certain credits. Write on line 10a your tax from Form 1040, line 40. Add the amounts, if any, from lines 41 through 44 of Form 1040, and write the total on line 10b. Also, add any WIN credit carryover you entered on Form 1040, line 46. Subtract line 10b from line 10a, and write the result on line 10c.

Line 11.—Compare amounts on lines 9 and 10c, and write the **smaller** of the two amounts on line 11. Also write this amount on Form 1040, line 45. This is your credit for child and dependent care expenses.

☆ U.S. GOVERNMENT PRINTING OFFICE: 1983—0-390-214/58-040-1110

6. Stocks, Bonds, Mutual Funds, and Capital Gains

Investing in some types of securities will lessen your tax bite. For example, municipal bonds pay interest that is, in most cases, totally tax-exempt to bondholders. Similarly, some public utilities issue partially tax-exempt securities.

To encourage the ownership of stocks and bonds by individuals, the capital gains tax was enacted many years ago. The capital gains tax rate is considerably lower than ordinary tax rates. It applies if the securities that earned the profit have been held for the requisite period of time, presently six months.

Here we give you the latest information with regard to capital gains and the dividend exclusion as well as vital data on the tax aspects of owning securities. If you invest, you must read this chapter.

Those Wonderful Capital Gains

Q When did the new six month holding period for capital gains begin?

A It applies to capital assets acquired after June 22, 1984. Assets acquired before that date must be held for the old twelve-month period before capital gains can be taken as a long-term item.

Q I am not sure I fully understand the concept of capital gains. Can you explain it to me?

A Capital gains attach to capital assets that an individual owns, such as a house, its furnishings, art objects, and stocks and bonds. When you sell one of these items, Uncle Sam wants to get his percentage of any profit you might get. If you have held the asset more than six months and you make a profit on its sale, 40 percent of the gain is reportable as income. The tax rate on that 40 percent is 20 percent according to the new tax law. (This applies to gains incurred after June 9, 1981.) Any asset held six months or fewer is a short-term asset and is taxed at ordinary income rates, which are higher than the capital gains rate unless you have offsetting capital losses.

Q When my mother died last year, I inherited her house. It was about nine months before I actually took title to the property because of estate valuations and other procedures that caused delays. From what date does the time run for capital gains purposes?

A The rule for inherited property is that time runs from the date of death, not the date from which you actually took possession of the property. However, you do not have to hold the property for six months to get long term capital gains treatment.

Q I have some stock that I bought about a year ago. I have made a nice gain on the stock, and now I want to sell it. I want to make sure, however, that I am getting a long-term capital gain rather than a short-term one, but I don't know how to determine the six-month period. I placed the order on February 10 and I received a confirmation from my broker on February 19. When does the holding period start running?

A For capital gains purposes, the holding period begins the day after the order to buy was executed. So if your broker bought the stock on the day you called, February 10, the holding period would start on February 11. The execution date should be noted on your confirmation.

What might be confusing to you is that when you sell stock, the holding period ends the day the sales order is executed. If, therefore, you call your broker on September 11, seven months later and your stock is sold on or after that date, you have qualified for capital gains treatment.

Dividend Exclusion

Q I guess I am like most taxpayers—I want to pay as little tax as possible. I get upset when I can't take all the deductions, credits, and exclusions I am entitled to. Here's my dilemma: I received more than $600 in stock dividends last year, but I can exclude only $100. Why am I not allowed the full $200?

A You are allowed $200 if you are married and if you file a joint return. It now makes no difference in whose name the stock is held as it did formerly.

Other Considerations

Q Two years ago I purchased an option on ten acres of farmland, but I did not exercise the option. Recently I sold the option at a profit. Can I claim a capital gain on that profit, or is it just ordinary income to me?

A Good news. You can take capital gains on the option because you have held it for more than six months. If you had allowed the option to lapse, you could have taken a loss that could have been offset against ordinary income.

Q I am a mutual fund shareholder. The fund that I have is a fund affiliated with a family of funds, all managed by the same company. Last year I exchanged one mutual fund for another in the family. Will I have to pay income tax on the exchange?

A No, not on the exchange. But if you had a gain on the shares of the first fund, you will be subject to capital gains tax for the year. If you suffered a loss, however, you can also qualify for a capital loss on the original fund.

Q I have heard it said that tax-exempt municipal bonds make good investment sense only for people in higher tax brackets. Is that so?

A Generally, yes. Here are some figures to prove it. Say you are in the 50 percent tax bracket, and you have the opportunity to choose between fully taxable bonds paying 10 percent and tax-exempt bonds paying 6 percent. Since your after-tax yield on the taxable bonds is 5 percent, the tax exempt bonds at 6 percent are a better buy.

Q Since my wife and I always file a joint return, I know that we are entitled to a $200 dividend exclusion on our stock. I own some stock individually in my name and so does she. Last year she earned about $40 in dividends and I earned $125. I have been told that I can take only $100 as an exclusion and she can take only the $40. What happens to the other $60 that she is entitled to, and why can't I take my full $125?

A **You were misinformed. You can exclude a maximum of $200 in dividends on a joint return regardless of who earns the dividends. You can take your full $125, your wife can add her $40, and the $165 total can be fully excluded on your joint return.**

Q Much to my surprise, the IRS informed me that the $1000 liquidating dividend that I received from one of my stock holdings should not have been included in the dividend income that I reported. How should it be reported? Why isn't it dividend income subject to exclusion?

A Liquidating dividends are made by corporations that are in the process of going out of business through either liquidation or bankruptcy. These dividends are considered payment for stock owned that may be worthless in the future. As such, liquidated dividends are treated as proceeds from the sale of stock, not as regular dividends.

Q I have often heard the term "wash sale" used, but I don't know what it means. Can you define the term?

A If you buy stocks and they show a loss, you can take a tax deduction. But if you sell your securities at a loss and within thirty days you turn around and buy back the identical securities, that is called a wash sale and any tax loss would be disallowed. It is, in effect, a thirty-day waiting period that the IRS imposes on you.

Q I invest heavily in the stock market. Can I deduct anything associated with these investments?

A Yes, many things. The largest expense you can deduct is that of brokerage commissions, but you can also deduct the cost of any related investment publications you subscribe to and any investment counseling fees you have incurred. Also, if you rent a safe-deposit box in which to store your certificates, you can deduct the cost of that rental.

Q My broker recently advised me to buy utility stocks that have tax-deferred dividends. Do all utilities have such dividends, and is there a limit on the amount I can defer?

A The 1981 tax law contained a provision allowing some utilities to give a stockholder shares of stock rather than cash dividends if the shareholder desires. The stock given must be equivalent in value to what the cash dividend would have been. You are allowed up to $750 worth of stock dividend deferral if you are single and $1500 if you file a joint return. Note, however, that not all utilities qualify; only those that have approved Dividend Reinvestment Plans are allowed to offer this benefit.

Whenever you sell your shares you will have to pay any taxes due, but if you hold the shares for six months or longer, you will pay at capital gains and not ordinary income rates. If you sell the stock rather than receiving the cash dividend, the entire proceeds are taxable.

Q I bought a home computer last year and I use it exclusively for my investments. I know that I can deduct the cost of the computer, but I also bought two expensive computer software packages for the investment work I do. Can I also deduct those costs?

A Yes, as long as you use the computer and the software exclusively for investment purposes, you can also deduct the software.

Q I own a few hundred shares of stock in a company that has been having some financial troubles. I am interested in going to the annual meeting of the company to find out what is really going on. The only problem is that the annual meeting is going to be held almost 1000 miles away from my home. If I go to the meeting, can I deduct my expenses?

A No. If you travel away from home to look after property you hold for investment, you can deduct those costs, but you cannot deduct expenses to go to an annual meeting.

Q I am an investor and last year I had a really bad year. Altogether I lost $9500 in the stock market. What can I do about recognizing the loss for tax purposes?

A If these losses were realized losses and not paper losses you are only allowed to take $3000 of the total losses on your return for this year. The other $6500 can be carried forward to future years but only to the extent of $3000 per year. There is no carryback on securities losses.

Schedule D, reproduced on the next page, is to be filed if you had any capital gains or losses, either short or long term, during the year.

SCHEDULE D (FORM 1040)

Department of the Treasury Internal Revenue Service (0)

Capital Gains and Losses

(Examples of property to be reported on this Schedule are gains and losses on stocks, bonds, and similar investments, and gains (but not losses) on personal assets such as a home or jewelry.)

▶ Attach to Form 1040. ▶ See Instructions for Schedule D (Form 1040).

OMB No. 1545-0074

1983

11

Name(s) as shown on Form 1040 | **Your social security number**

PART I.—Short-term Capital Gains and Losses—Assets Held One Year or Less

a. Description of property (Example, 100 shares 7% preferred of "Z" Co.)	b. Date acquired (Mo., day, yr.)	c. Date sold (Mo., day, yr.)	d. Gross sales price	e. Cost or other basis, plus expense of sale	f. LOSS If column (e) is more than (d) subtract (d) from (e)	g. GAIN If column (d) is more than (e) subtract (e) from (d)
1						

		Line	f. LOSS	g. GAIN
2	Short-term gain from sale or exchange of a principal residence from Form 2119, lines 7 or 11	2		
3	Short-term capital gain from installment sales from Form 6252, line 21 or 29	3		
4	Net short-term gain or (loss) from partnerships, S corporations, and fiduciaries	4		
5	Add lines 1 through 4 in column f and column g	5	( )	
6	Combine columns f and g of line 5 and enter the net gain or (loss)		6	
7	Short-term capital loss carryover from years beginning after 1969		7	( )
8	Net short-term gain or (loss), combine lines 6 and 7		8	

SAMPLE

PART II.— Long-term Capital Gains and Losses—Assets Held More Than One Year

a. Description of property	b. Date acquired	c. Date sold	d. Gross sales price	e. Cost or other basis, plus expense of sale	f. LOSS	g. GAIN
9						

		Line	f. LOSS	g. GAIN
10	Long-term gain from sale or exchange of a principal residence from Form 2119, lines 7, 11, 16 or 18	10		
11	Long-term capital gain from installment sales from Form 6252, line 21 or 29	11		
12	Net long-term gain or (loss) from partnerships, S corporations, and fiduciaries	12		
13	Add lines 9 through 12 in column f and column g	13	( )	
14	Combine columns f and g of line 13 and enter the net gain or (loss)		14	
15	Capital gain distributions		15	
16	Enter gain from Form 4797, line 6(a)(1)		16	
17	Combine lines 14 through 16		17	
18	Long-term capital loss carryover from years beginning after 1969		18	( )
19	Net long-term gain or (loss), combine lines 17 and 18		19	

Note: *Complete the back of this form. However, if you have capital loss carryovers from years beginning before 1970, do not complete Parts III or V. See Form 4798 instead.*

For Paperwork Reduction Act Notice, see Form 1040 instructions. **Schedule D (Form 1040) 1983**

PART III.—Summary of Parts I and II

20 Combine lines 8 and 19, and enter the net gain or (loss) here	20	
Note: *If line 20 is a loss, skip lines 21 through 23 and complete lines 24 and 25. If line 20 is a gain complete lines 21 through 23 and skip lines 24 and 25.*		
21 If line 20 shows a gain, enter the smaller of line 19 or line 20. Enter zero if there is a loss or no entry on line 19	21	
22 Enter 60% of line 21	22	
If line 22 is more than zero, you may be liable for the alternative minimum tax. See Form 6251.		
23 Subtract line 22 from line 20. Enter here and on Form 1040, line 13	23	
24 If line 20 shows a loss, enter one of the following amounts: **a** If line 8 is zero or a net gain, enter 50% of line 20; **b** If line 19 is zero or a net gain, enter line 20; or **c** If line 8 and line 19 are net losses, enter amount on line 8 added to 50% of the amount on line 19	24	
25 Enter here and as a loss on Form 1040, line 13, the smallest of: **a** The amount on line 24; **b** $3,000 ($1,500 if married and filing a separate return); or **c** Taxable income, as adjusted	25	

PART IV.—Complete this Part Only If You Elect Out of the Installment Method And Report a Note or Other Obligation at Less Than Full Face Value

☐ Check here if you elect out of the installment method.
Enter the face amount of the note or other obligation ▶ ....
Enter the percentage of valuation of the note or other obligation ▶

PART V.—Computation of Post-1969 Capital Loss Carryovers from 1983 to 1984

(Complete this part if the loss on line 24 is more than the loss on line 25)
Note: *You do not have to complete Part V on the copy you file with IRS.*

Section A.—Short-term Capital Loss Carryover

26 Enter loss shown on line 8; if none, enter zero and skip lines 27 through 30 then go to line 31	26	
27 Enter gain shown on line 19. If that line is blank or shows a loss, enter zero	27	
28 Reduce any loss on line 26 to the extent of any gain on line 27	28	
29 Enter smaller of line 25 or line 28	29	
30 Subtract line 29 from line 28. This is your short-term capital loss carryover from 1983 to 1984	30	

Section B.—Long-term Capital Loss Carryover

31 Subtract line 29 from line 25 (**Note:** *If you skipped lines 27 through 30, enter amount from line 25*)	31	
32 Enter loss from line 19; if none, enter zero and skip lines 33 through 36	32	
33 Enter gain shown on line 8. If that line is blank or shows a loss, enter zero	33	
34 Reduce any loss on line 32 to the extent of any gain on line 33	34	
35 Multiply amount on line 31 by 2	35	
36 Subtract line 35 from line 34. This is your long-term capital loss carryover from 1983 to 1984	36	

☆U.S. G.P.O. 1983-390-084 E.I. 43-0787287

7. Divorce, Alimony, and Child Support

Proper tax planning is an integral part of the divorce process. For instance, it makes a difference to both the husband and wife if alimony or child support is paid. Alimony is fully taxable income to the wife and totally deductible by the husband.

Child support is neither taxable to the wife nor deductible by the husband. If you are arranging a divorce settlement, what you *call* the payments that are to be made can make a big difference to you. An experienced attorney should be consulted for the full particulars.

Here in simple language we explain some of the consequences of divorce and their tax effects. Among the problems considered are deductibility of alimony, alternatives to alimony, and payments in lump sums.

The Alimony Deduction

Q I am going through a divorce settlement right now, and I want to take care of my alimony by assigning a certain number of shares of stock to my wife on a monthly basis. My lawyer says that I can't do that because of a recent change in the law. Is that so?

A Yes, it is. The Tax Reform Act of 1984 has done away with property such as real estate or securities as the subject matter for alimony. Now all alimony must be paid in the form of cash only, and the payments that you make will terminate at your wife's death. However, this only applies to support decrees and divorce agreements signed after 1984.

Q A friend of mine who was divorced a couple of years ago told me that I can't take my alimony payments as a deduction unless I itemize my deductions. Is he right?

A Your friend is living in the past. That used to be the rule, but now it is not necessary to itemize to take the alimony deduction.

Q I am presently going through divorce proceedings. My wife's attorney wants me to make a lump sum alimony payment to my wife, but my lawyer advised against it because, he said, the taxes would kill me. I thought alimony was deductible. Is it?

A Yes, it is, but not in this situation. To be deductible, alimony must be made in a series of periodic payments. Do not pay an alimony settlement in a lump sum if you can possibly avoid it.

Q I am now involved in divorce proceedings. I know that child support is not deductible, but is there anything I can do to lessen my taxes?

A You are right when you point out that child support payments are not deductible. You can, however, arrange with your former wife to take your children as dependents on your tax return. This must of course be written into your divorce agreement, but at least you could claim $1000 as a tax exemption for each child, and that would do something to lessen your tax load. An alternative is to pay only alimony, all of which is tax deductible.

Q When my divorce was finalized last year, I gave my former wife a piece of real estate that I owned as a property settlement; but now the IRS informs me that I cannot deduct the value of that real estate. Is this right?

A Yes, it is. Property settlements are nondeductible. If your separation agreement or divorce settlement had been written in such a way that the property you gave was in the nature of alimony and not a property settlement, even then you could have deducted the value of the real estate, because alimony must now consist of cash, not property.

Child Support Payments and Receipts

Q I think I have been the victim of poor legal advice. When my former husband and I got our divorce last year, my lawyer prepared the papers and I signed a form that didn't specify that a certain amount of the monthly maintenance to me be set aside for child support. Instead the paper that became part of the support decree gave me $500 per month in alimony, when in fact I was supposed to get $300 in alimony and $200 in child support. Now I find that I have to declare all the $500 as income. What can I do?

A You should sue your attorney for malpractice. If a specific amount is not set aside for child support in a divorce decree, then the entire amount is considered to be alimony and hence taxable to you.

Q My wife and I are now separated and our divorce will become final next year. We are each providing exactly 50 percent of my daughter's support. She lives with her mother. Who can claim my daughter as a dependent, I or my wife?

A Believe it or not, neither of you can. It is required that one of you provide *more* than 50 percent of the support to claim the child as a dependent. If in fact both of you provide exactly one half the support, the more than 50 percent test is not met. However, one of you can remedy the situation by paying just $1 more than the 50 percent needed. Make sure that in your divorce agreement the question of who takes the dependency exemption is worked out; otherwise, the IRS will constantly question or audit the person who is taking the exemption. Also think about a multiple support agreement whereby you take the exemption one year and your former wife takes it the following year. Ask your attorney or accountant about Form 2120 (which is reproduced in Chapter 20).

Divorced Taxpayer's Status

Q My divorce became final in May of last year. Can I take my former wife as a dependent for last year? We did live together for part of the year.

A No. The year you are divorced you lose the exemption for your former spouse. If your ex-wife had died during the year, you could have taken her as an exemption, but this is not so in the case of a divorce.

Q My wife and I separated 13 months ago. Can we still file a joint return even though we aren't living together?

A Your best bet is to work your taxes out both married filing jointly and separately. File whichever method that produces less tax.

Q My former husband stopped paying me alimony last year. He is supposed to pay until I remarry, which I have not done. I had to hire an attorney to compel my former husband to resume payments. I understand I can deduct the attorney's fee. Is that right?

A Yes. Since alimony is taxable, you are allowed to deduct legal expenses that are necessary to produce taxable income. You could also deduct any legal expenses incurred if you sued an employer or former employer in order to keep a job.

8. Doctor and Dentist Bills

Unfortunately we often have medical bills to pay, but fortunately we can deduct some of those expenses from our taxes. This chapter examines exactly how much can be deducted, the kinds of treatment that are deductible (you may be surprised), and the deductibility of medical insurance, medicine, drugs, and treatments.

Did you know that you may be able to avoid an audit of even a large medical expense deduction if you attach to your tax return an explanatory letter detailing any unusual medical deductions. When the IRS calls for an audit because of medical expenses, its representatives are looking for proof that you actually spent as much as you are claiming for medical expenses. If you furnish that proof when you file your return, the necessity of calling you in will be mitigated considerably.

The Medical Care Deduction Explained

Q I'm confused. How do I calculate the amount I spend for medicine and drugs into the total amount I can take as a medical care deduction?

A You are limited to 5% of your adjusted gross income. Except for prescription drugs and insulin you cannot deduct any other medications. The insulin and prescription drugs become part of the 5% limitation.

Q What is the rule with regard to the deductibility of hospitalization insurance? I have a major medical policy. Can I deduct any part of its cost?

A Not any more. You used to be able to deduct half of the cost of hospitalization insurance up to a limit of $150. This, however, has now been eliminated.

Q Last year I had some heavy medical expenses, and as is my habit I paid many of the bills in cash. One doctor told me that for my own good and for tax reasons I should pay him by check. Why?

A For one very good reason. You know that you are entitled to a medical expense deduction. The best way to prove that you actually incurred the medical expenses is to have the proper documentation. Checks provide that documentation. If you continue to pay by cash, make sure you get receipts or other evidence of payment from the doctor, dentist, or other practitioner. These bills are also considered valid documentation.

Allowable and Nonallowable Medical Procedures

Q My brother was confined to an alcoholism treatment center for three months last year. Is alcoholism considered a disease to the extent that a medical expense deduction can be taken for costs related to his confinement at the center?

A Yes. The costs of such confinement including fees paid for room, board, and doctors are deductible.

Q I recently took one of those intensive stop smoking courses. I was told that even though my doctor said it would be good for me to take it, I can't deduct it as a medical expense. Is that right?

A Yes, it is. Evidently the IRS does not consider smoking similar to drinking in this regard. You can take a deduction if you go to a treatment center to stop drinking, but the same doesn't hold true if you seek help to stop smoking.

Q I know that in some circles chiropractors are not looked on as real physicians. How does the IRS view them? Can I deduct chiropractic fees just as I would fees from a regular M.D.?

A Yes. Chiropractors' fees are considered eligible for the medical and dental care deduction. Psychiatric, psychological, and Christian Science practitioners' fees are also deductible.

Q I have two questions. I recently had some acupuncture treatment, and I was told that it is tax deductible. Is that right? Second, my wife is pregnant, and we would like to have an abortion performed. Is the cost of the abortion deductible?

A Yes to both questions, but the abortion has to be a legal one, that is, performed in a state that allows it.

Q My dentist performed extensive work on me last year, and as a result I now have a complete set of false teeth. Is all that work, including the cost of the new teeth, eligible for the medical care deduction?

A Yes. False teeth and all the costs associated with making them and inserting them are permissible medical care expenses.

Q To improve our appearance, both my husband and I had face-lifts last year. Can we claim the costs of that surgery as a medical deduction?

A Yes. Face-lifts are allowable medical expense procedures. So are acupuncture treatments and vasectomies. Of course medical expenses can be deducted only to the extent that they exceed 5 percent of the taxpayer's adjusted gross income.

Q My mother, who lives with us and is dependent on us for support, suffered a stroke last year. We installed an elevator-type device in the house to enable her to move from her bedroom upstairs to the downstairs areas. Can I deduct the cost of installing the elevator?

A Yes indeed. Any alterations to property that result from a medical condition are normally deductible as is the electricity to run them. The fact that your mother is dependent on you strengthens your case.

Q I recently had a physical examination, and my doctor told me that I must work out and exercise much more than I have been. There is a health spa nearby. Can I deduct as a medical necessity the fees I shall have to pay?

A No. Health spa fees are not an allowable medical deduction. Neither is the purchase of vitamins to maintain general good health or the expense of weight loss programs.

Q I have heard that some people have actually taken a tax deduction for building a swimming pool in their backyards. How is that possible? Could I get a deduction if I installed a pool?

A You could get such a deduction if you had a medical condition, such as a bad back, that required swimming as therapy. Such a pool must be prescribed by a physician. Of course you would also have to convince the IRS that the pool was built solely for medical purposes.

Q I recently read something in a newspaper that I can't believe is true. It was reported that a man claimed a tax deduction because a dentist prescribed clarinet lessons for his son who had a bad overbite. Did I read the item correctly?

A You sure did. Not only did dad get a tax deduction for the cost of the clarinet, but he also got a deduction for the cost of clarinet lessons. This is just another example of the point that if a doctor or dentist prescribes something for an ailment, there is not much the IRS can do, no matter how bizarre the treatment might seem.

Q My doctor, who has been treating me for a chronic ailment for a number of years, maintains two offices, one here in the midwest and the other in Florida where he lives in the winter. Can I deduct the cost of round trip air fares if I see him in Florida in the winter?

A Yes, if you see him and come right back to the midwest without taking a vacation while you are in Florida. There is nothing in the tax laws that requires your doctor's office to be right around the corner or down the street.

Q Because of a recent operation, I am unable to do housework. My doctor tells me I shouldn't do any until I am physically able, which may not be for a few more months. I have hired a woman to do my housework. Can I deduct her salary as a medical expense?

A No. This is true even though your doctor does not want you to do housework. Other medical expenses that are not deductible include diaper services, funeral and burial expenses, and the cost of maternity clothes. One possible way around the law is to hire a housekeeper who has been on the welfare rolls. Then you could claim the WIN credit. But if your hired help performs services that are the same as a nurse would perform, such as helping you in and out of bed or preparing meals, a portion of her pay may be deducted as a medical expense.

Q Recently we hired a neighborhood woman to perform nursing services for my infirm mother. There is only one problem: the woman we hired is not a licensed nurse. Can we still claim a medical care deduction?

A Yes. So long as the individual is performing nursing services, there is no necessity that he or she be licensed as a nurse. The deduction hinges on the nature of the work performed, not on the qualifications of the person performing them.

Q Under what circumstances can I take a deduction for my elderly mother's medical expenses?

A You can take the deduction if you contribute more than 50% of her support. By the way, the medical bills that you pay can be used to determine that 50% limit.

9. Primary Residences, Vacation Homes, and Real Property

The federal government has always favored and encouraged home ownership. Many tax laws, rules, and regulations have been written to give the homeowner a tax break. A prime example of this favored treatment is the relatively new rule that allows homeowners over the age of 55 to exclude for tax purposes the first $125,000 of profit on the sale of a house after July 20, 1981.

Homeowners under the age of 55 are afforded capital gains treatment on the sale of a house and of course all homeowners can deduct any interest paid on a home mortgage during the taxable year.

Buying a home has always been a wise tax strategy because it provides the buyer with a tax shelter that renting does not allow.

Selling a Home

Q My mother died last year and I inherited her house. Since I have a home of my own, I have decided to sell hers. How do I determine the value of the home for my tax purposes?

A If an estate tax return was filed for your mother, you should use the basis set forth there. If no estate tax return was filed, your best bet would be to have a real estate broker familiar with the area do an independent appraisal. The appraiser would have to determine the value of the house on the date of your mother's death.

Q We sold our home last June. What portion of the local property taxes can I deduct on this year's tax return?

A The general rule is that you can deduct property taxes on an apportioned basis using the number of days you actually owned the property. Typically, however, local property tax payments are worked out between the buyer and seller of a home as one of the conditions of the sale. Any taxes the new owner paid that were actually to be paid by you are added to the basis you use for calculating gain. Dig out your closing statement; all the figures should be there.

Q When I sold my home last year I had to pay a 6 percent commission to the real estate broker. Is that commission deductible?

A Yes, but only when you are calculating the profit on the sale of your home. Other deductible expenses include legal fees and state transfer taxes. Because the sale of a home is subject to capital gains treatment, you may be taxed on 40 percent of the profit you make on the sale of that house unless you either qualify for the $125,000 exclusion or reinvest the proceeds in a more expensive home. Also, if you moved more than 35 miles because of a job change, the realtor's commission may be deductible as a moving expense.

Q I sold my house last year and I gave the buyer a purchase money mortgage. She pays me a set amount of principal and interest every month. Now I am told that I must tell the IRS who she is. Is that true?

A Yes, it's true. The 1040 form now asks buyers to identify sellers and sellers to identify buyers where private financing is involved. The rationale here is that some taxpayers have been hiding income through private financing deals, and this double check is supposed to prevent that.

Q I bought a home last year. When I got the mortgage, I had to pay points to get the loan. Can I deduct these points?

A Most definitely. Points—or, as they are sometimes called, loan origination fees—are deductible in the year paid. If you sell property on which you have to pay points, like VA or FHA mortgages, you cannot deduct them. This is an area of particular complexity, and advice from a tax professional on the latest regulations and cases should be sought before acting.

Q I see where you can deduct points paid for the purchase of a home. I have a few houses that I rent out. Can I deduct the points I had to pay when I bought them?

A No. This is a deduction that is only available to an individual who obtains a mortgage for the purpose of buying a principal residence. You may not deduct points when a vacation home, commercial, or rental property is mortgaged.

Mortgages and Refinancing

Q Last year I sold a house I had owned for seven years. Because I had a twenty-year mortgage and I wanted to sell the house free and clear, I paid off the mortgage. But I also had to pay a prepayment penalty. Is that prepayment penalty deductible?

A Yes. Any penalty paid for prepaying a mortgage is considered a fully deductible interest payment. Make sure you have the amount of the prepayment penalty specifically and officially spelled out by the bank so that you can deduct the proper amount.

Q If I were to refinance my home, would I have to pay taxes on the amount I receive?

A No. Taking out a mortgage loan or refinancing an existing mortgage is considered for tax purposes to be a "nontaxable" event. However, if you have to pay points (processing fees) or a loan service charge to refinance, that amount is deductible as interest.

Q I own a few lots of valuable real estate for which I recently have been offered quite a bit of money. I have been told that if I give a purchase money mortgage, I can get a tax break. Can you explain this to me?

A If you accept a purchase money mortgage, which means that a buyer will pay off the purchase price over a number of years, you will have to pay tax on the income only as you receive it. You will not have to pay taxes on the full amount of the purchase price unless you are paid the entire amount within one year. Taxes are deferred on the amount not collected during the year.

The $125,000 Exclusion

Q My husband and I are both 62 years old and he has recently taken early retirement. We want to sell our home and move to a warmer climate. Naturally we'd like to pay as little capital gains on the sale of the house as possible. How can we do this?

A Fortunately you can get a very generous tax break if you meet certain qualifications. You can exclude a gain on the sale of the house up to $125,000 if you file a joint return and you have used the house as your principal residence for at least three of the past five years. This exclusion, however, is a once-in-a-lifetime thing. The law requires that a taxpayer be over 55 to qualify; since you are, any profit you make up to $125,000 is not subject to taxation.

Q My lawyer just told me something that I find hard to believe. She said that if I sell my house (I am 57 years old, my wife is 42) and take my $125,000 exclusion, my wife could not take the exclusion at some point in the future if she needs to. Is my lawyer right?

A Yes she is. Unfortunately once the exclusion is used by one spouse, it can't ever be used by the other spouse, even if you two should become divorced or if you should die. It is a rather harsh rule, but that is the way the law was written. Another point: if you use only part of the $125,000 exclusion, such as $35,000, you or your spouse can never use the other $90,000. It is lost forever.

Q My husband and I are over 55 and are moving from a single family home into a condominium. Do we still qualify for the $125,000 exclusion?

A Most definitely. The law specifically includes condominiums, cooperatives, and even houseboats and mobile homes. Enjoy your new home.

Postponing the Capital Gain

Q I understand that I don't have to pay any tax on the sale of my old home if I buy a new one within twenty-four months. Is that right?

A No. As the IRS is quick to point out, the gain on the sale of a home can be postponed but never entirely eliminated. If you purchase a new home within twenty-four months and its cost is the same as or higher than the adjusted sales price of the former home, you can postpone the gain by subtracting that gain from the basis of your new home. If you do not build or buy a replacement home within that period or the new home costs less than the old one, you must pay tax on the gain earned.

Q I am building a new home to replace my old one. Can I still postpone the gain if, because of construction delays, my new home isn't finished within the eighteen-month period after the sale of my old home?

A The rules are quite liberal with regard to construction of a new home. The rule is that you must *begin* building no later than twenty-four months after the sale. "Begin" has been defined as merely purchasing a lot, obtaining a mortgage, receiving approval of building plans, and obtaining a building permit. Actual construction need not have started.

Q Two years ago we moved out of our former home and bought a new one. However, we rented out our old house. I now want to sell that house, but I have been told that I cannot postpone the gain. Is that right?

A Yes. As soon as your old home assumes the status of a rental property, you are no longer eligible to postpone the gain on it, even though it was once your main residence.

Second Homes

Q I have a vacation home that I rented last year to an office colleague. I understand I don't have to report the rental income on my federal tax return. Is that right?

A It depends on the length of time you let the house. The IRS says you don't have to report rental income on a vacation home if you lease it for fourteen days or fewer. If, however, you let it for fifteen days or more, then that rental income must be reported.

Q I recently purchased a weekend retreat for myself and my family. The mortgage interest and property taxes will amount to about $2500 this year. Are there any special rules with regard to vacation homes, or can I deduct the $2500 just as if it were my primary residence?

A There are no special rules. Interest and taxes are fully deductible on a vacation home just as they are on your principal place of residence. The same holds true for casualty losses, such as a fire, that might be incurred.

Installment Sales

Q I just sold my house and I made a pretty good profit on it. I am retiring, so I asked the seller to give me a purchase money mortgage, which he agreed to do. Now I want to know how to report my gain for tax purposes?

A You have an election. You can either report all of your gain in one tax year or take advantage of the installment sales rules of the tax code and spread your taxable gain over the period of the mortgage.

Q I want to take advantage of the installment sales provisions of the tax code. What are the requirements for the type of personal property that qualifies, and what kind of down payment must I request from buyers?

A No requirements are spelled out by the IRS. You can sell any kind of personal property, and you need not ask for any kind of down payment. You can structure the transaction any way you want and the sale can be for any amount of money. And there is no set or specified period of time over which payments must be received.

Q Is personal property subject to the installment sales rules? I have a large collection of art prints that was left to me a few years ago which I now want to sell. I would like to spread out the payments, and my buyers are willing to pay me in installments. Can it be done?

A It sure can. Personal property, as well as real estate, falls under the installment sales rules.

Real Estate In General

Q I own a vacation home that I rent out to the general public and at times to members of my family at a fair market rent. What can I deduct?

A The law used to be that you could deduct mortgage interest payments and real estate taxes but only a portion of maintenance and depreciation expenses if you rented to a relative. This has now been updated. You can still deduct mortgage interest and real estate taxes but you can also deduct a higher percentage of depreciation and maintenance expenses. The percentage deductible varies with each owner, depending on personal use of the house and the number of days that the house is rented, whether to relatives or anyone else.

Q I sold my condominium last year. The attorney who handled the deal sent me a bill for services rendered. Can I deduct any portion of that bill?

A You can if the attorney gave you tax advice with regard to the sale and itemized the bill showing which part was for tax advice and which part was for the other legal work performed. The part allocated to the tax advice is deductible. You should ask for an itemized bill if one was not rendered.

Q The local man who prepared my tax returns says that I can deduct real estate taxes for my home on my federal return but cannot deduct local sewer and water taxes. Is he right?

A Yes he is. Although water and sewer taxes are related to real estate taxes, they are nevertheless considered separate nondeductible taxes for federal tax purposes.

Q I bought and rented out two single family homes last year. Where on the tax return do I report the income I made on them?

A You use Schedule E. That schedule is also used to report income from partnerships, estates, and trusts as well as any income from an S corporation. (See Schedule E at end of chapter.)

SCHEDULE E (Form 1040)

Department of the Treasury
Internal Revenue Service (0)

Supplemental Income Schedule

(From rents and royalties, partnerships, estates, and trusts, etc.)

▶ **Attach to Form 1040.** ▶ **See Instructions for Schedule E (Form 1040).**

OMB No. 1545-0074

1983

12

Name(s) as shown on Form 1040 | **Your social security number**

PART I.—Rent and Royalty Income or Loss

1 Are any of the expenses listed below for a vacation home or other recreational unit (see Instructions)? . . . . ☐ Yes ☐ No

2 If you checked "Yes" to question 1, did you or a member of your family occupy the vacation home or other recreational unit for more than the greater of 14 days or 10% of the total days rented at fair rental value during the tax year? . . . ☐ Yes ☐ No

Description of Properties (Show kind and location for each)

Property A ....

Property B ....

Property C

Rental and Royalty Income		Properties A	Properties B	Properties C		Totals (Add columns A, B, and C)
3 a Rents received . . .					} 3	
b Royalties received . . .						
Rental and Royalty Expenses						
4 Advertising . . .	4					
5 Auto and travel . . .	5					
6 Cleaning and maintenance . . .	6					
7 Commissions . . .	7					
8 Insurance . . .	8					
9 Interest . . .	9					
10 Legal and other professional fees . . .	10					
11 Repairs . . .	11					
12 Supplies . . .	12					
13 Taxes (Do **not** include Windfall Profit Tax here. See Part III, line 37.) . . .	13					
14 Utilities . . .	14					
15 Wages and salaries . . .	15					
16 Other (list) ▶						
....						
....						
....						
....						
....						
....						
....						
....						
....						
17 Total expenses other than depreciation and depletion. Add lines 4 through 16 . . .	17				17	
18 Depreciation expense (see Instructions), or depletion . . .	18				18	
19 Total. Add lines 17 and 18 . . .	19					
20 Income or (loss) from rental or royalty properties. Subtract line 19 from line 3a (rents) or 3b (royalties) . . .	20					

SAMPLE

21 Add properties with profits on line 20, and write the total profits here . . .	21	
22 Add properties with losses on line 20, and write the total (losses) here . . .	22	( )
23 Combine amounts on lines 21 and 22, and write the net profit or (loss) here . . .	23	
24 Net farm rental profit or (loss) from Form 4835, line 49 . . .	24	
25 Total rental or royalty income or (loss). Combine amounts on lines 23 and 24, and write the total here. If Parts II, III, and IV on page 2 do not apply to you, write the amount from line 25 on Form 1040, line 18. Otherwise, include the amount in line 39 on page 2 of Schedule E . . .	25	

For Paperwork Reduction Act Notice, see Form 1040 Instructions. **Schedule E (Form 1040) 1983**

Name(s) as shown on Form 1040 (Do not enter name and social security number if shown on other side) | Your social security number

PART II.—Income or Losses from Partnerships, Estates or Trusts, or S Corporations

If you report a loss below, and have amounts invested in that activity for which you are not at risk, you may have to file Form 6198. See instructions.

	(a) Name	(b) Check if foreign partnership	(c) Employer identification number	(d) Net loss (see instructions for at-risk limitations)	(e) Net income
Partnerships					
	26 Add amounts in columns (d) and (e) and write the total(s) here		26	( )	
	27 Combine amounts in columns (d) and (e), line 26, and write the net income or (loss)			27	
	28 Deduction for section 179 property (from Form 1065, Schedule K-1). (See Instructions for limitations.)			28	( )
	29 Total partnership income or (loss). Combine amounts on lines 27 and 28. Write the total here and include in line 39 below			29	
Estates or Trusts					
	30 Add amounts in columns (d) and (e) and write the total(s) here		30	( )	
	31 Total estate or trust income or (loss). Combine amounts in columns (d) and (e), line 30. Write the total here and include in line 39 below			31	
S Corporations					
	32 Add amounts in columns (d) and (e) and write the total(s) here		32	( )	
	33 Combine amounts in columns (d) and (e), line 32, and write the net income or (loss) here			33	
	34 Deduction for section 179 property (from Form 1120S, Schedule K-1). (See Instructions for limitations.)			34	( )
	35 Total S corporation income or (loss). Combine amounts on lines 33 and 34. Write the total here and include in line 39 below			35	

PART III.—Windfall Profit Tax Summary

36 Windfall profit tax credit or refund received in 1983 (see Instructions)	36	
37 Windfall profit tax withheld in 1983 (see Instructions)	37	( )
38 Combine amounts on lines 36 and 37. Write the total here and include in line 39 below	38	

PART IV.—Summary

39 TOTAL income or (loss). Combine lines 25, 29, 31, 35, and 38. Write total here and on Form 1040, line 18 ▶		39	
40 Farmers and fishermen: Write your share of GROSS FARMING AND FISHING INCOME applicable to Parts I and II	40		

PART V.—Depreciation Claimed in Part I.—Complete only if property was placed in service before January 1, 1981. For more space, use Form 4562. If you placed any property in service after December 31, 1980, use Form 4562 for all property; do NOT complete Part V.

	(a) Description of property	(b) Date acquired	(c) Cost or other basis	(d) Depreciation allowed or allowable in prior years	(e) Depreciation method	(f) Life or rate	(g) Depreciation for this year
Property A							
	Totals (Property A)						
Property B							
	Totals (Property B)						
Property C							
	Totals (Property C)						

☆ U.S. G.P.O. 1983-390-088 E.I. 43-0787287

10. Paying Interest

If you used a credit card last year, made payments on a mortgage, or paid off instalments on a personal loan, undoubtedly you paid interest charges. Interest is almost always tax deductible.

Owners of cooperative and condominium apartments get a double tax break that isn't available to regular homeowners. Not only are they entitled to the regular mortgage or loan interest deduction but they can claim a deduction for a portion of monthly maintenance or homeowners' association dues. The entire amount of maintenance or homeowners' dues is not tax deductible but normally the portion that is allowed makes the deduction worthwhile.

Q I promised my daughter and son-in-law that my wedding present to them would be the money every month to pay off the mortgage on a little house they bought. Can I deduct the interest on the mortgage?

A Not unless you signed the mortgage yourself. Otherwise, all you have done is to give a gift. Frequently doting parents try to take interest deductions on cars, personal loans, and other items that their children have actually signed for; this practice is contrary to the law.

Q I wonder if you could confirm something for me. I borrowed some money last year to buy some tax-exempt bonds. I have been told that the interest charged on the loan is nondeductible. Is that right?

A Yes, it is. Because you don't pay taxes on tax-exempt bonds, the government will not allow you a double tax break by allowing you to deduct the interest from money borrowed to buy such bonds.

The IRS has even gone so far as to prohibit interest deductions on other outstanding loans not connected with the purchase of tax-exempts.

Q Somebody told me that there is a limit on the amount I can deduct as interest in any one year. If that is so, what is the limit?

A There is a limitation on the amount of investment interest you can deduct in one year—$10,000. This is an annual limit.

Q I own some six-month money market certificates, which I purchased from a bank. My problem is this. I bought the certificates in August and they mature in February. Do I have to pay tax on the interest only in February or earlier as well?

A The IRS says you must pay tax on this interest when it is "credited" to your account. So if the bank computes the interest monthly and you receive a 1099 from the bank showing four-sixths of the total interest credited, that is what you have to report, even though you won't actually receive the interest until February.

Q Foolishly I cosigned a loan for my brother and he defaulted. I had to pay interest for six months. Now I've been told that I can't deduct those interest payments. Is that so, and if so, why?

A What you were told was correct. Cosigners or guarantors of loans, notes, or mortgages cannot deduct any interest payments that they make. However, they can take a short-term capital loss. Be careful about cosigning or guaranteeing loans in the future.

Q I finally sold my house last year but only after agreeing to pay the buyer's "points" for him. Can I take the deduction for those points?

A No. If you had bought the house yourself and paid the points out of separate funds, you could deduct. But if you as the seller pay the points for a buyer as an inducement to buy, you are not allowed the deduction.

Q I made good use of my overdraft checking account last year and paid quite a bit of interest for the privilege of using that account. Can I deduct that interest?

A Surely. It falls into the same category as credit card or charge account interest and it is deductible.

Q I have a son in medical school who has taken out a student loan. If I want to help him out by paying some of the interest on the loan, can I deduct that interest on my return?

A Not under the situation you propose. You can only deduct interest on your own obligation. Therefore, if you cosign the note you can take the deduction, but if you lend it to him you cannot. By the way, a guarantee of the note by you does not make it your obligation but cosigning it does.

11. Moving from Home to Home

Americans have always been on the move. A change in employment is probably the most common reason that today's Americans pull up stakes.

If you moved during the past year in order to get or to keep a job, you may be able to deduct some of the costs of that move.

Certain time and distance requirements that must be met before a deduction for a move can be taken will be detailed in the questions that follow. Good tax planning requires that you keep handy all receipts and information with regard to the move. If you are asked about them by the IRS, you will be able to prove the allowable expenses.

Q I am a self-employed business consultant who moved last year to a house that is 170 miles from my former residence. I work out of my home and I always have. Do I qualify for the moving expense deduction, even though I am self-employed?

A Yes, so long as you work full time for at least thirty-nine weeks during the first year of residency in the new house and a total of seventy-eight weeks during the two years immediately following your relocation.

Q Do I have to itemize my deductions to take a moving expense deduction?

A No. Moving expenses are deducted from adjusted gross income, so it is not necessary to itemize your deductions to take the moving expense deduction.

Q I think I have a bone to pick with my employer. I was moved from the East Coast to the West Coast last year so that I could work in the company's West Coast facility. I just got my W-2 form, and the company included in my taxable income the amount they paid the moving company to move me. Was that proper?

A Your company did the right thing. If the company pays for any part of your move or reimburses you for moving expenses, those amounts must be included in your taxable income and reflected on your W-2. But don't forget to deduct all the moving expenses, including those for which you were *not* reimbursed, like realtors' commissions.

Q I understand that the heavy motel bills my family and I incurred last year while looking for our present house are deductible. Is that so?

A Yes, but only up to $1500. Once you actually make the move, however, there is no limit on moving van or transportation expenses to your new residence. (See Form 3903 at the end of this chapter.)

Q I was transferred last year. I decided to rent an apartment in town rather than buy a home in the suburbs. I had to pay two months' rent ($1500) as a security deposit for the apartment I rented. Can I deduct that deposit as a moving expense?

A No, such deposits are nondeductible. The same holds true for prepayments of rent and losses incurred on the sale of a home. But if you had to buy a new lease, you could get a tax writeoff. If you incurred any temporary living expenses during that period, they would be deductible.

Form **3903** — Department of the Treasury, Internal Revenue Service (0)

Moving Expense Adjustment

▶ Attach to Form 1040.

OMB No. 1545-0062 — **1983** — 62

Name(s) as shown on Form 1040 | **Your social security number**

a What is the distance from your **old** residence to your **new** work place? ________ miles

b What is the distance from your **old** residence to your **old** work place? ________ miles

c If the distance in **a** above is 35 or more miles farther than the distance in **b** above, complete the rest of this form. If the distance is less than 35 miles, you may not take a deduction for moving expenses. This rule does not apply to members of the armed forces.

Line	Description			
1	Transportation expenses in moving household goods and personal effects			1
2	Travel, meal, and lodging expenses in moving from old to new residence			2
3	Pre-move travel, meal, and lodging expenses in looking for a new residence after getting your job	3		
4	Temporary living expenses in new location or area during any 30 days in a row after getting your job	4		
5	Add lines 3 and 4	5		
6	Enter the smaller of line 5 or $1,500 ($750 if married, filing a separate return, and, at the end of the tax year, you lived with your spouse who also started work during the tax year)		6	
7	Expenses of (check one): **a** ☐ selling or exchanging your old residence; or **b** ☐ if renting, settling an unexpired lease on your old residence		7	
8	Expenses of (check one): **a** ☐ buying your new residence; or **b** ☐ if renting, getting a lease on your new residence		8	
9	Add lines 6, 7, and 8		9	
10	Enter the smaller of line 9 or $3,000 ($1,500 if married, filing a separate return, and, at the end of the tax year, you lived with your spouse who also started work during the tax year)			10
	Note: *Use any amount on line **7a** not deducted because of the $3,000 (or $1,500) limit to decrease the gain on the sale of your residence. Use any amount on line **8a** not deducted because of the limit to increase the basis of your new residence. See **No Double Benefit** in the instructions.*			
11	Add lines 1, 2, and 10. This is your moving expense deduction. Enter here and on Form 1040, line 23 ▶			11
	Note: *If your employer paid for any part of your move (including the value of any services furnished in kind), report that amount on **Form 1040, line 7.** See **Reimbursements** in the instructions.*			

SAMPLE

General Instructions

Paperwork Reduction Act Notice.—We ask for this information to carry out the Internal Revenue laws of the United States. We need it to ensure that taxpayers are complying with these laws and to allow us to figure and collect the right amount of tax. You are required to give us this information.

Purpose of Form.—Use Form 3903 if you moved to a new principal work place within the United States or its possessions and you qualify to deduct your moving expenses.

Note: *Use **Form 3903F,** Foreign Moving Expense Adjustment, instead of this form if you are a U.S. citizen or resident alien who moved to a new principal work place outside the United States or its possessions.*

Additional Information.—For more information about moving expenses, please get **Publication 521,** Moving Expenses.

Who May Deduct Moving Expenses.—If you moved your residence because of a change in the location of your job, you may be able to deduct your moving expenses. You may qualify for a deduction whether you are self-employed or an employee. However, you must meet certain tests of distance and time, explained below.

Distance Test.—Your new work place must be at least 35 miles farther from your old residence than your old work place was. For example, if your old work place was 3 miles from your old residence, your new work place must be at least 38 miles from that residence. If you did not have an old work place, your new work place must be at least 35 miles from your old residence. (The distance between two points is the shortest of the more commonly traveled routes between the points.)

Time Test.—If you are an employee, you must work full time for at least 39 weeks during the 12 months right after you move. If you are self-employed, you must work full time for at least 39 weeks during the first 12 months and a total of at least 78 weeks during the 24 months right after you move.

You may deduct your moving expenses for 1983 even if you have not met the time test before your 1983 return is due. You may do this if you expect to meet the 39-week test by the end of 1984 or the 78-week test by the end of 1985. If you have not met the test by then, you will have to do one of the following:

- Amend your 1983 tax return on which you deducted moving expenses. To do this, use **Form 1040X,** Amended U.S. Individual Income Tax Return.
- Report as income on your tax return for the year you cannot meet the test the amount you deducted on your 1983 return.

If you do not deduct your moving expenses on your 1983 return, and you later meet the time test, you may file an amended return for 1983, taking the deduction. To do this, use Form 1040X.

Exceptions to the Distance and Time Tests.—You do not have to meet the time test in case of death or if your job ends because of disability, transfer for your employer's benefit, or layoff or other discharge besides willful misconduct.

You do not have to meet the time test if you meet the requirements, explained below, for retirees or survivors living outside the United States.

If you are in the armed forces, you do not have to meet the distance and time tests if the move is due to a permanent change of station. A permanent change of station includes a move in connection with and within 1 year of retirement or other termination of active duty. In figuring your moving expenses, do not deduct any moving expenses for moving services that were provided by the military or that were reimbursed to you and that you did not include in income. However, you may deduct your unreimbursed moving expenses, subject to the dollar limits. If you and your spouse and dependents are moved to or from different locations, treat the moves as a single move.

Qualified Retirees or Survivors Living Outside the United States.—If the requirements below are met, retirees or survivors who move to a U.S. residence are treated as if they moved to a new work place located in the United States. You are subject to the dollar limits and distance test explained on this form. Use this form instead of Form 3903F to claim your moving expenses.

Retirees.—You may deduct moving expenses for a move to a new residence in the United States when you actually retire, if both your old principal work place and your old residence were outside the United States.

Survivors.—You may deduct moving expenses for a move to a residence in the United States if you are the spouse or dependent of a person whose principal work place at the time of death was outside the United States. In addition, the expenses must be: (1) for a move that begins within 6 months after the decedent's death; and (2) must be from a former residence outside the United States that you lived in with the decedent at the time of death.

Moving Expenses in General.—You may deduct most, but not all, of the reasonable expenses you incur in moving your family and dependent household members. You may not include moving expenses for employees such as a servant, governess, or nurse.

Examples of expenses you MAY deduct are:

- Travel, meal, and lodging expenses during the move to the new residence;
- Temporary living expenses in the new location; and
- Pre-move travel expenses.

Examples of expenses you MAY NOT deduct are:

- Loss on the sale of your residence;
- Mortgage penalties;
- Cost of refitting carpets and draperies; and
- Losses on quitting club memberships.

Reimbursements.—You must include any reimbursement of, or payment for, moving expenses in gross income as compensation for services. If your employer paid for any part of your move, you must report that amount as income on **Form 1040, line 7.** Your employer should include the amount paid in your total income on Form W-2. However, if you are not sure the reimbursements have been included in your Form W-2, check with your employer. Your employer must give you a statement showing a detailed breakdown of reimbursements or payments for moving expenses. Your employer may use **Form 4782,** Employee Moving Expense Information, to give you the required breakdown of reimbursements or your employer may use his or her own form.

No Double Benefit.—You may not take double benefits. For example, you may not use the moving expense on line 7 that is part of your moving expense deduction to lower the amount of gain on the sale of your old residence. You also may not use the moving expense on line 8 that is part of your moving expense deduction to add to the cost of your new residence. (Use **Form 2119,** Sale or Exchange of Principal Residence, to figure the gain, if any, you must report on the sale of your old residence and the adjusted cost of the new one.)

Dollar Limits.—Lines 1 and 2 (costs of moving household goods and travel expenses to your new residence) are not limited to any amount. All the other expenses (lines 3, 4, 7, and 8) together may not be more than $3,000. In addition, line 3 (househunting trip expenses) and line 4 (temporary living expenses) together may not be more than $1,500. These are overall per-move limits.

There are some special situations:

- If both you and your spouse began work at new work places and shared the same new residence at the end of the tax year, you must treat this as one move rather than two. If you file separate returns, each of you is limited to a total of $1,500 for lines 3, 4, 7, and 8; and to a total of $750 for lines 3 and 4.
- If both you and your spouse began work at new work places but each of you moved to separate new residences, this is treated as two separate moves. If you file a joint return, lines 3, 4, 7, and 8 are limited to a total of $6,000; and lines 3 and 4 are limited to a total of $3,000. If you file separate returns, each of you is limited to a total of $3,000 for lines 3, 4, 7, and 8; and to a total of $1,500 for lines 3 and 4.

Line-by-Line Instructions

To see whether you meet the distance test, fill in the number of miles for questions **a** and **b** at the top of the form. If you meet the test in **c,** continue with the items that follow.

We have provided specific instructions for most of the lines on the form. Those lines that do not appear in these instructions are self-explanatory.

Line 1.—Enter the actual cost of packing, crating, moving, storing in transit, and insuring your household goods and personal effects.

Line 2.—Enter the costs of travel from your old residence to your new residence. These include transportation, meals, and lodging on the way, including costs for the day you arrive. You may only include expenses for one trip. However, all the members of your household do not have to travel together or at the same time. If you use your own car, you may figure the expenses in either of the following two ways:

- Actual out-of-pocket expenses for gas and oil (keep records to verify the amounts); or
- At the rate of 9 cents a mile (keep records to verify your mileage).

You may add parking fees and tolls to the amount claimed under either method.

Line 3.—Include the costs of travel before you move in order to look for a new residence. You may deduct the costs only if:

- You began the househunting trip after you got the job; and
- You returned to your old residence after looking for a new one; and
- You traveled to the general location of the new work place primarily to look for a new residence.

There is no limit on the number of househunting trips made by you and members of your household that may be included on this line. Your househunting does not have to be successful to qualify for this deduction. If you used your own car, figure transportation costs the same way as in the instructions for line 2. If you are self-employed, you may deduct these househunting costs only if you had already made substantial arrangements to begin work in the new location.

Line 4.—Include the costs of meals and lodging while occupying temporary quarters in the area of your new work place. You may include these costs for any period of 30 days in a row after you get the job, but before you move into permanent quarters. If you are self-employed, you may count these temporary living expenses only if you had already made substantial arrangements to begin work in the new location.

Lines 7 and 8.—You may include most of the costs to sell or buy a residence or to settle or get a lease. Examples of expenses you MAY include are:

- Sales commissions;
- Advertising costs;
- Attorney's fees;
- Title and escrow fees;
- State transfer taxes; and
- Costs to settle an unexpired lease or to get a new lease.

Examples of expenses you MAY NOT include are:

- Costs to improve your residence to help it sell;
- Charges for payment or prepayment of interest; and
- Payments or prepayments of rent.

Check the appropriate box, **a** or **b,** for lines 7 and 8 when you enter the amounts for these two lines.

☆ U.S. GOVERNMENT PRINTING OFFICE: 1983—0-390-226 58-040-1110

12. Education

Attending school, seminars, or continuing education classes is a lifetime avocation of many taxpayers. This chapter answers questions about the requirements you must meet in order to take the education deduction and how you can deduct the cost of keeping yourself current in your profession. Note specifically the rules with regard to education and changing occupations.

The IRS gives particular attention to people who take this deduction. If you qualify for it, be sure to follow the rules strictly.

If you are reimbursed by your employer for courses that you take to improve your job performance, you cannot claim a deduction for those courses.

Q Because I am thinking of changing professions, I recently took a series of courses to prepare me to become a real estate broker. Can I deduct the costs of those courses?

A No. The regulations state that you can deduct only costs of those courses necessary to maintain or improve skills required in performing the duties of your *present* work or business or to meet the requirements for keeping your salary, status, or job. Only expenses related to your current employment are deductible.

Q As an attorney specializing in admiralty law, I attended two different week-long seminars last year. Both seminars were held on the West Coast, but I live and work in New York. I know that the costs of the seminars are deductible, but can I deduct my travel expenses for both trips?

A Yes, so long as the seminars had an educational purpose and the main purpose of the trips was to broaden your education. In such cases, you can deduct not only the round trip travel expenses, but also the costs of meals and lodging. If, however, you took any side trips while on the West Coast and those trips were not associated with the educational seminars, costs associated with those side trips would be considered personal and therefore not deductible.

Q As an orthopedic surgeon, it is necessary for me to take continuing education courses so that I can sharpen my skills and keep informed of new developments. Are the costs of these courses deductible?

A Yes. This is the classic case of maintaining and improving skills. It is not necessary that you work for someone else to take the deduction.

Q My wife spent $450 for a bar review course prior to taking the state bar examination. Is that expense deductible?

A No. That is considered a personal expense, as are expenses incurred in taking an examination to become a certified public accountant or a chartered life underwriter.

Q I am presently a salesman, but my goal is to become a sales manager in my firm. To better qualify for the manager's job, I have taken several management courses at a nearby university. Can I deduct the cost of those courses?

A No. Because a promotion from salesman to sales manager means a move into management and away from selling per se, this is construed as qualifying you for a new trade or business; therefore the costs of the courses are not deductible.

Q My wife, who is working for her masters degree, received both a scholarship from the university and a special fellowship from a professional organization she is affiliated with. Is any part of the money she received reportable as taxable income?

A No. As long as she is working toward a degree she need not report the income from a grant, scholarship, or fellowship. However, if she had to render any service or work for the organization or school giving the grant the answer would be different. The aid therefore must be given with no strings attached to be nonreportable.

13. Travel, Entertainment, and Gifts

If you do any kind of business entertaining, whether you work for someone else or yourself, a myriad of sometimes complex rules must be observed. Probably the best piece of advice that can be offered is that all people who entertain business clients should keep careful and accurate records of all their entertainment expenses.

Receipts and credit card slips are the best evidence. If you note on each receipt (or in a diary of dates kept for that purpose) the *who, what, where,* and *business purpose* of each engagement, you should be able to meet any IRS challenge.

Deductible Expenses

Q I am self-employed and I took a two-week business-related trip last year. I know that I can deduct my air fares, rental car expenses, and meals and lodging for the trip. What other expenses can I deduct?

A Other business-related expenses that are deductible include tips, telephone calls, and cleaning and laundry expenses. If you used a public stenographer you can also deduct those fees. (See Form 2106 at the end of the chapter.)

Q Are there any circumstances under which I can deduct travel expenses for my spouse who accompanies me on a business trip?

A Unless you can prove a bona fide business purpose for your spouse's presence–perhaps he or she is an active partner in your business–you cannot deduct those travel expenses. Neither acting as a temporary typist nor helping you entertain customers sufficiently qualifies as a business purpose.

Q I own a few vacant lots in a city where I used to live, but it is over 300 miles away. Three times a year I travel to that city to clear the land and do other maintenance work that is needed. Can I deduct the costs of those trips? I usually take my car.

A You certainly can deduct the costs of those trips, at 20½ cents per mile if you drive. Likewise, if you fly or travel by train, you can deduct the costs of your fares to and from the city. If you stayed overnight in a hotel and ate meals while there, you could deduct those costs as well. The main purpose of your trip, however, must be for the purpose of maintaining or upgrading your property.

Q The nature of my business requires me to take frequent day trips to a city forty-five miles away. Exactly which expenses can I deduct and which can't I?

A The rules are clear. You can usually deduct transportation expenses for long day trips. You cannot, however, deduct meals and lodging unless you stay overnight. Another thing–get into the habit of entertaining customers at the business locale; that way your meal becomes a valid tax write-off.

Q Owing to an interesting combination of circumstances, I was able to attend four conventions last year. Two were held in Europe, one was in the Far East, and one was in Puerto Rico. I understand I can deduct all the travel expenses. Is that correct?

A Yes, it is. The rule has been liberalized. As long as the conventions had a business purpose and there was a legitimate reason for holding them overseas, then the deductions are in order.

Q What is the rule about deducting air fares to foreign conventions?

A You are limited to deducting the lowest coach or economy fare charged during that month by the airline you fly on. Further, a full deduction for transportation expenses is allowed only if one-half or more of the total days of the trip are devoted to business or business-related activities.

Q My plant is located in Boston, but my two best customers are in Chicago and I make a minimum of one trip a month to Chicago. I see one customer in the morning and the other in the afternoon, and I fly back to Boston in the evening. Can I deduct the cost of my meals while in Chicago?

A No. The costs of meals and lodging can only be deducted as a business expense if you are away from home *overnight*. Since you do not stay away from your Boston home overnight you cannot deduct meals. Of course your plane fares are deductible. However, if you entertain your customer, while discussing business, you are able to take an entertainment deduction.

Q Since I am in business for myself, I don't entertain elaborately, but I do occasionally take a client to a local restaurant where we have a few drinks and dinner. We normally discuss business during the meal. Can I take the entertainment deduction?

A Yes. Your business entertainment fits the definition of the "quiet business meal" that the IRS allows as a deduction. So long as the surroundings were conducive to a business discussion, you can take the deduction. If the place were loud and raucous, as is, for instance, a night club or a discotheque, the expense of the meal obviously would not qualify.

Q I started my own business some years ago and hired my wife, a former office manager, as a consultant on office operations for the business. We went to an office products convention last year. Can I legitimately deduct the cost of her trip?

A Yes. If your spouse actually works for you as an employee, consultant, or any other business capacity, you can deduct the cost of her trip. It is the business relationship, not the marital relationship, that is controlling.

Q My job requires that I do a lot of traveling to meet with customers and prospects. I am in business for myself and I want to know what is the most important thing to remember for tax purposes about travel and entertainment expenses?

A As far as travel and entertainment expenses are concerned, the three most important things to remember are documentation, documentation, and documentation. If you keep receipts, bills, and canceled tickets, you will be able to withstand any IRS challenges on travel and entertainment items. Most accountants recommend that you keep a diary of these expenses, and that is good advice.

Q I understand that there is a way I can deduct meal costs that I incurred on business trips last year without producing receipts for those meals. Is that right?

A You have an option. You can keep receipts and deduct the actual amount spent for meals while on a business trip, or you can deduct $14 a day for each day you were away from home.

If you deduct the $14 a day you do not need proof such as receipts or credit card stubs.

Entertaining Guests

Q I purchased a yacht last year, and I frequently take clients of mine for cruises. Can I deduct the costs of those cruises as legitimate business expenses?

A If you try to, you will probably have a fight on your hands with the IRS. You must prove that the primary purpose for the cruise was to conduct business. The IRS presumes that cruises on a yacht are made not purely, or in most cases even partially, for business reasons but mostly for pleasure; the IRS therefore considers cruises not deductible. To get the deduction, you must submit proof that you engaged in business and that the main *purpose* of the cruise was the transaction of that business. But any food served on the cruise may qualify for a business entertainment deduction.

Q I do a lot of entertaining in connection with my business, and in years past I have had difficulty proving travel and entertainment expenses to the IRS. Is there a preferred method of record keeping that I should employ to keep track of these expenses?

A If you keep a diary or log of expenses, the IRS cannot challenge you too strongly. As soon as you return home after spending money on business-related travel or entertainment expenses, write the following items in your diary: (1) the cost, (2) the date, (3) the business purpose, (4) the place, and (5) the business relationship of the person entertained.

Q As the owner of a small business I do a lot of business entertaining. I believe that I qualify for the entertainment deduction but I have one question. Do I actually have to get business out of the entertainment before I can take the deductions?

A No, you do not. As long as you had a "reasonable expectation" of obtaining business out of the entertainment you are still eligible for the deduction if you otherwise qualify.

Q I pay dues to an athletic club to which I belong. I often entertain clients by playing handball with them at the club. Can I deduct the costs of the dues as an entertainment expense? I am self-employed.

A If you can prove to the satisfaction of the IRS that you use the club for business more than 50 percent of the time, that the dues are paid as an ordinary or a necessary expense to further your business, and that the activities pursued directly relate to the conduct of your business, then you can deduct the dues. The same holds true for country club memberships, as well as for social and sporting club memberships.

Q I recently joined a club in town so that I can entertain business guests. The club, which is private, had a large initiation fee. Can I deduct the fee as a business entertainment expense?

A Unfortunately, no. Even though you can write off each visit when you entertain a client and despite the fact that you use it only for business purposes, you are not allowed to deduct the initiation fee.

Business Gifts

Q I am in business for myself, and maintaining customer goodwill is of primary importance to me. As a result, I give Christmas gifts to my clients every year. What is the rule with regard to deducting gifts?

A You can deduct gifts up to a total of $25 per client per year. The costs of packaging, mailing, engraving, or insuring are normally not deductible.

If, however, you should give an item such as a pen with your company's name on it, and the gift costs $4 or less, that item need not be included in the $25 limitation.

Form **2106**

Department of the Treasury
Internal Revenue Service (0)

Employee Business Expenses

(Please use Form 3903 to figure moving expense deduction.)

▶ **Attach to Form 1040.**

OMB No. 1545-0139

1983

54

Your name	Social security number	Occupation in which expenses were incurred
Employer's name	Employer's address	

PART I.—Employee Business Expenses Deductible in Figuring Adjusted Gross Income on Form 1040, Line 32

1 Reimbursed and unreimbursed fares for airplane, boat, bus, taxicab, train, etc.	1	
2 Reimbursed and unreimbursed meal, lodging, and other expenses while away from your tax home	2	
3 Reimbursed and unreimbursed car expenses from Part II	3	
4 Reimbursed and unreimbursed outside salesperson's expenses other than those shown on lines 1 through 3. **Caution:** *Do not use this line unless you are an outside salesperson (see instructions)*	4	
5 Reimbursed expenses other than those shown on lines 1 through 3 (see instructions)	5	
6 Add lines 1 through 5	6	
7 Employer's payments for these expenses only if not included on Form W-2	7	
8 If line 6 is more than line 7, subtract line 7 from line 6. Enter here and on Form 1040, line 24	8	
9 If line 7 is more than line 6, subtract line 6 from line 7. Enter here and on Form 1040, line 7	9	

PART II.—Car Expenses (Use either your actual expenses or the mileage rate.)

	Car 1	Car 2	Car 3
A. Number of months you used car for business during 1983	months	months	months
B. Total mileage for months on line A	miles	miles	miles
C. Business part of line B mileage	miles	miles	miles

Actual Expenses (Include expenses on lines 1 and 2 only for the months shown on line A, above.)

SAMPLE

		Car 1	Car 2	Car 3
1 Gasoline, oil, lubrication, etc.	1			
2 Other	2			
3 Total (add lines 1 and 2)	3			
4 Divide line C by line B, above	4	%	%	%
5 Multiply line 3 by line 4	5			
6 Depreciation (see instructions)	6			
7 Section 179 deduction (see instructions)	7			
8 Business parking fees and tolls	8			
9 Total (add lines 5 through 8). Enter here and in Part I, line 3	9			

Mileage Rate

10 Enter the smaller of (a) 15,000 miles or (b) the total mileage (Car 1+ Car 2+ Car 3) from line C, above	10	miles
11 Multiply line 10 by 20½¢ (11¢ if applicable, see instructions)	11	
12 Enter the total mileage, if any (Car 1 + Car 2 + Car 3) from line C that is over 15,000 miles	12	miles
13 Multiply line 12 by 11¢ and enter here	13	
14 Business part of car interest, parking fees, tolls, and State and local taxes (except gasoline tax)	14	
15 Total (add lines 11, 13, and 14). Enter here and in Part I, line 3	15	

PART III.—Information About Educational Expenses Shown in Part I or on Schedule A (Form 1040)

1 Did you need this education to meet the basic requirements for your business or profession? ☐ Yes ☐ No

2 Will this study program qualify you for a new business or profession? ☐ Yes ☐ No

Note: *If your answer to question 1 or 2 is "Yes," stop here. You cannot deduct these expenses, even if you do not intend to change your business or profession.*

3 If "No," list the courses you took and their relationship to your business or profession ▶

For Paperwork Reduction Act Notice, see Instructions on back.

Form **2106** (1983)

General Instructions

Paperwork Reduction Act Notice.—We ask for this information to carry out the Internal Revenue laws of the United States. We need it to ensure that taxpayers are complying with these laws and to allow us to figure and collect the right amount of tax. You are required to give us this information.

Purpose of Form.—This form is used to show employee business expenses. Use this form or a similar statement if you **are not an outside salesperson** and have reimbursed or unreimbursed transportation, travel away from home, and car expenses and other expenses that are reimbursed, or if you **are an outside salesperson** and have reimbursed and unreimbursed business expenses. You do not have to use this form or similar statement if you were required to and did account to your employer and any of the following apply to you:

- Expenses are equal to the total of your reimbursements and allowances,
- Expenses are more than the total of your reimbursements and allowances and you do not deduct the excess expenses, or
- Expenses are less than your reimbursements and allowances and your employer does not include the total reimbursements and allowances on Form W-2. In this case, include the amount by which the reimbursements and allowances are more than your expenses on line 7, Form 1040.

Also, complete and file Form 2106 if you have deductible educational expenses. See the instructions for Part III.

Expenses to Include.—Only include expenses you paid or incurred in 1983 in connection with services you performed as an employee.

Outside salesperson.—You are an outside salesperson if you do your selling away from your employer's place of business. **You are not** an outside salesperson if your main duties are service and delivery or if you are required to sell at your employer's place of business.

Accounting to your employer.— This is giving your employer documentary evidence and an account book, diary, or similar record in which you entered each expense at or near the time you made it.

Tax home.—Generally, your tax home is your main place of business or post of duty, regardless of where you maintain your family home.

Publications.—See the following publications for more information about employee business expenses and the records you must keep: **Publication 463,** Travel, Entertainment, and Gift Expenses. **Publication 508,** Educational Expenses. **Publication 529,** Miscellaneous Deductions. **Publication 534,** Depreciation. **Publication 587,** Business Use of Your Home.

Specific Instructions

Part I

Line 1.—Fares include fares for local business transportation as well as fares for business travel away from home. **Do not include** fares for commuting to and from work. Also include tips, baggage charges, charges for transporting sample and display material, and similar expenses.

Line 2.—Other expenses include tips, cleaning and laundry, telephone and telegraph, public stenographer's fees, and similar expenses.

Standard meal allowance.—Instead of actual cost, you generally may include your expenses for meals at $14 a day when you are in a general area less than 30 days and at $9 a day if you are in a general area 30 days or more. For more information, see Publication 463.

Line 4.—Include all your expenses not shown on lines 1 through 3. These include entertainment, gift, publications, and similar expenses and expenses for employment-related education, such as tuition, books, supplies, lab fees, etc. See the instructions for Part III.

Line 5.—Include reimbursed expenses other than those shown on lines 1 through 3 (see line 4 instructions). **Do not use** this line for reimbursed outside salesperson expenses. If you were reimbursed in full, enter the total expenses. If you were partially reimbursed, enter the expenses to the extent of the reimbursement. Enter any excess expenses on Schedule A (Form 1040), line 24. If you received a partial reimbursement that was intended to cover all expenses described on lines 1, 2, 3, and 5 without specifying the amount for each expense, use the formula in Publication 463 to figure the amount to enter.

Part II

Generally, you may figure your car expenses using either:

a. The **actual cost** of your car expenses (such as gas, oil, repairs, depreciation, section 179 deduction, etc.); or

b. The **standard mileage rate** which gives you a fixed deduction per business mile. **Do not use** this method if any of the following apply.

- The car is leased or used for hire;
- More than one car is used in your business at a time;
- You take a section 179 deduction on line 7;
- You figured depreciation in an earlier year using ACRS (Accelerated Cost Recovery System) or a method other than straight-line; or
- You took additional first-year depreciation.

If you are eligible to use the standard mileage rate, you may want to figure your deduction under both methods and use whichever one gives you the larger deduction.

Note: *If you use the standard mileage rate, you cannot use ACRS for that car.*

Actual Expenses

Line 2.—Include on this line your actual expenses for repairs, tires, supplies, insurance, taxes, tags, licenses, interest, etc.

Line 6.—The method of depreciation you may use depends on when you started using your car (placed the car in service). Do not deduct depreciation in excess of your basis or if your car is fully depreciated.

Cars placed in service before 1981 or for which standard mileage was used.—If you used either straight-line depreciation or the standard mileage rate in earlier years, you may use either straight-line depreciation or the standard mileage rate this year. If you used a method of depreciation other than straight-line, continue to use that method. If you want to change to straight-line depreciation or to another method of depreciation, see Publication 534. You cannot change to ACRS.

Percentage of business use.— If line A shows 12 months, multiply the amount of depreciation for the entire year by the percentage on line 4. If line A shows less than 12 months, multiply the resulting amount from the preceding sentence by the percentage arrived at by dividing the months on line A by 12. Enter the appropriate amount on line 6.

Cars placed in service after 1980.—If you placed a car in service after 1980 and you do not use the standard mileage rate, you must use one of two methods for figuring depreciation under ACRS:

- One ACRS method lets you deduct the following percentages of the business cost or other basis of your car regardless of what month you placed the car in service—

  1st year—25%
  2nd year—38%
  3rd year—37%

- The other ACRS method allows you to use a straight-line method over a recovery period of 3, 5, or 12 years with the half-year convention.

Do not consider salvage value in either of the ACRS methods.

Percentage of business use.—If you use ACRS, divide business miles by total miles for the year. If line A shows less than 12 months and you were not an employee all year, multiply the percentage on line 4 by the months on line A and divide by 12. If you sell (not trade) or stop using your car for business before the end of the year, line 6 is zero for that car.

Multiply the cost of the car (adjusted for trade-in, etc.) by the business use percentage for the year. From this amount subtract any section 179 deduction you have taken and half of any investment credit you take in 1983 (unless you take the reduced credit). Multiply the result by the ACRS percentage for the year and enter on line 6.

Investment credit.—If you placed a car in service during 1983, use **Form 3468,** Computation of Investment Credit, to determine the amount of investment credit you can take. If you take the investment credit, you will have to reduce your depreciation basis by ½ of the credit, unless you take the reduced investment credit.

Line 7.—You may deduct the cost related to the percentage of business use of your car up to $5,000 ($2,500 if you are married filing a separate return). This is the total section 179 deduction allowed for all property. Reduce the basis by the amount claimed. See Publication 534.

Mileage Rate

Use 20½¢ a mile for the first 15,000 miles of business use a year. Use 11¢ a mile for each mile over 15,000 business miles a year. You must also use 11¢ a mile if your car is fully depreciated. Generally, a car placed in service after 1979 is considered fully depreciated after 60,000 miles of business use at the maximum standard mileage rate.

Line 14.—The business part of parking and tolls is the amount you paid or incurred for business purposes. To figure the business part of interest and State and local taxes (except gasoline taxes) multiply the total of these items by the percentage you get by dividing line C by line B. For more information on the standard mileage rate, see Publication 463.

Part III

If you show educational expenses in Part I or on Schedule A (Form 1040), complete Part III.

You can deduct the cost of education that helps you keep or improve your skills for your business or profession.This includes education that your employer, the law, or regulations require you to get in order to keep your job or your salary. Do not deduct the cost of study that helps you meet the basic requirements for your business or profession or qualifies you for a new business or profession even if you do not intend to change to a new business or profession.

14. Sources of Income

Most people don't think of it, but income can flow from sources other than just salary or wages. Bonuses constitute income, as do royalties on the sale of an invention or a book. Even unemployment compensation is a form of income that may have to be reported on your tax return. Among some of the questions we answer in this chapter are: Does all this income have to be reported? If not, exactly how much does? Is an inheritance considered income?

Bonuses

Q I received a rather large bonus last year in addition to my salary. What is the maximum tax I have to pay on the bonus?

A Bonuses are treated no differently from regular salary payments. The maximum tax is 50 percent of the bonus, depending on your tax bracket of course. (See Income Averaging, Chapter 4.)

Various Types of Income

Q My accountant tells me I must cut down on the amount of unearned income I have. Why is that, and what is the difference between earned and unearned income?

A Let's start with the second part of your question first. Earned income comprises salary, commission, bonuses, and any other compensation you receive for working. Unearned income includes passive income items such as dividends, interest, rents, and so forth. Your accountant should have pointed out that there is no difference in the tax rate between earned and unearned income, as there used to be.

Q Is it true that the $10,000 I received from my deceased uncle's estate is not taxable to me?

A Yes. Like gifts and life insurance proceeds, inheritances are not considered taxable to the recipient. That's because the $10,000 may have already been taxed as part of the estate tax your uncle's estate was liable for.

Q I am contemplating joining a barter club. That's a club where people exchange products or services, and no money changes hands. What are the tax implications of bartering?

A Whatever product or service you receive in exchange for your product or service must be included in your gross income at the fair market value on the date received.

Q I was unemployed for a part of the year last year. I understand that I have to pay taxes on my unemployment benefits. Why? Is this regulation new?

A It is new, and you may have to pay taxes on some or all of your unemployment benefits if, when you add the total of all your unemployment compensation to your adjusted gross income, the amount is over $12,000 if you are single. If you are married and filing jointly, the limit rises to $18,000.

Q I was lucky last year—I won $10,000 in a state lottery game. Much to my chagrin, I discovered that withholding tax was taken out of my winnings. Can I do anything to reduce my tax bite?

A Since you can offset gambling losses against gambling winnings, if you have kept a record of every time you played the lottery and lost, then you can offset. Stubs, losing racetrack tickets, and the like, are the required documentation needed to satisfy the IRS. But you must itemize to deduct your losses.

Q Is a refund on my taxes considered taxable income in the year I receive it?

A If you receive a refund on your federal income tax, it is not considered taxable income. However, if you receive a refund on state or city income tax, it must be included in income in the year you received it, but only if you itemized deductions on your state or city income tax returns last year.

Q I hold a patent that has become increasingly more valuable through the years. I now have an opportunity to sell the patent to a large corporation that will pay me very nicely for it. If I sell the patent, can I get capital gains treatment?

A Yes. Capital gains or losses apply only to assets that are classified as "capital assets," and patents have been so classified provided that all substantial rights to the patent are transferred by the holder. Another example of a capital asset is vacant land held for investment purposes.

Q I have written several songs that I recently sold. Can I treat the income from the sale as a capital gain?

A Unfortunately, no. Authors, songwriters, playwrights, artists, and the like, must report as ordinary income the proceeds from the sale of their artistic labors. It makes no difference, by the way, whether the work is copyrighted or not; the same rule applies.

Q A jury awarded me $100,000 last year as the result of a libel suit. I received $75,000 for damage to my reputation; $25,000 was given in punitive damages because the person I sued was found to have deliberately libeled me. Isn't the entire $100,000 excluded from my income for the year?

A No, only $75,000 is excludable. The $25,000 that was awarded for punitive or exemplary damages must be included in your income for the year. The $75,000 is looked on by the IRS as reimbursement for the libel suffered. But punitive damages do not fall into that category. In a way they constitute a kind of windfall and thus have to be included in income.

Q Can you tell me what a 1099 form is and if I can expect to get one?

A A 1099 form is a nonemployee compensation reporting form which must be issued by any company, agency or bank that paid you any form of compensation from which taxes were *not* withheld. This is how dividends, interest and free-lance income is reported. A 1099 is similar to a W-2 form, but of course only total income is reported; no social security payments (FICA) or taxes are paid to the IRS. Therefore you must pay any taxes or social security payments due. Expect to receive a 1099 if you had dividend, interest or free-lance income during the year. A copy of the form is sent to the IRS by the reporting company, agency or bank.

Q I did my own return last year and I ran into a small problem while filling out Schedule B where interest and dividend income is reported. I have money in a money market fund and I didn't know whether to classify it as dividend or interest income. Which is it?

A It depends. If you have money in a money market account in a bank or savings institution it should be classified as interest, but if your money market fund is the older, independent type it must be classified as dividend income.

Alternative Minimum Tax

Q I have been hearing and reading about something called the Alternative Minimum Tax. What is it and will I be affected by it?

A The Alternative Minimum Tax was instituted to prevent some high-income taxpayers from avoiding paying any taxes at all. It is a complicated tax and you will only be affected if you have very large tax shelter deductions, capital gains, or investment tax credits.

There are no specific income cutoffs that can be given because each taxpayer's situation will be different but, one thing is for sure, unless you have a very large income you will probably not be affected.

Q My accountant told me that I am "over sheltered" and that I may have to pay the Alternative Minimum Tax this year. Is there anything I can do?

A Yes. If possible, bring in more income this year and defer expenses until next year. That way you will probably just have to pay the regular income tax instead of the AMT. Good luck.

Q When does the Alternative Minimum Tax come into play for an individual?

A You only pay the tax if it is more than the regular tax owed. There is, however, an exemption provided. For single filers, it is $30,000, but for people who file joint returns the figure is $40,000. Whatever is left after the exemption is taxed at a rate of 20%.

Q If I think that I will have to pay the Alternative Minimum Tax what should I do?

A Figuring the AMT is complicated and tricky. The best thing to do would be for you to go see a tax preparer (preferably a CPA) who has experience with the AMT. Let that person advise you. Don't try to do it yourself.

It should be pointed out that some tax preparers are not experienced with the AMT so be careful whom you choose.

If you are self-employed, do freelance work, or have a substantial amount of income from sources other than a regular salary, you will undoubtedly have to use one or all of the following three forms.

SCHEDULE C (Form 1040)

Department of the Treasury
Internal Revenue Service (0)

Profit or (Loss) From Business or Profession
(Sole Proprietorship)

Partnerships, Joint Ventures, etc., Must File Form 1065.

▶ **Attach to Form 1040 or Form 1041.** ▶ **See Instructions for Schedule C (Form 1040).**

OMB No. 1545-0074

1983
09

Name of proprietor | **Social security number of proprietor**

A Main business activity (see Instructions) ▶ ; product ▶

B Business name and address ▶ ......

C Employer identification number

D Method(s) used to value closing inventory:
(1) ☐ Cost (2) ☐ Lower of cost or market (3) ☐ Other (attach explanation)

E Accounting method: (1) ☐ Cash (2) ☐ Accrual (3) ☐ Other (specify) ▶ ......

	Yes	No
F Was there any major change in determining quantities, costs, or valuations between opening and closing inventory? If "Yes," attach explanation.		
G Did you deduct expenses for an office in your home?		

PART I.—Income

1 a Gross receipts or sales	1a	
b Less: Returns and allowances	1b	
c Subtract line 1b from line 1a and enter the balance here	1c	
2 Cost of goods sold and/or operations (Part III, line 8)	2	
3 Subtract line 2 from line 1c and enter the **gross profit** here	3	
4 a Windfall Profit Tax Credit or Refund received in 1983 (see Instructions)	4a	
b Other income	4b	
5 Add lines 3, 4a, and 4b. This is the **gross income** ▶	5	

PART II.—Deductions

SAMPLE

6 Advertising		23 Repairs	
7 Bad debts from sales or services (Cash method taxpayers, see Instructions)		24 Supplies (not included in Part III)	
8 Bank service charges		25 Taxes (Do not include Windfall Profit Tax here. See line 29.)	
9 Car and truck expenses		26 Travel and entertainment	
10 Commissions		27 Utilities and telephone	
11 Depletion		28 a Wages	
12 Depreciation and Section 179 deduction from Form 4562 (not included in Part III)		b Jobs credit	
		c Subtract line 28b from 28a	
		29 Windfall Profit Tax withheld in 1983	
13 Dues and publications		30 Other expenses (specify):	
14 Employee benefit programs		a	
15 Freight (not included in Part III)		b	
16 Insurance		c	
17 Interest on business indebtedness		d	
18 Laundry and cleaning		e	
19 Legal and professional services		f	
20 Office expense		g	
21 Pension and profit-sharing plans		h	
22 Rent on business property		i	

31 Add amounts in columns for lines 6 through 30i. These are the **total deductions** ▶	31	
32 Net profit or (loss). Subtract line 31 from line 5 and enter the result. If a profit, enter on Form 1040, line 12, and on Schedule SE, Part I, line 2 (or Form 1041, line 6). If a loss, go on to line 33	32	

33 If you have a loss, you must answer this question: "Do you have amounts for which you are not at risk in this business (see Instructions)?" ☐ Yes ☐ No
If "Yes," you must attach Form 6198. If "No," enter the loss on Form 1040, line 12, and on Schedule SE, Part I, line 2 (or Form 1041, line 6).

PART III.—Cost of Goods Sold and/or Operations (See Schedule C Instructions for Part III)

1 Inventory at beginning of year (if different from last year's closing inventory, attach explanation)	1	
2 Purchases less cost of items withdrawn for personal use	2	
3 Cost of labor (do not include salary paid to yourself)	3	
4 Materials and supplies	4	
5 Other costs	5	
6 Add lines 1 through 5	6	
7 Less: Inventory at end of year	7	
8 **Cost of goods sold and/or operations.** Subtract line 7 from line 6. Enter here and in Part I, line 2, above.	8	

For Paperwork Reduction Act Notice, see Form 1040 Instructions. **Schedule C (Form 1040) 1983**

☆U.S. G.P.O. 1983-390-080 E.I. 43-0787287

SCHEDULE SE (Form 1040)
Department of the Treasury
Internal Revenue Service (0)

Computation of Social Security Self-Employment Tax

▶ See Instructions for Schedule SE (Form 1040).
▶ Attach to Form 1040.

OMB No. 1545-0074
1983

Name of self-employed person (as shown on social security card)	Social security number of self-employed person ▶	

PART I.—Regular Computation of Net Earnings from Self-Employment

1 Net profit or (loss) from Schedule F (Form 1040), line 56 or line 89, and farm partnerships, Schedule K-1 (Form 1065), line 18b	1		
2 Net profit or (loss) from Schedule C (Form 1040), line 32, and Schedule K-1 (Form 1065), line 18b (other than farming). See instructions for kinds of income to report. **Note:** If you are exempt from self-employment tax on your earnings as a minister, member of a religious order, or Christian Science practitioner because you filed Form 4361, check here ▶ ☐ . If you have other earnings of $400 or more that are subject to self-employment tax, include those earnings on this line	2		

PART II.—Optional Computation of Net Earnings from Self-Employment

Generally, this part may be used **only** if you meet any of the following tests:

A Your gross farm profits (Schedule F (Form 1040), line 31 or line 87) were not more than $2,400, or

B Your gross farm profits (Schedule F (Form 1040), line 31 or line 87) were more than $2,400 and your net farm profits (Schedule F (Form 1040), line 56 or line 89) were less than $1,600, or

C Your net nonfarm profits (Schedule C (Form 1040), line 32) were less than $1,600 and also less than two-thirds (⅔) of your gross nonfarm income (Schedule C (Form 1040), line 5).

See instructions for other limitations.

3 Maximum income for optional methods	3	$1,600	00
4 Farm Optional Method—If you meet test A or B above, enter: two-thirds (⅔) of gross profits from Schedule F (Form 1040), line 31 or line 87, and farm partnerships, Schedule K-1 (Form 1065), line 18a, or $1,600, whichever is smaller	4		
5 Subtract line 4 from line 3	5		
6 Nonfarm Optional Method—If you meet test C, enter the smaller of two-thirds (⅔) of gross nonfarm income from Schedule C (Form 1040), line 5, and Schedule K-1 (Form 1065), line 18c (other than farming), or $1,600, or, if you elected the farm optional method, the amount on line 5	6		

SAMPLE

PART III.—Computation of Social Security Self-Employment Tax

7 Enter the amount from Part I, line 1, or, if you elected the farm optional method, Part II, line 4			7		
8 Enter the amount from Part I, line 2, or, if you elected the nonfarm optional method, Part II, line 6 . . .			8		
9 Add lines 7 and 8. If less than $400, you are not subject to self-employment tax. Do not fill in the rest of the schedule			9		
10 The largest amount of combined wages and self-employment earnings subject to social security or railroad retirement tax (Tier I) for 1983 is			10	$35,700	00
11 a Total social security wages from Forms W-2 and railroad retirement compensation (Tier I). **Note:** U.S. Government employees whose wages are only subject to the 1.3% hospital benefits tax (Medicare) should not include those wages on this line (see instructions)	11a				
b Unreported tips subject to social security tax from Form 4137, line 9, or to railroad retirement tax (Tier I)	11b				
c Add lines 11a and 11b			11c		
12 Subtract line 11c from line 10			12		
13 Enter the smaller of line 9 or line 12			13		
If line 13 is $35,700 or more, fill in $3,337.95 on line 14. Otherwise, multiply line 13 by .0935 and enter the result on line 14				.0935	
14 Self-employment tax. Enter this amount on Form 1040, line 50			14		

For Paperwork Reduction Act Notice, see Form 1040 Instructions. **Schedule SE (Form 1040) 1983**

☆ U.S. Government Printing Office: 1983—390-108 23-0916750

Form **1040-ES**

Department of the Treasury
Internal Revenue Service

Estimated Tax for Individuals

▶ **This form is primarily for first-time filers of estimated tax.**

OMB No. 1545-0087

1984

Instructions

Paperwork Reduction Act Notice.—We ask for this information to carry out the Internal Revenue laws of the United States. We need it to ensure that taxpayers are complying with these laws and to allow us to figure and collect the right amount of tax. You are required to give us this information.

This form is primarily for first-time filers. After your first payment-voucher is received in the Internal Revenue Service Center, IRS will mail you a 1040-ES package. Your name, address, and social security number will be preprinted on the vouchers. You should use these vouchers in making the remaining payments of estimated tax for the year. Using the preprinted vouchers will speed processing, reduce the chance of error, and help save your government processing costs.

This form can also be used if you did not receive a 1040-ES package, or if you lost it. Complete the appropriate payment-voucher and mail it with your payment to your Internal Revenue Service Center (see page 2 for address).

Estimated tax is the amount of tax you expect to owe for the year after subtracting the amount of tax you expect to have withheld and the amount of any credits you plan to take.

You do not have to pay estimated tax if your 1984 income tax return will show (1) a tax refund or (2) a tax balance due of less than $400.

A. Who Must Make Estimated Tax Payments.—The rules below are for U.S. citizens or residents and for residents of Puerto Rico, Virgin Islands, Guam, or American Samoa. (If you are a nonresident alien, use **Form 1040-ES (NR).**) You must make estimated tax payments if your estimated tax balance due is $400 or more **AND** if either item (1) or (2) below applies to you.

You expect your 1984 gross income:

(1) To include more than $500 from sources other than wages subject to withholding; **OR**

(2) To be more than:

- $20,000 if you are single, a head of household, or a qualifying widow or widower;
- $20,000 if you are married, can make joint estimated tax payments, and your spouse has not received wages for 1984;
- $10,000 if you are married, can make joint estimated tax payments, and both of you have received wages for 1984;
- $5,000 if you are married and cannot make joint estimated tax payments. (No joint estimated tax payments may be made if: (1) either you or your spouse is a nonresident alien, (2) you are separated under a decree of divorce or separate maintenance, or (3) you have different tax years.)

Note: *If you must make estimated tax payments and receive salaries and wages, you may not be having enough tax withheld during the year. To avoid making estimated tax payments, consider asking your employer to take more tax out of your earnings. To do this, file a new* **Form W-4,** *Employee's Withholding Allowance Certificate, with your employer and make sure you will not owe $400 or more in tax.*

B. How to Figure Your Estimated Tax.—Use the Estimated Tax Worksheet on page 3, the 1984 Tax Rate Schedules on page 4, and your 1983 tax return as a guide for figuring your estimated tax.

Most of the items on the worksheet are self-explanatory. However, the instructions below provide additional information for filling out certain lines.

Caution: Generally, you are required to itemize your deductions if:

- you have unearned income of $1,000 or more and can be claimed as a dependent on your parent's return;
- you are married filing a separate return and your spouse itemizes deductions;
- you file **Form 4563,** Exclusion of Income From Sources in United States Possessions; **OR**
- you are a dual-status alien.

For more information, see the 1983 Instructions for **Form 1040.** If you **MUST** itemize and line 2b of the Estimated Tax Worksheet is more than line 2a, subtract 2a from 2b. Add this amount to line 1 of the worksheet and enter the total on line 3. Disregard the instructions for lines 2c, 2d, and 3 on the worksheet.

The following tax law changes for 1984 may affect your 1984 estimated tax.

1. **Medical expense.**—The 1% of adjusted gross income (AGI) limitation on medicine and drugs expenses has been eliminated. Only prescription drugs and insulin expenses are deductible and these amounts will now be subject to the overall 5% limitation.

2. **Social security and railroad retirement benefits.**—These benefits may be includible in your income if your AGI (as adjusted) plus one-half of your benefits exceeds:

(a) $32,000 if you file a joint return;

(b) Zero if you are married, file a separate return, and lived with your spouse at some time during the tax year; or

(c) $25,000 if you have any other filing status.

Tax-exempt interest is includible in AGI for these purposes.

3. **Credit for the elderly and the permanently and totally disabled.**— The disability income exclusion has been repealed for years beginning after 1983. Beginning with 1984, the credit for the elderly has been expanded to include the permanently and totally disabled. Individuals 65 or older will continue to be able to take the credit. In addition, individuals under 65 who have retired with a permanent and total disability and receive income from a public or private employer because of that disability will be eligible for the credit.

If you are under 65 and receive a taxable pension from a public retirement system, you will no longer be able to take this credit unless you meet the permanent and total disability requirements.

4. **Partial deduction for charitable contributions.** The amount you can deduct as a charitable contribution if you do not itemize deductions has been increased. You can deduct 25% of the first $300 (the first $150 if married filing separately) of contributions to qualified organizations.

For more details, see **Publication 505,** Tax Withholding and Estimated Tax.

Line 7—Additional taxes.—Enter on line 7 any additional taxes from:

- **Form 4970,** Tax on Accumulation Distribution of Trusts;
- **Form 4972,** Special 10-Year Averaging Method;
- **Form 5544,** Multiple Recipient Special 10-Year Averaging Method; **OR**
- Section 72 penalty taxes.

Line 12—Self-employment tax.—If you and your spouse make joint estimated tax payments and both have self-employment income, figure the estimated self-employment tax separately. Enter the total amount on line 12.

C. How to Use the Payment-Voucher.—Each payment-voucher has the date when the voucher is due for calendar year taxpayers. Please use the correct voucher.

(1) Enter your name, address, and social security number in the space provided on the payment-voucher. If you are filing a joint payment-voucher, your spouse's name and social security number should be included on the voucher. If you file a joint payment-voucher and have different last names, please separate them with an "and." For example, "John Brown and Mary Smith."

(2) Enter the net amount of your payment on line 1 of the payment-voucher. If you paid too much tax on your 1983 Form 1040, you may have chosen to apply the overpayment to your estimated tax for 1984. If so, you may apply all or part of the overpayment to any voucher. Send the payment-voucher to IRS **ONLY** when you are making a payment.

(3) Tear off the voucher at the perforation.

(4) Attach, but do not staple, your check or money order to the payment-voucher. Make check or money order payable to Internal Revenue Service. Please write your social security number and "1984 Form 1040-ES" on your check or money order. Please fill in the Record of Estimated Tax Payments on page 2 so you will have a record of your payments.

(5) Mail your payment-voucher to the Internal Revenue Service Center for the place where you live. Use the address for your State shown on page 2.

D. When to Pay Your Estimated Tax.—The general rule is that you must make your first estimated tax payment by April 16, 1984. You may either pay all of your estimated tax at that time or pay in four equal amounts that are due by April 16, 1984; June 15, 1984; September 17, 1984; and January 16, 1985. Exceptions to the general rule are listed below.

(Continued on page 2)

1984 Estimated Tax Worksheet (Keep for your records—Do Not Send to Internal Revenue Service)

Line	Description		
1	Enter amount of Adjusted Gross Income you expect in 1984		1
2 a	If you plan to itemize deductions, enter the estimated total of your deductions. (If you do not plan to itemize deductions, skip to line 2c and enter zero)	2a	
b	Enter { $3,400 if married filing a joint return (or qualifying widow(er)); $2,300 if single (or head of household); $1,700 if married filing a separate return }	2b	
c	Subtract line 2b from line 2a (if zero or less, enter zero)		2c
d	If you do not itemize deductions, enter your allowable deduction, if any, for charitable contributions (see Instruction B.4 on page 1)		2d
3	Subtract line 2c or 2d, whichever applies, from line 1		3
4	Exemptions (multiply $1,000 times number of personal exemptions)		4
5	Subtract line 4 from line 3		5
6	Tax. (Figure your tax on line 5 by using Tax Rate Schedule X, Y, or Z in these instructions. DO NOT use the Tax Table or Tax Rate Schedule X, Y, or Z in the 1983 Form 1040 Instructions.)		6
7	Enter any additional taxes (see line 7 Instruction)		7
8	Add lines 6 and 7		8
9	Credits (credit for the elderly, credit for the permanently and totally disabled, credit for child and dependent care expenses, investment credit, residential energy credit, etc.)		9
10	Subtract line 9 from line 8		10
11	Tax from recapture of investment credit		11
12	Estimate of 1984 self-employment income $________; if $37,800 or more, enter $4,271.40; if less, multiply the amount by .113 (see line 12 instruction for additional information)		12
13	Tax on premature distributions from an IRA		13
14	Add lines 10 through 13		14
15 a	Earned income credit	15a	
b	Estimated income tax withheld and to be withheld (including income tax withholding on pensions, annuities, certain deferred income, etc.) during 1984	15b	
c	Credit for Federal tax on gasoline and special fuels (see Form 4136)	15c	
16	Total (add lines 15a, b, and c)		16
17	Estimated tax (subtract line 16 from line 14). If $400 or more, fill out and file the payment-voucher along with your payment; if less, no payment is required at this time. If you are applying an overpayment from 1983 to 1984 estimated tax, see Instruction C(2), page 1		17
	Caution: You are required to prepay at least 80% of your tax liability each year. If you prepay less than 80% of your actual tax liability, you will be subject to a penalty (see Instruction E). To avoid this, make sure your estimate is as accurate as possible. If you are unsure of your estimate, you may want to pay more than 80% of the amount you have estimated. In determining the amount of your estimated tax, you may take into account any of the exceptions to the underpayment penalty. For more information on these exceptions, please get **Publication 505.**		
18	If the first payment you are required to make is due April 16, 1984, enter ¼ of line 17 (less any 1983 overpayment that you are applying to this installment) here and on line 1 of your payment-voucher. You may round off cents to the nearest whole dollar. If you wish to pay more estimated tax than is shown on line 17, you may do so		18

Tear off here

Form **1040-ES** | **1984 Payment-Voucher**

Department of the Treasury
Internal Revenue Service

OMB No. 1545-0087

Return this voucher with check or money order payable to the Internal Revenue Service. Please do not send cash or staple your payment to this voucher.

(Calendar year—Due Jan. 16, 1985)

1 Amount of payment $________

2 Fiscal year filers enter year ending ________ (month and year)

File only if you are making a payment of estimated tax.

Please type or print

Your social security number | Spouse's number, if joint payment

First name and middle initial (of both spouses if joint payment) | Last name

Address (Number and street)

City, State, and ZIP code

For Paperwork Reduction Act Notice, see instructions on page 1. **Page 3**

(1) Other payment dates.—In some cases, such as a change in income, you may have to make your first estimated tax payment after April 16, 1984. The payment dates are as follows:

If the requirement is met after:	Payment date is:
• April 1 and before June 2	June 15, 1984
• June 1 and before Sept. 2	Sept. 17, 1984
• Sept. 1	Jan. 16, 1985

Note: *You may use the "Amended Estimated Tax Schedule" below to figure your amended estimated tax.*

You may pay your estimated tax in equal amounts. If the first payment you are required to make is due:

- June 15, 1984, enter ⅓;
- September 17, 1984, enter ½;
- January 16, 1985, enter all;

of line 17 (less any 1983 overpayment applied to 1984 estimated tax) on line 18 of the worksheet and on line 1 of the payment-voucher.

If you file your 1984 Form 1040 by January 31, 1985, and pay the entire balance due, then you do not have to make the payment which would otherwise be due January 16, 1985.

(2) Farmers and fishermen.—If at least two-thirds of your gross income for 1983 or 1984 is from farming or fishing, you may do one of the following:

- Pay all of your estimated tax by January 16, 1985; **OR**
- File Form 1040 for 1984 by March 1, 1985, and pay the total tax due. In this case, you do not need to make estimated tax payments for 1984.

(3) Fiscal year.—If your return is on a fiscal year basis, your due dates are the 15th day of the 4th, 6th, and 9th months of your fiscal year and the 1st month of the following fiscal year. If any date falls on a Saturday, Sunday, or legal holiday, use the next regular workday.

E. Penalty for Not Paying Enough Estimated Tax.—You may be charged a penalty for not paying enough estimated tax, or for not making the payments on time. The penalty does not apply if each payment is timely and the total tax paid:

- is at least 80% (66⅔% for farmers and fishermen) of the amount of income and self-employment taxes due (figured using the taxes and credits specified in **Publication 505**) as shown on your return for 1984; **OR**
- is based on one of the exceptions shown on **Form 2210,** Underpayment of Estimated Tax by Individuals (**Form 2210F,** Underpayment of Estimated Tax by Farmers and Fishermen).

  Also the penalty does not apply if you are a U.S. citizen or resident and you had no tax liability for the full 12-month preceding tax year.

Note: *You may be required to make payments of past due amounts to avoid further penalty. You may have to make these payments if you do not make your estimated tax payments on time, or if you did not pay the correct amount for a previous payment date.*

Example: On June 1, 1984, you find out that you should have made an estimated tax payment for April 16. You should immediately fill out the payment-voucher due April 16, 1984, and send in the required amount (¼ × 1984 estimated tax).

If you changed your name because of marriage, divorce, etc., and you made estimated tax payments using your old name, you should attach a brief statement to the front of your 1984 Form 1040. In it explain all the estimated tax payments you and your spouse made during 1984, the name of the Service Center where you made the payments, and the name(s) and social security number(s) under which you made payments.

F. Where to File Your Payment-Voucher.—Mail your payment-voucher to the Internal Revenue Service Center for the place where you live.

If you are located in:	Use this address:
New Jersey, New York City, and counties of Nassau, Rockland, Suffolk, and Westchester	Holtsville, NY 00501
New York (all other counties), Connecticut, Maine, Massachusetts, New Hampshire, Rhode Island, Vermont	Andover, MA 05501
District of Columbia, Delaware, Maryland, Pennsylvania	Philadelphia, PA 19255
Alabama, Florida, Georgia, Mississippi, South Carolina	Atlanta, GA 31101
Michigan, Ohio	Cincinnati, OH 45999
Arkansas, Kansas, Louisiana, New Mexico, Oklahoma, Texas	Austin, TX 73301
Alaska, Arizona, Colorado, Idaho, Minnesota, Montana, Nebraska, Nevada, North Dakota, Oregon, South Dakota, Utah, Washington, Wyoming	Ogden, UT 84201
Illinois, Iowa, Missouri, Wisconsin	Kansas City, MO 64999
California, Hawaii	Fresno, CA 93888
Indiana, Kentucky, North Carolina, Tennessee, Virginia, West Virginia	Memphis, TN 37501
American Samoa	Philadelphia, PA 19255
Guam	Commissioner of Revenue and Taxation Agana, GU 96910
Puerto Rico (or if excluding income under section 933) Virgin Islands: Non-permanent residents	Philadelphia, PA 19255
Virgin Islands: Permanent residents	Bureau of Internal Revenue Charlotte Amalie St. Thomas, VI 00801
A.P.O. or F.P.O. address of:	Miami—Atlanta, GA 31101 New York—Holtsville, NY 00501 San Francisco—Fresno, CA 93888 Seattle—Ogden, UT 84201
Foreign country: U.S. citizens and those excluding income under section 911 or 931, or claiming the housing deduction under section 911	Philadelphia, PA 19255

Record of Estimated Tax Payments

Payment number	(a) Date	(b) Amount	(c) 1983 overpayment credit applied	(d) Total amount paid and credited (add (b) and (c))
1				
2				
3				
4				
Total . . . . ▶				

Note: If you are not required to make the estimated tax payment due April 16, 1984, at this time, you may have to make a payment by a later date. See Instruction D(1).

Amended Estimated Tax Schedule (Use if your estimated tax changes during the year)

1 Amended estimated tax		1	
2 Less: **a** Amount of 1983 overpayment chosen for credit to 1984 estimated tax and applied to date	2a		
b Estimated tax payments to date	2b		
c Total of lines 2a and b		2c	
3 Unpaid balance (subtract line 2c from line 1)		3	
4 Amount to be paid (line 3 divided by number of remaining payment dates)		4	

Page 2

1984 Tax Rate Schedules

Caution: Do not use these Tax Rate Schedules to figure your 1983 taxes. Use only to figure your 1984 estimated taxes.

SCHEDULE X—Single Taxpayers

If line 5 is: Over—	but not over—	The tax is:	of the amount over—
$0	$2,300	—0—	
2,300	3,400	------- 11%	$2,300
3,400	4,400	$121 + 12%	3,400
4,400	6,500	241 + 14%	4,400
6,500	8,500	535 + 15%	6,500
8,500	10,800	835 + 16%	8,500
10,800	12,900	1,203 + 18%	10,800
12,900	15,000	1,581 + 20%	12,900
15,000	18,200	2,001 + 23%	15,000
18,200	23,500	2,737 + 26%	18,200
23,500	28,800	4,115 + 30%	23,500
28,800	34,100	5,705 + 34%	28,800
34,100	41,500	7,507 + 38%	34,100
41,500	55,300	10,319 + 42%	41,500
55,300	81,800	16,115 + 48%	55,300
81,800	------	28,835 + 50%	81,800

SCHEDULE Z—Heads of Household

If line 5 is: Over—	but not over—	The tax is:	of the amount over—
$0	$2,300	—0—	
2,300	4,400	------- 11%	$2,300
4,400	6,500	$231 + 12%	4,400
6,500	8,700	483 + 14%	6,500
8,700	11,800	791 + 17%	8,700
11,800	15,000	1,318 + 18%	11,800
15,000	18,200	1,894 + 20%	15,000
18,200	23,500	2,534 + 24%	18,200
23,500	28,800	3,806 + 28%	23,500
28,800	34,100	5,290 + 32%	28,800
34,100	44,700	6,986 + 35%	34,100
44,700	60,600	10,696 + 42%	44,700
60,600	81,800	17,374 + 45%	60,600
81,800	108,300	26,914 + 48%	81,800
108,300	------	39,634 + 50%	108,300

SCHEDULE Y—Married Taxpayers and Qualifying Widows and Widowers

Married Filing Joint Returns and Qualifying Widows and Widowers

If line 5 is: Over—	but not over—	The tax is:	of the amount over—
$0	$3,400	—0—	
3,400	5,500	------ 11%	$3,400
5,500	7,600	$231 + 12%	5,500
7,600	11,900	483 + 14%	7,600
11,900	16,000	1,085 + 16%	11,900
16,000	20,200	1,741 + 18%	16,000
20,200	24,600	2,497 + 22%	20,200
24,600	29,900	3,465 + 25%	24,600
29,900	35,200	4,790 + 28%	29,900
35,200	45,800	6,274 + 33%	35,200
45,800	60,000	9,772 + 38%	45,800
60,000	85,600	15,168 + 42%	60,000
85,600	109,400	25,920 + 45%	85,600
109,400	162,400	36,630 + 49%	109,400
162,400	--------	62,600 + 50%	162,400

Married Filing Separate Returns

If line 5 is: Over—	but not over—	The tax is:	of the amount over—
$0	$1,700	—0—	
1,700	2,750	---------- 11%	$1,700
2,750	3,800	$115.50 + 12%	2,750
3,800	5,950	241.50 + 14%	3,800
5,950	8,000	542.50 + 16%	5,950
8,000	10,100	870.50 + 18%	8,000
10,100	12,300	1,248.50 + 22%	10,100
12,300	14,950	1,732.50 + 25%	12,300
14,950	17,600	2,395.00 + 28%	14,950
17,600	22,900	3,137.00 + 33%	17,600
22,900	30,000	4,886.00 + 38%	22,900
30,000	42,800	7,584.00 + 42%	30,000
42,800	54,700	12,960.00 + 45%	42,800
54,700	81,200	18,315.00 + 49%	54,700
81,200	------	31,300.00 + 50%	81,200

Form **1040-ES** | **1984 Payment-Voucher**

Department of the Treasury
Internal Revenue Service

OMB No. 1545-0087

Return this voucher with check or money order payable to the Internal Revenue Service.
Please do not send cash or staple your payment to this voucher.

(Calendar year—Due Sept. 17, 1984)

1 Amount of payment $ ____________

2 Fiscal year filers enter year ending ____________ (month and year)

File only if you are making a payment of estimated tax.

Please type or print

Your social security number | Spouse's number, if joint payment

First name and middle initial (of both spouses if joint payment) | Last name

Address (Number and street)

City, State, and ZIP code

For Paperwork Reduction Act Notice, see instructions on page 1.

Tear off here

Form **1040-ES** | **1984 Payment-Voucher**

Department of the Treasury
Internal Revenue Service

OMB No. 1545-0087

Return this voucher with check or money order payable to the Internal Revenue Service.
Please do not send cash or staple your payment to this voucher.

(Calendar year—Due June 15, 1984)

1 Amount of payment $ ____________

2 Fiscal year filers enter year ending ____________ (month and year)

File only if you are making a payment of estimated tax.

Please type or print

Your social security number | Spouse's number, if joint payment

First name and middle initial (of both spouses if joint payment) | Last name

Address (Number and street)

City, State, and ZIP code

For Paperwork Reduction Act Notice, see instructions on page 1.

Tear off here

Form **1040-ES** | **1984 Payment-Voucher**

Department of the Treasury
Internal Revenue Service

OMB No. 1545-0087

Return this voucher with check or money order payable to the Internal Revenue Service.
Please do not send cash or staple your payment to this voucher.

(Calendar year—Due April 16, 1984)

1 Amount of payment $ ____________

2 Fiscal year filers enter year ending ____________ (month and year)

File only if you are making a payment of estimated tax.

Please type or print

Your social security number | Spouse's number, if joint payment

First name and middle initial (of both spouses if joint payment) | Last name

Address (Number and street)

City, State, and ZIP code

For Paperwork Reduction Act Notice, see instructions on page 1.

★U. S. Government Printing Office 390-126 E I #52-1074467

15. Bad Debts

When economic times are hard, personal bankruptcies and bad debts mount. If you lent money in the past year to people who have declared bankruptcy or can't pay you back because they simply don't have the money, you can at least write off the loss on your tax return. The circumstances detailing the bad debt deduction are set forth in this chapter.

Q I have a personal bad debt that I believe I am entitled to deduct. What are the mechanics of taking the deduction?

A If you have a nonbusiness bad debt, it is treated as though it were a short-term capital loss. It is limited to $3000 a year and is taken against ordinary income.

Q I loaned money to a friend last year. Since that time the friend has declared personal bankruptcy, and I shall be unable to collect what is owed me. Can I claim a bad debt deduction?

A Yes. Normally, bad debt deductions are thought of as business deductions only, but you can take a nonbusiness bad debt deduction in a situation such as you have described. The bad debt deduction for practical purposes is treated as a short-term capital loss that can be offset by a capital gain you might have.

Q Last year I cosigned a bank loan for my brother. He defaulted on the loan, and as guarantor I had to pay off the loan. I understand I cannot take a bad debt deduction. Why?

A If you guarantee a loan, you must prove that the loan was entered into with the expectation that a profit would be made on the transaction for which the loan was given. Since you gave a personal guarantee and you give no indication that the loan transaction was one for which you could derive a profit, a bad debt deduction cannot be taken.

Q I loaned my son the money for his college tuition a few years ago. I thought he would pay the money back, but he has failed to do so. Can I claim a bad debt deduction on my income tax?

A No. The IRS feels that loans you make to children for necessary educational expenses cannot properly be a valid basis for a bad debt deduction. You must establish a true creditor-debtor relationship to get the bad debt deduction. The IRS presumes that if you are lending money to a child, your expectation of getting it back is or should be weaker than if you lend money to a stranger.

Q I am a social worker in private practice and I have a few clients who have fallen behind in their payments to me. Can I write off these unpaid fees as bad debts?

A Unfortunately, no. If you are a cash basis taxpayer, there is no bad debt because income was never reported. If you are an accrual basis taxpayer, however, then a bad debt can be taken.

Q Can you tell me about the bad debt reserve which businessmen can use? I have my own business and I had some bad debts last year.

A Bad debts may be deducted on the charge off method or the reserve method. Under the charge off method, the bad debts are deducted as they occur. Under the reserve method, an estimated amount is deducted each year. The reserve method is helpful in years when your income is high and you need an offset to keep from paying higher taxes. Business bad debts are subtracted from gross income as shown on Schedule C.

Before you can use the reserve method, however, you must file Form 3115. If you don't, you can only charge the bed debt off in the year it is incurred.

16. Casualty and Theft Losses

Losing property as a result of fire, theft, or natural disaster is one of those unpleasant happenings that confronts taxpayers from time to time. Because people don't always insure their property against loss, the law allows taxpayers to take a loss deduction, subject of course to certain limitations.

To avoid potential problems with casualty and theft deductions, smart taxpayers have valuable property such as jewelry and art works appraised by experts as soon as it is acquired.

The fees of these expert appraisers are tax deductible and the appraisals should be kept in a tax deductible safe deposit box. Take photographs of less valuable items. If they are lost or damaged an expert may be able to appraise their value from the pictures.

Deductible Losses

Q Our garage was recently vandalized. Windows were broken and red paint was spattered all over the garage, which means that it will require repainting. My homeowner's insurance does not cover damage caused by vandalism. Can I take a tax deduction?

A Yes, as long as the amount of the damage exceeds 10 percent of your adjusted gross income. To obtain the deduction, the vandalism must have been sudden, destructive, and beyond your control. That seems to be the case here. (See Form 4684 at end of this chapter.)

Q Our pet cat broke a valuable Ming vase while "exploring" the living room. The vase had been appraised at $1800. Can we take a casualty loss deduction?

A No. What happened is not considered a casualty loss. You will have to look to your insurance for recompense.

Q Whenever it rains, improper drainage turns our street into a sea of mud. The city is unwilling to help us out and the problem persists. I have been told by a real estate broker that if I sell my house, I shall probably get less than what I bought it for because the street is notorious for poor drainage. If I do sell and get less for the house than I paid, can I take a casualty deduction?

A A general decline in the market value of property is not considered a casualty loss. A casualty loss must be sudden and unexpected and a calamity that causes damage very quickly. The answer is no.

Q I had some valuable trees in my yard. Because of an attack by Japanese beetles, all the trees were lost. Can I take a casualty loss deduction?

A No, for the simple reason that it takes Japanese Beetles a long time to do their dirty work. The rule is that an event resulting in a loss must be sudden and unexpected. If, however, the trees were attacked by pine beetles, which can destroy pines in less than two days, then the destruction would probably be considered "sudden."

Q Because I was very busy and because we had an early freeze last fall, I did not have antifreeze in my car; the engine block froze up and I had to replace it. Can I take a casualty loss deduction?

A Yes. There is no requirement that your casualty loss has to be entirely caused by outside forces. Your own negligence or poor judgment can also contribute to a deductible loss. Of course if you were fully compensated for the loss by your insurance company, you cannot take a deduction.

Q Our house was burglarized and ransacked last year. When we received the insurance compensation, we were not reimbursed for $500 of property damage. How much of that unreimbursed loss can I deduct on my tax return?

A It depends. All you can really deduct is the fair market value of the property. If the property was old, you have to take depreciation (or appreciation in the case of an art object) into account.

Q Because of a tremendous hurricane, my section of the state was declared a federal disaster area. Is it true that I can elect to take my casualty loss for either the taxable year in which the loss occurred or the prior taxable year?

A Yes. Only taxpayers in federal disaster areas are eligible to make that choice. The election must be made in writing, and, ninety days after it is made, it is irrevocable.

Q What difference does it make if I take my federal disaster area tax deduction this year (the year in which it occurred) or last year?

A Tax advisors normally tell their clients to file an amended return for the previous year and to take the deduction for the year immediately preceding the disaster. You will thus get a refund on your 1983 taxes together with interest on that refund and the chances are that you can use the money right now to help rebuild. The IRS usually rushes these refunds to taxpayers who file amended returns.

However, if you don't need the money immediately and you are in a much higher tax bracket this year than last, take the deduction this year.

Q Our area was hard-hit by floods last year and our home was flooded. We were partially covered by insurance so we did not suffer too bad a loss. However, we hired a commercial firm to aid us in cleaning up after the flood. Can we deduct the cost of cleaning up after the flood?

A Unfortunately no. If your insurance did not give you any money for clean-up, you have to pay for the clean-up yourself, and you are not allowed a deduction either.

Q My husband and I spent $2000 restoring our house from the effects of termite damage. Can I deduct that money?

A No. Termite damage is not considered a casualty loss and you must therefore bear the expense yourself.

Q I had a small accident with my car last year. The damage amounted to $450. I decided not to report the accident to my insurance company because I was afraid my insurance rates would be raised. Can I still report a casualty deduction on my taxes even though I didn't let the insurance company know about the damage?

A Yes, you can take a casualty loss deduction. As with all others, though, the loss must exceed 10 percent of your adjusted gross income.

Stolen Property

Q My office was broken into last year and two typewriters, a tape recorder, and a cash box were stolen. Altogether the cash and the cost of the machines amount to $3500. I didn't have any insurance. How much can I deduct?

A You can take the entire $3500 loss less any depreciation on the items stolen. Of course cash does not depreciate but the tape recorder and typewriters do, so a fair market value has to be determined before the question can be answered definitively.

Q We had some jewelry stolen last year. Fortunately we had some photographs of the pieces, and, by hiring a jewelry appraiser, we were able to ascertain its fair market value. Can we deduct the appraiser's fee as part of the theft loss?

A Yes. Just as in the case where you try to arrive at a fair market value of property given to charity, you can deduct the cost of an appraisal made for theft and casualty loss purposes. However, if the jewelry was a gift or was inherited, your deduction may be limited to your tax basis in the items stolen.

Form **4684**

Department of the Treasury
Internal Revenue Service

Casualties and Thefts

▶ See separate instructions.
▶ To be filed with Form 1040, 1041, 1065, 1120, etc.

OMB No. 1545-0177

1983

27

Name(s) as shown on tax return | **Identifying Number**

PART I.—Casualty or Theft Gain or Loss (Use a separate Part I for each different casualty or theft.)

	Item or article	Item or article	Item or article	Item or article
1 (a) Kind of property and description				
(b) Date of purchase or acquisition				
2 Cost or other basis of each item				
3 Insurance or other reimbursement you received or expect to receive for each item				
Note: *If line 2 is more than line 3, skip line 4 and complete lines 5 through 16.*				
4 Gain from casualty or theft. If line 3 is more than line 2, enter difference here and on line 17 or 22, column C. However, see instructions for line 21. Also, skip lines 5 through 16				
5 Fair market value before casualty or theft				
6 Fair market value after casualty or theft				
7 Subtract line 6 from line 5				
8 Enter smaller of line 2 or line 7				
Note: *If the loss was to property used in a trade or business, or for income-producing purposes, and it was totally destroyed by a casualty or it was a loss from theft, enter on line 8, in each column, the amount from line 2.*				
9 Subtract line 3 from line 8				

10 Casualty or theft loss. Add amounts on line 9. See instructions for **How Many Forms to Complete**	
11 Enter the part of line 9 that is from trade, business, or income-producing property here and on line 17 or 22.	
12 Subtract line 11 from line 10	
13 Enter the amount from line 12 or $100, whichever is smaller	
14 Subtract line 13 from line 12. See instructions for **How Many Forms to Complete**	
15 Enter 10% of adjusted gross income (line 33, Form 1040). See instructions before completing this line.	
16 Subtract line 15 from line 14. If line 15 is more than line 14, enter zero. Enter here and on line 17 or 22, column (B)(ii)	

PART II.—Summary of Gains and Losses (From separate Parts I)

(A) Identify casualty or theft	(B) Losses from casualties or thefts (i) Trade, business, rental or royalty property	(B) (ii) Other property	(C) Gains from casualties or thefts includible in income
Casualty or Theft of Property Held One Year or Less			
17			
18 Totals. Add amounts on line 17 for each column			
19 Combine line 18, columns (B)(i) and (C). Enter the net gain or (loss) here and on Form 4797, Part II, line 9. (If Form 4797 is not otherwise required, see instructions.)			
20 Enter the amount from line 18, column (B)(ii) here and on line 21 of Schedule A (Form 1040). Estates, trusts, partnerships, and S corporations, see instructions.			
Casualty or Theft of Property Held More Than One Year			
21 Casualty or theft gains from Form 4797, Part III, line 29			
22			
23 Total losses. Add amounts on line 22, columns (B)(i) and (B)(ii)			
24 Total gains. Add lines 21 and 22, column (C)			
25 Add amounts on line 23, columns (B)(i) and (B)(ii)			
Partnerships and S corporations, see instructions before completing lines 26(a), 26(b), and 27.			
26 If the loss on line 25 is more than the gain on line 24:			
(a) Combine line 23, column (B)(i) and line 24. Enter the net gain or (loss) here and on Form 4797, Part II, line 9. (If Form 4797 is not otherwise required, see instructions.)			
(b) Enter the amount from line 23, column (B)(ii) here and on line 21 of Schedule A (Form 1040). See instructions before completing this line.			
27 If the loss on line 25 is equal to or smaller than the gain on line 24, combine lines 24 and 25. Enter the net gain here and on Form 4797, Part I, line 2. (If Form 4797 is not otherwise required, see instructions.)			

For Paperwork Reduction Act Notice, see page 1 of separate instructions. Form **4684** (1983)

☆ U.S. GOVERNMENT PRINTING OFFICE: 1983 390-240 61-0882708

17. Home Office

Probably no area of tax regulation is more controversial than that of having an office in one's home. Recently the home office deduction requirements were changed. The newest, most up-to-date information is included here. Note especially the new data concerning home offices and second jobs. The chapter also discusses the deductibility or nondeductibility of home office furnishings and equipment.

Requirements for the Deduction

Q I commute many miles to work. Because I have to make many long distance calls, I often make them from an office in my home. My home office is just that, an office, and I don't use the room for any personal purposes. Am I eligible for the home office deduction?

A You seem to satisfy the exclusivity criterion to get the home office deduction, but you still must meet two other tests. The first is that you use the space regularly for work, and the second is that you use it for your employer's and not your own personal convenience. If you satisfy all three tests, you can get the home office deduction; but the IRS is strict about allowing the deduction.

By the way, you could probably deduct the costs of the calls if you are not reimbursed by the company for them.

Q Can I still take a home office deduction if I rent an apartment and use one room in the apartment exclusively for business?

A Yes. The mere fact that you rent an apartment makes no difference. You are still eligible to take the home office deduction if you otherwise qualify.

Deductible Items

Q I have a home office that I recently outfitted with furniture worth $2000. Can I deduct the entire amount on my tax return for the year?

A An assumption must be made here that the furniture has a useful life of more than one year. If the furniture does have such a useful life, you cannot deduct the $2000 in one year. Rather, you can depreciate the furniture because it would be a capital expenditure, and the furniture therefore is deductible through depreciation over its useful life of, say, five years. Additionally, you can claim an investment tax credit for the furniture in the amount of $200. Don't forget to take it. But if you can show that the furniture was used exclusively in your trade or business and had no personal function, you can deduct the entire $2000 in one year.

Q I cannot qualify for the office at home deduction, but I do make many business calls from my home telephone during the year. Can I take a deduction for those calls if my employer does not reimburse me for them?

A Yes. Whether you have a home office makes no difference, you are entitled to deduct the cost of business telephone calls made at home. Of course if your employer reimburses you for all the calls, you can't take the deduction; but if you are only partly reimbursed, you can deduct the unreimbursed portion. Be sure to keep records, though.

Q Can I deduct part of my electricity bill, telephone bill, and heating costs if I qualify for the home office deduction?

A So long as you can properly allocate the expenses between business use and personal use, a deduction is in order. Of course if some of the expenses are directly related to business, then an allocation is not necessary. For example, if your only long distance telephone calls were business calls, the cost of all of them can be completely deducted.

Q My husband and I conduct a mail order business from a room in our home. We both have other full-time jobs, so our mail order job is a moonlighting occupation. I read somewhere that we can deduct the costs of that home office. Is that so?

A Yes. Some recent court decisions have favored taxpayers who deducted office expenses for a second or moonlighting business. You should be cautioned that the IRS has not yet definitively ruled on the problem, and court decisions can be changed by regulation.

If you wish to take the deduction it is important that the room set aside for the business be used exclusively for the business and for nothing else. If you use the room for other purposes, even personal ones unrelated to the business, you may lose the entire deduction. Don't forget that you are also entitled to deduct from your heating and electrical costs the proportionate share that applies to that room. For example, if the room used exclusively for the business has an area of 200 square feet and your house or apartment has 2000 square feet, you can deduct 10 percent of the heating and electrical costs for the entire house.

18. Insurance, Annuities, and Disability Payments

Most people own a life insurance policy, but few understand the tax implications of that ownership. Annuities and disability insurance are also frequently misunderstood by the average taxpayer. Questions and answers concerning many aspects of insurance, such as borrowing against an insurance policy, are covered in this chapter. Insurance as it relates to your total estate plan is also highlighted here.

Taxability of Insurance Proceeds

Q I received $100,000 last year as the legal beneficiary of my father's life insurance policy. Is any of that taxable to me?

A No. If in fact the money you received was from a life insurance policy and not from an annuity, you receive such money tax-free, which makes life insurance such an important estate planning tool.

Q Last year I borrowed money on my life insurance policy. Can I deduct the interest I must pay on the loan?

A Yes. Policy loan interest is deductible just as interest would be if you took out a loan from a bank. However, you can take the deduction for the actual amount of interest you paid last year only if you are a cash basis taxpayer, which most individual taxpayers are.

Q Since I am planning to retire next year, I am thinking about all my options and the various tax consequences associated with each. What would happen if I elected to turn in my life insurance policy and get back its cash value in one lump sum?

A If the cash surrender value of your policy exceeds your lifetime premium payments, that amount of excess would be considered ordinary income. The IRS would tax you on that amount in the year you receive the lump sum payment. The same answer would be given if you took an annuity in a lump sum during the taxable year.

Q When I changed jobs I asked for and received a $100,000 fully paid life insurance policy, naming my spouse as beneficiary. I now find that I am being taxed on the amount my company paid for the policy. Does it make any difference that I own the policy and have it in my possession?

A No. The rule is that premiums paid by an employer are included in the income of the employee if the proceeds of the policy are irrevocably payable to the employee's spouse or estate. Who owns or possesses the policy makes no difference to the IRS.

Q My company has offered me something called "split dollar" life insurance. What is it, and what are its tax implications?

A Split dollar life insurance is life insurance that is paid for partly by you and partly by your employer, that is, you split the premium costs. You pay tax only on the difference between what you actually pay and what the government says you should pay. The latter figure is derived from something called the P.S. 58 table. Your employer should have worked out all the numbers for you so that you can make a reasoned judgment about whether you want to get split dollar insurance.

Annuities and the Annuity Exclusion

Q Can you explain to me what an annuity is? I have asked some other people and they were unable to tell me. Also, what are the tax implications of annuity ownership?

A An annuity is a contract generally purchased from an insurance company which pays you a fixed amount of money over a period of years. There are present and deferred annuities. With a present annuity you buy the contract and payments start immediately. A deferred annuity is bought years before payout begins.

Under a deferred annuity contract, earnings that accumulate before the payout period accumulate tax-free. You begin to pay taxes only when payout begins years later, usually when you are retired.

Q I bought a $10,000 annuity two years ago. Now, because of some financial setbacks, I would like to withdraw some funds from the annuity. I am supposed to start receiving payments from the annuity in eight years. What will be the tax consequence of my early withdrawal?

A Try to avoid an early withdrawal at all costs. The IRS now imposes a 5 percent penalty on premature withdrawals from an annuity contract. That is 5 percent of any amount that becomes part of your taxable income during the year. If you are over 59½, though, the penalty does not apply.

Q I am the holder of a joint and survivor annuity of my late husband's. I understand that I can exclude a part of the annuity income from my taxes. How much can I exclude?

A As the surviving spouse under a joint and survivor annuity, you can exclude exactly the same amount from each payment that your husband could when he was alive. To find out what that percentage of each payment was, check with the insurance company or whoever sold you and your husband the annuity.

Q I am thinking of buying a variable annuity for myself. I don't have to pay taxes on income earned before I start withdrawing money, do I?

A The period before an annuity starts paying out is called the accumulation period, and no tax is due on income earned during that period. Tax is paid when the payout period begins and throughout the payout period.

Disability Insurance

Q After suffering an accident last year I became disabled. I received some benefits from the health and accident insurance policy that I have at work. Are those benefits taxable to me?

A The answer depends on two conditions. First, whether you are "permanently and totally" disabled, and, second, who paid the premiums on the policy. If you paid the premiums, the benefits are nontaxable if you are permanently and totally disabled. If your company paid, the benefits may be taxable unless they constitute reimbursements for medical expenses incurred.

Permanent and total disability is defined as the inability to do any substantial gainful activity. The condition must be attested to by a physician.

Q Is all my disability income taxable, or does the government give me a small break?

A Because the IRS views disability income as a substitute for a salary, disability income is normally taxable. But there is a disability income exclusion of up to \$5200 a year or \$100 a week, whichever is less. However, to qualify for the exclusion you must be under 65, have retired on disability, have been permanently and totally disabled within the IRS's definition, and cannot have opted to treat your disability income as a pension or annuity.

Q I have received disability income payments for a number of years. For the first time in a long while I have been able to earn some income to supplement my disability payments. Is there a limit on how much I can earn and still qualify for the $5200 a year income exclusion?

A Most definitely. If your adjusted gross income including disability income exceeds $15,000 for the taxable year, then you lose $1 of exclusion for every $1 over that amount; this means that if your adjusted gross income exceeds $20,000, you cannot qualify for the exclusion at all.

Q My wife became disabled this year and received $10,000 from her employer, who said the money was for accrued annual leave that had accumulated. Do we have to report this income? After all, my wife is severely disabled and unable to work.

A Yes. As harsh as it sounds, lump sum disability payments that are attributed to accrued annual leave are considered ordinary income and are taxable.

19. Company Fringe Benefits

Working for a company has its benefits, and among them are the "fringes" that many employees get. Executives especially are entitled to certain perquisites that have important tax consequences. These consequences, alternatives, and limitations are explained in this chapter. Deferred compensation is especially troublesome, and it is given a full discussion here.

Profit-Sharing Plans

Q I have recently been promoted to the executive ranks of my company, and I am unfamiliar with the tax ramifications of some of my new benefits. I don't have to report as income my company's contribution to a profit-sharing plan, do I? I have been told that the plan is a qualified one.

A No. And you do not have to include in gross income your employer's contribution to a qualified pension or annuity that might be in your name.

Q What is the difference between a qualified deferred compensation plan and one that is nonqualified?

A There is a big difference. Under a qualified plan, one approved by the IRS, any income to the trust escapes taxation; and you are not taxed on the compensation until you receive it, which is most likely at retirement. If, however, the plan were nonqualified, you would have to pay taxes on the compensation when it is credited to your account.

Medical Reimbursement Plans

Q My company offers a medical reimbursement plan for its employees. The plan is funded through insurance bought for that specific purpose. Does the fact that the reimbursement plan is funded by insurance make any difference regarding taxability of the payments?

A No. Whether you are paid directly by your company or by an insurance intermediary, the result is the same. No inclusion of medical reimbursement expenses in income is necessary.

Q My company has a medical reimbursement plan whereby it reimburses me for any medical expenses incurred by me or my family. Are the reimbursements paid to me included in my gross income?

A No. Under such a plan, reimbursed medical expenses are not included in taxable income. Although this is the general rule, if the company's plan is written poorly, the IRS might challenge it. Since such amounts are not included in income, they naturally don't appear in adjusted gross income, so the 5 percent medical expense limitation does not apply.

Deferred Compensation

Q With retirement near, I have to make a decision about how I want my accumulated deferred compensation paid, either in a lump sum or in periodic payments during the length of my retirement. What are the tax implications if I take a lump sum payment?

A If you were active in a deferred compensation plan prior to and subsequent to January 1, 1974, at least a portion of any lump sum payment is taxable at capital gains rates. As far as the rest of the amount is concerned, you have an option. It can be taxed under a rather complicated ten-year forward averaging calculation or you can opt to tax both the ordinary and capital gains portions as ordinary income; and because you will be in a lower tax bracket, this could minimize your tax bite. Your company should work out the appropriate numbers for you.

Q I have been newly promoted into the executive ranks of my company and am confused by one of the fringe benefit offerings that I can have. Can you explain to me the tax implications of something called a salary reduction plan?

A These are also known as 401 (k) plans because of the tax code section. They operate in this manner: you can reduce your pay up to 10% per year and that money must be put into a retirement trust for you where it is invested in stocks, bonds, or a mutual fund of your choice.

The amount that you contribute to the plan each year is not taxed, even though you earned it and would normally be taxed on it if the 401 (k) plan did not exist. It is a tax sheltered way of providing for your retirement. You withdraw funds as needed during retirement.

Q Can you explain the terms "funded" and "unfunded" as they relate to deferred compensation plans?

A Surely. Under a funded plan, your company would have to pay the amount of the deferred compensation contribution to an independent trustee who keeps the money for your benefit. Under the unfunded plan, no money is paid to anyone, but you are relying on the future financial position of the corporation because it has made a promise to pay you. If it doesn't have the money when you retire, you might not receive any of the money promised.

Miscellaneous Fringe Benefits

Q My company recently began a program whereby employees can obtain any college degree and the company will help pay for it. I am working on my master's degree. Will I have to include the amount I am getting from the company in my gross income?

A Not if the educational assistance program is nondiscriminatory. But if the program is open only to a certain group of employees or pays only for certain types of courses (with the possible exception of courses on hobbies or sports), then the program could be considered discriminatory by the IRS, and the education benefit funds would then have to be included in income.

By the way, the courses you take under this program do not have to be directly related to your job in the company.

Q I have been informed by my company that I am eligible to have my finances, investments, and estate plan reviewed by an outside group of financial planners that my company has hired. But I was also told that the cost of this financial planning service will become part of my taxable income. Can I do anything about it?

A The entire cost of the service is included in gross income, but you get a corresponding tax deduction for that portion of the financial planning that is devoted to tax and investment advice. Therefore try to have the planners give you as much tax and investment advice as possible.

Q My employer is offering a new fringe benefit to employees, a legal services plan that will provide annually a certain amount of paid legal services to me and my family. Can the corporation tax me on the amount it contributes to the plan for my benefit?

A If the plan is a qualified one, then the costs of such premiums cannot be included in your gross income.

Q I want to provide as much tax-free income to my spouse as possible in the event of my death. My company provides a death benefit should an employee die while employed by the company. How much will my wife get from the death benefit, and how much of it will be tax free?

A The rule is that payments of up to $5000 to a deceased employee's spouse or beneficiary are excluded from income. Amounts in excess of $5000 could be included in the beneficiary's gross income unless it can be shown that the employer paid the amount as a gift to the beneficiary, which might be difficult to prove.

Q In reviewing my fringe benefits package, my financial advisor said that I should restrict myself to accepting only $50,000 of the group term life insurance offered by my employer. He said there were tax implications, but I don't recall what they were. Can you help?

A As an employee, you can exclude from income the premiums paid on group term life insurance by your employer up to $50,000. If you accept more than $50,000, part of your employer's premium cost will be reflected in your gross income. Exactly how much income is recognized is set out in IRS regulations. You should of course consult your financial advisor as to the advisability of accepting the new insurance or not.

Q For many years I have contributed to an Educational Benefit Trust (EBT) that was set up by my employer. Such trusts enable employees like myself to save money for our children's educations. The company also contributes to the EBT. Who pays taxes on the funds when they are paid out, myself or my children?

A The tax burden falls on you, but you don't pay the tax until the time the funds are actually paid to your children.

Another thing: contributions to an EBT by an employee are deductible in the year made if the plan is a qualified one.

Q As an executive, I am entitled to certain "perks" and my company is talking about a new one–providing annual physicals for all executives. What would be the tax consequences of putting in such a program?

A This increasingly popular benefit is not considered taxable income to the employee but is deductible by the company. This holds no matter whether the exam is a quick one or one of those comprehensive examinations that takes a full day to complete.

20. Family Transactions

Financial transactions between family members often give rise to tax consequences that neither family member intended at the time of making the transaction. For example, as simple an act as lending money to your children or selling stock to your sister, if not done properly, can cost you money. This chapter tells you how to structure family financial transactions so that taxes have the minimum impact on you and other members of your family.

Your Children

Q My daughter has a job every summer between college classes as a swimming pool maintenance worker. Her employer is an established company in town, and she earns approximately $2500 every summer. I understand that there is a way that she can keep from having withholding tax taken out of her pay. Can you enlighten me?

A Very simple. Any individual who earns less than $3300 a year can pick up a W-4 form from his or her employer. All that is necessary is to write the word *exempt* on line three of the form and then give the form back to the employer. That way taxes will not be withheld and your daughter will not have to wait almost a full year to get a refund because no taxes were due.

Q I understand that I can hire my two children for the summer and that I can still take them as my exemptions, as well as deducting their salaries as a business expense. Can I really?

A You sure can. But you must make sure that their job responsibilities and rate of pay are no different from those that would be given a nonfamily member hired to do the same job. For safety's sake have a nonfamily member keep a record of their working hours in case the IRS asks for it.

Other Family Financial Matters

Q I took a deduction on my tax return two years ago that the IRS subsequently disallowed. I sold 100 shares of stock that I had purchased at $50 per share to my sister at $20 per share, and I took the loss on my return. Why did the IRS disallow it?

A You can't take the loss deduction on the sale of any property to any family member. If you had sold the stock to anyone outside the family circle, then the loss would have been sustained. But the law is very clear when it comes to family members. This answer would be different, however, if you could prove that the fair market value of the stock was $20 per share.

Q I have read a number of articles where the writer has talked about income splitting among family members. Can you explain what income splitting is and give an example I can understand?

A Income splitting is a device whereby the principal breadwinner transfers money or income-producing assets from himself to another family member, usually a child or dependent parent, while incurring little or no tax liability. The child or parent is usually in a lower tax bracket than the breadwinner so he or she pays little or no tax on the gift. For example, suppose you are in the 40 percent tax bracket and you have $20,000 in bonds that earn $1500 per year. You would have to pay $600 in taxes if you kept the bonds. If you transfer them to your son or daughter, your child would get the $1500 and would have to pay a lot less in taxes. Hence you save money.

Q A salesman recently visited me. He was selling something he called a "family trust." He said that I could put all my assets into a trust with myself as trustee, and by doing that I could avoid paying almost all my taxes. It sounded too good to be true and I didn't buy. Was I right?

A You sure were. Family trusts, or, as they are sometimes called, "apocalypse trusts," are frauds and are not recognized by the IRS as legitimate tax shelters or tax avoidance devices. Although there are not as many people trying to peddle these trusts as there used to be, be wary of any who do show up. Those who sell them make a nice commission on the sale. Don't fall for their sales pitch, no matter what kind of "evidence" they may show you.

Q I recently became the sole support of my widowed mother. I would like to claim her as an exemption on my tax return. She had social security and dividend income of over $6000 last year. Can I take her as an exemption?

A No. To take a relative as an exemption that individual must earn less than $1000 a year. If your mother can shift $5000 of her income into tax-free securities, then you could properly take her as an exemption.

Q My 10-year-old niece became a child model last year and earned $5000 for the year. Her father received the money for her and put it all in a trust fund set up for the girl's education. Is that $5000 income to my brother or to my niece? After all, she never actually received the money, my brother did.

A The rule here is quite simple. Compensation received by a child for personal services is income to the child and not the parent; that is true whether or not the child actually receives the income.

Q My two sisters and I contribute to the total support of my mother, who is 92 years old. Is there a way that we can share the deduction for her?

A Yes. You can by rotating the deduction between the three of you. To do that you must file each year a Multiple Support Declaration (Form 2120) with the IRS stating which one of you will be claiming your mother as dependent for the year. Each year you can change the declaration by filing a new form and that way each of you gets the chance to claim your mother as a dependent. By the way, it makes no difference if one of you actually contributes more to your mother's support than any of the others. The multiple support declaration is still controlling. (See Form 2120 at the end of this chapter.)

Marriage Penalty Deduction

Q I understand that working married couples are now entitled to a tax deduction. I haven't seen anything about it. Can you explain?

A Beginning with the 1982 tax year, a new deduction has been introduced for working couples who file joint tax returns. Because working couples formerly had to pay a tax penalty for being married, the deduction is called the Marriage Penalty Deduction. For 1983 and 1984 it provides a 10 percent deduction on the earnings of the lower of the two incomes earned by the couple, up to a maximum of $30,000 income. The limit on the deduction would be $3000, or 10 percent of $30,000.

Q Both my wife and I work full time. I made $25,000 last year and she made $17,000. We both plan to put the maximum contribution of $2,000 each into our IRA accounts. How then do we figure the marriage penalty deduction?

A The deduction is based on the "qualified earned income" of the lower earning spouse. Qualified earned income is generally defined as wages or salary from a trade or business. If your wife works for you, however, the marriage deduction does not apply.

Before you can come up with the proper base figure upon which to calculate your deduction, certain deductions must be made from qualified earned income. These deductions include expenses related to the production of income from a trade or business, unreimbursed expenses paid or incurred in connection with the performance of services as an employee, any supplemental unemployment compensation benefits, and contributions to an IRA or Keogh plan.

You indicate that your wife wants to put $2,000 into her IRA. If she has no other deductions from qualified earned income her base would be $15,000. Since the deduction is 5 percent of the base amount, the marriage penalty deduction in this instance would be $750.

Q I want to take the marriage penalty deduction. What are the mechanics for putting it down on the tax return?

A You will be happy to know that the IRS has made available Schedule W, a new form that must be used to calculate the marriage penalty deduction. You must of course include it with your tax return when you file.

Q My son has been lucky enough to get a very high paying summer job this year and he will be making well over $5000. Since he also has a full scholarship to college we are wondering what kind of taxes he will have to pay on his earnings. Can you give us some advice?

A First of all, any amount earned above $3300 is subject to taxation. But consider the little known fact that anybody–including children who earn over $3300–can set up an IRA. If, therefore, your son establishes an IRA and puts $1700 into it, he can deduct that amount from his taxes and he will have no tax liability.

Form **2120** (Rev. Sept. 1981)

Department of the Treasury—Internal Revenue Service

Multiple Support Declaration

OMB No. 1545–0071 Expires 8–31–84

During the calendar year 19............, I paid more than 10% of the support of

....
(Name of person)

I could have claimed this person as a dependent except that I did not pay more than 50% of his or her support.

I understand that this person is being claimed as a dependent on the income tax return of ....
(Name)

...., and
(Address)

I agree not to claim an exemption for this person on my Federal income tax return for any tax year beginning in this calendar year.

.... (Your signature) .... (Your social security number)

.... (Date) .... (Address)

For Paperwork Reduction Act Notice, see back of form.

SAMPLE

Instructions

Paperwork Reduction Act Notice.—The Paperwork Reduction Act of 1980 says we must tell you why we are collecting this information, how we will use it, and whether you have to give it to us. We ask for the information to carry out the Internal Revenue laws of the United States. We need it to ensure that you are complying with these laws and to allow us to figure and collect the right amount of tax. You are required to give us this information.

If two or more persons together paid more than 50% of the support of an individual for a calendar year and each could claim that person as a dependent except that they did not individually pay more than 50% of the support, one of the contributors can claim the person as a dependent if:

(1) the taxpayer claiming the person as a dependent paid more than 10% of the support, and

(2) each contributor (other than the taxpayer claiming the dependent) who paid more than 10% of the support of the dependent agrees not to claim that person as a dependent for any tax year beginning in that calendar year.

Each person (other than the taxpayer claiming the dependent) who paid more than 10% of the support of the dependent must complete this declaration and give it to the taxpayer claiming the dependent, who in turn must file the declarations with his or her return.

The taxpayer claiming an exemption for the dependent should be prepared to support the right to claim the exemption if requested.

☆ U.S. GOVERNMENT PRINTING OFFICE: 1982—O-363:149 23-188-5979

Schedule W (Form 1040)
Department of the Treasury
Internal Revenue Service (0)

Deduction for a Married Couple When Both Work

▶ For Paperwork Reduction Act Notice, see Form 1040 Instructions.
▶ Attach to Form 1040.

OMB No. 1545-0074
1983
21

Names as shown on Form 1040 | Your social security number

Step 1 Figure your earned income

		(a) You	(b) Your spouse
1 Wages, salaries, tips, etc., from Form 1040, line 7. (Do not include any amount your spouse paid you.)	1		
2 Net profit or (loss) from self-employment (from Schedules C and F (Form 1040), Schedule K-1 (Form 1065), and any other taxable self-employment or earned income)	2		
3 Add lines 1 and 2. This is your total earned income	3		

Step 2 Figure your qualified earned income

		(a) You	(b) Your spouse
4 Adjustments from Form 1040, lines 24, 25a, 26, 30, and any repayment of sub-pay included on line 31. (See instructions below.)	4		
5 Subtract line 4 from line 3. This is your qualified earned income. (If the amount in column (a) or (b) is zero (-0-) or less, stop here. You may not claim this deduction.)	5		

Step 3 Figure your deduction

6 Compare the amounts on line 5(a) and line 5(b) and write the smaller amount here. (Write either amount if 5(a) and 5(b) are exactly the same.) ***Do not write more than $30,000***	6	
7 Percentage used to figure the deduction (10%)	7	x .10
8 Multiply the amount on line 6 by the percentage on line 7. This is the amount of your deduction. Write the answer here and on Form 1040, line 29 ▶	8	

SAMPLE

Instructions

Complete this schedule and attach it to your Form 1040 if you take the deduction for a married couple when both work. You may take the deduction if both you and your spouse:

- work and have qualified earned income, and
- file a joint return, and
- do not file **Form 2555** to exclude income or to exclude or deduct certain housing costs, and
- do not file **Form 4563** to exclude income.

There are three steps to follow in figuring the deduction on Schedule W.

Step 1 (lines 1, 2, and 3).—Figure earned income separately for yourself and your spouse.

Step 2 (lines 4 and 5).—Figure qualified earned income separately for yourself and your spouse by subtracting certain adjustments from earned income.

Step 3 (lines 6, 7, and 8).—Figure the deduction based on the **smaller** of:

- the qualified earned income entered on line 5(a) or 5(b) of Schedule W, whichever is less, **OR**
- $30,000.

Earned income.—This is generally income you receive for services you provide. It includes wages, salaries, tips, commissions, disability income, sub-pay, etc. (from Form 1040, line 7). It also includes income earned from self-employment (from Schedules C and F of Form 1040 and Schedule K-1 of Form 1065), and net earnings and gains (other than capital gains) from the disposition, transfer, or licensing of property that you created. Earned income does not include interest, dividends, pensions, annuities, IRA distributions, unemployment compensation, deferred compensation, or nontaxable income.

Caution: *Do not consider community property laws in figuring your earned income.*

Qualified earned income.—This is the amount on which the deduction is based. Figure it by subtracting certain adjustments from earned income. These adjustments (and the related lines on Form 1040) are:

- Employee business expenses (from line 24).
- Payments to an IRA (from line 25a).
- Payments to a Keogh plan (from line 26).
- Disability income exclusion (from line 30).
- Repayment of supplemental unemployment benefits (sub-pay) included in the total on line 31. See the instructions on repayment of sub-pay on page 13 of the Form 1040 Instructions.

Enter the total of any adjustments that apply to your earned income in the appropriate column on line 4.

Example.—You earned a salary of $20,000 and had $6,000 of employee business expenses (line 24 of Form 1040). Your spouse earned $17,000 and put $2,000 into an IRA (line 25a of Form 1040). Your qualified earned income is $14,000 ($20,000 minus $6,000) and your spouse's is $15,000 ($17,000 minus $2,000). Because your qualified earned income is less than your spouse's, the deduction is figured on your income. Therefore, the deduction is $1,400 ($14,000 x .10).

U.S. GOVERNMENT PRINTING OFFICE : 1983 O - 390-112

21. Pensions, Individual Retirement Accounts, and Keogh Plans

Every working person can have his or her own tax-sheltered retirement account. For individuals who work for someone else this type of account is called an Individual Retirement Account (IRA); for the self-employed it is called a Keogh plan.

The quicker you deposit money into either kind of account, the faster it will start to earn interest for you. For example, suppose you are considering making an IRA contribution of $2,000 in January 1983 but you know that IRA deductions for the 1983 tax year apply to any IRA contributions made until the final date for filing the return–April 15, 1984. If you wait until April 14, 1984 to make your IRA contribution for 1983, you will have lost almost 16 months of compounded interest on your pension account, which can amount to a significant loss of money to you when you retire.

Corporate Pension Plans

Q I know that if I work after I retire and if I earn a certain amount, I could lose some Social Security benefits. But if I receive some rather hefty pension payments from my former employer, are those payments subject to Social Security tax or other limitations?

A No. If the pension plan was a qualified plan, pension payments are not subject to Social Security taxes. If the plan was a nonqualified one, there is a possibility that the answer might be different, depending on the circumstances. The IRS must approve all these plans; if it doesn't, all advantages would be lost.

Q I retired from my company last year after twenty-five years of employment there. The company paid me a lump sum amount, but, as it turned out, the amount I received was less than the amount I actually paid into the plan. What can I do? The plan made some horrendous investments.

A You can claim a deduction for the difference between the amount you paid in and the amount you actually received. Whoever did the investing for your plan should be fired.

Q A few years ago my employer established an excellent pension plan that has shown very good returns on its investments. Since its performance has been so good I would like to add as much as I can to it as often as possible. I have read that under the recent tax changes I can add up to $2,000 to my employer's plan and it will be deductible just like an IRA. Did I read the item properly?

A Yes. You may contribute and deduct up to $2,000 to an employer's IRS qualified plan. However, and this is important, the plan must permit voluntary contributions by plan participants such as yourself. The new law was written so that you can make a partial contribution to your company plan and to a separate IRA as long as both contributions do not exceed $2,000 a year. Of course you still get to take the full $2,000 deduction even if you contribute to a company plan or your own IRA.

Q As a physician, I incorporated myself about five years ago. I have a pension plan that was properly set up and that I have been contributing to for that period of time. Now my pension adviser tells me that I can establish an IRA by contributing $2000 to my pension account. Can I really do that?

A Certainly. It is an excellent suggestion. By contributing IRA funds to your corporate pension plan, you need not set up a separate IRA account elsewhere. This is especially good if you are happy with the way your pension account is being administered.

Q I plan on retiring in four months and my company has informed me that they will be withholding taxes from my pension checks. Is this new and can I do anything to keep the company from withholding from my pension?

A As of January 1, 1983, firms are required by law to withhold federal taxes from pensions. However, your company should provide you with an election form that allows you to opt for non-withholding. If you do not file this form with your company, they are compelled to automatically withhold from your pension.

Individual Pension Plans

Q Besides holding a regular job, I moonlight as a consultant. Last year I made $15,000 doing that. Can I set up a Keogh Plan even though I only free-lance part time?

A Definitely. Keogh Plans are for self-employed individuals and are based on a percentage of self-employed income whether part or full time. You can put in and deduct 15 percent of your free-lance income—in your case, $2250. The maximum amount an individual can put into a Keogh is $20,000. One other point: your Keogh account must be set up prior to December 31 of the taxable year in which you want to claim the tax deduction.

Q Banks in my area advertise for IRA and Keogh plan customers, but I am confused. Some advertisements say December 31 is the last day to establish an account; others say April 14. Who's right?

A The confusion is understandable. There are different rules regarding IRAs and Keoghs. With an IRA you have until the due date of your return to establish an account and to contribute to it.

As far as Keoghs are concerned, you must establish the account before the end of the calendar year in which you plan to take the deduction. You can make contributions to the account until the return filing date.

Q I am 62 and fairly well set financially for the next few years, so I don't think I will have to draw on my IRA funds for quite a while. How long can I keep contributing to my IRA and also take the deduction for the contribution?

A You can make contributions and take the deduction for the contributions up until the year you turn 70½. At that time you must stop contributing to the account and of course you will not be allowed to take the deduction after that period either.

What's more, you must start taking the money out of your account before you turn 70½. If you allow the fund to build up after you turn that age, you will be subject to penalties.

Q Last year my bank was advertising that it would lend customers the $2000 to put into their IRA accounts if they didn't have the cash when they filed their returns. If you borrow the money, will that jeopardize the deduction for a contribution to an IRA?

A No, it won't. It might work out very well, especially if you can get the loan at a reasonable interest rate. If you do go that route you can also get a deduction for the interest you pay on the loan.

Q I worked for a company for two months last year, and then I was unemployed for a time before I got another job. My first employer had a qualified pension plan and my second does not. I wanted to start an IRA but was told I couldn't. Why is that?

A The old rule was that you could not start an IRA under these circumstances but as of January 1, 1982 it makes no difference whether your employer has a qualified plan or not. You can still establish an IRA if you wish.

Q My wife is a housewife. Can I deduct a contribution I make to her IRA?

A Yes. There is a $2250 limit that you can divide between your IRA and your wife's. You can allocate the $2250 anyway you wish between the two accounts, but you cannot put more than $2000 in any one account.

Q My husband and I are getting a divorce. He started a spousal IRA for me a few years ago. He now claims that the money is his. Whose is it?

A It's yours. It was put away for your benefit and you both took advantage of the tax deduction on your joint tax return. The law says that you get to keep the IRA divorce or no.

Q Is it a good idea to borrow the money for an IRA? My bank offers such a loan and I would like to take advantage of it if it works out well.

A Whether it is a good idea or not depends on the interest rate the bank is charging, but in most cases when you figure the advantages that an IRA gives you, it should be all right. One good thing: the interest that you pay on the loan you take out for your IRA is tax deductible.

Q Since I am self-employed, I opened an H.R. 10 or Keogh account. I have the account with my broker. Is any income to the account taxable to me this year?

A No. Just as with IRAs, income from Keogh accounts is tax exempt. One further word: make sure your broker is a valid trustee under the applicable laws. Brokers must satisfy certain requirements to become Keogh or IRA plan trustees. However, for the 1983 tax year you can be the trustee of your own plan.

Q Can I have more than one IRA account? After all, with inflation so high I would like to have as much money as possible put away for retirement.

A You are courting trouble and a possible fine by the IRS if you establish more than two IRAs in one year. Of course you can still only deduct $2,000 per year but if you want to establish two accounts one with a bank and the other with a broker or insurance company that is all right as long as you don't contribute and deduct more than $1,000 for each annually.

Q Can you explain to me what an IRA rollover is? I'm leaving my long-time corporate job and am going into business for myself.

A An IRA rollover comes about when an individual receives a lump sum distribution from a *qualified* pension plan. A person can defer taxation on that distribution by transferring the entire amount to an IRA within sixty days from the date of the receipt of the distribution. There is no limit on how much you can put into the IRA from the rollover. Another point: if you incorporate your new business, you may be able to rollover the IRA funds into a corporate pension plan.

Q When I signed up for my IRA, the bank officer explained to me that I could not take anything out of the account until I am 59½ years old. What happens if I retire at 55 and want the money then?

A An actual or cónstructive receipt of IRA funds before 59½ is not only included in the taxable income for the year of receipt, but you must also pay a 10 percent nondeductible penalty tax on the amount withdrawn.

The penalty is not imposed if the IRA owner dies or becomes disabled before reaching 59½ years.

Q I am self-employed and have set up a Keogh plan account. I was told by a friend that under the new law I can establish an IRA as well. Is that right?

A It sure is. Since January 1, 1984 you can put as much as $30,000 into your Keogh account and in addition you can deposit $2,000 into an IRA. This means that you can put a total of $32,000 away for your retirement and that amount can be fully deducted from your taxable income in 1984.

Q What is the new rule with regard to a non-working spouse and an IRA?

A If you wish to set up a joint IRA with your non-working spouse you can put away and deduct as much as $2,250 a year under present law. You must of course file a joint tax return, to be eligible for such an account.

Q I have my IRA with a securities firm that offers investment vehicles such as stock funds, bond funds, and money market funds. I can switch among these if I wish. Would such switches be considered rollovers?

A No. As long as the money is not sent back to you but remains on deposit with the investment firm, it is not considered a rollover. You are permitted a rollover once every 12 months. If you try to roll the account over more frequently, you may lose the tax advantage of an IRA.

Q Is it true that I can deduct an IRA contribution before I actually put the money in my IRA account? A friend mentioned that I could do that.

A Yes. The law used to be that you had to make your IRA contribution before filing your return. Now, however, if you file early, such as the second week in January, you need not put the money in your IRA account until April 15. That allows you to put your tax refund, if any, into your IRA account. This is only true for IRA plans, not self-employed Keogh plans. In a Keogh, the plan must have been established during the tax year, and the contribution must be made before the filing date for the deduction to be valid.

Q I haven't gotten the money together yet to make my IRA contribution for the tax year just ended. I know that I have until April 15 to make my IRA contribution in order to get the deduction. But suppose I file for an automatic four-month extension on sending in my tax return. What happens to my IRA contribution date?

A The law recently changed. Now you must make the contribution by April 15; extensions are no longer allowed.

Q Did I read somewhere that there is a new rule with regard to an increase in Keogh plan limitations?

A You did. As of the 1984 tax year, you can contribute to a Keogh plan the lesser of 20% of all your self-employment income up to a limit of $30,000. Formerly the limit was 15% or $15,000. The new law encourages self-employed people to put more away for their retirement and to get a bigger tax break right now.

Q Since I recently started my own business, I want to open a Keogh account for myself. There is only one problem, and that is starting the business cost much more than I anticipated and I have very little discretionary income available right now to open an account. Can I do anything?

A All you have to do is to start your Keogh plan before the end of the year but there is no limit as to what you can put in it when you open it. If you can find a bank or broker who will allow you to open an account with as little as $5, you can start the account now and contribute towards it until you file your return. All contributions made before the end of the tax year and those made up to the time of filing of the return may be deducted in the tax year.

Q What is a voluntary contribution to a Keogh plan?

A Beginning on January 1, 1984 you can contribute an additional 10% of your self-employment income to your Keogh Plan; this is over and above your maximum 20% or $30,000. However, and this is important, the voluntary contribution is not tax deductible. You add to the principal of your Keogh Plan with the additional contribution but you cannot deduct more than the 20% or $30,000 maximum. The increased interest that your additional contribution earns accumulates tax free.

Q I have read some confusing things about whether or not I can deduct the management fee that I pay every year for my IRA. Can you clear up my confusion?

A Be glad to. The fee that you pay is fully deductible but it is entered as a miscellaneous deduction on Schedule A. So, if you are charged an annual $50 management fee, for example, that $50 is a miscellaneous deduction which you are entitled to take each year it is charged. (See Schedule A on page 35.)

Q I own my own business. What is the new law with regard to borrowing from my Keogh Plan?

A If you own 10% or less of your business you can borrow up to $50,000 from your Keogh Plan account. You must, however, repay the loan within at least 5 years and you must pay interest on the money borrowed at a reasonable rate.

If you own more than 10% of your business you cannot borrow from your Keogh Plan without incurring a penalty.

22. Trusts

Although the subject of trusts is highly complex, every taxpayer should at the least know the rudiments of the short-term trust known as the Clifford Trust. Clifford Trusts are an essential estate and financial planing tool that you may want to employ at some point during your life. In this chapter you learn about Clifford Trusts and their uses and about the trust account known as the Uniform Gift to Minors Act Account.

Clifford Trusts

Q I have read several magazine articles where the writer has advocated the use of a Clifford Trust to finance a child's education. Since I am a parent with a twelve-year-old child, I want to examine the subject further. I am not at all sure I know what a Clifford Trust is. Can you tell me?

A These are short-term trusts that must run for a minimum of ten years and one day. Essentially they shift income from one taxpayer (in your case the parent) to a dependent who has little or no income tax liability because the total income of the dependent is minimal.

If you wanted to fund your child's education and it would cost $20,000, assuming you are in the 50 percent tax bracket, it would actually cost you $40,000 in pretax income to pay for the education. When you use a Clifford Trust, you transfer assets worth $20,000 to the trust, and your income is reduced by only $20,000. The result of all this is that you have effectively increased the income you can spend.

Remember, this is a temporary trust, and the principal amount that you put into a Clifford Trust is returned to you when the trust period has expired.

Q How can I fund a Clifford Trust? Is cash the only method?

A Cash is one means but not the only one. You can use any type of income-producing property, such as stocks and bonds or real estate.

Q I am thinking of transferring some stock into a Clifford Trust for the benefit of my children's education. What happens to any capital gains that result?

A Capital gains and losses are taxable to the individual who establishes the trust and not taxable to the beneficiary. This is true even if the trust does not distribute any cash to you as a result of the capital gain.

Q I have been advised to set up a Clifford Trust, but I am unsure who must pay the income tax on the trust. Do I pay or does my mother, who is the beneficiary?

A Your mother does if the trust is set up to distribute income currently—that is, if the income is paid to her as it is earned. If the trust is established so that the income is accumulated, then the trust would have to pay the taxes.

Q Can I appoint myself as trustee of a Clifford Trust that I established for the benefit of my twin daughters' education?

A Yes. Not only can you appoint yourself trustee, but you can continue to vote any stock that you put into the trust and make all investment decisions with regard to the trust. But remember, since the trust proceeds will eventually return to you, you will want to make investment decisions that not only make sense for your daughters but for yourself as well.

Trust Savings Accounts

Q Last year I set up a savings account for my son under the Uniform Gift to Minors Act (UGMA) account. Who is taxed on the income from that account, I or my son?

A Your son is taxed in all but the most unusual circumstances. If the income is used for necessities for the child such as food, shelter, clothing, or education that you would normally be liable to provide, then the income would be taxable to you. But one of the purposes of a UGMA account is to transfer the taxability of the income from you to your son, who has little or no tax liability.

Q Are there any disadvantages to setting up a custodian account for my child's education?

A One big one. If you name yourself custodian or trustee of the account and die while still trustee or custodian, the money in the account will become part of your estate for estate tax purposes. Therefore, name someone else as the custodian or trustee of the account.

Q I am the beneficiary of a trust fund that my recently deceased grandmother set up for me. Since this will be the first year I will receive any income from the trust how do I report it on the tax form?

A Depending on the type of income you receive you may have to report income on as many as three different schedules. Dividends from securities are to be reported on Schedule B. Capital gains on the other hand, whether long or short term, must be included on Schedule D. Any other income from the trust is to be shown on Schedule E. Your trustee should provide this for you before you file your taxes for the year.

Generation Skipping Trusts

Q Recently I read an article about generation skipping trusts that I can use for my grandchildren. I seem to have misplaced the article. Can you refresh my memory on them?

A Generation skipping trusts are an excellent estate planning tool. By setting up such a trust in your will you can take property out of your estate where it will not be subjected to estate taxes. Simply, it is a trust to which you donate assets. You leave part of the assets to your child or children for use during their lifetimes with the remainder going to your grandchildren. You are limited to leaving $250,000 worth of property for each child (not grandchild). So if you have two children, you could leave property worth $500,000 in generation skipping trusts.

Such trusts require the services of an attorney to set up, but it can be done when you have your will prepared.

23. Tax Shelters

Tax shelters are not as prevalent as they were a few years ago, but many people still invest in tax shelters without really knowing what they are. Tax shelters are investments that provide the individual investor with an immediate tax deduction while creating a potential gain for some future time. Here real estate and oil and gas drilling shelters are explained. Before you put money into any tax shelter, you should read this chapter.

One further word: Start thinking about tax shelters early in the year. If you see one that looks promising and an expert tells you that it looks good to him or her, invest right then. Don't wait until the end of the tax year. By the end of the year most of the good tax shelters are gone. Investing in a shelter involves early attention to tax matters, not last-minute planning.

Q Can you give me a simple definition of what a tax shelter is? Why are they held in such disrepute these days?

A Tax shelters are *investments* in ventures of a high-risk nature that are partially or fully deductible and that provide the investor with either partially or fully tax-exempt or at least tax-deferred income.

They are not really held in disrepute; rather, the IRS and Congress have limited their scope and effectiveness.

Q My brother-in-law used to give me financial advice. He would push all sorts of tax shelters, such as master recordings, films, cattle, and boxcar leasing. He said that much of that has been curtailed by the "at risk" provision of the Tax Reform Act of 1976. He didn't do a good job of explaining to me what the at risk provisions are. Can you explain them?

A Yes, and your brother-in-law is right. The Tax Reform Act did curtail the use of esoteric tax shelters such as the ones you describe. Simply, the at risk provision says that an investor cannot deduct a loss for more than the amount he initially invested in the tax shelter. Prior to the passage of that provision, some tax shelters were arranged so that you could deduct more in losses than you actually paid out or had, as is said, "at risk."

Q Are there any good tax shelters left? If so, what are they?

A In the Tax Reform Act of 1976, Congress emasculated most tax shelters except one, and that one is real estate. Real estate is from many points of view still the best investment you can make if you want to shelter current income from taxation.

Q Why is real estate still the best tax shelter?

A Real estate was not affected by the at risk provisions of the Tax Reform Act of 1976. You can still borrow a small amount of money for a down payment on a piece of real estate and take tax deductions for interest, depreciation, maintenance, and so on, that could easily be more than the amount you initially invested in the property.

Q My broker tells me that oil and gas drilling programs are a fairly good tax shelter. What do you think?

A Next to real estate, oil and gas exploration programs are still good tax shelters, but such programs should be evaluated by experts in the field before you decide to invest.

Even though oil and gas exploration programs are subject to the at risk provisions, investors in such programs can still take a deduction for something called intangible drilling and development costs. In some programs that deduction can amount to as much as 100 percent of the investor's investment. There are some other advantages as well, such as percentage depletion, that the investor can take advantage of. Consult an expert, though, before you invest.

Q I have been told that as a result of the tax law passed in 1981, tax shelters will be less popular than previously. Can you tell me why?

A The Economic Recovery Tax Act of 1981 reduces the top tax rate on investment income, such as dividends or interest, from 70 percent to 50 percent. Many taxpayers in the highest tax brackets considered the 70 percent tax rate to be too high so they purchased tax shelters to lessen their tax bite. With the top rate now at 50 percent some of their rationale for buying a tax shelter is mitigated. They can also avoid needless intervention on the part of the IRS in checking out the validity of the tax shelter.

Q I know that fees paid to an attorney for tax advice are deductible. How about money paid to a financial planner to look over a tax shelter deal I was considering?

A I'm afraid not. According to the IRS it is not the same as receiving tax advice from an attorney and it is not deductible.

Q I invested in a real estate limited partnership tax shelter last year. How will I be informed whether I can take a profit or loss for my taxes?

A You will receive a Schedule K-1 from the partnership which will summarize all of its gains, losses, deductions, and credits attributed to you during the year. You must transfer that information to your own 1040 because all deductions, losses, credits, and income flow through directly to you.

Q I want to sell my partnership interest in an oil and gas shelter. Will I get capital gains treatment if I sell it at a gain?

A A partnership interest is a capital asset and if you have held the interest for more than six months (the present long term capital gains period) and you have a gain, you qualify for capital gains treatment. If you held the interest less than the requisite period, any gain would become part of your ordinary income.

If you had tax shelter income during the year, Form 4797 must be included with your tax return:

Form **4797**

Department of the Treasury
Internal Revenue Service (0)

Supplemental Schedule of Gains and Losses

(Includes Gains and Losses From Sales or Exchanges of Assets Used in a Trade or Business and Involuntary Conversions)

▶ **To be filed with Form 1040, 1041, 1065, 1120, etc.—See Separate Instructions**

OMB No. 1545-0184

1983

28

Name(s) as shown on return | **Identifying number**

PART I.—Sales or Exchanges of Property Used in a Trade or Business, and Involuntary Conversions From Other Than Casualty and Theft — Property Held More Than 1 Year (Except for Certain Livestock)

Note: *Use Form 4684 to report involuntary conversions from casualty and theft.*

Caution: *If you sold property on which you claimed the investment credit, you may be liable for recapture of that credit. See Form 4255 for additional information.*

a. Description of property	b. Date acquired (mo., day, yr.)	c. Date sold (mo., day, yr.)	d. Gross sales price	e. Depreciation allowed (or allowable) since acquisition	f. Cost or other basis, plus improvements and expense of sale	g. LOSS (f minus the sum of d and e)	h. GAIN (d plus e minus f)
1							

2 Gain, if any, from Form 4684, line 27 . . . . .

3 Section 1231 gain from installment sales from Form 6252, line 21 or 29 . . . . .

4 Gain, if any, from line 29, Part III, on back of this form from other than casualty and theft. . . . . .

5 Add lines 1 through 4 in column g and column h . . . . . ( )

6 Combine columns g and h of line 5. Enter gain or (loss) here, and on the appropriate line as follows:

(a) For all except partnership returns:

(1) If line 6 is a gain, enter the gain as a long-term capital gain on Schedule D. See instruction E.

(2) If line 6 is zero or a loss, enter that amount on line 7. (S corporations, enter on Schedule K (Form 1120S), line 7.)

(b) For partnership returns: Enter each partner's share of line 6 above, on Schedule K-1 (Form 1065), line 8.

SAMPLE

PART II.—Ordinary Gains and Losses

a. Description of property	b. Date acquired (mo., day, yr.)	c. Date sold (mo., day, yr.)	d. Gross sales price	e. Depreciation allowed (or allowable) since acquisition	f. Cost or other basis, plus improvements and expense of sale	g. LOSS (f minus the sum of d and e)	h. GAIN (d plus e minus f)

7 Loss, if any, from line 6(a)(2) . . . . .

8 Gain, if any, from line 28, Part III on back of this form . . . . .

9 Net gain or (loss) from Form 4684, lines 19 and 26a . . . . .

10 Ordinary gain from installment sales from Form 6252, line 20 or 28 . . . . .

11 Recapture of section 179 deduction (see instructions) . . . . .

12 Other ordinary gains and losses (include property held 1 year or less):

13 Add lines 7 through 12 in column g and column h . . . . . ( )

14 Combine columns g and h of line 13. Enter gain or (loss) here, and on the appropriate line as follows:

(a) For all except individual returns: Enter the gain or (loss) from line 14, on the return being filed. See instruction F for specific line reference.

(b) For individual returns:

(1) If the loss on line 7 includes a loss from Form 4684, Part II, column B(ii), enter that part of the loss here and on line 21 of Schedule A (Form 1040). Identify as from "Form 4797, line 14(b)(1)". . . . . .

(2) Redetermine the gain or (loss) on line 14, excluding the loss (if any) on line 14(b)(1). Enter here and on Form 1040, line 15 . . . . .

For Paperwork Reduction Act Notice, see page 1 of separate Instructions. Form **4797** (1983)

PART III.—Gain From Disposition of Property Under Sections 1245, 1250, 1251, 1252, 1254, 1255

Skip lines 23 and 24 if you did not dispose of farm property or farmland, or if a partnership files this form.

15 Description of sections 1245, 1250, 1251, 1252, 1254, and 1255 property:	Date acquired (mo., day, yr.)	Date sold (mo., day, yr.)
(A)		
(B)		
(C)		
(D)		

Relate lines 15(A) through 15(D) to these columns ▶ ▶ ▶ ▶	Property (A)	Property (B)	Property (C)	Property (D)
16 Gross sales price				
17 Cost or other basis plus expense of sale				
18 Depreciation (or depletion) allowed (or allowable)				
19 Adjusted basis, subtract line 18 from line 17				
20 Total gain, subtract line 19 from line 16				
21 **If section 1245 property:**				
(a) Depreciation allowed (or allowable) after applicable date (see instructions)				
(b) Enter smaller of line 20 or 21(a)				
22 **If section 1250 property:** (If straight line depreciation used, enter zero on line 22(f).)				
(a) Additional depreciation after 12/31/75				
(b) Applicable percentage times the smaller of line 20 or line 22(a) (see instruction G.4)				
(c) Subtract line 22(a) from line 20. If line 20 is not more than line 22(a), skip lines 22(d) and 22(e)				
(d) Additional depreciation after 12/31/69 and before 1/1/76				
(e) Applicable percentage times the smaller of line 22(c) or 22(d) (see instruction G.4)				
(f) Add lines 22(b), and 22(e)				
23 **If section 1251 property:**				
(a) If farmland, enter soil, water, and land clearing expenses for current year and the four preceding years				
(b) If farm property other than land, subtract line 21(b) from line 20; if farmland, enter smaller of line 20 or 23(a)				
(c) Excess deductions account (see instruction G.5)				
(d) Enter smaller of line 23(b) or 23(c)				
24 **If section 1252 property:**				
(a) Soil, water, and land clearing expenses				
(b) Amount from line 23(d), if none enter zero				
(c) Subtract line 24(b) from line 24(a). If line 24(b) is more than line 24(a), enter zero				
(d) Line 24(c) times applicable percentage (see instruction G.5)				
(e) Subtract line 24(b) from line 20				
(f) Enter smaller of line 24(d) or 24(e)				
25 **If section 1254 property:**				
(a) Intangible drilling and development costs deducted after 12/31/75 (see instruction G.6)				
(b) Enter smaller of line 20 or 25(a)				
26 **If section 1255 property:**				
(a) Applicable percentage of payments excluded from income under section 126 (see instruction G.7)				
(b) Enter the smaller of line 20 or 26(a)				

SAMPLE

Summary of Part III Gains (Complete Property columns (A) through (D) through line 26(b) before going to line 27)

27 Total gains for all properties (add columns (A) through (D), line 20)	
28 Add columns (A) through (D), lines 21(b), 22(f), 23(d), 24(f), 25(b) and 26(b). Enter here and on Part II, line 8	
29 Subtract line 28 from line 27. Enter the portion from casualty and theft on Form 4684, line 21; enter the portion from other than casualty and theft on Form 4797, Part I, line 4	

PART IV.—Complete this Part Only if You Elect Out of the Installment Method And Report a Note or Other Obligation at Less Than Full Face Value

☐ Check here if you elect out of the installment method.

Enter the face amount of the note or other obligation ▶ ____________

Enter the percentage of valuation of the note or other obligation ▶ ____________

☆ U.S. GOVERNMENT PRINTING OFFICE: 1983—0-390-245 58-040-1110

24. Gift and Estate Taxes

The Economic Recovery Tax Act of 1981 made many changes but undoubtedly its greatest effects were felt in the areas of gift and estate taxation. Although the average taxpayer may not pay any gift tax during his lifetime, his or her heirs may be faced with some estate taxes after the taxpayer's death. Some of the changes of the new law are discussed in this chapter.

Because the changes introduced by the 1981 Act were so extensive, it is advisable for every taxpayer to update his or her will so that it will conform to the new realities of estate taxes. You should seek competent legal counsel to aid you in the amendment of your last will and testament.

Recent Tax Law Changes

Q I've been reading a lot about estate tax law changes made in 1981 and 1982 and I am a bit confused. What changes made in the tax bill, in your opinion, are most important for individual tax planning?

A Undoubtedly, the most far reaching changes concerning individual tax planning are those made in gift and estate taxes. Without getting too technical, since January 1, 1982 the law has allowed most property to pass from spouse to spouse through a will without any estate tax liability whatsoever. This eliminates the need for husbands and wives to own property such as the family home jointly during their lifetimes.

Beginning in 1982 estates worth $225,000 and less were not taxed at all and this figure will rise gradually through 1987 to $600,000. In 1983 the figure was $275,000 and $325,000 in 1984. This provision is intended to allow owners of small businesses to pass on their business tax-free to family members. It is of course applicable to all estates, not just those of small business owners.

Q Does all of this mean that estate tax planning is no longer necessary?

A Certainly not. Planning is still necessary to effect proper transfers of property among family members so that estate tax limits will not be reached. Also, in some cases a deceased spouse may leave an estate of over $600,000 (in 1987) and if that is a real possibility the surviving spouse's estate should be well planned. Thus estate planning will still be necessary.

Q For many years now I have been making annual gifts to my children in the form of cash. Because I didn't want to pay gift tax, I had to limit the gifts to $3,000 per child. I understand that there is a changed limit under the 1981 tax law. Is this true, and if so what is the new limit?

A The limit is now $10,000 per donee. You are entitled to give $10,000 to each of your children each year without incurring any gift tax liability. If you file a joint return and your spouse agrees, each of you can give $10,000 every year for a total of $20,000 tax-free to each of your children.

Q In light of the 1981 tax law, what kind of income tax planning should I engage in for this year?

A If you can possibly defer receiving some income until next year, do it because the overall tax rate will be lower then. On the other hand, you should take as many legitimate deductions this year as you can. For example, you could prepay next year's real estate taxes and make charitable gifts before December 31. Also, if you plan to make a large purchase next year, such as an auto or boat, consider buying it this year instead, to take advantage of this year's sales tax deduction.

Gift and Estate Taxes Generally

Q My wife and I are in a position where we want to help our grandchildren. We can afford to make some large gifts to them. I know that the law allows me a lifetime gift allowance of $175,000, over and above an annual $10,000 gift limit. Won't that limit be reached pretty quickly if I want to make substantial gifts?

A The 1981 tax act raised the limits on the lifetime allowance. For 1983, the limit is $275,000. It jumps to $325,000 in 1984, $400,000 in 1985, $500,000 in 1986, and finally $600,000 in 1987. This tax-free allowance applies to both lifetime gifts and bequests. Of course, gifts or bequests given to spouses under the free marital transfer are not affected. The $10,000 annual gift limit is also unaffected by the lifetime allowance. The lifetime allowance refers to gifts and bequests above the $10,000 annual limit.

Q I understand that the Economic Recovery Tax Act of 1981 made some very important changes with regard to gift and estate taxes. What change will have the biggest effect on estate planning?

A Undoubtedly, the provision called the "free marital transfer," which allows one spouse to leave to another all of his or her property tax-free. Besides allowing tax-free transfers by way of will, it permits spouses to give each other unlimited gifts during their lifetimes.

Q My attorney did some estate planning for me last year. Now he advises me that only part of his fee is deductible. Is that right?

A Yes. When it comes to estate planning, only those portions of the lawyer's fees than can be allocated to tax advice are deductible. Your attorney should have noted the proper allocation on his bill.

You could also deduct a portion of fees for tax advice if your attorney worked with you on investments that have tax consequences.

Q Is there an exemption from estate taxes on my Keogh Plan?

A Yes, but it is only $100,000. Any accumulation in your plan above that amount might be subject to taxation if the rest of your estate exceeds $400,000 in 1985 or $500,000 in 1986.

Q My attorney recently sent me a letter telling me that I should update my will because it was executed prior to September 12, 1981. Is he just trying to get more money out of me or does it have significance?

A It definitely does have significance. Prior to that time the maximum marital deduction amounted to one-half of your estate or $250,000, whichever was larger.

Now, however, there is an unlimited marital deduction and, if you do not update your will, you will be bound by the former deduction limits rather than the unlimited one.

25. Small Businesses

Owning a small business involves many problems, not the least of which is paying taxes that are owed as a result of the profit made in the business. Some tax difficulties can be alleviated by organizing your business properly before you start. No longer is the single-owner business (sole proprietorship) or the partnership necessarily the best way to organize your company.

Small business owners should retain accounting and tax experts who will help them to pay less taxes and organize their finances in a proper manner.

If you are starting a new business you should pay particular attention to the information on Subchapter S corporations and the advantages of organizing your business that way. You should be aware of some new rules and regulations regarding depreciation and investment credits. By properly utilizing this information you may be able to increase the profit-making potential of your business.

Q I recently bought a business from an owner who wanted to retire. As part of the deal to purchase the business, I also bought the building in which the business is housed. The seller owed some back taxes on the real estate and I had to pay them off to get clear title to the property. Can I deduct those taxes as real estate taxes paid?

A No. The taxes you paid are added to the cost of the property for tax purposes and become part of what is called your "cost basis" in the property.

Q I recently opened a bar and grill. In my state the license fees to open such an establishment are pretty hefty. Are these fees deductible business expenses?

A Yes. If you must pay license or regulatory fees to state or local governments to open or stay in business, they are deductible in the year to which the fees apply. For example, if you opened your business in 1982 and the fees apply to that year, they are deductible on your tax return for 1982. If, however, you are a cash basis taxpayer and you make those payments in 1983, you may not take the deduction until 1983.

Q Under the tax laws, how is a sole proprietorship defined?

A You are considered a sole proprietor of a business if you are self-employed *and* you are the sole owner of an unincorporated business. As such you must file Schedule C of Form 1040 to report your income (or loss) from that business. The profit or loss you report on Schedule C is then transferred over to the proper line on your Form 1040.

Q I am a practicing psychologist. I have a vast professional library that I use extensively. One of my colleagues mentioned that I can depreciate the books in the library. Is that so?

A It sure is. Books for a professional which are used in the ordinary course of business or in researching topics associated with your work are depreciable.

Q As a business consultant who is in business for myself I am called upon frequently to give speeches and make presentations before large groups. Am I permitted to deduct the costs associated with these activities such as typing and duplicating?

A Yes. This would come under the heading of promotional activities and as such these expenses are deductible if you are in business.

Q My colleagues and I want to start a business. A friend told us to consider organizing as a Subchapter S corporation. Two questions: Can you explain to me what a Subchapter S corporation is? What are the tax advantages of organizing that way?

A Subchapter S corporations (or S Corporations) are inventions of the Internal Revenue Code. Provisions of the Code allow certain owners of small business corporations to elect to be taxed as though they were partners. Corporate income is taxed directly to the shareholders of the corporation rather than through the medium of a corporation.

Electing Subchapter S treatment avoids double taxation. Corporate income is normally taxed twice: when earned by the corporation and when distributed to the shareholders in the form of dividends.

In most other respects, however, the S corporation is like any other corporation. For instance, as in any corporation, salaries paid to shareholder-employees are tax deductible. Salaries are not generally deductible by owner-partners, however.

Corporations that qualify under Subchapter S are limited in the number and type of shareholders they can have and they must maintain a certain capital structure. To set up an S corporation properly, seek competent legal aid.

Q Besides the tax advantages of starting an S corporation, are there any other reasons for using one?

A There sure are. The chief advantage of the corporate form of organization is that the stockholders enjoy limited liability. That is, their personal assets are not at risk if something goes wrong and the corporation is sued. Only the assets of the S corporation can be taken by creditors–not the houses, cars, or bank accounts of the stockholders. In a sole proprietorship, however, virtually all of the owner's assets can be taken in a lawsuit.

Another advantage is that all of your medical expenses can be taken care of by the corporation at no expense to you. Such expenses are tax deductible by the corporation.

Q I run a small business and I have two full-time employees working for me. My accountant told me that I cannot set up a Keogh plan for myself unless I establish one for my employees as well. Was she correct?

A Yes, if your employees have worked for you for three or more years. Only full-time employees (over 1000 hours a year) would be eligible. Under any other circumstances you can set up your own Keogh plan without taking employees into account. However, the rules and regulations involved here are quite complex, so you should consult with a pension expert before you forge ahead.

Q Can you explain the "investment credit"? I recently purchased some new property for my business and I want to know whether I can take the investment credit on my taxes for this year.

A Taxpayers who buy new or used depreciable property and place that property in service during the tax year may be eligible for the investment credit. Eligibility turns on whether the property is "qualifying property." Qualifying property must be depreciable as recovery property under the ACRS *or,* like other depreciable property having a useful life of at least three years, it must be tangible personal property. Exceptions are air conditioning or space heater units, buildings, or other structural components. The property must have become an integral part of the business for production of income and it must be placed in service during the year for use predominantly in the United States.

The allowable credit is 10 percent of the eligible investment but the credit is limited to the income tax shown on your return or $25,000 plus 80 percent of the tax that is more than $25,000–whichever is less.

Q I recently bought a home computer that I use exclusively for business. Can I deduct the cost of the computer as a business expense even though it is located in my home?

A If you purchased a computer that you use exclusively for business, you can recover the cost of that computer by depreciating it over a five-year period by using an accelerated method of depreciation called the Accelerated Cost Recovery System (ACRS).

In addition, if you depreciate the computer under the ACRS, you can deduct 10 percent of the cost of the computer in the year of its purchase. This is called an investment credit and it allows you an extra tax break on the purchase of property that you buy for your business. However, in this case you might want to elect to write off the first $5,000 of cost this year. If the computer cost less than $5,000 you can deduct the whole amount this year.

Q I recently went into business for myself and I am incorporated. I was advised to establish a medical reimbursement plan for myself. Why?

A Under a medical reimbursement plan your company will reimburse you for your medical expenses, and the total amount reimbursed can be taken as a deduction by your company. The money that you receive is not counted as taxable income. It is another of the advantages of having your own business. If you have employees, your medical reimbursement plan must cover them as well.

Q I am in charge of setting up the insurance program for our newly formed business. Is it true that all insurance premiums, if they relate to the business, are deductible?

A Generally, yes. Premiums paid for business insurance policies are deductible expenses. This includes fire, flood, theft, auto, workmen's compensation, and group hospital and health insurance for your employees. Disability and life insurance policies, however, are not deductible.

Q I am a physician and the cost of my malpractice insurance premium has gone sky-high. I read somewhere that I can deduct the cost of the premium. Is that so?

A It sure is. It makes no difference whether you work for yourself or someone else; the deduction can still be taken.

Q As a small business owner I frequently use an employment agency to help me fill my personnel vacancies. To make it easier on the prospective employees, I pay the agency's commission. Is that fee deductible by me?

A Yes. It is a cost of doing business, just as paying a salary would be, and as such it is deductible by the business.

Q I am contemplating starting a new business, and I have found the perfect factory space I need. If I lease the building, what kind of tax deductions can I take if I make some improvements on the building?

A Any improvements you make that maintain the property are deductible. Other costs deductible by a lessee are costs associated with canceling a lease and the value of improvements made that are given back to the lessor at the end of the lease term that were not already recovered by you.

Q One of the small business publications I subscribe to mentioned that businessmen who travel now get $14 a day in meal expenses as a deduction. Can you confirm this?

A It's true. If you are away from home on business, the IRS will allow you to take $14 a day meal money and you don't need receipts to prove you spent that much. If, however, you want to deduct higher daily meal expenses you must have documentary proof such as credit card receipts.

Q My business is presently in a cash bind and I need to borrow money. A financially astute colleague mentioned to me that I can borrow from my pension plan with the company. I thought that an individual couldn't borrow from a pension plan. What is the answer?

A You cán borrow from a pension plan other than a Keogh but with certain restrictions. If you have a corporate pension plan you are permitted to borrow up to 50% of the accrued benefits in the plan but only up to a maximum of $50,000. So, if your account has built up more than $100,000 in benefits you can only borrow up to $50,000.

By the way, the loan must be allowed under the terms of the pension plan trust agreement and the same terms must be available to all of your employees as well. Finally, you must pay back the loan within 5 years and you must charge yourself a "competitive" (undefined by the IRS) rate of interest.

Q I am considering leasing a computer for my business. I have talked to a number of leasing companies but I haven't made up my mind yet. Are there any tax implications that I should know of that may make my decision easier?

A Yes, there is one. Some leasing companies may pass the investment tax credit that is available with computers along to you. Most won't, though, so you'll have to check around. This credit is in addition to the lease payment deduction that you can take if the computer is solely used for business.

Partnerships

Q I have been a member of a partnership for several years. I am contemplating selling my partnership interest to another individual. Can I get capital gains treatment if I sell?

A Partnership interests are a capital asset and as such are subject to capital gains treatment. Be careful though—any current income that you have earned from the partnership during the taxable year results in ordinary income; so when you sell, sell your partnership interest and not any income earned from the partnership up to the date of the sale.

Q I am a member of a partnership. Some of the partnership money was invested in municipal bonds last year. I am aware that I am to report any income I get from the partnership as ordinary income and that the partnership itself is not a taxable entity. Will the income from tax-exempt bonds be passed along as tax-exempt income to me and my fellow partners?

A Definitely. You are completely correct when you say that for tax purposes partnership income is passed directly through the partnership to each individual partner. The same holds true for tax-exempt income as well.

Q I invested in a real estate partnership with some acquaintances six months ago. Much to my surprise, we made a profit of $25,000 on the sale of a piece of property soon after the partnership was formed. How much of that profit do I have to report as income?

A The controlling factor here is your partnership agreement. If that agreement was properly drawn, it should provide for a distribution of gains and losses among the various partners. If you have four other partners, for instance, and the agreement says you share profits equally, you would have to report $5000 as income, provided there were no losses to report (in which case the losses would offset the gain).

Contribution of Property

Q A friend of mine recently proposed a transaction but I don't know what the tax consequences are. He offered me an interest in his business if I would contribute a piece of real estate I own. He said we would become partners. Should I get involved?

A Contributing property to a partnership in exchange for a partnership interest is a nontaxable event, so you won't have any additional taxes to pay to enter the business this way if you want to. You will have to determine whether your piece of property is more valuable to you as it is now or as an asset of a partnership in which you share.

Partnerships in General

Q If a partnership is not a taxable entity in and of itself and is just a conduit for income to the partners, why is it necessary for the partnership to file a tax return?

A The people at the IRS are not trusting souls. They want to be able to track all your income so that you can't hide it in any kind of business venture they don't know about. The partnership return is therefore just an information return giving the IRS the data they need about the income of the partners.

Q A friend of mine is a partner in a beauty salon. She said that she was assessed a fine by the IRS for failure to file a partnership return. Can that be so? I thought the partnership return was just an information return.

A Information return or not, the penalty is $50 a month for failure to file a complete partnership return. Unless an information return is filed, the IRS has no notification about a taxpayer's earnings from a partnership. Fraud is a possibility if taxpayers don't report all their income.

Q I am involved in a profitable business partnership. My accountant told me that the IRS is now cracking down on partnerships. Is that so?

A Not exactly cracking down, but they are going to be stricter about auditing partnerships. If a question arises as to partnership income, the IRS now has the authority to resolve the question by auditing one partner in the partnership. It used to be that they had to audit all partners; in the case of large, complicated partnerships, this was a large headache for the IRS. Long delays and appeals by each partner are no longer tolerated.

Depreciation

Q My business depends largely on goodwill. Is goodwill something that can be depreciated?

A Goodwill is neither depreciable nor amortizable. If and when you sell your business, a portion of the selling price can be allocated to goodwill, but it is not depreciable. Trade secrets, stock-in-trade, and usable inventories also cannot be depreciated or amortized.

Q I bought a building for $125,000 last year as an investment. The way the transaction was structured, $25,000 was allocated to the land and $100,000 to the building. I paid only $25,000 cash for the property; the rest was given in the form of a mortgage. What is my basis in the building for purposes of depreciation?

A Your basis is $100,000. Land of course is not depreciable, but the full purchase price of the building is. It makes no difference how large or small the mortgage is on the property. When it comes to determining the basis for depreciation purposes, the entire purchase price, if reasonable, will in most cases be the proper basis. The purchase price less the cost of land might be considered unreasonable if it is, for example, a gift or an inheritance.

Q My brother is a farmer. He was told by his accountant that he could actually depreciate his herd of dairy cattle. That idea seems too far-fetched to me. Who is right?

A The accountant is right. If the dairy herd is used to produce milk that your brother sells or if the cattle are regularly sold for slaughter, then the herd would be considered a depreciable business asset. Copyrights, patents, and royalties fall into the same category; they, too, are depreciable.

Q I recently received a patent on an invention that may make me a good deal of money. Somebody mentioned to me that I can depreciate that patent. Is that possible?

A Yes, it is. Patents and copyrights are items that can be depreciated. They are depreciated over their useful life, which is the period for which the patent or copyright is granted by the government.

Q I purchased a home computer, which I use solely to work on my investment portfolio. I understand that I can depreciate the cost of that computer over a five-year period. Do I just write off 20 percent a year?

A No. For five-year depreciable items such as this you must adhere to the following schedule: 15 percent of the cost is depreciable in the first year, 22 percent in the second year, and 21 percent in each of the last three years. But if you used the computer only 50 percent of the time for your investments and 50 percent for personal entertainment, those percentages of 15, 22, and 21 would be applied to 50 percent of the cost.

For example, if your computer cost $4000 and you use it for investment purposes 50 percent of the time, you must base the 15 percent writeoff the first year on $2000 of the cost, or $300. But if you use the computer totally for your investments, it would be based on the full $4000 cost giving you a depreciation writeoff of $600 in the first year.

Q I own two houses. I live in one and rent out the other. I understand that there are new depreciation rules with regard to rental property of this kind. Can you tell me what the rules are?

A You are probably referring to the fact that you can now depreciate rental real estate over an 18-year period. Prior to the passage of the Economic Recovery Tax Act of 1981 you had to depreciate rental real estate over a longer period of time.

Q What is the new depreciation period on automobiles used for business purposes?

A A car used for business purposes can now be depreciated over a three-year period. However, only an auto purchased or put into service in 1981 or later qualifies.

Don't forget that you might want to write off the first $5,000 of the cost of the car in the year in which you bought it. If the auto cost over $5,000 the remaining amount can be depreciated over the three-year period.

Social Security Payments

Q I retired recently and my neighbor shocked me by saying that some of my social security benefits may be taxed. Is that true?

A Yes, it may be. It depends on how much income you have each year. If you are single, filing individually, and your income from all sources including tax exempt sources is over $25,000, you will be taxed on one-half of the amount of social security benefits above that figure. So, if you are single and your income totalled $38,000, including social security benefits of $8,000, you will be taxed on $4,000 worth of benefits.

For married taxpayers filing jointly the base is $32,000. One note: no matter how much you earn, not more than one-half of all social security benefits received can be subject to taxation.

Form **1065**

Department of the Treasury
Internal Revenue Service

U.S. Partnership Return of Income

▶ For Paperwork Reduction Act Notice, see Form 1065 Instructions.

For calendar year 1983, or fiscal year beginning________, 1983, and ending________, 19__

OMB No. 1545-0099

1983

A Principal business activity (see page 4 of Instructions)	Use IRS label. Other-wise, please print or type. Name	D Employer identification number
B Principal product or service (see page 16 of Instructions)	Number and street	E Date business started
C Business code number (see page 16 of Instructions)	City or town, State, and ZIP code	F Enter total assets at end of tax year $

G Check method of accounting: (1) ☐ Cash (2) ☐ Accrual (3) ☐ Other

H Check applicable boxes: (1) ☐ Final return (2) ☐ Change in address (3) ☐ Amended return

I Check if the partnership meets *all* the requirements shown on page 4 of the Instructions under **Question I** . . . . ▶☐

J Number of partners in this partnership ▶ ________

	Yes	No
K Is this partnership a limited partnership (see page 3 of Instructions)?		
L Is this partnership a partner in another partnership?		
M Are any partners in this partnership also partnerships?		

	Yes	No
N (1) Was there a distribution of property or a transfer of a partnership interest during the tax year?		
(2) If "Yes," is the partnership making an election under section 754? If "Yes," attach a statement for the election. (See page 4 of the Instructions before answering this question.)		
O At any time during the tax year, did the partnership have an interest in or a signature or other authority over a bank account, securities account, or other financial account in a foreign country (see page 4 of Instructions)?		
P Was the partnership the grantor of, or transferor to, a foreign trust which existed during the current tax year, whether or not the partnership or any partner has any beneficial interest in it? If "Yes," you may have to file Forms 3520, 3520-A, or 926. (See page 5 of Instructions.)		
Q Are there any specially allocated items of income, gain, loss, deduction, credit, etc. (see page 5 of Instructions).		

Income

Line	Description		
1a	Gross receipts or sales $ ______ 1b Minus returns and allowances $ ______ Balance ▶	1c	
2	Cost of goods sold and/or operations (Schedule A, line 7)	2	
3	Gross profit (subtract line 2 from line 1c)	3	
4	Ordinary income (loss) from other partnerships and fiduciaries	4	
5	Nonqualifying interest and nonqualifying dividends	5	
6a	Gross rents $ ______ 6b Minus rental expenses (attach schedule) $ ______		
c	Balance net rental income (loss) ▶	6c	
7	Net income (loss) from royalties (attach schedule)	7	
8	Net farm profit (loss) (attach Schedule F (Form 1040))	8	
9	Net gain (loss) (Form 4797, line 14)	9	
10	Other income (loss)	10	
11	**TOTAL** income (loss) (combine lines 3 through 10)	11	

Deductions

Line	Description				
12a	Salaries and wages (other than to partners) $ ______ 12b Minus jobs credit $ ______ Balance ▶			12c	
13	Guaranteed payments to partners (see page 6 of Instructions)			13	
14	Rent			14	
15a	Total deductible interest expense not claimed elsewhere on return (see page 6 of Instructions)	15a			
b	Minus interest expense required to be passed through to partners on Schedule K-1, lines 13, 20a(2), and 20a(3) and Schedule K, lines 13, 20a(2), and 20a(3) (if Schedule K is required).	15b			
c	Balance ▶			15c	
16	Taxes			16	
17	Bad debts (see page 7 of Instructions)			17	
18	Repairs			18	
19a	Depreciation from Form 4562 (attach Form 4562) $ ______ 19b Minus depreciation claimed on Schedule A and elsewhere on return $ ______ Balance ▶			19c	
20	Depletion (***Do not deduct oil and gas depletion.*** See page 7 of Instructions.)			20	
21a	Retirement plans, etc. (see page 7 of Instructions)			21a	
b	Employee benefit programs (see page 7 of Instructions)			21b	
22	Other deductions (attach schedule)			22	
23	**TOTAL** deductions (add amounts in column for lines 12c through 22)			23	
24	Ordinary income (loss) (subtract line 23 from line 11)			24	

SAMPLE

Please Sign Here

Under penalties of perjury, I declare that I have examined this return, including accompanying schedules and statements, and to the best of my knowledge and belief it is true, correct, and complete. Declaration of preparer (other than taxpayer) is based on all information of which preparer has any knowledge.

▶ ________ Signature of general partner ▶ ________ Date

Paid Preparer's Use Only

Preparer's signature ▶	Date	Check if self-employed ▶ ☐	Preparer's social security no.
Firm's name (or yours, if self-employed) and address ▶		E.I. No. ▶	
		ZIP code ▶	

SCHEDULE A.—Cost of Goods Sold and/or Operations (See Page 7 of Instructions.)

1	Inventory at beginning of year	1	
2	Purchases minus cost of items withdrawn for personal use	2	
3	Cost of labor	3	
4	Other costs (attach schedule)	4	
5	Total (add lines 1 through 4)	5	
6	Inventory at end of year	6	
7	Cost of goods sold (subtract line 6 from line 5). Enter here and on page 1, line 2	7	

8a Check all methods used for valuing closing inventory:

(i) ☐ Cost

(ii) ☐ Lower of cost or market as described in regulations section 1.471-4 (see page 8 of Instructions)

(iii) ☐ Writedown of "subnormal" goods as described in regulations section 1.471-2(c) (see page 8 of Instructions)

(iv) ☐ Other (specify method used and attach explanation) ▶

b Check if the LIFO inventory method was adopted this tax year for any goods (if checked, attach Form 970) ☐

c If you are engaged in manufacturing, did you value your inventory using the full absorption method (regulations section 1.471-11)? ☐ Yes ☐ No

d Was there any substantial change in determining quantities, cost, or valuations between opening and closing inventory? ☐ Yes ☐ No
If "Yes," attach explanation.

SCHEDULE B.—Distributive Share Items (See Pages 8, 10-11, and 15 of Instructions.)

	(a) Distributive share items		(b) Total amount
1	Net long-term capital gain (loss)	1	
2	Other net gain (loss) under section 1231 and specially allocated ordinary gain (loss)	2	
3a	If the partnership had income from outside the United States, enter the name of the country or U.S. possession ▶		
b	Total gross income from sources outside the United States	3b	

SCHEDULE L.—Balance Sheets
(See Pages 4 and 8 of Instructions and Question I on Page 1 Before Completing Schedules L and M.)

		Beginning of tax year		End of tax year	
	Assets	(a)	(b)	(c)	(d)
1	Cash				
2	Trade notes and accounts receivable				
a	Minus allowance for bad debts				
3	Inventories				
4	Federal and State government obligations				
5	Other current assets (attach schedule)				
6	Mortgage and real estate loans				
7	Other investments (attach schedule)				
8	Buildings and other depreciable assets				
a	Minus accumulated depreciation				
9	Depletable assets				
a	Minus accumulated depletion				
10	Land (net of any amortization)				
11	Intangible assets (amortizable only)				
a	Minus accumulated amortization				
12	Other assets (attach schedule)				
13	**TOTAL** assets				
	Liabilities and Capital				
14	Accounts payable				
15	Mortgages, notes, and bonds payable in less than 1 year				
16	Other current liabilities (attach schedule)				
17	All nonrecourse loans				
18	Mortgages, notes, and bonds payable in 1 year or more				
19	Other liabilities (attach schedule)				
20	Partners' capital accounts				
21	**TOTAL** liabilities and capital				

SCHEDULE M.—Reconciliation of Partners' Capital Accounts (See Page 8 of Instructions.)
(Show reconciliation of each partner's capital account on Schedule K-1, Item F.)

(a) Capital account at beginning of year	(b) Capital contributed during year	(c) Ordinary income (loss) from page 1, line 24	(d) Income not included in column (c), plus nontaxable income	(e) Losses not included in column (c), plus unallowable deductions	(f) Withdrawals and distributions	(g) Capital account at end of year

☆U.S. Government Printing Office: 1983—390-319 23-0916750

26. Tax Planning and Strategies

Saving on taxes should not be some thing you think of just while you are filling out your tax return but a year-round process.

This involves planning and implementing procedures and ideas when they occur and when they are most appropriate during the year.

Whenever you get involved in any kind of financial transaction you should consider the tax consequences of that course of action. Obviously, certain planning ideas and strategies will be better than others from a tax saving point of view.

In the chapter that follows some procedures, systems, and strategies that you might want to implement will be detailed.

Q I received a $10,000 bonus a week ago and I put the money in my savings account. I just realized that if I keep the money there I will have to pay taxes on the interest earned on it. Is there a way I can get out of paying taxes on the interest?

A You can pay taxes next year instead of this year if you take the $10,000 and purchase a Certificate of Deposit or Treasury Bill that matures after January 1 of next year. That way you will postpone paying the tax until your taxes for next year are due. Remember, taxes are only paid when income is received and the interest on a C.D. or T. Bill will not be paid until next year.

Q I want to take as many deductions this year as I can and fewer next year because I anticipate making a lot more this year than next. Do you have any suggestions as to what I should do?

A There are a number of things you can do. For example:

1. If you have a loan that is to be repaid next year, pay it off this year. That way you'll get the interest deduction this tax year.
2. Double up on your charitable contributions. If you give to one charity annually, send them twice as much this year and let them know that the contribution is for two years instead of one. Charitable contributions are deductible in the year made.
3. If possible, prepay real estate taxes. This is more feasible in December. If your town allows it, pay two years at once.
4. If you plan on buying a big ticket item, such as an automobile, buy it this year instead of next year. That way you can deduct the sales tax paid.

Q It looks like I will be underwithheld this year. I don't want to incur any penalties for underwithholding. Is there anything I can do?

A Yes. Simply request your employer to withhold the necessary amount before December 31. By doing that you will avoid the penalties. Your employer must, however, get the OK from you to do this. They won't do it on their own.

Q I had some stock that I lost money on last year. I want to donate that stock to a charity. Can I take a short term capital loss on the stock?

A No. Once you donate securities to a charity you lose the short term capital loss. A better strategy would be for you to sell the securities, donate the proceeds, and then you can take the capital loss which would be the difference between what you paid and what you sold the securities for.

Q It makes sense to contribute property that has appreciated in value but what about giving away property, such as stocks, that have declined in value?

A Don't give that property away. If you do you'll lose the opportunity to take a tax loss. A better strategy would be to sell the stock and contribute the proceeds to the charity. That way you get a deduction and you can take a loss as well.

Q I am an engineering consultant. I have a steady customer for whom I do work every December, and I tell him not to pay me until after January 1. I do this because I am a calendar year taxpayer and I want to report as little income as possible for the year ending December 31. Is what I am doing legal?

A Definitely. You can do whatever you want to minimize taxes for yourself so long as what you are doing is legal; and your actions are undoubtedly legal. The IRS might argue that you "constructively received" the money for your services when you rendered them in December; but if you were to go to court over the matter, the IRS would lose the case, as they have in similar ones.

27. Miscellaneous

Here are the questions and answers on such diverse topics as hobbies, the deductibility of uniforms, job search, and malpractice. Attention is also given to your particular filing status and the dependents exemption. There are a lot of little-known "goodies" hidden in this chapter, so read it with an eye to your own particular tax situation.

Filing Status

Q Our accountant told us something I don't believe. Here's our situation. Both my husband and I are self-employed, but we don't work with each other. We have always filed estimated joint returns and have filed joint final returns as well. This year our accountant advises us to file separate final returns. Can we, even though we have filed joint estimated returns during the taxable year?

A Your accountant is right. The fact that you have filed estimated joint returns has no effect on your filing status for your final return. If the calculations work to your benefit, by all means file separately.

Q Both my wife and I work. Last year my wife incurred some large unreimbursed medical expenses. I have been told that if we file separate returns instead of the joint ones we always have, we can save a lot of money in taxes this year. Is that true?

A It may be. This is one of the few situations where it may be more beneficial to file separately than jointly. The only way to know, however, is to do your taxes jointly and then separately and see which way results in the greater tax savings.

Q My husband and I always file a joint return. However, because I was out of the country on business from February 10 to April 30, I filed for an extension. Do both of us have to qualify for an extension for it to be granted?

A No. If one of the two spouses who are filing a joint return needs an extension, it will be granted for both parties. It is not necessary that your husband file separately even though he may have been able to file before April 15.

You are of course entitled to a four-month extension for filing your return. This means you can file until August 15 without incurring any legal penalties.

Q Can you explain to me what surviving spouse status is and whether I am eligible to file for that status? My husband died last year, and, although we were married for forty years, we never had any children.

A Surviving spouse status is beneficial because it allows eligible taxpayers to use joint return rates when filing. Surviving spouse status is available for the first two years after the death of a spouse when the surviving spouse maintains a home for a dependent child. Although your husband died last year, you don't qualify as a surviving spouse because you are childless. But you can file a joint return for the year of death, and take your late husband as an exemption for that year.

Dependents Exemption

Q I am unmarried and I would like to file as head of household. However, my mother, who lived with me, died in March of last year. The instructions for the tax forms say that the taxpayer to file as head of household must furnish half the cost of maintaining the household for the *entire year* for a dependent. Since my mother died in March, does this mean that I am ineligible to file as head of household?

A No. You read the instructions correctly but they are not interpreted that way. If a dependent dies or is born during the year, you are considered to have maintained that person's principal residence for the part of the year that person was alive. You can then file as head of household. In addition, you can take the full $1000 dependency exemption for your mother for the year of her death.

Q My daughter got married in June of last year. Before her wedding, she was living at home. Can I claim her as an exemption for last year even though she is now married?

A Only if your daughter and her husband file separate returns. If she files jointly with her husband, you cannot take the exemption. It should be worth their while to file separately. They should calculate their taxes both ways and if they would have to pay only, for example, $50 more by filing jointly, you should give them the $50. If you are in the 40 percent tax bracket, the extra $1000 exemption is worth $400 to you—you come out $350 ahead.

Q My twins who are in college each earned $5000 last summer working on small construction jobs. Can I still claim both of them as exemptions on my tax return?

A If you provided at least half their support last year, you can claim them as deductions. Normally if a child earns more than $1000, the parents can lose the dependency exemption, but an exception is made in the case of children who are full-time students or under the age of 19. Of course if they used the $5000 apiece to completely support themselves in college by paying room, board, tuition, and all other expenses, you probably did not provide 50 percent of their support.

Q For more than a year and a half we have had a foreign student (Korean) living in our home while she went to school. The girl is a close friend of my daughter, so she pays no rent and we provide more than half the student's support. I have been told that we cannot claim the student as a dependent. Why not?

A A stranger who lives in your household and to whose support you contribute more than half would normally qualify for dependency status, but one element is missing here. A dependent must be a citizen of the United States, Canada, Mexico, Panama, or the Canal Zone. Obviously a Korean citizen does not qualify.

Q My sister-in-law is totally disabled, and while my spouse and I were married she became completely attached to me since I took total care of her. We always claimed her as a dependent because she lived with us and had no independent means of support. Since I got my divorce I have continued to care for my sister-in-law and she continues to live with me. Can I still claim her as a dependent even though I am now divorced? She is after all the sister of my former spouse.

A You certainly can continue to claim her as your dependent. Once a dependent relationship is established it cannot be ended by divorce or death. Once an in-law, always an in-law for tax purposes.

Job Search

Q I attended a career counseling program last year and paid for the services myself because I was unemployed at the time. Can I deduct those fees?

A Yes. If the career counseling was part of a job search program then the fees are deductible as long as your job search involved the same line of work you had before you lost your job.

Q I recently met an insurance agent who was touting something called job insurance. He claimed that it would pay my salary if I lost my job and that the premium payments are deductible. Is that in fact true?

A Yes it is. You can deduct the premiums as an employee business expense and if the policy is the type that will help you to find a new job, that portion of the premium devoted to that service is also deductible as a job hunting expense.

Q Last year I lost my job as an accountant because my company relocated and I didn't want to leave this city. To get my present job, I had to pay an employment agency a fee of $200. Can I deduct that fee if I itemize my deductions?

A Yes, and you can also deduct any other job hunting expenses you might have incurred, such as the cost of having resumes printed and of taxi fares. The only limitation is that your new job must be in the same field as your former one. So if you are working as an accountant, you can take the deduction; but if you are now managing a health spa, you cannot.

Q I have just graduated from college and I am looking for my first job. I am allowed to deduct all my job-hunting expenses, right?

A No. This is one of the exceptions to the rule that job-hunting expenses are deductible. Newly graduated students looking for their first job cannot deduct job-hunting expenses; neither can individuals who are looking for a job in a line of work different from their previous employment. In other words, a former salesperson cannot deduct job-huntng expenses incurred while seeking a job as an x-ray technician or any job different from that of a salesperson.

Various and Sundry Information

Q I read that the IRS is looking at returns prepared by individuals it characterizes as "problem preparers." How do I know if the person who I have used the past few years is a "problem preparer?"

A Your local IRS office has a list of "problem preparers." If you check with them they should be able to tell you whether the preparer is on the list. By the way, you should be aware of the fact that no matter who prepares your return, you, as the taxpayer, are responsible for any mistakes, omissions, or problems encountered.

Q Even though I now have an executive position, I maintain my trade union membership. Can I claim my union dues as a deduction?

A As long as you remain a member of a union, union dues are deductible. So are dues paid to any professional organization, such as a bar association or medical society. **This only applies however if you itemize your deductions.**

Q I work for a small company, and because my job involves a limited amount of physical exertion, the company requires that I have a physical examination every year. Can I deduct the costs of these physicals?

A Yes, if the physicals are required as a condition for retaining employment. Of course your company cannot reimburse you if you expect to take the deduction. Only unreimbursed job-related outlays are deductible.

Q Two years ago I purchased a substantial savings certificate from my local bank The certificate was to mature in four years. Last year I found a house I wanted to buy, and I decided to cash the certificate in so that I would have enough money for a down payment. Can I deduct the amount I had to pay to the bank for the privilege of prematurely withdrawing the money?

A You probably didn't actually have to pay a fine to the bank; rather, the bank deducted a certain amount of unearned income from what you would have received. Whatever you forfeited, however, is deductible.

Q I discovered a profitable hobby last year. I started to keep bees. I plan to sell the honey from the bees to some local markets. I read a few books on beekeeping, and I took a course on the subject. Setting up the operation cost me a good deal of money. Can I deduct these expenses even though beekeeping is not my primary source of earnings?

A Although the answer is not a definitive one, it is probably yes. This is a tricky area that the IRS is constantly alert to. The rule is that you must enter the activity with a "reasonable expectation" of making a profit. Whether you actually make one is immaterial.

Q I am a member of the Air Force Reserve. Last year I spent about $50 to clean and launder my uniform. Can I deduct that $50?

A Yes. Members of armed forces reserve units can deduct laundry and cleaning costs, but their counterparts in active service or in military academies cannot.

Q I have recently taken a new job as an executive with a large retail store. I am entitled to a 30 percent employee's discount whenever I purchase anything in the store. Are these discounts taxable to me?

A No. Discounts of the type you describe are routine in the retail business and are not considered part of the employee's taxable income.

Q I am a physician. Last year I spent a lot of money defending myself against a malpractice suit. Although I have malpractice insurance, it did not cover all my expenses. Can I deduct the unreimbursed expenses?

A Yes. Individuals, whether physicians or not, can deduct the costs of defending their professional acts.

Q I am contemplating starting a new business, and I have found the perfect factory space I need. If I lease the building, what kind of tax deductions can I take if I make some improvements on the building?

A Any improvements you make that maintain the property are deductible. Other costs deductible by a lessee are costs associated with canceling a lease and the value of improvements made that are given back to the lessor at the end of the lease term that were not already recovered by you.

Q In another state I owned a few acres of land that I used for investment purposes. Last year that property was "condemned" by the state because the state wants to build a state office building on the site. How can I treat the condemnation award for tax purposes?

A If you realized a gain on the condemnation, that is, if the state paid you more than your basis in the property, you can make an election. You can postpone the gain by replacing it with similar property of the same use or you can be taxed on the gain in the normal way if you don't replace the property.

However, if you incurred a loss on the conversion, you cannot make the election. The loss is either deductible or not, without regard to any replacement rules.

Q At a cocktail party the other evening, I heard two acquaintances talking about tax-free exchanges. What are they?

A Normally when property is bought, sold, or exchanged, that transaction results in a gain or loss that must be recognized immediately for tax purposes. However, tax-free exchanges postpone the taxable effect of some transactions. For example, if you sell a house and buy another within eighteen months, the gain on the sale can be postponed if you meet certain criteria.

Another example would be if you exchanged one piece of income-producing real estate for another lot of "like kind." And some insurance and annuity policy exchanges can result in tax-free transactions.

Q I do a lot of free-lance work, and sometimes I don't get paid until months after I do the work. I am thinking of changing my accounting method from cash basis to accrual basis. What should I know before I make the change?

A So long as your accounting method "clearly reflects" income, you can consider using the accrual method. The accrual method allows you to show income when you have done everything you must do to earn the income, even though you may not have actually received it yet.

If you make the change, you must obtain the consent of the Commissioner of Internal Revenue, because the accounting method you adopt on your first return is supposed to be the one you keep forever.

However you must realize that most individual taxpayers use the cash basis rather than the accrual basis, precisely because of the problem of getting IRS approval to change. It might be wiser for you to stick with the cash basis.

Q My employer thinks it important for me to be a member of several professional accounting groups and pays the dues to each organization I belong to. Can the employer include the cost of the dues in my taxable compensation?

A No. The dues are not considered compensation to you and you should not be taxed on them at all.

Q I have been told that I probably should file an estimated tax return. Can you tell me what the requirements are to estimate my taxes?

A You must file a declaration of estimated tax if you expect to earn more than $500 from sources that are not subject to withholding, such as dividends, interest, or, more commonly, free-lance work. Also if you expect to earn more than $20,000 this year you must file a declaration. In both cases though you should expect your tax to be at least $300.

Q Last year I paid my taxes late. I didn't have the money when April 15 rolled around. What will happen if I pay late again this year?

A It will cost you a little less this year. The interest rate, which had been 20 percent, dropped to 16 percent on January 1, 1983, and it dropped even further, to 11 percent, on July 1.

Q I still have my tax returns of the last ten years. Do I need all of them or can I throw some of them out?

A Under most circumstances, the IRS will not or cannot ask you to produce returns that go back more than seven years. You shouldn't throw tax returns away at all if you can help it, because you can never tell when the IRS might claim that a return you filed previously was fraudulent, and in such a case there is no statute of limitations.

Q Because we no longer use it, our motor home is sitting in our driveway collecting rust. Somebody told me that I can rent it out and get a tax deduction, but I am skeptical. How can that be done?

A Don't be skeptical; it is possible. You will have to find a motor home dealer who handles rentals, and you'll have to persuade him to add your unit to his rental fleet. By doing that, you are now considered to be in the leasing business and are entitled to write off all your expenses, repairs, insurance, and depreciation—a nice tax deduction for a previously unused asset.

Q Every year when I do my taxes I try to determine whether I would be better off taking the standard deduction (now called zero-bracket amount) or itemizing my deductions. Are there any guidelines?

A If you are married filing jointly, itemize if your deductions are more than $3400; if you are married filing separately, you should itemize if deductions total either half that amount or $1700. If you are single or the head of a household, you should itemize if your deductions total more than $2300.

Q Last year I converted my unused garage into office space that I use regularly and exclusively for business purposes. The garage needed extensive repairs to be made usable. Can I deduct the costs of the repairs even though the garage is attached to my home?

A As you probably know, repairs to a personal residence are nondeductible expenses. However, repairs to a "business" property are deductible as a business expense. If you have received approval from the IRS to take a business deduction on the garage—that is, the IRS has never challenged your business deduction—you can take the repair deduction. But there is a thin line between what is a repair that is deductible and what is a renovation that would have to be depreciated.

Q My son has been offered a job as night manager in a small but growing hotel. Part of the compensation is a furnished suite in the hotel where he and his wife are expected to live. Can the hotel include the rental value of the room in his taxable income?

A No. If an employee is furnished living quarters for the convenience of the employer, then the suite is not and cannot be considered part of the employee's taxable compensation. And any meals furnished your son on the premises are also tax free.

Q Why can't I take a depreciation deduction for my house? It depreciates like any other building, doesn't it?

A It sure does. But according to the law, you can take depreciation only on real estate used either in your trade or business or to generate income. Since your residence does not fall into either of these categories, you are not allowed to take a depreciation deduction. Of course, if you have a home office in your residence you will be able to deduct some expenses with regard to that office.

Q I am confused about the matter of sales taxes. Am I restricted to using the figures set out in the sales tax tables that appear near the end of the tax booklet that I received?

A Definitely not. As a matter of fact if you made some large purchases during the year, such as a car or furniture, you should dig out those sales slips and figure your sales tax deduction from them. Large purchases during the year usually raise the sales tax deduction over the amounts set out in the table.

Q What can you tell me about the new tax return called the 1040 EZ?

A Here goes. This simplified return can be used only by a single filer who has no dependents. Furthermore, you must make less than $50,000 a year derived all from wages. No dividend income of any kind must be paid to you and you are limited to $400 or less in interest income. Finally, if you are over 65 or blind you cannot use the 1040 EZ.

Q As a free-lance artist I joined a professional organization of free-lancers. We have regular meetings and I am an active participant in the organization's activities. Am I allowed to deduct annual dues and meeting costs that I incur?

A You sure are. The only thing you have to do is identify by name the organization on your tax return. Your annual dues and meeting costs are fully deductible.

Q I use my home computer for virtually everything. Last year I bought a software program to help me prepare my taxes. Since the cost of preparing a tax return is tax deductible, does a tax software program fall into that category?

A Yes it does. Just as if you took your return to a CPA, attorney, or commercial preparation firm to be prepared and you could deduct the fee, you can also deduct the cost of the tax preparation package. You cannot, however, deduct the cost of the computer itself unless you use it for business.

Q I am retired and I receive a pension check every month. I gave permission to my former employer to withhold taxes from each check. How do I account for the money that was withheld?

A You should receive a W-2P from your former employer. That form should show the total amount withheld during the previous year. Simply transfer that amount to the line "Federal income tax withheld" in Form 1040. It becomes a credit for taxes paid just as taxes were withheld from your salary when you were working.

Q I just received my tax forms and the 1040 A that I have been filing for years looks different. Have they changed it?

A You are sharp-eyed. Two new items have been added to the 1040 A. Now taxpayers who wish to use the 1040 A can deduct their IRA contributions and then take the child care credit if they qualify.

Formerly, if a 1040 A filer wanted to take those items, it was necessary to file the 1040 long form. Now that is no longer necessary.

1983

Department of the Treasury - Internal Revenue Service

Form 1040EZ Income Tax Return for Single filers with no dependents (0)

OMB No. 1545-0675

Name & address

If you don't have a label, please print:

Please write your numbers like this. 1 2 3 4 5 6 7 8 9 0

Write your name above (first, initial, last)

Present home address (number and street)

City, town, or post office, state, and ZIP code

Social security number

Presidential Election Campaign Fund
Check box if you want $1 of your tax to go to this fund. ▶

Figure your tax

		Dollars	Cents
1 Wages, salaries, and tips. Attach your W-2 form(s).	1		
2 Interest income of $400 or less. If more than $400, you cannot use Form 1040EZ.	2		
3 Add line 1 and line 2. This is your **adjusted gross income.**	3		
4 Allowable part of your charitable contributions. Complete the worksheet on page 19. Do not write more than $25.	4		
5 Subtract line 4 from line 3.	5		
6 Amount of your personal exemption.	6	1,000	00
7 Subtract line 6 from line 5. This is your **taxable income.**	7		
8 Enter your Federal income tax withheld. This should be shown in Box 9 of your W-2 form(s).	8		
9 Use the tax table on pages 29-34 to find the **tax** on your taxable income on line 7. Write the amount of tax.	9		

Attach Copy B of Form(s) W-2 here

SAMPLE

Refund or amount you owe

Attach tax payment here

10 If line 8 is larger than line 9, subtract line 9 from line 8. Enter the **amount of your refund.**	10		
11 If line 9 is larger than line 8, subtract line 8 from line 9. Enter the **amount you owe.** Attach check or money order for the full amount, payable to "Internal Revenue Service."	11		

Sign your return

I have read this return. Under penalties of perjury, I declare that to the best of my knowledge and belief, the return is true, correct, and complete.

Your signature Date

X

For IRS Use Only—Please do not write in boxes below.

For Privacy Act and Paperwork Reduction Act Notice, see page 38.

You can use this form if:

- Your filing status is single.
- You do not claim exemptions for being 65 or over, OR for being blind.
- You do not claim any dependents.
- Your taxable income is less than $50,000.
- You had **only** wages, salaries, and tips, and you had interest income (other than All-Savers interest) of $400 or less.

If you can't use this form, you must use Form 1040A or 1040 instead. See pages 4 through 6. If you are uncertain about your filing status, dependents, or exemptions, read the step-by-step instructions for Form 1040A that begin on page 6.

Completing your return

It will make it easier for us to process your return if you do the following:

1. Keep your numbers inside the boxes.
2. Try to make your numbers look like these 1 2 3 4 5 6 7 8 9 0
3. Do not use dollar signs.

Name and address

Use the mailing label we sent you. After you complete your return, carefully place the label in the name and address area. Correct any errors right on the label. If you don't have a label, print the information on the name and address lines.

Presidential election campaign fund

Congress set up this fund to help pay for Presidential election campaigns. You may have one of your tax dollars go to this fund by checking the box.

Figure your tax

Line 1. Write on line 1 the total amount you received in wages, salaries, and tips. This should be shown on your 1983 wage statement, **Form W-2**, (Box 10). If you don't receive your W-2 form by February 15, contact your local IRS office. Attach the first copy or Copy B of your W-2 form(s) to your return.

Line 2. Write on line 2 the total interest income you received from all sources, such as banks, savings and loans, and credit unions. You should receive an interest statement (usually **Form 1099-INT**) from each institution that paid you interest.

You cannot use Form 1040EZ if your total interest income is over $400, or you received interest income from an All-Savers Certificate.

Line 4. You can deduct 25% of what you gave to qualified charitable organizations in 1983. But if you gave $100 or more, you can't deduct more than $25. Complete the worksheet on page 19 to figure your deduction, and write the amount on line 4.

Line 6. Every taxpayer is entitled to one $1,000 personal exemption. If you are also entitled to additional exemptions for being 65 or over, for blindness, for your spouse, or for your dependent children or other dependents, you cannot use this form.

Line 8. Write the amount of Federal income tax withheld.This should be shown on your 1983 W-2 form(s) (Box 9). If you had two or more employers and had total wages of over $35,700, see page 23. If you want IRS to figure your tax for you, complete lines 1 through 8, sign, and date your return. If you want to figure your own tax, continue with these instructions.

Line 9. Use the amount on line 7 to find your tax in the tax table on pages 29-34. Be sure to use the column in the tax table for **single** taxpayers. Write the amount of tax on line 9. If your tax from the tax table is zero, write 0.

Refund or amount you owe—Compare line 8 with line 9.

Line 10. If line 8 is larger than line 9, you are entitled to a refund. Subtract line 9 from line 8, and write the result on line 10.

Line 11. If line 9 is larger than line 8, you owe more tax. Subtract line 8 from line 9, and write the result on line 11. Attach your check or money order for the full amount. Write your social security number and "1983 Form 1040EZ" on your payment.

Sign your return

You must sign and date your return. If you pay someone to prepare your return, that person must also sign it below the space for your signature and supply the other information required by IRS. See page 25.

Mailing your return

File your return by **April 16, 1984**. Mail it to us in the addressed envelope that came with the instruction booklet. If you don't have an addressed envelope, see page 28 for the address.

☆ U.S. GOVERNMENT PRINTING OFFICE: 1984-423-334 E.I. 43-0787287

Appendix. Audit Technique Handbook for Internal Revenue Agents—Selected Pages

Planning The Examination

210 *(4-23-81)* 4231
Introduction

(1) This chapter discusses preliminary planning of the examination, scope of the examination and workpaper preparation.

(2) The scope of Tax Auditor non-business returns is normally set by Classification unless the return is subject to pre-contact analysis. The auditor will not routinely extend the examination to other issues without the consent of his/her manager. Therefore, preliminary planning of these returns is customarily restricted.

(3) However, on pre-contact analysis cases for Tax Auditors and for Revenue Agent returns, preliminary planning is essential. This planning does not pre-empt an employee from expanding or contracting the scope of the audit based on his/her judgment after the examination has begun.

(4) Workpapers should conform to the standards set forth in Chapter 300 for their preparation. Pro-forma audit aids are included for use by Office Auditors in the examination of the most often examined issues.

220 *(4-23-81)* 4231
Approach to the Assignment

221 *(4-23-81)* 4231
Introduction

Because of variations in operational methods employed in various offices, all or part of this discussion may be inappropriate to some examiners. However, to the extent possible, this section should be given close scrutiny and application.

222 *(4-23-81)* 4231
Prior Examination Record

(1) Form 5546, Examination Return Charge-Out, may indicate the results of a prior examination and if it was a no-change, the issue(s) involved.

(2) In other instances, you may discover during the examination, that a prior audit occurred which may affect the current examination. You should give consideration to the possible existence of recurring issues and ensure that the taxpayer has had an opportunity to take the necessary corrective action determined in the prior examination.

223 *(4-23-81)* 4231
Time

In planning your examination, care must be exercised to spend no more time than is necessary to decide upon a proper course of action.

224 *(4-23-81)* 4231
Scrutiny of Associated Documents

(1) Documents which may relate to the income tax liability may be attached to the income tax return or be included in the case file when the tax return is assigned to the examiner.

(2) Examples of these documents are:

(a) Information Returns Program (IRP) Reports.

1 An IRP transcript or IRP listing may be associated with the tax return. The document may contain information regarding wages, pensions, dividends, interest, gambling winnings, and other items that should be reported on the income tax return.

2 The examiner should determine whether or not the items shown on the IRP transcript or listing are properly reflected on the income tax return. Where it is not possible to make a determination based on information contained in the tax return alone, as when only total dividends or interest are shown, the examiner should secure the information from the taxpayer;

(b) Examination Information Reports (Form 5346);

(c) Notice of Examination of Fiduciary, Partnership, or Small Business Corporation Return, Form 918-A;

(d) Claim, Form 843;

(e) Tentative Carryback, Form 1045;

(f) Notice of Determination of Self-Employment Income, Form SSA-1000;

(g) Currency Transaction Reports, Form 4789; and,

(h) Informant Communications.

(3) All information contained in any attachment to the income tax return should be thoroughly and completely scrutinized to ascertain whether or not all of the information contained in the document is adequately reflected on the tax return.

225 *(4-23-81)* 4231
Research of Unfamiliar Items

(1) On pre-contact Tax Auditor cases and Revenue Agent cases, when an examiner has completed his/her scrutiny of the return, prior examination reports, related documents, informers' letters, and other attachments, problems will often arise because of unfamiliarity with the subject.

(2) A brief period of time spent in research of these problems will in many cases avoid considerable wasted effort later. For example, if a return contains income from mineral royalties and certain deductions therefrom which are not clear to the examiner, a research into the general peculiarities of reporting such income and deductions may resolve the examiner's questions without the necessity of any further verification.

(3) The income tax law is far too complex for each agent to immediately perceive its ramifications and provisions in all returns assigned him/her from a scrutiny of the return. An examiner cannot perform adequately unless he/she is familiar with the issues on the return which scrutiny raises. In addition to these issues, additional ones will be raised during the examination which will require similar research. The tax law, regulations, Treasury decisions, rulings, court cases, the published services, and a myriad of other sources of information are the tools of the trade. No one can work without tools, and no one can improvise substitutes for such tools.

(4) The work of an income tax examiner is professional and should be viewed in that light. Nothing detracts from professional performance as much as lack of preparation for the immediate job at hand.

226 *(4-23-81)* 4231
Scope of the Examination

(1) For Tax Auditors, the scope of the examination on non-business returns not requiring pre-contact analysis will be set by Classification. However, the Tax Auditor may expand the examination when significant issues arise as a result of information secured during the examination. Also, instances may arise where, in the judgment of the Auditor a significant item was not identified during classification. In the latter instance approval of the group manager is necessary, when possible, before the scope may be expanded.

(2) For Revenue Agent returns and for Tax Auditor returns requiring pre-contact analysis, the scope of the examination will ordinarily be set by the examiner. Judgment should be exercised in determining what issues should be pursued. However, gross receipts must be probed in most of these examinations. For minimum tests, see IRM 4241.5 and IRM 4253.2. See also, Chapter 300 of this handbook.

(3) In a case involving payments to a widow, examination of the returns of the corporation and the widow should be coordinated and, if possible, conducted concurrently.

(4) Each case should be factually developed to include:

(a) the relationship of the widow, or deceased, to stockholders or directors of the corporation;

(b) the extent to which the widow, the deceased, or relatives of either hold, or held stock in the corporation;

(c) a determination, through interviews with responsible parties, as to why the payment was made;

(d) information as to whether consideration was given to the needs of the widow; and

(e) a determination as to whether the payor-corporation has a plan, practice or policy of making payments.

227 *(4-23-81)* 4231
Workpapers—Definition and Purpose

(1) An examiner's workpapers are the connecting link between the tax return and the examiner's report. Workpapers include all the evidence gathered by the examiner to show the work performed, methods and procedures followed and conclusions reached. They should also include all notes made before, during and after the examination.

(2) Perhaps the most important quality of workpapers is that they are the best evidence of the scope of the examination and the diligence with which it was completed. These papers further constitute the background for the determination of the tax liability.

(3) Workpapers prepared by an examiner may be utilized in the preparation of the report and its review as reference in cases where the determination is to be litigated, and as a source of more detailed information which may be requested later in writing.

(4) Each of the workpapers should be headed up clearly, showing the name of the taxpayer, tax year examined, date workpapers prepared, the name or initials of the examiner, and the issues or items being examined. The pages should be indexed, numbered, and securely stapled together.

(5) See Chapter 300 for discussion of the standards for workpaper preparation.

228 *(4–23–81)* 4231

Pro-Forma Audit Aids—Office Examination

(1) Pro forma audit aids have been developed for use by tax auditors on the following frequently examined items:

(a) Income probe
(b) medical
(c) taxes
(d) interest
(e) contributions
(f) casualty loss
(g) miscellaneous
(h) moving expense

(2) The use of these forms is mandatory on all Office Examination cases where one or more of these items are examined. The aids were designed to assist the Tax Auditor and to provide some degree of uniformity in examination techniques and workpaper documentation.

(3) Examples of pro-forma aids are in Exhibit 200–1. The reminders listed on the pro-forma are to ensure that the Tax Auditor, at a minimum, considers these features. They are not designed to include all possible audit procedures. The examiner must exercise judgment as to what additional audit techniques are necessary based on the circumstances in each case.

229 *(4–23–81)* 4231

Comparison of Audits by Public Accountants with Audits by Internal Revenue Agents

(1) Application of this section is limited to Revenue Agents due to the scope of Tax Auditor Examinations.

(2) The objective of the ordinary examination of financial statements by an independent auditor is the expression of an opinion on the fairness with which they present financial position and results of operations. The auditor's report is the medium through which he/she expresses his/her opinion or, if circumstances require, disclaims an opinion. In either case, he/she states whether his/her examination has been made in accordance with generally accepted auditing standards. These standards require him/her to state whether, in his/her opinion, the financial statements are presented in conformity with generally accepted principles of accounting and whether such principles have been consistently applied in the preparation of the financial statements of the current period in relation to those of the preceding period.

(3) In an audit, the independent accountant is responsible to many persons or organizations, such as the client, creditors, bank, investors, courts, and Government agencies. In accepting an engagement, an accountant often plans the scope of an audit according to the terms of the arrangements made with the client. The limitations of the audit may require qualifying statements in his/her report. The overall work performed, of course, is governed by established accounting principles and professional conduct standards.

(4) By comparison, the end product of an income tax examination is the determination of the correct taxable income, as defined by the Internal Revenue Code, and the determination of the correct income tax liability of the person or entity under examination. In making an examination, the agent has a twofold responsibility: To the taxpayer and to the Government of the United States. The responsibility to both parties is the same in that the agent is required to make a proper determination of the tax liability.

(5) In making the audit the agent is expected to pursue his/her examination to a point where he/she can, with reasonable certainty, conclude that all items necessary for a substantially proper determination of the tax liability have been considered. He/she is expected to extend his/her audit to include all unusual and questionable items. In some cases, it will be necessary to conduct an extensive audit to properly determine the tax liability; in other cases, the examination can be completed after inquiry into only one or two items on the return.

(6) A tax examination frequently will be extended beyond the scope originally intended because of situations not apparent at the outset. The amount of verification work to be done in any single tax examination is a matter of individual judgment for which no rigid rule can be established.

(7) There are differences between net income for general accounting purposes and taxable income for Federal income tax purposes. However, such differences become insignificant when compared with the vast number of transactions which are treated identically for both purposes. It should not be forgotten that the determination of taxable income and the resultant tax liability is contingent upon the net income determined for general accounting purposes.

230 *(4–23–81)* 4231

Initial Interview

(1) The initial interview is the most important part of the examination process. The first few minutes should be spent making the taxpayer comfortable and explaining the examination process and appeal rights. This would also be a good time to ask the taxpayer if he/she has any questions.

(2) Sufficient information should be developed to reach informed judgments as to:

(a) financial history and standard of living;

(b) the nature of employment to determine relationship with other entities and the existence of expense allowances, etc.; this could include the exchange of merchandise or services (bartering);

(c) any money or property received which was determined to be tax exempt and/or nontaxable income; and

(d) the potential for moonlighting income.

(3) If warranted by issues on the return or responses to previous questions, the following information should be developed:

(a) the real and personal property owned, including bank accounts, stocks and bonds, real estate, automobiles, etc., in this country and abroad.

(b) any purchases, sales, transfers, contributions or exchanges of personal assets during the period; and

(c) the correctness of exemptions and dependents claimed;

(4) Remember, the taxpayer is being examined and not just the return. Therefore, develop all information to the fullest extent possible. If the appearance of the return and response to initial questions lead the examiner to believe that indirect methods to determine income may be necessary, the factors in Chapter 500 should also be covered at this time.

(Next page is 4231–17)

Exhibit 200-1

Income Probe ◇

T/P	**ROSE**
YEAR(S)	**1979**
AUDITOR	**OAK**
DATE	**12/24/80**
PAGE	**A-1**

Minimum Tests

Non-business returns

Question taxpayer regarding possible sources of income not reported; i.e.,

1) State income tax refunds,
2) Moonlighting income, and/or
3) Bartering, etc.

Business returns

1) Evaluate internal control
2) Question taxpayer in re:
   a) sources of income,
   b) standard of living,
   c) purchase of assets,
   d) balance of cash-on-hand and in bank, and
   e) payments on loans and receipt of borrowed funds.

If there are indications of unreported income or that taxpayers records are inadequate or do not reflect all transactions, consider the use of an indirect method as outlined in Chapter 800 of IRM 4231.

Verified	*Per Return*	*Adjustment*	*Source Document*
$5500	$5000	$500	STATE INCOME REFUND AND MOONLIGHTING INCOME

Exhibit 200-1 Cont. (1)

Medical, IRC 213 ◇

T/P	**ROSE**
YEAR(S)	**1979**
AUDITOR	**OAK**
DATE	**12/24/80**
PAGE	**B-1**

Reminders
See IRM 4231

(1) Verify amounts claimed and determine that the deduction has been taken in proper year.
(2) Ascertain whether any insurance reimbursement has been made or is expected.
(3) Segregate medicines so that the proper limitations can be applied.
(4) Determine that the percentage limitation, the maximum amount limitation and the dependency qualification have been correctly applied.
(5) Determine that the expense was incurred primarily for the diagnosis, cure, mitigation, treatment or prevention of disease, or for the purpose of affecting any structure of the body.

Medical Expenses Paid To	*Verified*	*Per Return*	*Adjustment*	*Source Document*
DRXY	$500	$1000	$500	MEDICARE PAYMENTS CHECKS/RECEIPTS

Exhibit 200-1 Cont. (2)

Taxes, IRC 164

◇

T/P	ROSE
YEAR(S)	1979
AUDITOR	OAK
DATE	12/24/80
PAGE	B-2

Reminders
See IRM 4231

(1) Verify amounts claimed and determine that the deduction has been taken in proper year.
(2) Determine whether the tax is of the type deductible in accordance with the rules and regulations.
(3) Ascertain that no foreign income taxes have been claimed as a deduction where election has been made to claim the foreign tax credit.
(4) Verify that the taxpayer has not claimed duplicate deductions for taxes, i.e., Itemized Deductions and Rental Expense.
(5) Verify that any proration of current real estate taxes in the year of purchase or sale is correct.

Taxes Paid To	*Verified*	*Per Return*	*Adjustment*	*Source Document*
YYA MORTGAGE CO.	$600	$2000	$1400	COMPUTER PRINTOUT AND CHECKS BANK RECORDS

Exhibit 200-1 Cont. (3)

Interest Expense, IRC 163

◇

T/P	ROSE
YEAR(S)	1979
AUDITOR	OAK
DATE	12/24/80
PAGE	B-3

Reminders
See IRM 4231

(1) Verify amounts claimed and determine that the deduction has been taken in proper year.
(2) Ascertain whether interest payments are made on a valid, existing debt owed by the taxpayer.
(3) Interest paid as a guarantor does not constitute an interest deduction.
(4) Verify that loans from related individuals are valid and that they are not gifts.
(5) Check for double deduction, i.e., itemized deduction and rental expense.
(6) Look at the instruments of debt for verification, i.e., mortgage statements, loan contracts, cancelled checks, credit card statements.
(7) Brokerage accounts, interest expense on margin accounts.
(8) Amounts paid by purchaser in connection with the occupancy of home prior to the date of enforceable liability on the mortgage may be rent payments.

Interest Paid To	*Verified*	*Per Return*	*Adjustment*	*Source Document*
Brother Bill	$5,000	$10,000	$5,000	NOTE OF INDEBTNESS

Exhibit 200-1 Cont. (4)

Contributions, IRC 170 ◇

T/P	ROSE
YEAR(S)	1979
AUDITOR	OAK
DATE	12/24/80
PAGE	B-4

Reminders
See IRM 4231

(1) Verify amounts claimed and determine that the deduction is claimed in the proper year.
(2) Determine whether the payments were made to qualified organizations.
(3) Determine that percent limitation is correctly computed, has not been exceeded, and that any contribution carryover is correct.
(4) Determine if contributions claimed are nondeductible personal expenses and ascertain if donor received benefits or consideration in return for contributions.
(5) In a case where property is contributed ascertain: type of property, cost and fair market value at time of gift, and whether donor retains any control over property.
(6) Some non-cash contributions have the potential of being a tax shelter scheme, for example:
  (a) Gemstones,
  (b) Books (RR 80-329),
  (c) Art work,
  (d) etc.

If a tax shelter scheme is uncovered, the examiner should see group manager.

Contributions Cash & Noncash	*Verified*	*Per Return*	*Adjustment*	*Source Document*
Cash	$1,500	$3,500	$1,000	CANCELLED CHECKS

Exhibit 200-1 Cont. (5)

Casualty Loss IRC 165 ◇

T/P	ROSE
YEAR(S)	1979
AUDITOR	OAK
DATE	12/24/80
PAGE	B-5

Reminders
See IRM 4231

(1) Ascertain that a loss has actually occurred.
(2) Determine that the taxpayer is the owner.
(3) Be alert to the possibility that cash stolen may not have been included income.
(4) If personal residence is involved in the loss deduction, ensure that the basis of property has been reduced for all gains previously unrecognized.
(5) Be alert to the possibility that the taxpayer may be engaged in arson-for-profit activities.
(6) Determine that the amount claimed is equal to the difference in value before and after the loss.
(7) Check for insurance procedures.
(8) Remember $100 limitation.

Computation of Casualty Loss

(1)	FMV of Property Immediately Before Casualty	9,600
(2)	Less: FMV of Property Immediately After Casualty	-0-
(3)	FMV of Property Actually Destroyed or Stolen	9,600
(4)	Adjusted Basis of Property (cost)	12,000
(5)	Loss Taken into Account for Purposes of IRC 165; Lesser amount of property actually destroyed line (3) or adjusted basis of property (cost) line (4)	
(6)	Less: Insurance Received or Expected to be Received	-0-
(7)	Allowable Loss	9,600
(8)	Less: Limitation per Casualty	(100.00)
(9)	Allowable Deduction	9,500
(10)	Deduction per Return	10,500
(11)	Adjustment	1,000

Exhibit 200-1 Cont. (6)

Miscellaneous Expense ◊

T/P	**ROSE**
YEAR(S)	**1979**
AUDITOR	**OAK**
DATE	**12/24/80**
PAGE	**B-6**

Reminders
See IRM 4231

(1) Verify amounts claimed and determine that the deduction is claimed in the proper year.
(2) Ascertain whether any reimbursement has been received.
(3) If the miscellaneous expense claimed is an education expense:
   (a) Determine if the expenses were primarily incurred for the purpose of maintaining or improving skills or meeting express requirements for retention of status. If so, does it qualify:
      (1) For a new trade or business
      (2) Meet minimal education requirements
   (b) If the educational expenses involves overseas travel, the tour folio, registration receipt, and transcript of studies from the overseas educational institution should be reviewed.

Expenses Paid	*Verified*	*Per Return*	*Adjustment*	*Source Document*
Sea Cruise Educational Lines	$1,150	$2,150	$1,000	Checks Tour Folio,

Exhibit 200-1 Cont. (7)

Moving Expense IRC 217 ◊

T/P	**ROSE**
YEAR(S)	**1979**
AUDITOR	**OAK**
DATE	**12/24/80**
PAGE	**B-7**

Reminders
See IRM 4231

(1) Where a moving expense deduction is claimed and Form 3903 (Moving Expense Adjustment) is not attached to the return, you should secure an analysis of the expense, both reimbursed and nonreimbursed.
(2) Verify expenses from original documents. Examples include Bills of Lading, lodging receipts, escrow statements.
(3) Verify that items are properly classified on Form 3903 for limitation purposes.
(4) Verify that the new job is at least 35 miles farther from the taxpayers former home than the old job location was.
(5) Verify that the employee has worked full time for at least 39 weeks during the 12 months right after the move.
(6) Verify that the move is closely related to the start of work.

Expense	*Verified*	*Per Return*	*Adjustment*	*Source Document*
Trans-H/H Goods	$500	$1,500	$1,000	Bill of Lading
Exp. Incurred Moving to New Location	1,500	2,500	1,000	Checks Receipts
Pre-Move Househunting Exp.	2,000	2,000	—	
Temporary Living Expenses	1,000	3,000	2,000	Hotel Receipts
Residence Sale/Lease Exp.	250	2,250	2,000	Bill of Sale
Residence Purchase/Lease Exp.	—	—	—	
Totals	$5,250	$11,250	$6,000	

(Next page is 4231-29)

(2) When an individual return is assigned and it has as an associated document, Form 918A, the agent is placed on notice that another district is examining the partnership or fiduciary return, on which return this taxpayer is shown as a beneficiary or partner. All issues, other than the partnership, fiduciary, or small business corporation issues, should be completed for the members' returns. If the examination of all other issues is completed prior to the completion of the partnership, fiduciary, or small business corporation examination, an agreement should be obtained for the resolved items using forms prescribed by IRM 428(10), Report Writing Guide for Income Tax Examiners. A statement will be inserted in the "Other Information" section of Form 4549, Income Tax Examination Changes, stating that the items contained in the Form 4549 do not include adjustments attributable to the examination of the related entity and that adjustments, if any, as a result of the examination of the related entity, will be proposed upon completion of the related entity examination. For unagreed cases, reports will be prepared as prescribed by IRM 428(10), Report Writing Guide for Income Tax Examiners. No appeals action will be taken on any items until the resolution of the partnership items.

(3) After the assessment of the agreed portion, if any, the return will be forwarded to the Returns Program Manager to be placed in the suspense file pending receipt of Form 918–A, Part 2. Upon receipt of Form 918–A, Part 2, the member's return will be forwarded by the Returns Program Manager to the appropriate group for closing, if necessary.

(4) If a return is assigned indicating income from a partnership or fiduciary located in another district, and Form 918A is not received, it may be assumed, unless notified otherwise, that the fiduciary or partnership has not been selected for examination. The examination may be recommended in such cases if it appears appropriate during the examination of the beneficiary or partner. Agents should prepare and forward to the Returns Program Manager Form 5346, Examination Information Report, to recommend such examination.

234.4 *(8–30–76)* 4231
Informers' Letters

(1) Returns assigned for examination in some cases have associated letters received from informers. These letters in general make allegations concerning impropriety of the returns in question.

(2) Some allegations are anonymous, while others are signed by the writer. The value of such letters, insofar as they provide leads to potential deficiencies, is difficult to determine prior to examination. However, comparison should always be made, where possible, of the contents of the letter with the contents of the return to ascertain, if possible, the treatment given the item by the taxpayer.

234.5 *(8–30–76)* 4231
Research of Unfamiliar Items

(1) When an agent has completed his/her scrutiny of the return, prior examination reports, related documents, informers' letters, and other attachments, problems will often arise because of unfamiliarity with the subject.

(2) A brief period of time spent in research of these problems will in many cases avoid considerable wasted effort later. For example, if a return contains income from mineral royalties and certain deductions therefrom which are not clear to the agent, a research into the general peculiarities of reporting such income and deductions may resolve the agent's questions without the necessity of any further verification.

(3) The income tax law is far too complex for each agent to immediately perceive its ramifications and provisions in all returns assigned him/her from a scrutiny of the return. An examiner cannot perform adequately unless he/she is familiar with the issues on the return which scrutiny raises. In addition to these issues, additional ones will be raised during the examination which will require similar research. The tax law, regulations, Treasury decisions, rulings, court cases, the published services, and a myriad of other sources of information are the tools of the trade. No one can work without tools, and no one can improvise substitutes for such tools.

(4) The work of an income tax examiner is professional and should be viewed in that light. Nothing detracts from professional performance as much as lack of preparation for the immediate job at hand.

(5) Another example concerning appropriate research before contacting a taxpayer may be found in a return claiming the benefits of a particular tax convention with a foreign country. Few agents have occasion to familiarize themselves thoroughly with these treaties. Only re-

search and preparation can equip an agent to properly weigh such problems indicated on the return.

234.6 *(8–30–76)* 4231
Survey vs. Examination

(1) At this point in the application of audit techniques the examiner is faced with his/her first decision. Shall he/she contact the taxpayer and examine his/her records or is the return unworthy of examination? (See IRM 4215.)

(2) In making this decision the examiner should consider the results of his/her scrutiny of the return and associated documents, and of his/her research on the unfamiliar items. His/her decision should be predicated on retaining in his/her inventory those cases which show the greatest enforcement potential in terms of inducing and maintaining voluntary compliance by the taxpayer. In the event of a survey the agent must follow the procedures in IRM 4281.2.

Communicating With Taxpayer

410 *(8-30-76)* 4231
Making the Appointment

411 *(8-30-76)* 4231
Introduction

The methods for making an appointment to examine a tax return will vary with circumstances, among districts or even within the same district. The suggested methods that follow are divided between metropolitan areas and large geographical areas.

412 *(4-27-77)* 4231
Metropolitan Areas—Field Examinations

(1) In arranging for a convenient time and place to begin an examination it is usually advisable to contact the taxpayer by telephone. However, under no circumstances should the telephone be used to verify items appearing on a tax return. Inspection of records or other data cannot be made by telephone. It is emphasized that the initial contact is to be made with the taxpayer, not his/her representative. If a corporation is involved, contact is to be made with an executive who was directly connected with the preparation of the return, such as the treasurer. In the case of partnerships, the contact is to be made with a partner. Often upon such initial contact, the examiner will be referred to an accountant or an attorney for finalizing the appointment. This referral is generally acceptable as explained in (2) below.

(2) If a taxpayer, or his/her representative who has a power of attorne, on file with the Service, and who is not disqualified from practicing before the Service, requests, orally or in writing, that contacts with the taxpayer be made through the representative, such request will be complied with provided that compliance therewith does not unreasonably delay or hinder the examination, or the factual development during the examination process. However, if repeated attempts to comply with such a request result in unreasonable delays or hindrances to the examination, or the factual development during the examination process, the examiner will discuss the situation with his/her Group Manager and request permission to contact the taxpayer direct. Where the manager gives approval to deviate from the request of the taxpayer or representative, the examiner must be prepared to include in the case file sufficient facts to show how the examination was being delayed or hindered by complying with the request of the taxpayer or representative.

(3) When contacting the taxpayer's representative, it is usually advisable to telephone for an appointment before visiting his/her office. This procedure may be waived, with the examiner's Group Manager approval.

(4) If an examiner is requested to make an examination at any place other than the taxpayer's place of business, he/she should attempt to dissuade the taxpayer from such practice. It is extremely unlikely that all records which the examiner will want during the examination would be at such other place. Even though all ledgers and journals may be there, the underlying supporting data are usually elsewhere.

(5) In making an appointment the agent should not insist on a specific date, but should attempt to make appointments at the taxpayer's convenience.

(6) Cases arise when telephone contact is impractical or impossible. Form L-57, Appointment Letter, (which must be manually signed) is prescribed for use in such cases in arranging appointments with taxpayers. Examiners should familiarize themselves with the procedures for using such letters and should assure that they are prepared neatly and properly addressed, giving the taxpayer clear details of the information desired.

(7) Once the appointment is made, the agent is duty bound to keep it to the best of his/her ability. No trivial excuse for postponement is to be used. The best method for adhering to dates made is to record appointments in a pocket diary. In addition, agents should not expect taxpayers to be ready to commence an examination on 1 or 2 days' notice. Therefore to best utilize his/her time, each agent should schedule appointments for a considerable time in advance. Consideration should be given to allow intermittent blank dates to be used for such purposes as writing final reports, research of the law, and follow up of previous examinations when such return visits are unavoidable.

(8) Each examiner shares the responsibility with his/her supervisor to ensure that an adequate inventory of assigned cases is on hand at all times. With a reasonable inventory, the agent will experience little difficulty in making appointments for tax examinations.

(9) Cases once begun should not be allowed to become inactive due to the agent's choice. In a reasonable manner taxpayers and representatives should be requested to be prompt in securing additional information where needed. Agents should not risk justifiable criticism for laxity on their part in concluding an examination.

413 *(4-27-77)* 4231
Large Geographical Areas—Field Examinations

(1) Agents on duty at offices which require considerable travel to meet taxpayers are confronted with a more difficult problem in making appointments. The telephone method is of lesser value and, in addition, costly.

(2) Considerable advance planning is necessary in these situations to ensure optimum use of time and travel funds. As cases are assigned, they should be grouped by general area of location. Appointments should then be made by mail, sufficiently in advance so that the taxpayer's reaction to the appointment date may be received and necessary changes made as required. In addition, a reserve supply of cases should be on hand to fill in during idle time which will occur due to unforeseen circumstances.

(3) In the event there is such nonscheduled idle time available and a case carried in reserve is to be worked, to the extent possible the taxpayer should be notified immediately by local phone. Arrival at a taxpayer's place of business without advance notice is not desirable.

(4) When contacting the taxpayer's representative, it is usually advisable to telephone for an appointment before visiting his/her office. This procedure may be waived, with the examiner's Group Manager approval.

(5) In accordance with local instructions, the Group Manager should be advised of variations in the planned itinerary as they occur.

420 *(8-30-76)* 4231
Records Needed

(1) There are several principles adaptable to all appointment making by the examiner. In actually making an appointment, the agent should ensure that the taxpayer or his/her representative is fully aware of what is required for the examination. The term "books and records" has various meanings to people. No one should preselect, for the examiner, what he/she "thought" would be needed. The agent should explain to the taxpayer what he/she wants at the time the appointment is made. This point is especially important when a field examination must be held away from the taxpayer's place of business, or held in an office interview.

(2) While record requirements cannot be prejudged, certain requirements are obvious from the return itself. A partnership examination requires the partnership agreement, a fiduciary examination requires the will or trust instrument, and a corporation examination requires the minute book. Scrutiny of the return may indicate the desirability of seeing copies of related returns. Unusual items on the face of the return will require specific documents or information. The agent should take every precaution to ensure that the examination is not delayed or interrupted by the absence of any necessary material.

(3) If an agent decides he/she should inspect retained copies of returns for any reason, such as to determine whether to examine the year subsequent to the assigned return (as provided in IRM 4217), or for purposes of the employment tax (under the package audit procedures in IRM 4034), the initial request for retained copies should be made when making the appointment.

(4) With smaller taxpayers, who have not had experience with previous tax examinations, care must be exercised in arranging for the examination to ensure that the taxpayer understands that the request for an appointment is not unusual in nature and that all books and records for the year under review should be assembled for the examination. If a taxpayer at the time of an appointment questions the examiner as to why the return is scheduled for examination, the examiner should not say that the examination is "routine," but merely that under the various selection procedures employed by the Service the return was chosen. In some criminal cases taxpayers have stated that their Constitutional rights were violated where for one reason or another the examining agent said the examination was "routine."

430 *(8-30-76)* 4231
Commencing the Examination

431 *(8-30-76)* 4231
Public Relations

(1) In dealing with the public on tax matters, each internal revenue agent is not only an officer of the Government but also, in effect, a representative of the taxpayer. Under the revenue laws the objective of the Service is to determine and collect the correct tax; no more and no less, and with a minimum of inconvenience to the taxpayer. It is therefore appropriate for an examiner to fulfill his/her obligation to the Government, thereby ensuring that the tax is not understated; and also to consider his/her obligation to the taxpayer to make certain that the tax is not overstated. The revenue produced by an agent is not the measure of his/her efficiency.

(2) When the agent puts himself/herself in the taxpayer's place, with the purpose of finding the real problem, he/she may avoid a premature recommendation of additional tax that may be reversed on appeal. Such an impartial approach will do much to gain the respect of the public. The examiner should take the time and exercise the patience necessary to ensure that the taxpayer properly understands the issue raised. He/she should explain the provisions of law which require the correction of the return and give full weight to all evidence and information furnished by the taxpayer, so that the taxpayer is satisfied that no injustice is done. Each agent should read Rev. Proc. 64-22, 1964-1 C.B. (Part 1), 689, concerning some principles of internal revenue tax administration.

432 *(8-30-76)* 4231
Attempts to Interfere with Administration of Internal Revenue Laws

(1) In the execution of your duties and in your general conduct, you should always be cognizant of the taxpayer's rights as an individual. However, do not lose sight of your own rights as an individual. It is your duty to make a full report immediately, preferably in writing, to your immediate supervisor if you are threatened (including a threat to a member of your family) or forcibly assaulted, impeded or interfered with in the execution of your duties. For more specific instructions on this matter, see IRM 9142.3.

(2) If you are approached with an offer or prospective offer of money or other gratuity to influence your official action, your course of action will differ from the above. Bribe offers are often made indirectly and subtly, rather than in a direct fashion. You must be perceptive and alert in recognizing such bribe overtures and must promptly report them so that trained personnel can evaluate the facts and initiate investigation when sufficient evidence warrants. If you have reasonable grounds for believing that an attempt to bribe you has been or will be made, it is your duty to:

(a) Avoid any statement or implication that you will or will not accept the bribe, and try to hold the matter in abeyance.

(b) Immediately report the matter, by telephone where necessary, to the servicing Inspection office in your region or district. The telephone numbers of Inspection offices are posted on bulletin boards in every Internal Revenue office. The calls may be made collect.

(c) Submit as soon as possible a memorandum to Inspection stating the full circumstances concerning the matter. The memorandum will be routed according to the direction given you by the Regional Inspector or his/her representative.

(d) Thereafter cooperate fully in any ensuing investigation and avoid any unnecessary discussion of the case with anyone.

433 *(8-30-76)* 4231
Taxpayers' Representatives

Material for this subsection will be supplied later.

434 *(8-30-76)* 4231
Restatement of Purpose of the Examination

At this point, the beginning of the audit, the examiner should have clearly in mind the purpose of the examination, namely, to determine the correct tax liability. Time spent on irrelevant discussion after the initial period of introduction is wasted. To the extent that an agent allows himself/herself to be sidetracked, or involved in irrelevant work, by the taxpayer or his/her representative, he/she is wasting his time and not accomplishing his/her mission. Even though the taxpayer or his/her representative is willing to waste time, and most are not, the Service is not. The objectives are to examine as many returns as possible without sacrificing quality, and without spending time on needless petty details not material to the purpose of the examination.

435 *(8-30-76)* 4231
Accountants' Workpapers

(1) Guidelines for obtaining accountants' workpapers is taken from IRM 4024.2 as follows:

"Access may be had to audit workpapers of an independent accountant or an accounting firm. Examiners will direct their initial request for accountants' workpapers to the taxpayer. However, examiners will not request access to such workpapers as a matter of standard examining procedure in every case. The access sought should be only to the portion of the workpapers believed to be material and relevant to the examination. In determining materiality and relevance in this context, the examiner should keep in mind that the taxpayer's records are the primary source of information and the accountant's workpapers should normally be used only as a collateral source access to which should be requested with discretion. Since audit workpapers are ordinarily the property of the accountant or accounting firm, access normally will be provided by the accountant at his office, the office of the taxpayer, or some other suitable location."

(2) In most cases, if the accountant is not cooperative, the agent would probably save time by gathering the required information himself/herself without recourse to the workpapers. However, IRM 4024.3 contains procedures when it becomes necessary to issue a summons to obtain them.

440 *(8-30-76)* 4231
Rules on Statute of Limitations

441 *(8-30-76)* 4231
General Rule

Generally, all income taxes must be assessed within three years after the return was filed (the last day prescribed by law for filing a return if the return was filed earlier). The original return (not the amended return) starts the running of the assessment period.

442 *(8-30-76)* 4231

Exceptions to General Rule

(1) There are exceptions to the three-year limitation period on assessment in the following instances.

(a) *False Return*—In the case of a false or fraudulent return with intent to evade any tax there is no limitation for assessment. The tax may be assessed and suit instituted for collection without assessment *at any time after such false or fraudulent return is filed.*

(b) *No Return*—In the case of a failure to file a return, the tax may be assessed or a proceeding in court for the collection of such tax may be begun without assessment at *any time after the prescribed due date for filing the return.*

(c) *Extension by Agreement*—The time prescribed for the assessment of any tax may, prior to the expiration of such time, be extended for any period of time agreed upon, in writing, by the taxpayers and the District Director. The extension becomes effective when the agreement has been executed by both parties. The period agreed upon may be extended by subsequent agreements in writing made prior to the expiration of the period previously agreed upon. Example: 1960-1040 return due April 15, 1961. The statute of limitations is April 15, 1964. However, an agreement is signed to extend the statute to April 15, 1965. If no further agreement is made, the statute of limitations in this particular case is four years.

(d) *Prompt Assessments*—If a written request for prompt assessment is made, assessment must be made within 18 months after the written request is filed. The effect of this request is to limit the time in which an assessment can be made. However, it does not extend the time within which an assessment may be begun or a proceeding in court without assessment may be begun beyond two years from the date of the return. In other words, the statute of limitations is determined 18 months from the receipt of the request, providing the 18 months does not extend beyond the three-year period, otherwise the statute of limitations is three years from the due date of the return. Example: Request for prompt assessment on a 1961 return received June 15, 1962, assessment must be made by December 15, 1963; and request for prompt assessment on 1961 return received January 15, 1964, assessment must be made by April 15, 1965. In the first instance, the 18 months falls within the three-year statutory period. In the second instance, the 18 months would extend to July 15, 1965. Since this would extend beyond the three-year statutory period for the 1961 return, the assessment would be required to be made by April 15, 1965.

(e) *Omission from Gross Income*—If the taxpayer omits from gross income amounts properly includable in the return which is in excess of 25 percent of the gross income, tax may be assessed or a proceeding in court may be begun without assessment at any time within six years after the return is filed.

(f) *Personal Holding Company Tax*—If a corporation which is a personal holding company for any taxable year fails to file with its income tax return, a schedule setting forth the items of gross income described in IRC 543(a) received by the corporation and the names and addresses of individuals who owned at any time during the last half of the taxable year more than 50 percent in value of the outstanding capital stock of the corporation within the meaning of IRC 544, the personal holding company may be assessed or a proceeding in court for collection may be begun without assessment at any time within six years after the return for such year was filed.

(g) *Certain Income Tax Returns of Corporations*—

1 *Trust or Partnerships*—If the taxpayer determines in good faith that it is a trust or partnership and files a return accordingly and later it is held that it is a corporation, the return filed in good faith will be considered to be the return of the corporation and the Statute of Limitations starts to run from the time the fiduciary or partnership return was filed.

2 *Exempt Corporations*—Similarly, if the taxpayer in good faith files as an exempt organization and is later held to be a taxable corporation, the Statute of Limitations starts to run from the time the return was filed as an exempt corporation.

(h) *Net Operating Loss Carryback*—The limitation on the time for assessment runs from the year the carryback originates rather than from the earlier year to which it applied. In other words, a deficiency attributable to the application of a net operating loss for the calendar year 1961 and applied to the three previous years must be assessed on or before March 15, 1965 for a corporation, and April 15, 1965 for an individual.

(i) *Foreign Tax Carryback*—Beginning January 1, 1958, a deficiency due to a carryback of a foreign tax credit may be assessed within one year after the expiration of the period for assessing a deficiency. This, in effect extends the statute for assessment another year.

(j) *Joint Return After Separate Return*—Where both spouses filed returns prior to making a joint return, the date for determining the statute is the date the last separate return was filed but not earlier than the due date. However, in the event a joint return is filed after separate returns, which results in an assessment, the limitation shall not be less than one year after the date of the actual filing of the joint return. This, in effect, permits assessment when the joint return is filed just prior to the expiration of the statute on the separate returns. For example: Separate returns filed April 15, 1961, statute would expire April 15, 1965. A joint return was filed April 14, 1965, in which case the statute is extended to April 14, 1966, permitting sufficient time for assessment.

443 *(8-30-76)* 4231

Statutory Periods for Filing Claims

The Internal Revenue Code expressly provides for refunds and credits for overpaid internal revenue taxes. A refund or credit is required where refund claims are filed within the applicable statutory period. Form 843 is not the only document used for claiming a refund. The returns 1040, 1040B, 1040NB, 1040NB-a, 1120, 1040-X and 1120-X disclosing an overpayment will constitute a claim. An amended return disclosing an overpayment also constitutes a claim. A request made in writing indicating an overpayment for a particular year within the statutory period of limitation constitutes an informal claim and will be given consideration. However, caution should be exercised in accepting materials other than a Form 843 or an amended return. If there is any doubt as to the acceptability of an informal claim, it should be brought to the attention of the supervisor for an administrative decision.

444 *(8-30-76)* 4231

General Rule—Claims

(1) The statutory period for filing claims differ depending on whether or not a return was filed.

(a) *Where a return is filed*—If the return originally results in a tax, any claim for credit or refund of an overpayment must be filed within three years from the time the return was filed or within two years from the time the tax was paid, whichever period expires later. A return disclosing an overpayment constitutes a claim. Even though a return is filed late, it is the claim for refund of the overpaid tax and the taxpayer's rights are fully protected. However, a return to recover excessive withholding tax and estimated tax payments must be filed within three years from the due date of the return.

(b) *Where no return is filed*—A claim for credit or refund must be filed by the taxpayer within two years from the time the tax was paid. In other words, a claim will be entertained if it is filed within two years from the date of actual payment. However, the amount to be refunded is limited to the portion of the tax actually paid within such two years.

445 *(8-30-76)* 4231

Exceptions to the General Rule—Claims

(1) *Bad Debts or Worthless Securities*—Claims relating to bad debts or worthless securities or to the effect that the deductibility of such debt or loss has on the application of a carryover may be filed within *seven years* from the date for filing the return without regard to extensions of time for filing the return.

(2) *Claim for Foreign Taxes*—In the case of an overpayment of income tax allowed for taxes paid or accrued to a foreign country, a claim for credit or refund must be filed within ten years from the due date of the return (determined without regard to any extension of time for filing such return).

(3) *Extension of Time by Agreement*—A claim for credit or refund may be filed after the ordinary period has expired where the taxpayer and the Commissioner have, by agreement (form 872), extended the period for assessment of the tax. Claim may be filed during the extended period and during six months thereafter. (The agreement referred to above becomes effective when signed by the taxpayer and the District Director or an Assistant Regional Commissioner.)

(4) *Net Operating Loss Carryback*

(a) In general, the limitation on the time for refunds runs from the year the carryback originates rather than from the earlier year to which it is applied.

(b) Example: If an overpayment of the 1957 tax was caused by a carryback of net operating loss originating in the return for the calendar year 1959, it is recoverable if claim for refund is filed by March 15, 1963, if a corporation and April 15, 1963, if an individual.

(c) Corporations which sustain net operating losses and individuals, partnerships, estates and trusts that sustain business net operating losses may get a credit or refund of overpayments due to carrybacks before the usual time by filing an application for tentative carryback adjustment. In the case of a calendar year taxpayer, the application must be filed on or after the return for that year is filed but not later than December 31 of that year.

(d) Example: Taxpayer sustained a net operating loss on his 1961 return. His return was filed on April 15, 1962. The application for a tentative carryback adjustment must be filed anytime before December 31, 1962. This procedure provides the taxpayer with a quickie refund. However, this adjustment is subject to audit at a later date and any erroneous part of the allowance is recoverable and adjustment made against the taxpayer. If the taxpayer is not satisfied, he is still entitled to file a claim for refund within the statutory period.

446 *(8-30-76)* 4231

Suspension of Running of Period of Limitations

(1) The running of the Statute of Limitations may be suspending for various reasons which will be given below. It is important to be cognizant of these situations.

(a) *Issuance of a Statutory Notice of Deficiency*—The mailing of deficiency letter prior to the expiration of limitations suspends the running of the Statute of Limitations for 90 days if the notice is addressed to a person within the United States and 150 days if the notice is addressed to a person outside the United States and for 60 days thereafter if no appeal is filed. However, if an appeal to the Tax Court is placed on the Tax Court docket, the office has 60 days from the date on which the Tax Court decision becomes final in which to make an assessment. It should be noted that the Statute of Limitations in this instance can extend far beyond the original period of limitation.

(b) In bankruptcy and receivership cases, the assessment period is suspended for a period starting with the date of adjudication of bankruptcy or appointment of a receiver and ending thirty days after notice of appointment of trustee or receiver is received by the District Director. However, the suspension period may not exceed two years.

(c) Where collection is hindered or delayed because property of the taxpayer is situated or held outside the United States, the statute of limitations is suspended for the duration of such delay or hindrance but the total suspension may not exceed six years in the aggregate.

(d) The Trade Expansion Act of 1962 amended IRC 6501(h) to provide that a deficiency for a year in which a carryback loss was applied may be assessed five years after filing of the return for the year which gave rise to the carryback, or within 18 months after the date on which the taxpayer filed a copy of certificate of eligibility of adjustment assistance, whichever period is later.

447 *(8-30-76)* 4231

Obtaining Consents to Extend Statutory Period of Limitations

(1) When the expiration of the assessment period on a return is imminent, examiners may be required to contact a taxpayer for the purpose of having him/her sign an agreement form, usually referred to as a consent, to extend the statutory period of limitations. But see the procedures in IRM 4541. Most taxpayers are very cooperative and do not hesitate to sign the prescribed form.

(2) After explaining the purpose of the consent form, if the taxpayer hesitates or refuses to sign it, at no time should any statements be made that would attempt to coerce a taxpayer into signing it, such as statements that if the consent is not signed, jeopardy assessment proceedings will be started immediately against the taxpayer.

(3) The granting of a consent to extend the statutory period of limitations is strictly a voluntary action on the part of the taxpayer. We should make the best possible impression upon the public and not seek voluntary waiver of a statutory right by making threats of action to obtain an agreement.

Accounting Records and Methods

510 *(8-30-76)* 4231

General

(1) Taxpayers are required by law and regulations to maintain accounting records in sufficient detail to enable them to make a proper return of income. The Commissioner is authorized to examine records or any other data which may be relevant for ascertaining the correctness of the return or for making a return where none has been made. He/she is also authorized to summon any person, deemed proper, to appear with such records at a reasonable time and place and give testimony, under oath, which may be relevant or material. See (21)80 regarding summons.

(2) The primary (informal) records common to all types of businesses, accounting systems and reporting methods are those documents such as invoices, vouchers, bills, receipts, and tapes upon which are recorded the individual transactions of buying and selling merchandise, supplies, services, assets used in the business, and capital assets. When inventories are an income-determining factor, the primary records include detailed inventory lists. Also to be included in primary records are such evidences of financial transactions as canceled checks, duplicate deposit slips, bank statements and notes.

(3) The secondary (formal) records, regardless of the accounting method employed by the taxpayer, are the permanent books, worksheets, tallies, etc., which list or summarize those individual documents, with adjustments when necessary, in proper classifications designed to aid the taxpayer in determining, at the end of any given period, his/her financial status and profit or loss for the period. These secondary records may consist of a single book or record, a simple set of books, or a complicated set of records in which numerous analyses, consolidations, or summarizations are made before the final result is obtained.

(4) The only taxpayers not required to keep secondary records are those whose sole source of gross income is from salaries, wages, or similar compensation for personal services rendered, or from farming. (See Chapter 800, Farmers.) All taxpayers are required to keep the primary records, and even those not required to keep secondary records are required to be prepared to show how each item of income and expense on the return was computed. All records shall be retained so long as the content may become material in the administration of any internal revenue law. In view of this requirement, agents should refer taxpayers who have questions regarding retention of records to the applicable regulations.

520 *(8-30-76)* 4231

Adequacy of Records

(1) The adequacy of a taxpayer's records depends on their existence, completeness, and substantial accuracy. It is recognized that all taxpayers do not exercise the same degree of care in recordkeeping, and that while some are extremely meticulous, others are considerably less so. The appearance of the records is not important so long as the accuracy and completeness are not affected.

(2) Because of the infinite variety of taxpayers, trades, businesses, professions, types and sources of income, deductions, etc., a specific definition of what would be considered adequate records applicable in each and every case, is not possible or practical. The determination of whether any particular taxpayer has maintained adequate records must necessarily be a matter of judgment and a factual matter in each case.

(3) If it is found that a taxpayer has failed to comply substantially with the law and regulations for maintaining adequate books and records, the examiner will orally inform the taxpayer that the books and records maintained are not sufficiently detailed for the preparation of a proper return of income. Care should be taken, however, to avoid any criticism of the work of employees, accountants or attorneys. Subsequent to orally informing the taxpayer of the inadequacies of his/her records, the examiner will follow the procedures in IRM 4297. This provides basically that the examiner include in his/her transmittal letter a clear concise statement specifying in what respects the taxpayer's records are inadequate in order that this wording can be readily inserted in an inadequate record notice to the taxpayer.

(4) There will be cases where the taxpayer's records are inadequate only to a degree or with respect to a particular item or items. If the item or items involved are not important, either individually or as a class, then minor inadequacies exist, and it will be sufficient to inform the taxpayer orally of the need for improvement and to incorporate in the transmittal letter of the report a comment relative to such inadequacies and the fact that the taxpayer was so informed. On the other hand, if it is found that the taxpayer

has failed to keep adequate records to substantiate entertainment and other business expenses, the examiner will follow the procedures in IRM 4265. This provides for the preparation of Form 4298 as well as informing the taxpayer as to the inadequacies of his/her records.

(5) The form the examination takes from this point will depend upon the extent of the inadequacy. In the case of wholly inadequate records, or a complete lack of records, it may be helpful to use the guidelines in Chapters 700 and 900, as well as the aids described in Chapter (21)00. If there are indications of fraud the examiner should proceed in accordance with Chapter (10)00.

(6) Where the records are only partially inadequate, it may be helpful to utilize a combination of the guidelines in Chapters 600 and 900, and the aids in Chapter (21)00 as may be applicable.

(7) Prior to making an examination of the books, some ways to determine whether the records are adequate are:

(a) read prior examination reports, if available, for indications of careless recordkeeping and ask about the records from the agent who examined the prior year return;

(b) obtain the accountants' audit report, read the qualifying statements and note any mention of inadequate records;

(c) inspect the trial balances and balance sheet as of the beginning and end of the year;

(d) where necessary reconcile income per books with income per return and observe whether earned surplus and capital accounts in the books agree with these same accounts in the balance sheets.

(8) The information obtained from the above techniques will permit an agent to have an informed opinion concerning the adequacy of the records. However, it has been found that fraud occasionally exists even when the records are well kept and audited by reputable accountants because of taxpayers' activities not recorded in the books and not made known to the accountants.

(9) The agent should at all times be alert to any of the questionable practices discussed in Chapter (10)00 on fraud. If the preaudit inspection indicates a complete set of well-kept books, the agent will be prepared to concentrate on those specific items he/she believes warrant examination.

(10) If the records appear to be inadequate, the examiner must determine an approach from his/her own observations. Trial balances should be requested from the taxpayer and checked with the books. If none are available, the agent should prepare them himself/herself. A copy of the beginning and ending balance sheets and the income statement should be obtained or prepared and checked to the trial balances. The general journal should be scrutinized to find any adjustments for large clerical errors, important corrections of control accounts, omitted income, etc. Upon request, the taxpayer may be unable to produce any particular journal or ledger account. The lack of a balancing trial balance (taken by either the taxpayer or agent), or a particular journal or ledger account, or the presence of adjustments indicating seriously faulty accounting may call for a "net worth" approach rather than an item-by-item audit, depending on the seriousness of the inadequacy.

(11) It is possible that the agent may have to resort to detailed verification of particular accounts or journals. Detailed auditing should be kept to a minimum. If the area of error is large, the taxpayer should be requested to make suitable verification and correction before the agent proceeds. After satisfying himself/herself that the books reflect all of the taxpayer's business activities for the period, the agent should proceed to an examination of particular items for the purpose of determining their tax consequences. Of course, good judgment should be exercised so that no time is wasted, therefore, while awaiting additional information from the taxpayer, the agent may examine any particular items which appear to be complete.

530 *(8-30-76)* 4231
Accounting Systems

531 *(8-30-76)* 4231
Single-Entry System

(1) The single-entry system of bookkeeping is essentially a system in which are maintained only records of cash and personal accounts. There is considerably less uniformity in the use of this system than in the use of the double-entry system. The single-entry system is often used by small businesses, such as small retail or commission merchants, professional firms, estates, or trusts which are concerned chiefly with cash receipts and disbursements. "Single-entry" is a generic term frequently applied to any method of day-to-day recordkeeping which does not use the double-entry system.

(2) In this system the details of income and expense can be obtained only by an analysis of the daily records. These records usually consist of a journal and a cashbook. A ledger is kept for certain accounts to which postings are made from the books of original entry.

(3) The journal is used to record all noncash transactions affecting accounts receivable and accounts payable. The pages are ruled to provide columns for date, description, and ledger folio. Two money columns are also provided. In the left money column amounts are entered which are to be posted to the left side of various ledger accounts, and in the right money column are amounts to be posted to the right side of various ledger accounts. These left and right sides are frequently not designated as debit and credit although they are used in the same manner, i.e., left is debit and right is credit. In the "description" column of the journal, the word "to" often identifies a debit and "by" a credit. Because income and expense accounts are usually not kept in a ledger, the journal entries are the only records affecting accounts receivable or payable, or capital.

(4) The cashbook is used to enter cash receipts and disbursements. This cashbook constitutes both a book of original entry and the cash account.

(5) The ledger usually contains only the capital (net worth) account and the individual accounts receivable and payable to which postings are made from the journal and the cashbook. Therefore, no trial balance may be taken but only a list of balances.

(6) The system described above is what may be called a formal single-entry method. Its origin goes back to the early days of bookkeeping. Besides this method, there are various means of recording transactions which, although single entry, are often haphazard and even more incomplete than this method. Quite often they will be encountered in connection with strictly cash businesses. The only record common to all will be some sort of cashbook. Inventories, where applicable, will probably be estimated.

(7) The examination of a return based upon any of the records mentioned above presents peculiar problems which are not usually encountered in the average double-entry system. The examiner must make a decision soon after beginning the examination as to how deeply he/she should delve into the accounting methods of the taxpayer in order to assure himself/herself that they are substantially adequate before making an examination of particular items on the return. There are several questions which should be asked at this time, some of which are as follows.

(a) Has the taxpayer available net worth statements or balance sheets as of the beginning and end of the year?

(b) Does he/she have worksheets analyzing the income and expenses for the year and do they tie in with the tax return?

(c) Does the net income (or loss) per these worksheets agree with the net increase (or decrease) of net worth as shown by a comparison of the beginning and ending balance sheets?

(d) Have recent prior years been examined and does the year currently under examination show a return comparable to those of other years?

(e) Is the examiner familiar with the type of business and do the results of this year's operations compare favorably with this experience?

(f) Have the books been audited by a reputable accountant and did he/she prepare the return from worksheets which are available?

(8) The answers to the questions above and any others which may fit particular situations will indicate the extent of the examiner's audit.

(9) If this initial survey leaves a doubt in the agent's mind about the trustworthiness of the records, it behooves him/her to investigate, insofar as practicable (depending on the size of the business, extent of the inadequacy, etc.), the balance sheets at beginning and end of the period under investigation. If a comparison of taxable income determined by the net worth or bank deposit method with the amount reported on the return reveals that no substantial difference exists, examination of specific items of income and deductions should be undertaken. Agents are cautioned against attempting minute reconciliations except in those cases where it has been determined that fraud exists or the taxpayer is prepared to contest a sizable deficiency. The techniques described in Chapter 900, Examination of Returns—Inadequate Records, may be employed in arriving at net worth at the beginning and end of the year. Outside sources of information such as those described in Chapter (21)00 may also be utilized.

(10) The agent should be continually aware of the need for mathematical verification of single-entry records.

(11) If the inadequacy necessitates a reconstruction of income and expense accounts, the following schedules may be used or adapted:

(a) Computation of sales

Cash sales (cashbooks)	...	XX
Sales on account:		
Collections from customers (cashbooks)	XX	...
Less: Accounts receivable (beginning balance sheet)	XX	...
Collections from sales for the period	XX	...
Add: Accounts receivable (ending balance sheet)	XX	XX
Total sales	...	XX

(b) Computation of purchases

Cash purchases (cashbook)	...	XX
Purchases on account:		
Payments to creditors (cashbook)	XX	...
Less:		
Accounts payable (beginning balance sheet)	XX	...
Payments for purchases for the period	XX	...
Add:		
Accounts payable (ending balance sheet)	XX	XX
Total purchases	...	XX

(c) Computation of expenses

Prepaid items (beginning balance sheet)	...	XX
Cash payments for allowable expenses (cashbook)	XX	...
Less:		
Accrued expenses (beginning balance sheet)	XX	XX
Total	...	XX
Add:		
Accrued expenses (ending balance sheet)	...	XX
Total	...	XX
Less:		
Prepaid expenses (ending balance sheet)	...	XX
Expenses for period	...	XX

(12) Even in instances where all circumstances appear favorable to good reporting, it is advisable, with this type of accounting system to check balance sheets to detect omitted items. It should be noted that while inventories, fixed assets, prepaid items, etc. are not recorded in the formal single-entry ledger, the taxpayer will probably have some sort of memorandum accounts, records, or lists wherein data pertaining to these assets is kept. The agent should visually inspect the premises to determine that all fixed assets are included, as well as to note the general prosperity of the enterprise.

(13) After satisfying himself/herself that he/she has arrived at the correct net worth increase or decrease (either from taxpayer's records, his/her own investigation, or a combination of both), the agent should, where required, proceed to examine the deductibility of expenses and costs in accordance with the techniques described in Chapter 600.

532 *(8-30-76)* 4231
Double-Entry System

532.1 *(8-30-76)* 4231
Introduction

(1) Double-entry bookkeeping is a system of accounting where the theory is applied that assets equal liabilities plus capital. "Capital" includes the daily increase or decrease of net worth from the operations of the business as reflected in the nominal accounts, i.e., income and expense accounts. This system records transactions so that every net increase in assets is accompanied by a corresponding increase in either liabilities or capital and every net decrease in assets requires a like decrease in liabilities or capital. The increases or decreases of particular asset, liability or capital accounts are accompanied by corresponding decreases or increases in other asset, liability, or capital accounts.

(a) By this continual action and corresponding reaction, a properly maintained set of double-entry books is always in balance; i.e., the total of all debits equals the total of all credits.

(b) The double-entry system consists of two types of formal (secondary) records: The journals and the ledgers.

532.2 *(8-30-76)* 4231
Journals

(1) The journals are called the books of original entry because entries are made therein from the invoices, bills, vouchers, etc., which comprise the primary records. These journals consist of—

(a) *Salesbook*—This may be a book in which each charge sale is entered or it may be a binder in which the duplicate charge sale invoices for a period are gathered together. Both types of books are totaled periodically (usually monthly) and posted to the control accounts receivable (debit) and sales (credit) in the general ledger. The individual customers' accounts are debited daily as sales occur.

1 Sales returns and allowances which are frequently accounted for in the back of these same books are totaled and posted periodically as a debit to sales returns and allowances and as a credit to accounts receivable in the general ledger. Details are posted to individual customers' accounts in the subsidiary ledger.

2 Cash sales are usually handled solely through the cashbook, although it is possible to use both books and post the debit (cash) from the cashbook and the credit (sales) from the salesbook.

(b) *Purchase book*—This book is used for recording charge purchases of merchandise for resale or materials and supplies for incorporation in a finished product. Purchase returns and allowances are frequently recorded in the same book. The purchase book is totaled periodically (usually monthly) with postings made to purchase (debit) and accounts payable (credit) in the general ledger. The returns and allowances are posted as a debit to accounts payable and a credit to purchase returns and allowances in the general ledger.

(c) *Voucher register*—This book is used for recording all purchases of merchandise, materials, supplies, and services that are to be paid for by check. When the voucher register is used, the purchase book is not needed. Each invoice (or group of invoices) which is to be paid by one check is entered in the book on a single line and an identifying number placed on both the voucher and the register. When paid, the check number is placed in an appropriate box on the same line as the original entry. The total of the items not having check numbers plus any unentered invoices represents the accounts payable at the end of any period. Postings are made periodically to appropriate cost or expense accounts (debits) and accounts payable (credits).

(d) *Cashbooks*—

1 Herein are recorded the cash receipts and check disbursements. Since most currency disbursements are small, they are usually recorded in a petty cash book and a single check is drawn, when needed, to replenish the currency fund. When a voucher register is not in use, expenditures, other than for merchandise or materials, are usually not recorded until paid and then they are entered in this book and postings made from it to the asset or expense accounts in the general ledger, at month end. Where a voucher register is in use, the only posting from the disbursements part of the book is to accounts payable (debit) and cash (credit).

2 All receipts from whatever source should be recorded in the receipts part of the book, and at the end of the month the postings are to cash (debit), accounts receivable (credit), cash sales (credit), capital accounts (credit), etc.

(e) *General journal*—This is not a specialized journal like the others mentioned above, but may be used to record any type of transaction. Postings must be made individually from each entry instead of in total from specialized columns. This book is normally used to record such nonrecurring transactions as the original investment in the business, purchase or sale of assets, admission of new or additional capital or assets into the business, and withdrawal of assets. It is also used to record year-end adjustments to, and closing of, accounts. In the early days of bookkeeping all transactions went through the general journal, and some small businesses, with relatively few transactions, still follow this practice.

(f) *Standard journal*—Many businesses use this book for recording regularly recurring monthly and quarterly adjustments rather than clutter up the general journal. By use of special columns for each account affected, periodic postings may be made in total rather than individually.

532.3 *(8-30-76)* 4231
Ledgers

(1) The ledgers are called the books of final entry because transactions are finally entered therein through posting from the books of original entry. These ledgers are:

(a) *General ledger*—Herein is kept an account for every balance sheet and profit and loss item to which are made the periodic postings mentioned above. At the end of each accounting period, proper adjustments are made to the accounts through the general journal after which a balance sheet and statement may be made up from the open accounts. The nominal (income and expense) accounts are then closed, and the net balance, representing the net income or loss transferred to the capital account (retained earnings of a corporation or proprietary accounts of the owner or partners).

(b) *Subsidiary ledgers*—To relieve the general ledger of congestion and to facilitate posting, most businesses have a control account for receivable and one for payables in the general ledger, and keep the individual accounts in subsidiary ledgers. In addition, many businesses maintain a control account for expenses. Any general ledger account is capable of being used as a control where the taxpayer so desires.

(c) *Private ledger*—This is a type of ledger not found frequently. Its object is to place those accounts containing information pertaining to matters considered secret or personal by the proprietor in a separate book which is available only to a selected few. Agents are cautioned against allowing any information gathered from such a source to be seen by any employee of taxpayer except one properly entrusted with it. The ledger may be kept either in the manner of a subsidiary with a control account in the general ledger and a separate checking account and cashbook or as a mere segregation of general ledger accounts.

(2) The system outlined above is fairly basic among taxpayers operating small to average-size businesses with double-entry books. There are peculiarities in certain businesses which necessitate the use of slightly different terminology, adaptation of journals, etc. These variations are not of such importance that they will pose any particular problems to the examiner.

Some of the important variations are discussed in Chapter 600. It is important for the agent to develop ability to quickly determine the approach to be used in examining a double-entry set of books. Unlike a single-entry system, where the possibility exists that items may be omitted from the inventory and appraisal of assets as of year-end, no such problem is presented in a complete double-entry system. It is possible, of course, in the best run system that tax evasion may be practiced by deliberate omission of income. This and other methods of evasion will be discussed in Chapter (10)00 on fraud. It is also true that errors may occur in year-end accruals of income and expenses and in merchandise inventory evaluations; but these errors tend to correct themselves between periods, and the agent's problem is one of verification of these and other items to which leads have already been furnished by the records as discussed in Chapter 600. Once an examiner has established to his/her own satisfaction the trustworthiness of the particular double-entry set of books, he/she can find leads to practically all the information he/she desires within the books themselves.

540 *(8-30-76)* 4231
Accounting Methods

541 *(8-30-76)* 4231
General

(1) The system of accounting described in 530 may be operated under any one, or a combination, of several accounting methods. It is not mandatory that taxpayers with more than one business use the same accounting method for each, nor must a taxpayer use the same method of accounting in his/her personal affairs as in his/her business.

(2) Generally, taxable income must be computed under the method of accounting on the basis which the taxpayer regularly computes his/her income in keeping his/her books. If no method of accounting has been regularly employed or if the method employed does not clearly reflect income, the computation shall be made in accordance with such method as, in the opinion of the Commissioner, does clearly reflect income. It is the responsibility of the agent, in such a situation, to determine what method does clearly reflect income and proceed to compute a corrected net income on that basis. A method of accounting will not be regarded as clearly reflecting incomes unless all items of income and expenses are treated with reasonable consistency. However, consistency alone should not be the test for a clear reflection of income. A taxpayer must secure the consent of the Commissioner before changing the method of reporting income.

542 *(8-30-76)* 4231
Basic Methods

(1) The following are the acceptable basic methods of accounting.

(a) The cash receipts and disbursements method means there shall be included in gross income all items of income actually or constructively received (whether in cash or property at its readily realized market value) and there shall be deducted from gross income only the amounts actually paid out other than withdrawals and capital expenditures. Certain items, even on the cash method, may not be wholly deducted in any one year but must be prorated. These include insurance premiums covering more than one year, payments to obtain long-term leases, etc. Where a taxpayer keeps no books or records of account, it may generally be concluded that the cash receipts and disbursements method is being used, and that ordinarily under such circumstances he/she cannot be on the accrual basis.

(b) The accrual method of accounting contemplates that net income will be determined by including in gross income all items of income when earned, even though not received and deducting all expenses as soon as incurred whether paid or not. Under this method, generally speaking, net income is measured by the excess of income earned over expenses incurred. In any case where it is necessary to use inventories, no method of accounting in regard to purchases and sales will correctly reflect income except the accrual method. The inventories should be taken and evaluated in a consistent manner from year to year.

(c) Excepting a "cost plus" contract or one permitting specific charges to be made for material used, the costs of labor and material applied to a job uncompleted at year-end do not constitute an inventory item for a construction, building, or installation contractor; consequently, the existence of such costs does not oblige the use of the accrual method of accounting. This conclusion is supported by two considerations: one, such costs are deemed to be unrelated to merchandise held or produced for sale to customers (a contractor is generally considered to be selling services); two, title to the improvement or alteration of real property vests in the owner of that property from moment to moment as the contract is in the process of performance.

(d) A hybrid method is one which involves the use of elements of both the cash and accrual methods. This method is permissible as long as it clearly reflects income, is used in a consistent manner from year to year, and violates none of the rules regarding use of inventories, proration of insurance, etc. An example of the use of such a method is found in the case of a small retailer who uses the accrual method on sales and cost of goods sold and the cash receipts and disbursements method on expenses. The installment method, described separately below, is also an example of a hybrid method.

543 *(8-30-76)* 4231
Installment Method

(1) Persons who regularly sell personal property on the installment plan may report as income therefrom, in any one year, the gross profit portion of the payments received in that year. The gross profit portion is computed on the gross profit rate applicable to the year in which the sale took place. Deductions for expenses (other than for bad debts and loss on repossessions) are taken in the same manner as on the cash or accrual basis.

(2) Taxpayers who use this method must maintain their books of account so that an accurate computation can be made on such basis. In particular, they must make a yearly computation of the gross profit ratio for the year (this must be available for all years for which there are still outstanding installment accounts receivable), and they must identify collections for the year in which the account was created.

(3) Installment accounting records are usually, maintained under the double-entry system; and except for the distinctly "installment" accounts (installment accounts receivable, reserve for unrealized profits or deferred gross profit on installment sales, as it is sometimes called, provision for bad debts—installments), the general ledger accounts are kept in the usual manner. The books of original entry are also maintained in the customary way except for a few variations; for instance, the cashbook may have additional columns for analyzing collections as to the year in which the account originated. Usually this is not the case; instead, the individual customer's ledger cards are analyzed and the necessary information transcribed onto schedules for use in determining, at year end, the amount of realized profit for each year to which collections pertain.

(4) In those businesses where sales are made on the cash or credit basis in addition to the installment plan, each type of sale must be recorded separately. Incidentally, sales price includes finance and service charges. Where the gross profit ratio on cash or credit sales is different from installment sales (and this is usually the case), it will be necessary to maintain such records of costs as will enable the taxpayer to compute a proper gross profit ratio for installment sales. The usual method is to cost installment sales currently and allow the remainder of cost to apply to other type sales without maintaining separate cost records for them.

(5) Sales allowances, if applying to current year sales, act as a direct reduction of sales.

Installment sales	XXX	
Installment accounts receivable		XXX

(6) If sales allowances apply to a prior year, the cost portion is a current expense and the unearned profit should be closed out of the unearned gross profit on installment sales account. The offsetting credit for the whole amount is installment accounts receivable.

Sales returns and allowances	XXX	
Unearned gross profit	XXX	
Installment accounts receivable		XXX

(7) At year end the gross profit ratio is computed, and an entry made closing out the installment sales account to cost of goods sold (or some other trading account) for the cost portion and unearned gross profit for the profit portion.

Installment sales	XXXXXX	
Cost of goods sold		XXXXXX
Unearned gross profit		XXXXXX

(8) At the same time an entry is made taking out of the unearned gross profit account the realized profit on prior and current years' sales, based upon current collections, and crediting income summary.

Unearned gross profit	XXXXXX	
Income summary		XXXXXX

(9) Bad debts are taken either on an actual or provision for bad debts basis. The amount of the bad debt deduction is the unrecovered cost portion of the uncollected installment accounts receivable. A separate provision for bad debts

must be kept for installment accounts and for credit accounts. The provision on the books may be either on the unrecovered cost basis or the total receivable basis. If the former, the entry to adjust the provision will be a debit to bad debts and a credit to the provision for bad debts—installments for the amount necessary to bring the provision up to the cost portion of estimated doubtful accounts.

Bad debts	XXXX	
Provision for bad debts—installments		XXXX

(10) Individual chargeoffs will involve an entry charging the provision for bad debts—installments, unearned gross profit and crediting installment accounts receivable.

Provision for bad debts—installments	XXX	
Unearned gross profit	XXX	
Installment accounts receivable		XXX

(11) If the book provision is carried on the basis of the total receivables estimated to be doubtful, then, additions to the provision are debited to bad debts (for the unrecovered cost) and unearned gross profit for the profit portion.

Bad debts	XXXX	
Unearned gross profit	XXXX	
Provision for bad debts—installments		XXXX

(12) Individual chargeoffs are for the full amount of the receivable. The entry is a debit to provision for bad debts—installments, and a credit to installment accounts receivable.

Provision for bad debts—installments	XXX	
Installment accounts receivable		XXX

(13) Gain or loss on repossessions is the difference between the fair market value of property repossessed and the unrecovered cost of the merchandise. The transaction affects the accounts as follows: debit purchases (for the fair market value), unearned gross profit (for balance of unearned gross profit), gain or loss on repossessions (credit if gain), and credit installment accounts receivable.

Purchases	XXX	
Unearned gross profit	XXX	
Gain or loss on repossessions	XX	
Installment accounts receivable		XXX

(14) Merchandise sold in prior years and returned in the current year is handled in a similar manner. Merchandise sold and returned in the same year is handled as a canceled sale.

(15) It is frequently found that the installment dealer keeps his/her books on a strict accrual method including year-end adjustments and closings. None of the usual ledger accounts peculiar to installment accounting are maintained. When this method is employed an analysis of the installment accounts receivable will show, at year end, the balances owing for each year of sale. The provision for bad debts will also be maintained on the accrual basis, and an analysis will be provided showing the amount applicable to each year's receivables. The gross profit ratio for each year is applied to the net balance of receivables for that year minus the provision for bad debts for the year, and the result is the unrealized profit for each year, all of which are added together to make the total unrealized profit at the end of the year. The tax return is then prepared showing all the necessary details on the accrual basis. The unearned gross profit at the beginning of the year (computed as above) is added to the net income, and the unearned gross profit at the end of the year (computed similarly) is deducted. The result is the taxable net income on the installment method. The provision for bad debts at beginning and end of the year must be taken into consideration in order to effect an adjustment to current accrual method accounting of the gross profit element contained in the current bad debt deduction. If taxpayer does not make a provision for bad debts but takes specific charge-off of installment bad debts, no such adjustment is necessary.

(16) When auditing a set of installment method books, the agent should verify deductions and items of noninstallment income in accordance with instructions in Chapter 600. The installment element of income should be audited somewhat as follows.

(a) The gross profit ratios for each year for which there is still unearned gross profit at the end of the taxable year should be verified. This should be done by reference to the schedules maintained for that purpose and comparison with the pertinent ledger accounts. Particular attention should be paid to any year in which there is a sizable drop in the profit ratio. The element of gross profit should include all applicable items, such as invoiced cost, and freight in.

(b) The balances of installment accounts receivable controls at beginning and end of the year should be compared with the corresponding totals of analysis sheets for the individual accounts and any sizable adjustment necessary to balance the controls should be investigated. Any reduction of control balances during the year from other than installment collections should also be investigated.

(c) The installment accounts receivable at the beginning of the year should be analyzed by years in order to ascertain whether any old open balances were improperly carried over from prior years, and, if so, an effort should be made to determine why the individual accounts receivable are still outstanding.

(d) The ratios should be applied to collections during the year and traced to debits in the total unrealized profit. Any other debit in the unrealized profit account should be traced to the corresponding credit.

(e) Current year's sales and sales for both current and prior years charged back in current year should be scrutinized and any sizable debits investigated.

(f) Current year's cost of goods sold should be audited in accordance with instructions in Chapter 600.

(g) Taxpayer's computation of bad debt deduction should be checked to make certain that only the cost factor is considered. Where a provision for bad debts is made, the amount of the provision in relationship to the balance of receivables should be considered.

(h) If there is a provision for reinstated accounts, it should be examined to determine if accounts are charged off too readily. Recoveries handled through any other account should likewise be examined for the same purpose.

(i) The taxpayer's policy on valuing repossessed merchandise should be investigated to make certain that any year-end inventory is properly priced; i.e., has not been reduced to an unrealistic value.

550 *(8-30-76)* 4231
Special Features

551 *(8-30-76)* 4231
Cost Accounting

551.1 *(8-30-76)* 4231
Introduction

(1) The ordinary accounting system is one designed to show, among other things, the cost of all the business operations for a particular period. A cost accounting system is one designed to show the cost of each job, process, or product completed or work in process. Some cost systems are also designed to account for variances between previously estimated or standardized costs of a particular product or process and the actual cost.

(2) Although cost systems are usually thought of in relationship to large manufacturers or fabricators, they are also used by smaller businesses such as automobile dealers.

(3) The term "cost accounting system" as used here applies to the type of double-entry system wherein is recorded the various allocations and adjustments necessary to reflect the cost factors. Where the business keeps its cost records entirely separate from the general books of account, the agent, except for inventory pricing, is not faced with the type of problem discussed here; therefore, he/she should conduct his/her examination in the usual manner.

(4) There are three types of cost accounting systems in general use.

(a) *Job cost* refers to the system kept in a plant (or that portion of a plant) where goods are manufactured or fabricated on specific orders only. Costs are therefore accumulated on a departmental basis for each such order of job.

(b) *Process cost* refers to the system in use in a plant (or that portion of a plant) where goods are manufactured continuously or in bulk and it is not desirable (it is often impossible) to distinguish between orders. Costs and quantities processed are determined by department. Average costs are obtained per unit and the accumulated costs are followed from department to department. Inventories of work in process are valued on the basis of these accumulated costs.

(c) *Standard costs* is used in conjunction with either job or process cost and consists of setting up standards of cost and quantity for materials, labor, and overhead. Entries are made on the basis of these estimates and variances with actual costs and quantities are recorded.

551.2 *(8-30-76)* 4231
Description of Cost Accounting Systems

(1) Cost accounting systems include the following ledgers with related general ledger control accounts: Material, work-in-process, fac-

tory overhead, and finished goods. Also, a standard journal for recording recurring monthly journal entries is usually used.

(2) Under job and process cost systems, materials, when purchased, are entered in the control account from the voucher register or purchase book and details of the purchases are entered in the subsidiary ledger which is usually a set of cards—one for each type of material. Payroll, when accrued, is entered from the journal by a debit to work-in-process and a credit to payroll accrued. Sometimes labor is allocated between direct and indirect, in which case the indirect portion would be charged to overhead. Overhead is entered monthly from the voucher register, purchase book, or cashbook, plus accruals from the journal, with details posted to the proper accounts in the subsidiary ledger. Monthly journal entries are made charging work-in-process for materials put in process, labor expended in manufacturing and overhead applied to production. The overhead applied is an estimate based on experience so that at year end the variance between the total monthly applications and the actual constitute over- or under-applied overhead which is closed directly to the income summary account. The cost of goods or jobs completed during the month is removed from the work-in-process account and placed in finished goods.

(3) At year-end the cost of finished products or jobs sold is removed from work-in-process (or finished goods, if used) and charged to cost of goods sold. The remainder in the work-in-process account is the cost of products or jobs incomplete as of year end.

(4) Under a standard cost system, raw materials are entered at standard cost in the stores account. The difference between standard and purchase price is entered in an account called material variance—price. Materials are put into production at standard cost. Any variances between standard and actual quantities of raw materials placed in production are recorded at standard cost as material variance—quantity. Work in process is always charged with standard quantities at standard prices. Labor is subject to two possible variances, rate and time. These are recorded as labor variance—rate and labor variance—time when accruing payroll. Since overhead is applied to work in process on a standard time (labor) basis multiplied by a standard overhead rate variances from actual overhead must be accounted for by an entry to overhead variance at month-end to balance the factory overhead account. Usually no attempt is made to allocate the variance between the portion caused by labor variance and that by overhead variance. While the variance accounts are usually closed to the income summary account at year-end, the portion applicable to inventories of raw materials, work-in-process, and finished goods should be carried over to the succeeding period.

(5) The agent examining records maintained under any of the systems outlined above for the first time may be somewhat confused by the seeming complexity of the various adjustments necessary to accomplish the desired results. However, the situation clears when it is borne in mind that most of these adjustments do not affect net profit (except insofar as inventories are concerned), but bring about refinements of the accounts to enable management to observe and control the profitableness or unprofitableness of particular departments and operations.

(6) The audit should be made with these main questions always in mind.

(a) Are sales and other income accounted for in the proper period?

(b) Are the purchases, labor costs, and overhead expenses allowable as first entered from the books of original entry?

(c) Are inventories properly counted and priced?

(d) Are general expenses allowable?

(7) Reconciliation of books with return, analysis of surplus, scrutiny of balance sheets, etc., should be made according to methods described in this and other chapters.

(8) The audit of sales and other income in a manufacturing business, which for audit purposes does not differ from any other type of business, will be done according to procedures outlined in succeeding chapters.

(9) Cost of goods manufactured and sold should be verified from the control accounts to the journals, or from the journals alone depending on the judgment of the agent. No attempt should be made to follow the various month-end distributions and applications of material, labor, and overhead from the original accounts through the work-in-process accounts. The verification should take the usual form for these materials, labor, and overhead accounts; i.e., the search should be for items of a capital nature, personal expenses of officer-stockholders or proprietors, excessive or unearned salaries on wages, and excessive depreciation.

(10) The beginning and year-end inventories and accrual accounts should be closely scrutinized in order to tie in the system as a whole. In other words, the costs will have been verified as they were first charged on the books and all intervening distributions and applications ignored. The open end of the system is comprised of balance sheet accounts carrying over to the succeeding periods or accruing in the current period items to be charged off or paid for in the future. Inventory details should be audited from taxpayer's detailed inventory cards or sheets on a spot-check basis to ascertain if pricing is according to the requirement of the Code and regulations, and if the three elements of cost in in-process inventories (materials, labor, and overhead) are handled on a consistent basis. Agents should be alert to the possibility that overhead may have been omitted from inventory. (See Chapter 600.) Any sizable writeoffs of alleged obsolete or spoiled goods should be given particular attention. If variance accounts are used and large variances exist, a rough calculation should be made to determine if the variances have been allocated among work-in-process, cost of goods sold, and finished products inventory to avoid distortion of the income for the period. Of course, no reserves for anticipated inventory losses are allowable, neither may inventories be arbitrarily priced at replacement cost.

(11) General expenses should be verified as outlined in Chapter 600.

552 *(8-30-76)* 4231
Automatic Data Processing

552.1 *(8-30-76)* 4231
General

There are two general types of automatic data processing systems: One system, EAM, uses Electronic Accounting Machines which utilize punched cards to process data and prewired panels or plugboards to control their operations. The other system, EDP, uses Electronic Data Processing equipment which includes a central processing unit called a computer and its peripheral equipment, such as storage units, printers, and punched card or magnetic tape devices. A set of operating instructions is communicated to the electrical circuitry of the latter system which permits the computer to follow these instructions and control the operation of the system.

552.2 *(8-30-76)* 4231
EAM or Punched Card Systems

(1) In these systems information from source documents is transcribed or coded by punching holes into cards. By the use of these holes the cards are "read" by mechanical or electrical means as they pass through one or more machines for each operation. Each card often contains only one item or one transaction, so the system is sometimes called a unit record card system.

(2) This card punch, the sorter, and the accounting machine (tabulator) are the usual machines found in a punched card system. The card punch is used to punch holes in a card in accordance with a predetermined code or scheme. The sorter arranges the cards according to their data to meet a specific requirement. The sorter may arrange the cards alphabetically or numerically; it may group like items together; or it may select one or more items from a larger group of items.

(3) The purpose of the accounting machine is to print alphabetical and numerical data from punched cards in an orderly fashion and to total data by proper classification. Other types of machines may also be found in a punched card system, such as a calculator capable of performing addition, subtraction, multiplication and division.

(4) From the agent's point of view the most important items of the EAM system are the printed records from the accounting machine. These printed records, sometimes called "printouts," may differ in format from journals and ledgers found in manual systems. Nevertheless, experience has shown that after one becomes accustomed to working with them, they often prove easier to read and analyze than manual records, because they are more legible.

(5) The agent on his/her initial visit, should discuss the overall system with the taxpayer or his/her representative to determine the types of print-outs which are available and should become familiar with any coding which appears on the printouts, such as codes for account names or account subdivisions. Additional printouts should be requested when necessary, but care must be taken not to cause needless expense to the taxpayer.

(6) In general, the punched card system presents few problems which cannot be solved through conventional auditing techniques.

552.3 *(8-30-76)* 4231
Electronic Data Processing Systems

(1) These systems usually consist of a combination of units including input, storage, pro-

cessing, and output devices. The principal element of these systems is the processing unit, a high-speed electronic computer.

(2) The processing unit controls and supervises the entire computer system and performs the actual arithmetic and logical (place in sequence, compare, rearrange, etc.) operations on data. In order for it to perform the desired operations, careful and precise instructions must be written for each task to be performed. The entire process of analyzing the operation to be performed, determining the best method of achieving the desired results, and writing the instructions is known as programming. Programs are written sometime before the system becomes operational, but may be changed. They may be written in a high level programming language (i.e., one close to ordinary English, such as, COBOL) or in machine language (i.e., one intelligible to a processing unit with little or no translation). In any case, the program is transcribed upon a medium accept able to the system, such as magnetic tape, punched tape or punched cards. The instructions or program may then be "read" into a storage unit before a particular operation is to be performed.

(3) When data is to be processed, information from source documents is transcribed upon a medium acceptable to the system and "read" into the system.

(4) Once they are within the system both the instructions and the data are in the form of electrical units or impulses. Therefore, the processing of the data within the computer is accomplished by manipulating them through electrical circuits. Many operations may be performed within the processing unit, such as arithmetical computations, comparisons, and rearrangements of data. These capabilities permit many bookkeeping operations to be performed within the computer, such as calculating payrolls, updating inventories and accounts receivable.

(5) The results of the processing are "written" out onto magnetic tape, punched tape or cards, or other unreadable mediums and they may not be printed out in English at the same time.

(6) Thus the conventional "audit trail" may be missing from part of the full accounting cycle from source documents to summary for tax purposes. However, the processing unit must follow a prescribed set of instructions; and, in many cases, these instructions may be considered a part of the audit trail. For example, a set of instructions, or program, for updating accounts receivable through the computer will likely remain constant once the best program for that particular system is devised. When good internal control exists over both the accounting activities, up to the point data is introduced into a computer, and the results of the processing in the computer, a review of the program procedures may be sufficient to satisfy the auditor of the adequacy of the records. He/she should also make conventional auditing checks of the accounting processes not computerized.

(7) Rev. Proc. 64-12, 1964-1 C.B. (Part 1) 672, sets forth the Service's guidelines for determining the adequacy of records maintained within an automatic data processing system, as follows.

(a) *General and Subsidiary Books of Account*—A general ledger, with source references, should be written out to coincide with financial reports for tax reporting periods. In cases where subsidiary ledgers are used to support the general ledger accounts, the subsidiary ledgers should also be written out periodically.

(b) *Supporting Documents and Audit Trail*—The audit trail should be designed so that the details underlying the summary accounting data, such as invoices and vouchers, may be identified and made available to the Internal Revenue Service upon request.

(c) *Recorded or Reconstructible Data*—The records must provide the opportunity to trace any transaction back to the original source or forward to a final total. If printouts are not made of transactions at the time they are processed, then the system must have the ability to reconstruct these transactions.

(d) *Data Storage Media*—Adequate record retention facilities must be available for storing tapes and printouts as well as all applicable supporting documents. These records must be retained in accordance with the provisions of the Internal Revenue Code of 1954 and the regulations prescribed thereunder.

(e) *Program Documentation*—A description of the ADP portion of the accounting system should be available. The statements and illustrations as to the scope of operations should be sufficiently detailed to indicate the application being performed, the procedures employed in each application (which, for example, might be supported by flow charts, block diagrams or other satisfactory descriptions of input or output procedures), and the controls used to insure accurate and reliable processing. Important changes, together with their effective dates, should be noted in order to preserve an accurate chronological record.

(8) Summarized below are some audit suggestions which may be useful in examining an electronic data processing system.

(a) Don't be awed by the mass of intricate machinery. You are concerned with what it does, not how it does it.

(b) Familiarize yourself, in general, with the manual of operations, with the objective of learning what visible records are produced, as well as the source of the information contained in the records.

(c) Plan your audit. Analyze your audit requirements. Allow the tax manager time to secure or prepare the necessary information not already at hand.

(d) Apply your audit techniques which have proven useful on manual systems.

(e) Refer to minute books, appropriation binders or files, budgetary control records, executive minutes. error listings, and manually prepared journal vouchers for possible audit leads.

(f) Intensify your audit of periods of transition from manual to machine systems.

(g) Investigate scope of taxpayer's internal audit program. Internal auditors' workpapers may be of great value.

(h) Make use of tax files, schedules, and workpapers prepared by the tax department, available workpapers of auditors, SEC reports, and reports of other Governmental agencies.

(i) Be firm in insisting that any reasonable request be complied with.

(j) Seek permission of the taxpayer to ask questions of his/her EDP personnel. There are very few "experts."

(k) Refer to the Manual of Operations, or talk with the EDP supervisor, to check assertions by the taxpayer's accountant or tax department that particular information is not available or cannot be produced.

(l) Experience has shown that the computers have a high degree of accuracy. However, don't rely 100% on the accuracy of the analyses and printouts prepared by the taxpayer. Make some test checks of the source documents. And, don't overlook the fact that the machines can be programmed to nonprint or nonadd any specified figure or amount.

(m) Upon completion of the audit, suggest procedures which will expedite an audit of subsequent years.

(n) Insist that the taxpayer's original source documents be retained and filed in some logical sequence.

(o) Don't expect to find that all systems are alike. Each system will be as different as the needs of the business dictate.

(p) The field of electronic data processing is continuing to develop and only a brief outline of the common basic elements in computer usage has been given here.

Audit Standards for Examiners

310 *(4-23-81)* 4231
Introduction

(1) As previously stated in Chapter 100, the purpose of auditing a tax return is to determine the taxpayer's correct tax liability—no more or no less. A quality audit is the examination of a taxpayer's books and records in sufficient depth to fully develop relevant facts concerning issues of merit; ascertaining the true meaning of applicable tax laws; and correctly applying such laws to the relevant facts.

(2) One responsibility of Examination is to conduct on a timely basis quality audits of selected tax returns to determine the correct tax liability. Examination standards were developed as the level of achievement required for you to discharge this responsibility. Examination procedures necessary to achieve the standards are explained in the sections of the Manual indicated. Efforts have been made to define all standards as fully as possible; however, certain terms in the standards are intangible or subjective, and, as such, do not lend themselves to explicit definition. These include terms such as reasonable and professional judgment. Although the explanations have been written in a manner to show you the intended meaning of the terms, you must use your technical knowledge, training, and experience to correctly apply these concepts to the examination process.

320 *(4-23-81)* 4231
General Standards

(1) The examiner has a responsibility both to the taxpayer and to the government to determine the correct tax liability and to maintain a fair and impartial attitude in all matters relating to the examination.

(a) *Explanation*— The Service's goal of achieving the highest degree of voluntary compliance depends entirely on the cooperation and confidence of the taxpaying public. The fair and impartial attitude of an examiner aids in increasing voluntary compliance. An examiner must approach each examination with an objective point of view.

(2) Employees must maintain the highest level of integrity and avoid circumstances that might impair or give the appearance of impairing their independence.

(a) *Explanation*

1 Examiners will disqualify themselves from the examination or survey of any return assigned to them when either of the following circumstances apply:

a The examiner's personal transactions with the taxpayer have been or are significant in relation to the examiner's or taxpayer's financial position; or

b The examiner's business, social, or other relationships with the taxpayer are of a nature that might impair, or give the appearance of impairing, the examiner's impartiality and independence. (See policy statement P-4-6.)

2 The circumstances in a and b apply equally to examinations of Internal Revenue Service employees and officials.

3 When the assignment of a return to an examiner meets the circumstances above, it will be the responsibility of the examiner to return the case to the examiner's manager with an appropriate explanation. In situations where the examiner is doubtful whether this policy applies, the case in question will always be returned to the examiner's manager.

4 Additional information can be found in IRM 4036, 4042, and 0735.1, Handbook of Employee Responsibilities and Conduct.

(3) The classification, examination, and review of returns will be performed by persons who have adequate technical training and experience.

(4) Professional judgment should be exercised in the identification of significant items, pre-audit planning, performance of the audit, preparation of the report, and subsequent quality review.

(a) *Explanation*

1 An important aspect of a quality examination is the use of professional judgment during various phases of the examination process. It starts with a classifier using judgment to identify significant items, continues with an examiner determining scope and depth, and ends with a reviewer ensuring that sound professional judgment was used during the entire process.

2 Professional judgment is developed through knowledge, training, and experience.

(5) Management personnel will be responsible for the effective use of all allocated resources.

330 *(4-23-81)* 4231
Standards For Examining Returns

(1) The scope of the examination should be limited or expanded to the point that the significant items necessary for a correct determination of tax liability have been considered.

(a) *Explanation—Tax Auditors*

1 The scope of the examination on non-business returns not requiring pre-contact analysis will be set by classification. The classification checksheet should list significant items that warrant examination. However, the Tax Auditor may expand the examination when significant issues arise as a result of information secured during the examination. Also, instances may arise where, in the judgment of the Auditor a significant item was not identified during classification. In the latter instance approval of the group manager is necessary, when possible, before the scope may be expanded.

(b) *Explanation—Revenue Agent*

1 The scope of the examination will be set by the revenue agent. For non-DIF returns, significant items will be identified by the classifier on the classification checksheet. However, the examiner is not precluded from extending the scope of the examination beyond the identified items or from eliminating certain items if circumstances warrant. For DIF returns, classification will not identify significant items, and the revenue agent will have sole responsibility for determining the scope of the examination.

(2) Adequate evidence should be obtained through inspection, inquiry, and analysis of supporting documents to ensure full development of relevant facts concerning issues of merit.

(a) *Explanation*

1 Evidence is the sum total of all information presented by the taxpayer, representative, or third parties regarding an issue. Evidence can include the taxpayer's books and records, the taxpayer's oral statements, statements of the taxpayer's representative, statements of third parties, or documentation submitted by or obtained from third parties. If the issue involves specific recordkeeping required by law, then documentation should be presented as evidence. However, where the issue does not normally involve formal documentation, oral statements may be adequate evidence. Adequate evidence, therefore, does not require complete documentation.

2 Inspection is the critical examination of evidence presented to determine its applicability to the issue questioned and whether it is adequate substantiation for the issue under examination. Based upon the professional judgment of the examiner, it may be necessary not only to inspect the taxpayer's documents or books and records, but also to inspect the taxpayer's place of business, review his/her standard of living, and evaluate third party information.

3 Inquiry is the technique of asking a question or a logical sequence of questions, written or oral, that will secure information regarding the issue being examined or that will determine the relevance of evidence presented. The examiner may pose questions to the taxpayer(s), their representative, and, when appropriate, third parties.

4 Analysis refers to the process of arranging, sorting or scheduling the evidence presented in a logical manner to facilitate reaching conclusions regarding the issue under examination.

(3) Examination results will reflect technically correct conclusions based on consideration of all relevant facts and the proper application and interpretation of the tax laws.

(a) *Explanation*

1 When an examination is pursued to the proper depth, all relevant facts will have been accumulated. To reach technically correct conclusions, the examiner must apply the appropriate tax laws to the facts. The conclusions reached should be based on an objective interpretation of the law, whether it is in the taxpayer's or government's favor.

2 An examiner has various research materials available that will aid in arriving at technically correct conclusions:

a IRC;
b Regulations;
c Commercial Tax Services;
d Published decisions;
e Rulings; and
f Actions on decisions

3 If the examiner is still unable to reach a conclusion, the group manager should be consulted. Formal requests for technical advice should be made if appropriate (see IRM 4550). The examiner should also be aware of formal suspense issues (IRM 4559).

(4) Workpapers will fully disclose the scope, depth, and techniques used in the examination and will support all conclusions.

(a) *Explanation*—The examiner's workpapers are the connecting link between the tax return and the examination report. The workpapers summarize all the evidence gathered by the examiner to indicate the depth and scope of the audit, the techniques used, and the conclusions reached. In addition to being used to prepare the examination report, workpapers are used:

1 In reviewing the case to determine if a quality audit was performed;

2 As a source of information for examiners of subsequent year returns or claims;

3 By Appeals in unagreed cases; and

4 As part of the administrative file for litigation cases.

(b) *Workpaper Requirements*

1 The workpapers should contain all notes made before, during, and after the examination, including a history sheet which shows all contacts made with the taxpayer(s), representative(s), third parties, etc., during the course of the audit.

2 The workpapers must be legible.

3 All significant items, whether or not changed, should be commented on in the workpapers.

(c) *Pro Forma Audit Aids*

1 Pro forma audit aids have been developed for frequently examined items. They are designed to assist the examiner and to provide uniform examination techniques and workpaper documentation. The use of these aids is mandatory.

2 The reminders listed on the pro forma aids ensure that those features are considered, but they are not all inclusive. Therefore, the examiner must determine which features are applicable in each case and whether other aspects should also be considered.

340 *(4-23-81)* 4231

Definition of Significant

(1) Invariably, the definition of significant will depend on your perception of the return as a whole and the separate items that comprise the return. There are several factors, however, that you must consider when determining whether an item is significant. These factors are:

(a) Comparative size of the item—A questionable expense item of $6,000 with total expenses of $30,000 would be significant; however, if total expenses are $300,000, ordinarily the item would not be significant.

(b) Absolute size of the item—Despite the comparability factor, size by itself may be significant. For example, a $50,000 item may be significant even though it represents a small percentage of taxable income.

(c) Inherent character of the item—Although the amount of an item may be insignificant, the nature of the item may be significant. For example, airplane expenses claimed on a plumber's schedule C may be significant.

(d) Evidence of intent to mislead—This may include missing, misleading or incomplete schedules or incorrectly showing an item on the return.

(e) Beneficial effect of the manner in which an item is reported—Expenses claimed on a business schedule rather than claimed as an itemized deduction may be significant.

(f) Relationship to/with other item(s) on a return—No deduction for interest expense when real estate taxes are claimed may be significant. Similarily, the lack of dividends reported when Schedule D shows sales of stock may be significant.

(2) Generally, automatic adjustments (obvious errors or omissions on the return) in excess of the 241 LEM IV tolerance will be considered significant items.

(3) During classification, all significant items will be identified for examination on the classification checksheet for those returns requiring checksheets.

(4) Consideration should be given to items that are not shown on the return, but would normally appear on returns of the same examination class. This applies not only to unreported income items, but also for deductions, credits, etc. that would result in tax changes favorable to the taxpayer.

(5) The examiner's report will be clear, concise, and legible, accurately computing the tax, taking into account all automatic adjustments and using the method most beneficial to the taxpayer.

(a) *Explanation (Office Examination)*

1 IRM 428(10), Report Writing Guide for Income Tax Examiners, contains detailed instructions and procedures which should be followed in preparing examination reports.

2 Automated report writing equipment will be used where available.

3 The report should include all necessary information so that both the taxpayer and reviewers will have a clear understanding of the

adjustments made to the return and the reason(s) for those adjustments. If a standard paragraph exists for an adjustment, it must be used as the explanation.

4 Automatic adjustments are those changes to items on the return necessitated by the adjustment of other items. For example, a change to the medical expense deduction based on a change to adjusted gross income is an automatic adjustment. Another example is a change from itemized deductions to the zero bracket amount when, as a result of another adjustment, the zero bracket amount becomes more beneficial.

5 If it appears that a more beneficial method of tax computation is available to the taxpayer, the examiner should secure any information necessary to make such computation, and that method should be used to determine the correct tax liability. The tax change tolerances in 241 of LEM IV will be adhered to in all examinations.

(b) *Explanation (Field Examination)*

1 IRM 428(10), Report Writing Guide, contains detailed instructions and procedures which should be followed in preparing examination reports.

2 The report should include all necessary information so that both the taxpayer and reviewers will have a clear understanding of the adjustments made to the return and the reason(s) for those adjustments.

3 Automatic adjustments are those changes to items on the return necessitated by the adjustment of other items. For example, a change to the medical expense deduction based on a change to adjusted gross income is an automatic adjustment. Another example is an adjustment to allowable investment credit due to a change in the tax liability limitation which is caused by another adjustment.

4 If it appears that a more beneficial method of tax computation is available to the taxpayer, the examiner should secure any information necessary to make such computation, and the method should be used to determine the correct tax liability. The tax change tolerances in 241 of LEM IV will be adhered to in all examinations.

(Next page is 4231-37)

Audit Techniques

510 *(4-23-81)* 4231
Individual Returns

511 *(4-23-81)* 4231
Introduction

The examiner should become familiar with the name(s), address, occupation(s), and filing status shown on the return. Reference to this information will be important as the examination progresses.

512 *(4-23-81)* 4231
Filing Status

(1) If the return indicates that a joint return, head of household, or surviving spouse status has been claimed, determine the validity of the status.

(2) If separate returns have been filed by persons entitled to file jointly, ascertain the similarity of treatment with respect to standard or itemized deductions.

(3) Examiners should pursue filing status when other features indicate that the status is questionable.

513 *(4-23-81)* 4231
Dependency Exemption Cases

513.1 *(4-23-81)* 4231
Proof of Dependency

(1) Taxpayers have the burden of proof when claiming an exemption deduction. However, in certain situations they may not have the information to complete this requirement. One such situation occurs when the dependent does not live in the household of the taxpayer, or lives there only a part of the year.

(2) In cases of the foregoing type, taxpayers will be furnished questionnaires to secure the necessary information from the head(s) of household in which the dependent resided. The questionnaire will be accompanied by the district's preaddressed envelope for direct mailing by the other taxpayer if he/she so desires. The questionnaire provided is Form 2038 (Questionnaire—Exemption Claimed For Dependent).

(3) If the examiner is satisfied that the taxpayer has furnished the major support, the exemption for the dependent(s) will be allowed. Conversely, if the examiner is satisfied that the taxpayer has not furnished major support, the exemption for the dependent(s) will be disallowed. These determinations may be possible even though total support amounts are not available. In these situations, the inquiry procedure in (4) below will not be necessary unless the case is unagreed. However, Form 5346 (Examination Information Report) should be prepared when it appears that the same dependent may have been claimed by another taxpayer. If the examination originating from the Form 5346 results in allowing the dependents and the return is otherwise acceptable as filed, the regular no-change procedure may be followed. In such cases, the originating district will be advised of the findings by use of Form 5346.

(4) When the taxpayer is unable to furnish sufficient information to show major support of dependent(s) residing in another household, even though he/she did attempt to secure the information by use of the questionnaire, districts may request the information direct from the taxpayer. For this purpose, Letter 977(C/DO) (Third Party Inquiry—Questionable Exemption) will be used when appropriate and necessary. Requests will be limited to cases in which the taxpayer has shown that substantial support payments were made, but additional facts are necessary to determine who furnished the major support for the dependent(s). Letter 977(C/DO) advises the taxpayer that his/her return is not being examined.

(5) When the inquiry procedure does not result in obtaining sufficient facts to resolve the exemption issue, the other taxpayer's return, if filed in the same district, will be inspected for duplicate exemption(s) and, if necessary, will be examined. However, when the dependent resides with a taxpayer in another district, Form 4217 (Duplicate Exemption and Alimony Inquiry) will be used to request a collateral examination. This request will first be reviewed as prescribed in IRM 4416:(1).

(6) If the receiving district determines that a duplicate exemption is not involved, a reply to that effect will be sufficient; however, collateral examination procedures will apply to all other cases.

(7) The related case procedure in IRM 4224.1 will apply only in unagreed cases involving more than one taxpayer, both under examination, and claiming the same dependent(s). This does not include cases in which it is not

known whether or not the other taxpayer is under examination.

513.2 *(4-23-81)* 4231
Children of Divorced or Separted Parents

(1) For taxable years beginning after December 31, 1966, IRC 152(e) provides that, as a general rule, the parent having custody of a child for the longer period of time during the year is entitled to the deduction for personal exemption.

(2) This rule applies only if the combined support furnished by the parents amounts to more than one-half of the total support of the child for the year, and only if the child is in the custody of either or both of his/her parents for more than one-half of the year.

(3) "Custody," in the normal case, is determined according to the law of the jurisdiction in which either the decree of divorce or separate maintenance was entered, or the separation agreement was executed.

(4) The above general rule provides two exceptions under which the parent not having custody (or having custody for the shorter period) becomes entitled to the deduction. They are:

(a) If he/she contributes at least $600 toward the support of child and the decree of divorce or separate maintenance, or a written agreement between the parents, provides that he/she is to receive the deduction; or

(b) if he/she provides $1,200 or more of support and the parent having custody for the longer period does not clearly establish that he/she provided a greater amount of support.

(5) When one of the parents claims the deduction for a child pursuant to a written agreement between them, reasonable effort should be made to verify the existence of the written agreement.

513.3 *(4-23-81)* 4231
Disclosure of Dependency Information

(1) An officer or employee of the Service is prohibited from disclosing to a taxpayer information furnished by the taxpayer's former spouse about amounts claimed for support of their child. The taxpayer may be informed only that the amount expended by him/her is not sufficient to establish his/her right to the claimed dependency deduction.

(2) An exception to the disclosure of dependency information is provided for taxable years beginning after December 31, 1966. The exception applies when the parent not having custody claims to have furnished more than $1,200 of support and the parent having custody claims that such amount was not furnished, or claims to have furnished the greater amount of support. In such a case, each parent is entitled to receive an itemized statement of the expenditures upon which the other's claim of support is based. This itemized statement will be limited to the information in Form 2038. A request for such information need not be in writing, nor must a request be made before an examiner is permitted to disclose such information. Disclosure of such information may be informal and not necessarily in writing except when so requested.

520 *(4-23-81)* 4231
Income

521 *(4-23-81)* 4231
Introduction

Examiners must be alert to detect the possibilities of omitted income. Some indications of possible unreported income may be apparent on the face of the return. If income reported appears insufficient to meet the cost of living and other disbursements including those claimed on the return and substantiated during the examination, examiners should ask questions designed to uncover potential sources of income not reported on the return. Two sources are moonlighting income and income from bartering. The reasons for failure to report the income should be developed and the file documented accordingly. Minimum probes are located at IRM 4241.5 and 4253.2.

522 *(4-23-81)* 4231
Income—Wages and Salaries, Unemployment Benefits, etc.

(1) Review compensation arrangement to determine special privileges (paid vacations, use of company car, etc.).

(2) Particular consideration should be given to the source of taxpayer's income as certain occupations and trades are more susceptible than others to omitted income. Some examples are:

(a) Members of certain trades usually work for contractors from whom they receive a W-2. Due to the nature of their work, they may do part-time work for homeowners and others who may not file W-2's. They should be directly questioned as to the possible existence of such income.

(b) Itinerants, such as fruit-pickers and seasonal workers, may have income from other sources during the off-season.

(c) Practical nurses may be employed by individuals, as well as by hospitals or rest homes and the wages received from individuals may not be covered by a Form W-2.

(d) Returns of taxpayers reporting income from occupations where tips are commonly received should be carefully reviewed to determine if this income was reported. Taxpayers who receive tip income may not maintain complete and accurate records. The examiner should test check to determine the accuracy of the amounts reported.

1 If an adjustment to FICA tax on tip income is made, Form 885-T will be prepared in a minimum of an original and one copy. A copy of only the Schedule T-A will be attached to the front of the case file. The Schedule T-A will serve as a flag to the self-employment control clerk and will be sent to Social Security Administration. The top portion of the form will constitute the employment tax report going to the taxpayer.

2 The following special instructions will be followed in preparing Schedule T-A (Form 885-T).

a *Section A*—Include increase or decrease in tip income not reported to employer. Decreases should be shown in brackets. The total adjustment should be distributed equally to the four quarters unless the taxpayer submits information which establishes that the tips were not earned every month.

b *Section B*—Enter the taxpayer's occupation that accounts for the tip income. Enter the social security number of the taxpayer whose tip income is being adjusted.

c *Section C*—The taxpayer's name and address *must* be correct. This information and the social security number should be verified with the taxpayer.

d *Section D*—This block should always be answered. Social Security Administration needs this information to determine the proper adjustment of taxpayer's earnings record.

e *Section E*—Refile number will be entered by the service center.

(3) Low income of one spouse may indicate the other spouse received income and possibly did not receive a Form W-2 or 1099. The possibility of unreported income is increased if the amount of income reported seems inadequate in view of the reported exemptions and deductions. In these circumstances, the examiner should ask specific questions to determine if additional income was received.

(4) For taxable years beginning after December 31, 1978, unemployment compensation may be taxable. Examiners should be alert to unemployment benefits which may not have been reported.

(5) Be alert to outside employment, prizes, tips, etc.

(6) Development of information verifying reported deductions or income may reveal facts indicating the taxpayer is the beneficiary of an estate or trust and should have reported distributable income from that source.

523 *(4-23-81)* 4231
Income from Bartering

(1) When verifying income, the examiner should be alert to the possibility of "bartering" or "swapping" techniques or schemes. Such noncash exchanges may be done directly; however, the greater volume of these exchanges is handled through reciprocal trade agencies. Both services and inventory may be exchanged for "credits." These "credits" can then be used to obtain other goods or services. Bartering does result in taxable income and should be reported as such.

(2) Some areas of possible tax abuse are as follows:

(a) Nonrecognition of current income.

(b) The trading of services or inventory for capital assets (which would convert ordinary income to capital gain) or for fixed assets (which should be depreciated over the useful life of the assets).

(c) The exchange of inventory or services for personal goods and services, such as vacations, houseboats, luxury cars, use of vacation home or condominium, or payment of personal or stockholder debts.

(3) In addition, examiners should be alert for the following:

(a) Deductions and/or payments for credit liability insurance or insurance guaranteeing lines of credit.

(b) Deductions and/or payments for membership fees, annual dues, or service charges to specialized reciprocal trading companies.

(c) The write-off or mark-down of inventory, especially for excess or supposedly obsolete inventory.

(d) The factoring or sale of accounts or notes receivable to specialized reciprocal trading firms.

524 *(4-23-81)* 4231
Dividend Income

(1) The examination of dividend income reported by the taxpayer should not be limited to the information documents attached to the return. If more than $100 is excluded, the ownership of securities by both husband and wife should be ascertained.

(2) The method used by the taxpayer in determing dividend income should be secured. Understanding the method used may suggest the most appropriate way to check for accuracy. A list of securities owned at the beginning of the taxable year, used in conjunction with subsequent sales and acquisitions, will afford the most exact results.

(3) If the taxpayer merely records dividends when received and also keeps some securities in the broker's custody, the broker's monthly statements should be checked for dividends credited to the account. Most taxpayers who have security trades during the year retain their monthly statements. These statements should be checked when verifying dividend income.

(4) The examiner should verify the accuracy of claims that dividend income is either fully or partially tax-exempt, or nontaxable, such as distributions representing partial return of capital.

(5) Be aware of duplication of credits such as foreign dividends received and recorded net of foreign tax paid, and a further credit being taken on the return.

(6) Be alert for stock splits which increase the number of shares upon which the taxpayer would receive dividend income.

525 *(4-23-81)* 4231
Interest Income

(1) Be alert to income from interest on income tax refunds and savings accounts which may not appear on the tax return or taxpayer's records.

(2) Verify claims that interest from state or municipal bonds is either fully or partially tax-exempt.

(3) Taxpayers should be asked whether they have cashed or transferred any Government bonds, held any matured Government bonds, or had any savings accounts during the taxable year. When ownership of Series E Bonds is transferred, interest income earned must be reported in the year of transfer.

(4) The verification of interest income should also be made in conjunction with the examination of capital transactions. Interest bearing securities sold during the year should be compared to interest reported. The interest accrued to date of sale is sometimes reported as part of the proceeds, rather than as interest income.

(5) Verify that savings and loan interest, as well as credit union interest, through commonly called dividends, has been treated as interest income for tax purposes.

(6) Verify that other interest income items such as interest on paid up insurance policies, interest on prior year tax refunds, interest on G.I. insurance dividends on deposit with the Veterans Administration, and interest on insurance dividends on deposit with an insurance company which are withdrawable upon demand have been reported.

(7) If property was sold in prior or current years and a purchase money mortgage or second mortgage constituted part payment, interest income should be reflected in the return. Verify that mortgage collections have been allocated to principal and interest.

(8) Verify that interest received on a condemnation award has been included as ordinary income.

526 *(4-23-81)* 4231
State Tax Refunds

Verify that state income tax refunds which caused a decrease in tax in prior years have been included in income in the year refunded. In some instances, taxpayers include in income only the actual amount of state income tax refund received and not the refund figure per the state tax return. Taxpayers may take the position that the difference, credited to state estimated taxes, is not included in income since expenses of equivalent amount would also have to be included and, therefore, a wash results. This is not true in cases where a taxpayer is subject to the minimum tax due to excess itemized deductions. In these situations, any increase in AGI or itemized deductions results in an increase in the tax preference item subject to the minimum tax computation. Similarly, in the maximum tax computation, any increase in AGI will reduce the percentage of income subject to the maximum tax.

527 *(4-23-81)* 4231
Alimony Income

(1) If the initial interview discloses the taxpayer is divorced, explore the possible receipt of alimony income.

(2) Combination alimony and child support payment agreements should be scrutinized for the portion reportable as alimony.

528 *(4-23-81)* 4231
Pensions and Annuities

528.1 *(4-23-81)* 4231
Basic Elements and Verification

(1) The four basic elements used in determining the taxable portion of amounts received as a pension or annuity are:

(a) the investment in the contract or the cost of the annuity;

(b) tax-free cost recovery in the past;

(c) the expected return; and

(d) payments received during the taxable year.

(2) The examiner should verify the source of the payments, verify investment in the contract, expected return, and amounts received with proper allowance for refund features.

(3) If employer-employee annuity, determine whether proper reporting has been made.

(4) Military retirement pay, based upon age or length of service, is taxable. However, the amount of reduction in retirement or retainer pay to provide a survivor annuity for a spouse or children is not included in income.

(5) Veterans' disability compensation paid either to the veteran or the family is exempt from tax.

(6) Old age pensions granted for consideration for other than past services are taxable as compensation and are not treated as annuities.

(7) Old age pensions received under the Social Security Act or under the Railroad Retirement Act are entirely exempt from tax.

528.2 *(4-23-81)* 4231
Employer-Employee Financed Plans

The Code distinguishes between employer-employee financed annuities where the employee's cost will be recovered within 3 years, and between other so-called general rule annuities. If the taxpayer claims the cost is recoverable within 3 years, the examiner should verify this fact.

528.3 *(4-23-81)* 4231
Purchased Annuities

(1) Some purchased annuity contracts contain a life insurance feature. If the life insurance remains in effect after payments are received by the annuitant under the contract, that portion of the amount paid which is attributable to the insurance feature should be eliminated from the cost of the annuity. It may be necessary for the taxpayer to secure this information from the insurance company.

(2) Most insurance companies furnish annuitants with a statement showing the exact amount to be entered on Form 1040. The amounts are keyed directly to the annuity schedules on that form. Where the taxpayer produces such a statement, it may usually be accepted without further verification.

529 *(4-23-81)* 4231
Capital Gains and Losses

(1) The technique to be used in the examination of the gains and losses reported on a return will vary depending on the nature of the asset. The two broad classifications of assets, both under the law and for purposes of audit approach, are capital assets and all other assets.

(2) The verification of gains and losses involves several elements; the selling price, expenses of sale, the adjusted basis of the property, and the holding period.

529.1 *(4-23-81)* 4231
Selling Price

(1) The settlement statement is the best approach to verify the transaction. The taxpayer should be requested to submit the settlement statements.

(2) Sales of securities, options, and commodity market transactions are normally effected through brokers. When such is the case, the brokerage "bought" and "sold" slips and the broker's monthly statements are the best ap-

proach to this phase of an examination. The transaction slips state the purchase price or sales price, the commissions, the transfer taxes (Federal and local), and accrued interest where appropriate. In addition, the dates of the transaction are clearly set forth.

(3) If the transactions reported were not made through a broker, the proceeds and expenses of sale should receive closer scrutiny. Disposition of securities in a closely held corporation should be checked as to the valuation of property received, when in a form other than cash. This valuation should be based on fair market value. A common error is the reporting of gain or loss based on the retained earnings.

529.2 *(4-23-81)* 4231
Expense of Sale

Capital transactions are rarely reported in which there is no appropriate expense of sale. These expenses include legal, accounting, and brokerage fees. When gains or losses appear on a return and no such expenses are set out, the examiner should determine that they have not been claimed as ordinary deductions.

529.3 *(4-23-81)* 4231
Adjusted Basis of the Property

(1) Particular attention should be given the adjusted basis. The examiner should determine whether the adjusted basis properly reflects any nonrecognized gain realized from a prior sale.

(2) In computing capital improvements, an analysis should be made to determine that the value of the taxpayer's labor is not included. In addition, casualty losses previously allowed are a reduction of the basis whereas appropriate reconstruction after the casualty is an addition to the cost.

(3) Appraisal statements are usually acceptable for verifying the basis of property, especially where personal property or portions thereof, have been converted to rental use. These statements should be made by a qualified appraiser and show a logical and acceptable basis for fixing the probable value at the date the property was received or converted. Such appraisals are sometimes a basis for making an FHA loan.

(4) Where the property was inherited, determination of the correct basis may be done by an inspection of copies of the estate tax return or appraisal statements. Where it was received as a gift, inspection may be made of the gift tax return.

529.4 *(4-23-81)* 4231
Holding Period

(1) Because the Code varies its treatment of gains or losses depending upon the holding period of the capital asset, the dates of acquisition and disposal are important. They are also important in connection with losses arising out of wash sales and in cases of property acquired in a tax free exchange.

(2) The general rule for determining the holding period is that such period begins the day after contractual purchase (regardless of later delivery or payment date) and ends on the day of contractual sale. Therefore, in verifying sales on a security exchange, the contract date, not the settlement date, is governing.

(3) Further refinements have been made by the Service. In the case of a cash basis taxpayer, the loss on a transaction is deemed to have been realized upon the date of sale despite the fact that the proceeds were received in a subsequent taxable year. Conversely, the gain on a transaction is realized upon receipt of the proceeds. These rules are important since there is usually a flurry of so-called "tax-selling" near the close of a calendar year.

529.5 *(4-23-81)* 4231
Personal Residence

(1) The Code provides unique treatment with respect to gains on the sale or exchange of a residence.

(2) When information is not available from the return and taxpayers are claiming nonrecognition of all or part of the gain, they should be asked to complete Form 2119, Sale or Exchange of Personal Residence. In many cases, it will be necessary to use facts stemming from years other than the one under examination. The is true because of the latitude of time provided in the Code for replacement or reinvestment. It is important for the examiner to realize that completion of the form by the taxpayer is not the equivalent of an examination of the transaction. The amounts entered on the form should be verified.

(3) In addition to the purchase price, the taxpayer usually claims capital additions in the adjusted basis. Unlike the case of rental property, no deductions are allowable for repairs to a residence. To verify the taxpayer's claim for improvements during the holding period, the examiner must clearly understand the distinction between expense and capital items.

(4) Receipted bills of contractors who perform the work would be useful. Comparison of the amount shown on such a bill should be made with the amount of disbursement. The inspection of a cancelled check, for instance, may reveal that the amount of the bill was reduced because of protest by the taxpayer.

529.6 *(4-23-81)* 4231
Multiple Dwellings

(1) Frequently property is sold which consists in part of the taxpayer's residence. The approach to verifying such transactions should take the form of dividing the sale into two parts, one for the residence, the other for the rental property. Treating the sale in two parts may result in a nonallowable loss on the residence portion and a taxable gain on the rental portion.

(2) In dividing the sale transaction, proper allocation must be made for original cost and capital additions between the personal and rental portions of the asset. All depreciation allowed or allowable is an adjustment to the basis of the rental portion only. Similarly, the selling price and expenses of sale must also be allocated between the two segments. The separate gain and loss is measured for each segment, personal and rental, and proper tax treatment applied to each. Regarding the sale as a single transaction allows the taxpayer to offset a nondeductible loss against a taxable gain.

(3) Various methods are available for allocating costs and selling prices between the personal and rental portions. One acceptable method is the ratio of rental value of the two segments. The allocation of capital additions between the personal and rental parts must be tempered by taxpayers' normal inclination to spend more money on their own residence. This should be taken into account absent reasonable substantiation for prorating the costs.

(4) The sale of property that is part personal and part rental, if held the statutory number of months, will be treated as an IRC 1231 transaction for the rental portion. This portion should be verified in the same manner as though it were an independent sale of property held solely for rental income.

(5) IRC 1231 specifies capital gain treatment for sales of certain ordinary assets. Where gains from such sales are reported, look for any casualty losses in the business schedule or among the itemized deductions; gains or losses on similar depreciable property arising from the distribution of partnership assets; and, for gains or losses from involuntary conversions. The Code relief provision requires consideration of these items in the aggregate, prior to classification between ordinary and capital gain.

(6) Often in the sale of depreciable assets or land, the agreement includes the sale of other items such as goodwill and inventories. These extraneous assets must be handled separately and the selling price allocated on the basis of their respective fair market value.

529.7 *(4-23-81)* 4231
Ordinary Income vs. Capital Gains

(1) In determining whether income from the sale of assets should be taxed as ordinary income rather than as capital gains, the examiner should look for:

(a) sales of depreciable property to related taxpayers;

(b) dealings in a manner which would constitute a trade or business, i.e., subdivision of a tract of land and sale of its lots upon which substantial improvements have been made;

(c) redemption of stock by a closely held corporation; and

(d) dealings with related individuals (substance vs. form).

529.8 *(4-23-81)* 4231
Nonbusiness Bad Debts

(1) Ascertain whether there was a valid, existing debt or whether the amount may be a gift as between family members.

(2) Determine that the debt is worthless and that the deduction is claimed in the year during which the debt became worthless.

(3) Ascertain whether the amount claimed exceeds the adjusted basis of the debt.

(4) Ascertain whether the loss has been correctly reported as a short-term capital loss.

529.9 *(4-23-81)* 4231
Installment Sales

(1) The examiner must be thoroughly familiar with the installment sales provision of the Code and regulations and be certain that all requirements are met. Verify that taxpayers have properly computed the amount realized in the year of sale.

(2) When examining installment sales, determine whether the taxpayer has properly included:

(a) payments in the taxable year other than the initial payment;

(b) earnest money deposit or option payments;

(c) any accrued interest, taxes or other liabilities of the taxpayer paid by the purchaser;

(d) any mortgage paid off for the taxpayer by the buyer;

(e) any mortgage assumed by the purchase over the taxpayer's adjusted basis in the property;

(f) any notes receivable from third parties or other property given the taxpayer; and

(g) noncash down payments, i.e., a trailer, house, car, etc., turned over to the seller.

(3) When a case involves installment sales of real estate parcels or subdivisions, the cost of the realty may contain an amount to cover estimated costs for future improvements. In such event, the taxpayer will be asked to sign Form 921 or 921A (Consent Fixing Period of Limitation Upon Assessment of Income and Profits Tax) as appropriate, extending the time in which a deficiency in tax may be assessed.

529.(10) *(4-23-81)* 4231
Capital Losses

(1) Ascertain whether *capital losses* are reflected as ordinary losses in such cases as:

(a) nonbusiness bad debts;

(b) certain casualty and theft losses which may be required to be offset against capital gains.

(2) Ascertain whether sales which reflected no gain or loss are bona fide. Sales to related individuals below fair market value could result in a gift tax liability to the taxpayer.

(3) Verify that any loss on the sale of rental property has been reported as a business loss and deducted in full in the year of loss.

529.(11) *(4-23-81)* 4231
Capital Loss Carryover

When a taxpayer has a capital loss carryover; the computation of the loss in the year in which it arose and the computation of income for any other year to which the loss should have been carried is subject to verification. Where the loss year and/or the intervening years have not been examined, the taxpayer's retained copies of the returns should be inspected. The examiner should make any adjustment necessary in the intervening year.

530 *(4-23-81)* 4231
Exclusions From Income

531 *(4-23-81)* 4231
Introduction

When a taxpayer reports that the payment is excludable from income, the examiner should verify the source of the payment and in addition verify the following.

532 *(4-23-81)* 4231
Earned Income From Sources Without the United States

(1) There are four basic elements which should be verified for this issue:

(a) determine if the exclusion is claimed as a bona fide resident or for physical presence in a foreign country;

(b) ascertain that the time requirements have been met;

(c) ascertain that no deductions are claimed which are attributable to the excluded income.

(d) ascertain that the excluded income qualifies as earned income.

(2) Residence abroad—In order to determine item (1)(a) above, the examiner should secure such information as the name of the foreign country, the employer's name, and the time period involved. If the taxpayer returned to the United States, find out the reason; e.g., vacation, resignation, completion of work abroad, or temporary assignment in the United States in connection with the job in the foreign country.

(3) Activity in domestic life of foreign country—To further determine item (1)(a) above, ascertain: the type of visa secured for entry into the foreign country; whether the taxpayer has applied for foreign citizenship; whether the taxpayer is required to pay foreign income taxes; address in foreign country; type of dwelling resided in (i.e., purchased home, hotel or other rented quarters, company furnished quarters); address where family resided; local foreign schools attended by taxpayer's children; and citizenship of children and spouse.

(4) Employment abroad—In connection with Item (1)(b) above, the following information would be helpful: name of employer; nature of work performed; and basis of employment, i.e., permanent, for an indefinite period, length of contract; whether or not there is an option to extend the term; and, whether or not taxpayer will return to the United States at the completion of a project. When determining item (1)(d) above, ascertain types of income received by taxpayer, such as salary or wages, commissions or fees, etc.

(5) For further guidance in this area, refer to latest edition of Publication 54, Tax Guide for United States Citizens Abroad.

533 *(4–23–81)* 4231
Disability Income Exclusion

(1) The examiner should verify the age and dollar limitations which are required for this exclusion.

(2) Verify the disability income has been included in income on the return.

(3) The use of Form 2440, Disability Income Exclusion, is recommended in checking this exclusion. Note that Form 2440 includes a required physician's statement. The form contains clear instructions for claiming the exclusion.

534 *(4–23–81)* 4231
Scholarship and Fellowship Grants

(1) When examining this issue, the following questions should be answered:

(a) Is the grantor a tax-exempt organization, or a government unit or agency?

(b) What is the purpose of the grant, the period of the grant, and for whose primary benefit is the grant?

(c) What portion, if any, of the reported grant, constitutes compensation for services rendered or to be rendered?

(d) Is reimbursement for travel and other expenses specifically stated in the grant?

(e) Has the limitation been applied to the amount excludable from income where the recipient is not a candidate for a degree?

(2) A letter from the grantor specifically answering the above questions is usually necessary to verify the issue. Some grantors issue their own publications wherein they indicate the tax consequence to the recipients. Such statements by the grantor should be viewed only as their opinion.

535 *(4–23–81)* 4231
Prizes and Awards

Verify that salespersons have reported expense-paid trips which they have received for exceeding sales quotas. By obtaining a statement from the employer, or determining percentage of time devoted to various activities and reviewing the trip brochure, the examiner should be able to ascertain the purpose and value of the trip.

540 *(4–23–81)* 4231
Adjustments to Income

541 *(4–23–81)* 4231
Moving Expenses

(1) Where a moving expense deduction is claimed and Form 3903 (Moving Expense Adjustment) is not attached to the return, the examiner should secure an analysis of an expense, both reimbursed and unreimbursed. Particular attention should be given to the nature of the expense incurred in connection with the move. Indirect or unrelated expenses such as the cost of refitting rugs or draperies, and penalties for breaking leases, are not deductible moving expenses. Reimbursement of nonqualifying expense constitutes gross income.

(2) In some situations, a statement from the employer, if one is involved, may be desirable. Such a statement should include:

(a) circumstances of the employee's move;

(b) specific expenses and the amount for each type of expense for which reimbursement was made;

(c) amount of reimbursement or allowance included in wages on the Form W-2 Statement;

(d) period of employment in the new location; and

(e) the existence of an agreement between the employer and the taxpayer with reference to arrangements for reimbursing the taxpayer on the sale of a personal residence or an agreement whereby the company purchases the residence that would otherwise be sold at a loss.

(3) Verify expenses from original documents, if possible. Examples include bill of lading, lodging receipts, escrow statements. Verify that expenses used in the computation of this deduction are not included in the computation of the sale of the residence.

542 *(4–23–81)* 4231
Rents, Royalties

542.1 *(4–23–81)* 4231
Rental Income

(1) Scrutinize transactions with related taxpayers and controlled entities. Look for such features as: shifting income, renting for an inadequate consideration to owner, etc.

(a) Verify the net loss from rentals is not attributable to the fact that the property was rented to a relative or friend for an amount less than the fair market rental value of the property.

(b) Determine if the rental loss involves a vacation home used part of the time by the taxpayer.

(2) Determine whether there may have been income from sources for which no corresponding asset is recorded.

(3) Be alert to possible rental contracts which may be conditional sales.

(4) Depreciation, repairs, and other expenses should be analyzed.

(5) Be alert to prepaid rent or lease deposit items that may not be included in income.

(a) Question the taxpayer directly about the weekly or monthly rent received for each unit and periods of vacancy, if any.

(b) Where rents are received in advance on either the cash or the accrual basis and there is no substantial limitation on disposition, they constitute taxable income when received (constructive receipt). Verify these amounts have been included in income.

(c) A bonus paid by the lessee to the lessor upon execution of the lease constitutes income, as does a lump sum amount paid by the lessee in consideration for the cancellation of a lease. Verify that these amounts have been included in income.

(d) Question the taxpayer about tenants providing services in lieu of rental payments. Verify that the taxpayer has reported the value of the services as income if a deduction has been taken for the value of such services.

(6) Determine whether the taxpayer has coin-operated laundry machines located at the rental units and has reported the income.

(7) Look for fictitious rental income for taxpayer's occupancy. Taxpayer may be attempting to make all expenses deductible without apportionment.

542.2 *(4–23–81)* 4231
Royalties

(1) The royalty contract should be scrutinized to determine that the taxpayer has an economic interest, not an economic advantage.

(2) If the taxpayer has given up all rights in the property from which income is derived, verify the amounts received are reported as the sale or exchange of the property rather than royalty income.

(3) The terms of the contract must be scrutinized to determine whether the taxpayer has sold the property, i.e., divested rights, title and interest, or granted a franchise or right for use only, resulting in ordinary income. Verify the income has been properly reported.

(4) Royalties received from copyrights or patents are usually paid on a unit basis, such as, number of books, machines, tickets sold, etc. Determine the number of units printed and sold.

(5) Copyrights and patents have useful lives. Examiners should determine when the work was created as this fact will affect the useful life for depreciation purposes.

543 *(4–23–81)* 4231
Alimony

(1) Request a copy of the document under which payments are made such as, court decree and amendments thereto, written separation agreement, or decree of support. Analyze terms and dates that are material in determining deductibility.

(2) Determine that the amount claimed is an allowable deduction under the applicable provisions of the law.

(3) Verify the amounts paid from cancelled checks or other evidence of payment.

(4) Verify that payment of premiums on an insurance policy irrevocably assigned to a former spouse are reported as alimony income.

(5) Determine the disposition of the marital residence. Transfer of the jointly owned residence may be a taxable event. Payments on a home mortgage, as well as interest and real estate taxes, are not alimony payments if the nonresident spouse is making the payments and has retained an interest of ownership in the property. The payments, in part, however, may constitute an allowable deduction as interest and taxes.

(6) Where possible, check the return of the recipient to see that the amount is included as income or file an Information Report, Form 5346, if the return is out of the immediate jurisdiction.

544 *(4-23-81)* 4231
Individual Retirement Accounts (IRA's)

(1) Examiner should determine that the taxpayer meets the qualifications for an IRA. Check to see that contributions do not exceed the maximum amount allowed. Such excess may be subject to an excise tax.

(2) Ascertain whether the taxpayer ever withdrew retirement money prior to age 59½ (usually not permitted). If the taxpayer is over age 70½, ascertain if taxpayer began drawing out these accumulated funds. The institution holding the funds may be able to provide this information to the taxpayer.

(3) Taxpayers should be questioned as to whether they have "rolled-over" their investment. "Roll-overs" are permitted only once in a specified time period.

(4) Ascertain that the funds received are taxed as ordinary income.

545 *(4-23-81)* 4231
Keogh (H.R. 10) Plans

Self-employed persons are entitled to set up qualified pension plans for themselves and full-time employees. These are sometimes called Keogh or H.R. 10 Plans, the amount contributable depends on the amount of earned (personal service) income. Verify that the taxpayer is not an inactive owner or partner receiving investment income.

546 *(4-23-81)* 4231
Tax-Deferred Annuity Plans

These plans are prevalent among the teaching profession and usually, but not always, the annuity has already been excluded from the amount on the W-2. When this adjustment to income is claimed on a return, determine whether or not the item is included in the W-2 Form.

547 *(4-23-81)* 4231
Employee Business Expenses

547.1 *(4-23-81)* 4231
General

(1) Examiners should obtain an analysis of all expenses both reimbursed and unreimbursed. Discuss with the taxpayer the employer's reimbursement policy. If these is any question as to the amount of the reimbursement or as to the fact that the taxpayer was obligated to incur expenses, the examiner should ask the taxpayer to secure a letter from the employer. The letter should contain a positive statement as to whether the employer was reimbursed and if so, how much and whether the amount is included in the Form W-2. The examiner should consider the employees' position in the company in evaluating the letter from the employer.

(2) Once the question of reimbursement has been determined, the taxpayer's deduction must be substantiated. The expenses should be broken down into the broad categories of transportation, meals, and lodging, etc.

(a) Examine selected items within each of the broad categories.

1 Expenses for cash and credit cards should be verified.

2 If a diary is kept, ascertain the manner and method used in maintaining it. Test a sufficient number of entries to determine the reliability and credibility of the diary. The examiner does not have to accept the diary as being correct even though it conforms with the recordkeeping requirements of Reg. 1.274-5.

3 If the amount of expenses claimed in the diary is disproportionate when compared with the business activities and income of the taxpayer, or if the examiner has reasonable grounds for questioning the credibility of the taxpayer's entries, the taxpayer should be requested to submit further substantiation.

(b) The examiner should review documentary evidence such as receipts, paid bills, or similar evidence to support the expenditures. Where the taxpayer generally has good records, the lack of occasional receipts or other element will not prevent the records from being adequate.

(c) The examiner should determine if the taxpayer is in substantial compliance with the law and regulations. The term "substantial compliance" is not defined in the regulations and is a question of degree. It is an area where the examiner must exercise judgment depending on the facts and circumstances in each case. In exercising judgment, the examiner should consider and document in the workpapers such factors as the number of missing elements, the nature of the missing documentation, the reason why the element was not substantiated in accordance with the adequate records requirements, and the availability of other information to substantiate the expenditure.

(d) Examiners can accept taxpayer's statements, if the statements are not improbable or unreasonable, self-contradictory, or inconsistent with surrounding facts and circumstances. If oral statements are part of the factual record, the workpapers should include:

1 The substance of the oral statement. If considered necessary, an affidavit may be secured from the taxpayer for this purpose.

2 The surrounding facts and circumstances, if any, which collaborate or contradict the oral statement.

3 The conclusion reached and the determinant factors. If the issue involves specific recordkeeping required by law and regulations (e.g., IRC 274), then oral evidence alone *cannot* be substituted for necessary written documentation.

547.2 *(4-23-81)* 4231
Unreimbursed Expenditures of State Department Employees

(1) Authorized Certifying Officers of the State Department at overseas posts certify certain unreimbursed expenditures considered necessary in carrying out the duties of a Foreign Service employee's official position abroad. The certification covers two types of expenditures:

(a) those which would have been reimbursed under Title IX of the Foreign Service Act had sufficient funds been available (representation and official residence expenses); and

(b) expenditures which would have been reimbursed from general purpose allocations had sufficient funds been available (restricted almost exclusively to authorized use of the employee's personal car on official business).

(2) The Authorized Certifying Officers also certify similar expenditures by personnel of the United States Information Agency abroad.

(3) The State Department does not certify representation expenses of its Foreign Service officers and employees while they are stationed in the United States, since there is no accounting to the Department by the employee for such expenses. However, the Department has a procedure by which an employee furnishes his/her immediate supervisor with information concerning expenditures for which he/she wishes to claim tax deductions. If the supervisor believes the expenses were ordinary and necessary and were in the interest of the United States Government, he/she furnishes the employee with an endorsement to that effect which the employee may file with his/her tax return.

(4) Even though a Department of State or United States Information Agency employee submits a certification or endorsement, such as described in (1) or (3) above, the examiner may, when appropriate, require additional substantiation.

550 *(4-23-81)* 4231
Computation of Tax

551 *(4-23-81)* 4231
Minimum Tax

(1) Examiners should scrutinize returns and ask taxpayer if they had any transactions involving the following items of tax preference.

(a) Accelerated depreciation on real property—

1 Low-income rental housing under IRC 167(k) or amortization of certified historic structures under IRC 191

2 Other real property

(b) Accelerated depreciation on personal property subject to a lease

(c) Amortization of certified pollution control facilities

(d) Amortization of railroad rolling stock

(e) Amortization of on-the-job training facilities

(f) Amortization of child care facilities

(g) Reserves for losses on bad debts of financial institutions

(h) Stock options

(i) Depletion

(j) Intangible drilling costs

(k) Capital gains

(l) Large itemized deductions

(2) Examiners should verify that each member of a partnership has taken into account the distributive share of the partnership's items of income and deductions that are items of tax preference.

(a) For beneficiaries of estates and trusts, the total items of tax preference for the year are apportioned between the estate or trust and the beneficiaries on the basis of the income of the estate or trust allocable to each.

(b) Tax preference items on forms 1120S (U.S. Small Business Corporation) are apportioned pro rata among the shareholders in the same way any corporate losses would be apportioned. If capital gains are taxed to both the corporation and the shareholder, the capital gains can be an item of tax preference at both the corporate and individual level.

(3) Form 4625, Computation of Minimum Tax—Individuals, should be used to compute the add-on minimum tax. Form 6251, Alternative Minimum Tax Computation, should be used to compute the alternative minimum tax.

552 *(4-23-81)* 4231
Maximum Tax

(1) Examiners should verify whether the earned income on Form 4726, Maximum Tax on Personal Service Income, is limited to wages, professional fees, and other amounts received as compensation for personal services actually rendered. Passive income such as interest and dividends should not be included in earned income.

(2) Where the taxpayer is an officer-stockholder of a closely-held corporation, a determination will be made as to the reasonableness of the taxpayer's compensation for personal services. Only that portion of income received which is deemed reasonable for the services rendered qualifies as earned income.

(3) Examiners should:

(a) Be aware of the effect of capital investment. Where a taxpayer is engaged in an unincorporated trade or business in which both personal services and capital are material income-producing factors, earned income is limited to a reasonable allowance for personal services.

(b) Be alert for situations where the taxpayers include 100 percent of their profits from a trade or business as earned income.

(c) Recognize that "inactive" or "limited" partners, or those receiving distributions from "out of district partnerships," usually contribute little or no personal services to the business.

(4) Verification should be made of the taxpayer's allocation of IRC 62 deductions between earned and unearned income.

(5) Determine if the taxpayer has actually rendered the services for which he/she has been compensated. If the income is for future services, it does not qualify as earned income.

553 *(4-23-81)* 4231
Income Averaging

(1) Examiners should consider this option which is available to taxpayers, especially when large adjustments are being proposed.

(2) The examiner should ask the taxpayer to provide copies of prior year returns which are needed to make this computation. Examiners should question taxpayers about prior audits which may have increased base year taxable income.

560 *(4-23-81)* 4231
Credits

561 *(4-23-81)* 4231
Introduction

This section discusses the most common credits. Although several of these credits will be found only on business returns, they are all listed in this section. The examiner should question the taxpayer as to any allowable credits which may not have been claimed on the return.

562 *(4-23-81)* 4231
Credit for the Elderly

(1) Examiners should verify taxpayer age, filing status, AGI and type of retirement plan since these items directly effect the computation of the credit.

(2) Taxpayers should be asked whether they are receiving Social Security, Railroad Retirement, or other excludible pensions. Verify that these items have been used to reduce the amounts on which the credit was determined.

(3) Schedules R & RP (Form 1040), Credit for the Elderly, are useful worksheets for computing the credit.

563 *(4-23-81)* 4231
Investment Credit

(1) The investment credit is a mandatory credit. Taxpayers claiming this credit should attach Form 3468 (Computation of Investment Credit) to the return.

(2) In verifying the credit, the examiner should ascertain that the allowable credit does not exceed the total of the correct income tax and the correct statutory credits for retirement income and foreign tax. Adjustment of one or more of these items may affect the investment credit.

(3) The general rules for determining basis are applicable in the verification of the basis of new section 38 property.

(4) The examiner should verify that the basis of used section 38 property or the basis of new section 38 property acquired as a replacement for property which was destroyed by casualty, etc., has been properly computed.

(5) Schedule D, Gains and Losses from Sales or Exchanges of Property, and Form 4797, Supplemental Schedule of Gains and Losses, should be reviewed for disposition of property which qualified for the investment credit. If appropriate, the examiner should consider recapture provisions. The recapture rule is also applicable if the property ceases to qualify as section 38 property.

564 *(4-23-81)* 4231
Foreign Tax Credit

(1) Ascertain that the foreign tax has been paid or accrued and is an income, war profits, or excess profits tax and has been imposed on the taxpayer.

(2) A foreign tax credit or deduction claimed is an immediate flag to the examiner that income from foreign sources should also be reflected on the return. Where all foreign income is exempt from gross income, no credit or deduction for foreign taxes is allowable.

(3) Verify a credit has not been taken for excess tax payments which would be refunded by a foreign country with which the U.S. has a tax treaty if a claim were filed.

(4) Form 1116, Computation of Foreign Tax Credit, should be used as a worksheet to compute this credit.

565 *(4-23-81)* 4231
Energy Credit

(1) This credit is allowed for energy saving items installed in a taxpayer's principal residence.

(2) Examiners should verify:

(a) the item qualifies for the credit

(b) the cost of the item from source documents

(c) the taxpayer has reduced the basis of the residence by the credit claimed.

(3) Form 5695, Energy Credits, is useful to compute this credit.

(4) In connection with the verification of credits for energy conservation property or the examination of producers or distributors of insulation, examiners should refer apparent violations of flame resistance and corrosiveness safety standards set by the Consumer Product Safety Commission to the Director, Examination Division, Attention CP:E:G:E.

566 *(4-23-81)* 4231
Earned Income Credit

(1) Verify the taxpayer's income and dependents.

(2) Determine if others in the household may be claiming the credit for the same exemption.

(3) Ask the taxpayer if they have filed Form W-5, Earned Income Credit Advance Payment Certificate, with their employer.

(4) Inspect Form W-2, Wage and Tax Statement, for amount of advance EIC payment.

(5) Adjust the Earned Income Credit whenever a change is made to adjusted gross income.

567 *(4-23-81)* 4231
Child Care Credit

(1) The examiner should verify the amounts claimed and determine that the credit is taken in the proper year.

(2) The examiner should determine the reasonableness of payments, the relationship of the payee, and whether the services were provided to a qualifying individual.

(3) For taxable years beginning after December 31, 1978, examiners should be alert to changes in the law regarding payments to relatives.

(4) Since some child care expenses can also qualify as medical expenses, examiners should check for double deductions.

(5) Form 2441, Credit for Child and Dependent Care Expenses, is a useful worksheet in computing child care expenses.

(6) When cash wages of $50 or more have been paid in a calendar quarter for domestic services, the examiner should verify that Form 942, Employer's Quarterly Tax Return for Household Employees, has been filed.

(7) If the wages paid were $1,000 or more in a calendar quarter, the examiner should verify that Form 940, Employer's Annual Federal Unemployment Tax Return, has also been filed.

568 *(4-23-81)* 4231
Work Incentive (WIN) Credit

(1) Verify that the wages were paid —
(a) Under a qualified program, and
(b) to eligible employees

(2) Verify that the deduction for wages has been reduced by the amount of the credit.

(3) Verify that the taxpayer has not claimed the Targeted Jobs Credit if WIN credit has been claimed.

(4) Form 4874, Credit for Work Incentive (WIN) Program Expenses, should be used as a worksheet to compute this credit.

569 *(4-23-81)* 4231
Jobs Credit

(1) Verify the wages were —
(a) subject to FUTA
(b) paid to a qualified individual
(c) within the maximum limitation

(2) Verify all employees have been certified by a local designated agency (generally the State Employment Security Agency).

(3) Verify that the deduction for wages has been reduced by the amount of the Jobs Credit.

(4) Form 5884, Jobs Credit, should be used as a worksheet to compute this credit.

56(10) *(9-3-81)* 4231
Royalty Owners Credit

(1) This credit is allowed for individuals that have paid or had withholding of Windfall Profit Tax on domestic crude oil production.

(2) Examiners should verify whether:
(a) taxpayer qualifies for the credit,
(b) taxpayer does not have to share the credit with another member of taxpayer's family,
(c) the credit equals the amount of withholding for Windfall Profit Tax,
(d) royalty owner credit not previously claimed,
(e) taxpayer is claiming any other credit or refund for overpaid Windfall Profit Tax, and
(f) taxpayer has reduced amount of Windfall Profit Tax deduction by credit claimed.

570 *(4-23-81)* 4231
Schedule A—Deductions

(See Pro-forma Aids in Exhibits 200-1 through 200-1 cont.(7))

In verifying deductions claimed by a taxpayer, examiners should also be alert to the possibility of unclaimed deductions. If one examination reveals such unclaimed items, they should be allowed in the examination report.

571 *(4-23-81)* 4231
Medical Expense

(1) Verify amounts claimed and determine that the deduction is claimed in the proper year.
(a) Determine whether medical expenditures of a capital nature increase the value of the property.
(b) Determine that costs of transportation do not include amounts spent for board and lodging.

(2) Ascertain whether any insurance reimbursement has been made or is expected.

(3) Determine that the expense was incurred primarily for the diagnosis, cure, mitigation, treatment of prevention of disease, or for the purpose of affecting any structure or function of the body (including transportation and medical insurance).

(4) Medicines should be separated so that the proper limitation can be applied.

(5) Determine that the percentage limitation, the maximum amount limitation and the dependency qualification have been correctly applied.

(6) Be aware that amounts allowed as child care expense cannot also be claimed as medical expense.

572 *(4-23-81)* 4231
Taxes

(1) Verify amounts claimed and determine that the deduction has been taken in the proper year.

(2) Determine whether the tax is of the type deductible in accordance with the rules and regulations.

(3) Ascertain that no foreign income taxes have been claimed as a deduction where election has been made to claim the foreign tax credit.

(4) Examiners should verify that the taxpayer has not claimed duplicate deductions for taxes, i.e., itemized deduction and rental expense.

573 *(4-23-81)* 4231
Interest

(1) Verify amount claimed and determine that the deduction has been taken in the proper year.

(2) Determine whether the payments are for interest or for other items, such as discounts,

finance charges or principal. Finance charges on revolving charge accounts are considered to be interest and are deductible.

(3) Ascertain whether the interest payments are made on a valid, existing debt owed by the taxpayer. If there is a joint and several liability, the entire amount of interest is deductible by the payor. Interest paid as a guarantor does not constitute an interest deduction.

(4) Ascertain whether the debt was incurred to carry or purchase the income from which is tax-exempt, or was incurred to purchase a single premium life insurance, endowment or annuity contact after March 1, 1954.

(5) Loans from related individuals should be analyzed to determine that the interest rate paid does not exceed the normal rate for available money.

(6) When verifying an interest deduction, the examiner should inspect the instruments of indebtedness, such as mortgage statements, loan contract, etc. Cancelled checks are not usually evidence of the liability or payment of interest, and generally, should be supported by documentation.

(7) If the taxpayer maintains brokerage accounts, the statements should be analyzed. Interest charged on margin accounts should not be netted against interest or dividend income. It must be claimed as an itemized deduction.

(8) Examiners should verify that the same interest deduction is not claimed twice, i.e., Itemized Deductions and Rental Expense.

(9) Examiners should be alert for situations where taxpayers have claimed deductions for accrued interest on existing liabilities and foreclosure proceedings have subsequently occurred. Verify the taxpayer has included the difference between the liability per the books and the liability which was relieved by the foreclosure as income.

(10) If the taxpayer moved during the year under examination, the examiner should check the allocation of interest on the closing statement.

(11) If the taxpayer assumed a mortgage during the year under examination, the examiner must make a proper allocation between the buyer and the seller since the lender will normally issue a statement on total interest paid during the year for that mortgage.

574 *(4-23-81)* 4231
Contributions

(1) Verify amounts claimed and determine that the deduction has been taken in the proper year.

(2) Determine whether the payments were made to qualified organizations. An individual may claim a charitable contribution deduction to a church that has not been recognized by the Service as tax exempt. Such deduction is not barred merely because the church has never applied for recognition of exempt status. Similarly, when an organization has applied but has not provided the Service with sufficient information upon which to make a favorable determination of exempt status, a charitable deduction is not automatically barred.

(3) Determine that percentage limitation is correctly computed, has not been exceeded, and that any contribution carryover is correct.

(4) Determine if contributions claimed are nondeductible personal expenses and ascertain if donor received benefits or consideration in return.

(5) Where a taxpayer claims out of pocket expenses in rendering donated services to a qualified organization, the examiner should determine whether there was reimbursement by the organization.

(6) In a case where property is contributed, ascertain:
(a) whether ordinary income property, capital gain property, or a combination are involved,
(b) cost and fair market value at time of gift, and
(c) whether donor retains any control over the property. If inventory or stock in trade is involved, be alert to double deductions.

(7) When examining unsubstantiated cash contributions, examiners should ask themselves this question: Is the total amount of contributions claimed reasonable in relation to the amount available out of which contributions could have been made? Such available cash must take into consideration the amount of gross income less the other deductions claimed on the return, personal living expenses, income tax withheld and any estimated tax payments.

575 *(4-23-81)* 4231
Casualty and Theft Losses

(1) Ascertain that a loss has actually been incurred. Property may have been fully depreciated, nonexistent, sold, previously expensed, lost, etc. It may be necessary to verify the adjusted basis of the property. In such a case, the taxpayer should be required to submit evidence as to the original cost, subsequent improvements, and the amount of depreciation claimed in prior years.

(2) Be alert to the possibility that cash stolen may not have been included in income.

(3) Trace handling of losses involving inventory or stock in trade to ascertain that a double deduction is not claimed.

(4) Ascertain that the loss is claimed in the proper year—casualty losses generally in the year incurred—theft or embezzlement in the year discovered.

(5) Determine if gains from involuntary conversion are reported which would change the tax treatment of the casualty and theft losses.

(6) Determine that the amount claimed is equal to the difference in value before and after the loss (limited by cost or other basis), and that the taxpayer was the owner of the property. If a personal residence is involved in the loss deduction, the examiner should ensure that the basis of the property has been reduced for all gains previously unrecognized.

(7) Ascertain that insurance proceeds or claims, salvage proceeds, or salvage value have been properly taken into account.

(8) Casualty losses affecting items, incidental to real property, such as trees or shubbery, must be verified as a loss of a minor portion of the asset. The shrinkage in market value, limited to adjusted basis, which forms the allowable deduction, must be determined by reference to the property as a whole, both as to FMV and adjusted basis.

(9) Be alert to the possibility that the taxpayer may be engaged in arson-for-profit activities.

(a) Indicators of possible arson schemes with potential tax consequences are:

1 Failure to report insurance proceeds which exceed the basis of the property destroyed by fire.

2 Failure to report the correct adjusted basis of the property destroyed.

3 Failure to reduce a casualty loss claimed on a return by the insurance proceeds received.

4 Reducing insurance proceeds by payoffs to "torches"—individuals starting the fires.

(b) Examiners should consider using in-depth examination techniques in cases where the taxpayer is suspected of being engaged in arson-for-profit activities.

576 *(4-23-81)* 4231
Educational Expenses

(1) Determine if the expenses were primarily incurred for the purpose of maintaining or improving skills or meeting express requirements for retention of status.

(2) Examiners should be alert to the special situation of school teachers. Often the requirement of a local board are different than those of a State Board of Education. A teacher may be incurring educational expenses in order to meet the minimum requirements of one of the boards.

(3) If the educational expense involves overseas travel, the tour folio, registration receipt, and transcript of studies from the overseas educational institution should be reviewed. Consideration should be given to the amount of time devoted to educational pursuits.

(4) Verify amounts claimed and determine that the deduction is claimed in the proper year.

(5) Ascertain whether any reimbursement has been received from an employer, governmental agency, or other third party.

577 *(4-23-81)* 4231
Union Dues

Verify the amount claimed includes only Labor Union dues and initiation fees and does not include payment for sickness, accident or death benefits.

578 *(4-23-81)* 4231
Return Preparer Penalties

(1) Examiners should ascertain whether a return was prepared for compensation by someone other than the taxpayer.

(2) If the taxpayer has utilized the services of a preparer, and preparer penalties may be applicable, the examiner should refer to IRM 426(27).5 for Return Preparer Penalties.

580 *(4-23-81)* 4231
Business Returns

581 *(4-23-81)* 4231
General

581.1 *(4-23-81)* 4231
Introduction

Before beginning an examination, examiners must have a knowledge of the type of service performed or merchandise sold. They should also know the approximate volume of business, the expected gross profit ratio or markup practices, and the method of accounting. In addition, the taxpayer should be questioned about banking methods used and whether all receipts are deposited.

581.2 *(4-23-81)* 4231
Basis of Accounting

(1) Examiners must determine at the beginning of an examination the basis of accounting, that is, whether cash or accrual, and in the course of the examination must see that whatever basis is used is consistently maintained as to all accounts.

(2) Unusual items of income and deductions which tend to distort a taxpayer's income should in every case receive special attention and comment.

(3) Items of income and expense deductions which occur in each taxable period should be scrutinized for any inconsistency in the manner of handling.

581.3 *(4-23-81)* 4231
Examination of Employer's Accounting Procedures for Employees' Expenses

(1) Examination of an employer's return may disclose allowances or reimbursements made by the employer for travel, entertainment, and other such business expenses incurred by employees, including officers of a corporation. Unless the total amount of allowances or reimbursements is insignificant, the examiner will ascertain during each such examination whether the taxpayer uses acceptable accounting procedures in requiring an accounting of business expenses incurred by employees.

(2) If the examiner determines that the accounting required by the employer from the employees adequately reflects the correctness of travel, entertainment, and other such business expenses incurred by officers and employees, he/she will include a statement regarding his/her finding in his/her report transmittal or workpapers.

582 *(4-23-81)* 4231
Gross Receipts or Sales

(1) In the initial testing of the sales account the following techniques may be considered:

(a) Test methods of handling cash to see if all receipts are included in income. Scan daily cash reconciliations and related book entries and bank deposits. Note any undeposited cash receipts on hand at the end of the year.

(b) Test reported gross receipts by the gross profit ratio method. (See gross profit ratio test, Text 584)

(c) Note items unusual in origin, nature, or amount in the books of original entry and test them by reference to original sales slips, contracts, job record book, bank deposits, etc. Also, check selected entries made at different times of the year, including some at the beginning of the year. Test check footings and postings to the general ledger.

(d) Review bank statements and deposit slips for unusual items. Test check deposits by comparing selected items to cash receipts and income entries on the books. Determine the net increase or decrease in the bank balances at the beginning and end of the year. If a taxpayer has not reconciled the bank statements, the examiner must do so for this analysis. Compare the ending balance to the balance per books.

(e) Scan the sales account in the ledger for unusual entries. Test entries from the general journal and sales journal. Compare total receipts to total business income bank deposits and reconcile any differences.

(f) Be alert to the possibility of income which may be taxable even though not appearing on the books (dealer reserve income, constructive, receipt, income from foreign sources etc.)

(2) If the results of these initial tests compare favorably with gross receipts reported, further verification would generally be based on the particular circumstances of the case. For example, a high percentage of cash receipts which are not regularly deposited or properly accounted for would be a basis for further testing.

(3) If further verification is necessary, the following techniques should be considered.

Nonbusiness Returns

710 *(8-30-76)* 4231
Introduction

(1) The examination of a nonbusiness return very seldom involves the audit of a set of books. However, if books do exist the audit techniques described under adequate records, Chapter 600, should be followed.

(2) The following guidelines are not intended to be a complete coverage of every question that may arise in the audit of a nonbusiness return, but they are intended to serve as an aid in the solution of the most common problems that will be encountered.

720 *(8-30-76)* 4231
General

721 *(8-30-76)* 4231
Occupation

(1) The occupations line of a tax return is of most significance during the precontact stage of an examination. Its principal significance comes from its relationship to other items which are or should be on the return. Examples of such inter-relationships are:

(a) Is income from tips of waiters, cab drivers, Pullman porters, etc. reported on the return? It normally should be.

(b) The occupation of a salesperson associated with the employer's name as shown on the return is often of use in judging allowability of expense deductions, or determining whether they should be deducted as an employee business expense or an itemized deduction. Examples are as follows.

1 A salesman at a local retail store usually should not claim entertainment expense.

2 An automobile salesperson's business expenses should usually appear only as an itemized deduction (except for possible transportation expense). As many of these salesmen are furnished a car by their employer, potential personal use should be ascertained for inclusion in income.

3 Milk or beer truck driver-salesmen, or combination insurance collector-salesmen should not deduct employee business expenses other than for local transportation.

4 Any salesman in out-of-town travel status who does not include car expenses among his business expenses should be asked why. If the car is furnished him by the company is there any personal use of it?

(c) Members of certain trades usually work for contractors from whom they receive a W-2. Due to the nature of their work, they are apt to do part-time work for homeowners and others who are not likely to file W-2s. They should be directly questioned as to the possible existence of such income. Carpenters, painters, plumbers, electricians and the like are in this category.

(d) Executives, public employees, salesmen and union men who deduct expenses are often reimbursed for them. As examples, union men who deduct travel expense (other than local transportation) usually receive some payment to cover that expense; a city building inspector is usually furnished mileage. Examiners should question if such expense offset exist.

(e) A wife whose occupation is listed as housewife would be inconsistent with a child care deduction. Of course there could easily be a good explanation for this apparent inconsistency.

722 *(8-30-76)* 4231
Exemptions and Dependents

(1) If there is no exemption claimed for a wife (or husband), particularly where dependent children are listed, or even where an exemption is claimed for a wife, attention should be given to whether a separate return is being filed by the spouse. This item is significant with respect to the right to use the standard deduction or the tax table, the top limitation of the standard deduction, or the right to compute the tax under the joint return provisions.

(2) A difficulty encountered in this category is the determination of the excess of fifty-percent support required in nonmultiple support cases. If the claimed dependent resides in the taxpayer's home the difficulty is increased because amounts spent for the general support of such a dependent, such as for food, clothing and lodging, are not of the type that can be substantiated by ordinary documentation. The examiner should take into consideration the total income of the taxpayer and number of persons in the family unit. The determination of what constitutes support should be made in accordance with the principles set forth in Rev. Rul. 235, 1953-2 C.B. 23, as modified by Rev. Rul. 58-302, 1958-1 C.B. 62, and Rev. Rul 64-222, 1964-2 C.B. 47.

(3) In determining the amount furnished by the dependent himself/herself, the age of the dependent should lead to a question as to whether social security benefits exist. Welfare payments, relief and incidental earnings of the

dependent should also be considered. If the dependent is other than a child of the taxpayer, raise the question as to whether other persons related to the dependent are also contributing to the support.

(4) The taxpayer should be questioned as to the age of his/her youngest child. Sometimes a child born after the end of the taxable year but before the filing date is claimed as an exemption.

730 *(8-30-76)* 4231
Income

731 *(8-30-76)* 4231
Salaries, Wages, Bonuses, etc.

(1) Subsection 721, Occupations, includes certain techniques applicable to income of this nature. Additional techniques available for use where appropriate are as follows.

(a) Ask taxpayer whether his/her spouse worked during the year. Frequently where the spouse earned less than $600.00 during the year, the income is omitted from the tax return under a mistaken belief the spouse is a dependent.

(b) Ask taxpayer if he/she received any Christmas or other bonus during the year and, if so, whether it was included in his/her Form W-2. If taxpayer did receive a bonus, and does not know if it was so included, the information should be secured from his/her employer.

(c) If taxpayer's occupation is such that he/she was employed by a number of different employers during the year, so that he/she had several W-2s, it is possible that one or more W-2s were not listed on the tax return. This is particularly true of construction workers, itinerant farm laborers and the like. In these cases it is wise to have the taxpayer account for his/her employment chronologically throughout the year. He/she should be requested to produce his/her retained W-2 copies for in some cases the originals are removed from the filed Form 1040 before the agent receives it. The retained copies might also include W-2s which the taxpayer did not list on his/her return, because he/she had not yet received them at the time the return was filed.

(d) The possibilities in (c) above apply also where the returns of minor children and students are being examined. In certain cases husbands should also be questioned whether their wives worked as domestic servants for often W-2s are not filed in such cases since there is no withholding tax involved.

(e) Tip income is difficult to establish. Cab drivers' tips are sometimes established by applying 15% to their individual bookings or meter readings. Their employers may show these bookings on their W-2s. If they do not, but the drivers' salaries are a percentage of bookings, the bookings can be determined by working backward from the W-2 as in the following example.

Salary per W-2	$1,750.00
Percentage of bookings which is paid as salary	35%
Bookings as reconstructed (100/35 × $1,750.00)	$5,000.00
Estimated tip income, 15% thereof	$750.00

1 Waitresses' tips are difficult to estimate. In rare cases it may be advisable to ascertain the restaurant sales for the year, divide by the average number of waitresses, and then assume that 15% thereof is the individual's tips for the year. In those cases where a waitress is furnished meals at the start or end of the work day it is likely they were not furnished for the convenience of the employer and are accordingly taxable to the employee. The waitress should be questioned as to this possibility.

2 It is the practice in some hotels to add a percentage to the total of each bill rendered for banquets and other catered events to cover tips to waiters. These tips are then distributed to the waiters by the hotel, or disbursed to the head waiter who in turn is expected to distribute them to the waiters. In examining the returns of such waiters, the hotel records provide a convenient source of information from which to verify income from tips.

3 Under legislation enacted in 1965, cash tips will count toward Social Security and Railroad Retirement Benefits beginning January 1, 1966. The law requires an employee who receives $20 or more in cash tips in any one month to report them to his/her employer by the 10th day of the following month. However, all tip income must be included on an employee's income tax return even though it is less than $20 a month and not required to be reported to his/her employer for tax withholding purposes.

4 The Service has issued Form 4070 (Employee's Reports on Tips) which may be used by employees to report cash tips to their employers. This form along with a booklet, Document 5636 (Employee's Daily Record of Tips and Report of Tips to Employees) is available so that employees can keep a daily record of tips. As audit techniques are developed under these new provisions, they should be reported on Form 3038. (Audit Technique Item).

(f) If listed salaries indicate a husband and wife are working for their own closely held corporation, the examiner should determine whether the corporate return has been selected for examination. If it has not, consideration should be given to whether the wife actually worked for the corporation. If she did no work, the corporation return should be examined.

732 *(8-30-76)* 4231
Sickness and Accident Pay Exclusion

(1) The use of Form 2440 is recommended in checking an exclusion under IRC 105(d). Particularly note the instructions on Form 2440 (Statement to Support Exclusion of Sick Pay). A copy is provided as Exhibit 7. If the form is properly filled out, the correctness of the amount excluded on the return can be readily determined.

(2) The following are likely to be the more prevalent sources of error where sick pay is concerned.

(a) *Failure to include in income the benefits received from all sources*—Some employees receive benefits from more than one source for the same period of absence-from-work. Employers and insurance companies are the usual sources of such payments, but, where the employee is a union member, he/she should be questioned whether he/she also received benefits from a union welfare fund. Many such funds are supported not by dues, but by assessments against contractors who hire the individual union members. They are thus employer financed plans.

(b) *Exclusion of payments that are not in income because they are specifically not taxable*—The principal example of this is the case of the worker covered by the Railroad Retirement Act. Such a worker receives a specified amount per day from Railroad Retirement for all absence due to sickness after a specified number of days. This payment is not subject to tax. Because of this, it is not included in any W-2. Employees may not be aware of this and may attempt to exclude it on the tax return.

(c) *In the case of a salesman reporting sick pay, it should be determined if the amount is actually a salary*—In some cases the amount may be the weekly "draws" against his/her earned commissions. His/her employer may not even have an accepted plan.

1 If there is an exclusion of income under IRC 104 or 105(b), the examiner should determine whether there is any medical expense deduction in the current or preceding year. Where there is, the possibility exists that the amount claimed as excludable should offset the medical deduction in the current year, or by reported as income if the medical deduction was claimed in a prior year. In States where workmen's compensation payments contain a specific element of medical reimbursement, such reimbursement should be isolated.

2 Where a taxpayer has been injured and received a payment (whether through suit or otherwise), and the payment does not designate whether it covers medical expenses, other damages, or both, consideration should be given toward applying a portion of it to the recovery, or as an offset, to any claimed medical expenses.

733 *(8-30-76)* 4231
Travel and Entertainment

(1) A detailed discussion of audit techniques in this area will be furnished at a later date in Chapter 600. The limited discussion in this subsection concerns certain expenses which are usually not reflected in a set of books.

(2) If the return does not include a schedule of expenses, the examiner should have the taxpayer complete Form 2106. A copy is provided as Exhibit 8. A taxpayer's occupation can be an aid in determining whether he/she is reimbursed. Generally speaking, salaried persons are reimbursed by their employers for expenses incurred. If there is any question as to the reimbursement or as to the fact that the taxpayer was obligated to incur expenses, the examiner should ask the taxpayer to secure a letter from his/her employer. Since most employers are interested in the financial welfare of their employees, the wording of such a letter may be vague. It is not sufficient that the letter merely states that the employee is obligated to travel in the interest of his/her employer. The agent should insist on the letter containing a positive statement as to whether or not the employee was reimbursed and, if so, how much and whether the amount is included in the Form W-2. Such a letter would be of doubtful value if the employer is a corporation in which the taxpayer is the principal stockholder or if the employer is a related individual.

(3) This situation is usually apparent when the taxpayer's name is the same or similar to the employers, for example:

Taxpayer	Employer
John and Mary Doe	John Doe, Inc.
Richard Roe	Roe and Doe and Co.
John Smith	M. Smith, Co.

(4) In such a situation the examiner should find out whether the employer's return is being examined by another agent, in which case any information as to reimbursement can be secured from the other agent. If the return is not being examined, the agent can inspect the retained business return for the deduction for travel and entertainment expense and determine whether both returns should be examined concurrently.

(5) In cases where the deduction is reconstructed from secondary evidence and the amount is substantial, the agent should reconcile the amount so determined by preparing an analysis of cash availability.

(6) In other words, the total of all funds received from salaries, commissions, drawings on account, investments and savings, less estimated amounts spent for living expenses, actual savings and investments will reflect the maximum amount that could have been spent for entertainment.

(7) In determining expenses allowable for the operation of an automobile, the approximate total mileage involved can often be ascertained from reference to any repair bills at the beginning and at the end of the year, because quite often the bill will reflect the mileage reading.

(8) Assistance in the allocation of automobile expenses between business and personal use can sometimes be received by reference to the automobile insurance policy which usually states whether other members of the family operate the vehicle. If the taxpayer uses the car in traveling to and from work, the measurable mileage for that purpose alone, when related to the total year's mileage, may be considerably over the taxpayer's own estimated personal portion.

(9) In some cases, taxpayers may claim a deduction in terms of a flat allowance per mile for automobile operating expenses. See Rev. Proc. 74-23, 1974-2 C.B. 476.

(10) Additional guidelines in the form of answers to specific questions relating to this topic are contained in 1963-1 C.B. 447, and 1963-2 C.B. 129.

734 *(8-30-76)* 4231
Dividend Income

(1) The audit of dividend income reported by the taxpayer should not be limited to the information documents attached to the return.

(2) The verification should include classification, time of receipt, and total reported. If more than $100 is excluded, the ownership of securities by both husband and wife should be verified.

(3) The method used by the taxpayer in determining his/her dividend income should be secured. Understanding the method used may suggest the most appropriate way to check for accuracy. A list of securities owned at the beginning of the taxable year, used in conjunction with subsequent sales and acquisitions, will permit the most accurate check.

(4) If the taxpayer merely records dividends when he/she receives them, and also keeps some securities in the broker's custody, the broker's monthly statements should be checked carefully for dividends credited to the account. Most taxpayers who have any security trades during the year retain their monthly statements. The verification of dividend income should include checking these statements.

(5) Information regarding dividend payments by publicly held corporations is available in many forms in audit division libraries. Sources of information include Moody's, Poor's and Fitch's Dividend Services, issued annually.

(6) Farmers' cooperative dividends are not true dividends and are treated in several different ways. Farmers' returns should be examined carefully to see that patronage dividends are properly handled. If shown as dividends, they are not subject to the dividend credit if received from a tax-exempt farmers' cooperative.

(7) Distributions by corporations, which are in whole or in part nontaxable, are tabulated in various services such as Prentice-Hall and Commerce Clearing House Capital Adjustment Services and in the Internal Revenue Manual (see IRM 455(10) and Exhibits to IRM 4550). Corporations whose distributions most commonly have irregular features include railroads, mining companies, investment companies, mutual funds, and utility companies.

(8) Dividends paid by taxpayers in connection with short sales of securities may not be subtracted from dividend income. Publication 17, Your Federal Income Tax, should be consulted for explanation on reporting dividends on stock sold short as well as for further details on reporting other dividends.

(9) Savings and loan and credit union interest, though commonly called dividends, is treated as interest income for tax purposes.

(10) In cases where dividends are reported from foreign corporations, care should be taken to see that a taxpayer has not deducted foreign taxes paid on these dividends before reporting them and then, elsewhere on the return, taken a credit for these same taxes.

735 *(8-30-76)* 4231

Interest Income

(1) The verification of interest income should also be made in conjunction with the audit of capital transactions. If interest bearing securities were sold during the year check to see if any interest should have been reported. The interest accrued to date of sale is sometimes included as part of the proceeds, instead of as interest income.

(2) Where bonds have been acquired "flat," i.e. with interest in default, a check should be made to determine that any interest received which accrued after the purchase date is reflected as interest income. The aforementioned Capital Adjustment Services indicate the details and interest payment dates of bonds with interest in default.

(3) If the taxpayer maintains brokerage accounts the statements should be analyzed. Interest charged on margin accounts may not be netted against interest or dividend income. It must be claimed as an itemized deduction. In the analysis, determine whether interest paid to carry tax-exempt securities has been deducted.

(4) The taxpayer should always be asked whether he/she has cashed any Government bonds, held any matured Government bonds or had any savings accounts during the taxable year. Some States require that the individual have an account as a prerequisite to leasing a safe deposit box in a savings bank. If a deduction for the rental of the box is claimed in such cases, the existence of a savings account is indicated. Similarly, if the taxpayer uses savings bank money orders or cashier's checks to substantiate deductions, inquiry should be directed to a savings account.

(5) Other interest income items often erroneously omitted from returns include interest on paid up insurance policies and interest on prior year tax refunds. If property was sold in prior or current years and a purchase money mortgage constituted part payment, interest income should be reflected in the return. A common error is to regard all collections on account of the mortgage as principal until it is fully paid.

(6) Interest income from closely held corporations in which the taxpayer is a principal should receive close scrutiny. Consideration should be given to the procedures in IRM 4263 concerning the need for examination of the corporation return where warranted.

736 *(8-30-76)* 4231

Net Operating Loss Deduction

Occasionally, on a nonbusiness return, a net operating loss deduction will appear because the taxpayer is no longer in business or the net operating loss arose from a casualty loss. In either case the computation of the loss in the year in which it arose and the computation of income for any other year to which the loss should have been carried is subject to verification. If the loss arose from a casualty see 746.

737 *(8-30-76)* 4231

Gains and Losses from Sale or Exchange of Property

(1) The technique to be used in the audit of the gains and losses reported on a return will usually vary depending on the nature of the asset disposed of. The two broad classifications of assets, both under the law and for purposes of audit approach, are capital assets and all other assets.

(2) *Capital Assets*—The verification of gains and losses involves several elements: The selling price, expenses of sale, the adjusted basis of the property, and the holding period.

(a) The most common capital transactions appearing on nonbusiness returns are sales of securities. Normally they are effected through brokers, if they are listed securities. When such is the case, an analysis of the brokerage "bought" and "sold" slips and the broker's monthly statements is the best approach to this phase of an examination. The transaction slips state the purchase price or the sales price, the commissions, the transfer taxes (Federal and local), and accured interest where appropriate. In addition, the dates of the transaction are clearly set forth.

(b) Verification of capital transactions from brokers' slips and statements should be made in conjunction with auditing of interest and dividend income as set forth in 734 and 735. This dual check can indicate both errors in the dividend and interest reported and also omitted transactions.

(c) If the capital transactions reported were not made through a broker, the proceeds and expenses of sale should receive a closer scrutiny. Disposition of securities in a closely held corporation should be checked for the valuation of property received, when in a form other than cash. This valuation should be based on fair market value. A common error is the reporting of gain or loss based on the surplus or deficit. See (21)(10)0 dealing with valuation of property.

(3) *Holding Period*—Because the Code varies its treatment of gains or losses depending

on the holding period of the capital asset, the dates of acquisition and disposal are important. They are also important in connection with losses arising out of wash sales and in cases of property acquired in a tax free exchange. See IRC 1223 pertaining to holding period in such cases.

(a) The general rule for determining holding period is that such period begins the day after contractual purchase (regardless of later delivery or payment date) and ends on the day of contractual sale. Therefore in verifying sales on a security exchange, the contract date, not the settlement date, is governing. Further refinements have been made by the Service. In the case of a cash basis taxpayer, the loss on a transaction is deemed to have been realized upon the date of sale, despite the fact that the proceeds were received in a subsequent taxable year. Conversely the gain on a transaction is realized upon receipt of the proceeds. These rules are important since there is usually a flurry of so-called "tax selling" near the close of a calendar year.

(4) *Expense of Sale*—Capital transactions are rarely reported in which there is no appropriate expense of sale. These expenses include legal, accounting, and brokerage fees. When gains or losses appear on a return but expenses of sale do not, the agent should determine whether they have been claimed as ordinary deductions. Frequently these expenses are netted against the selling price, which is satisfactory.

(5) *Personal residence*—Because of current economic trends, sales of personal residences most often result in a gain, which is taxed as a capital gain. Because the Code provides unique treatment with respect to some gains on the sale or exchange of a residence, Form 2119, Statement Concerning Sale or Exchange of Personal Residence, is a useful worksheet to use in beginning the audit of such gain. A copy is provided as Exhibit 9.

(a) When the information is not available from the return and the taxpayer is claiming nonrecognition of any of the gain, he/she should be asked to complete the form. In many cases, it will be necessary to use facts stemming from years other than the one under examination. This is true because of the latitude of time provided in the Code for replacement or reinvestment. It is important to realize that completion of the form by the taxpayer is not the equivalent of auditing the transaction. The amounts entered on the form must be verified.

(b) As in the case of any real property, the closing statement is the best source for checking the transaction. Where at all possible the purchase and sale statements should be obtained. If the taxpayer cannot obtain this data, the other party to the transaction and the mortgagee, if any, are good sources of information.

(c) In addition to the purchase price the taxpayer usually claims capital additions in the adjusted basis. Contrary to rental property, no deductions are allowable for repairs to a residence. Therefore when reporting rental income, the taxpayer's inclination may be to shade his/her judgment in favor of expense instead of capital charge. On the other hand, in reporting the sale of a residence, his/her inclination may be to regard all prior repairs and expenses as capital additions. In verifying the taxpayer's claim for such improvements during the holding period, the classification between expense and capital items must be clearly in mind. In most communities the building codes require the filing of plans and securing permits to make material renovations or additions. This evidence should be requested or secured if the agent has no other means of determining the facts.

(d) When the sale of a residence is reported, particular attention should be given the adjusted basis. It is necessary to determine whether it was properly reflected in terms of the nonrecognition of any gain realized from a prior similar transaction. In computing the cost of a residence and capital additions an analysis should be made to determine that no value of the taxpayer's labor is included therein. In addition, casualty losses previously allowed are a reduction of the basis whereas appropriate reconstruction after the casualty is an addition to the cost.

(6) *Multiple dwellings*—Because of the preponderance of multiple dwellings in some parts of the country, frequently property is sold which consisted of a part of the taxpayer's residence. The approach to verifying such transactions should take the form of dividing the sale into two parts, one of a residence, the other of rental property. Treating the sale in two parts frequently results in a nonallowable loss on the residence portion and a taxable gain on the rental portion.

(a) In analyzing the sale, proper allocation must be made for original cost and capital additions between the personal and rental portions of the asset. All depreciation allowed or allowable is an adjustment to the basis of *the rental portion only.* Similarly the selling price and expenses of sale must be allocated to the two segments. A separate gain or loss is determined for each segment, residence and rental, and proper tax treatment is applied. To regard the transaction as one then allows the taxpayer to offset nondeductible loss against taxable gain.

(b) Various methods are available for allocating costs and selling prices between the residence and rental portions. Our acceptable method is the ratio of rental value of the two segments. The allocation of capital additions between the personal and rental parts must be tempered by the taxpayer's possible inclination to show that he/she spent a disproportionate amount on his/her own residence. This should be taken into account where no definite substantiation as to the proration is available.

(c) The sale of property which is partially rented and partially a residence, if held more than six months, will be treated as an IRC 1231 transaction for the rented portion. This portion should be verified in the same manner as though it were an independent sale of property held solely for rental income. The check is similar to that involved in the sale of business property. See 665.

(d) Assets such as a residence may be classified temporarily as rental property. An example is a residence in a resort area, all or part of which is occasionally used for production of rental income.

(7) *Personal automobile*—Another asset which has a dual classification between business and personal is an automobile used partly for business and partly for personal convenience. The sale of such an asset should be audited as two transactions in the same manner as the dual purpose real property. Because of IRC 1231, the gain on the business portion may be reportable as a capital gain, but it is still to be determined independently of the personal portion, which is always a capital transaction, a taxable gain or a nonrecognized loss.

(8) *Liquidation of corporations*—In examining reported capital gains and losses particular attention should be given to sales reported as liquidations, partial or complete, of corporations in which the taxpayer was a principal. The Code provides sections for construction of the distribution as an ordinary dividend in some cases.

(9) *Treatment of certain ordinary assets as capital assets, IRC 1231*—This section of the Code specifies capital treatment for gains from sales of certain ordinary assets. Where gains from such sales are reported in the capital gains schedule, the approach should include a careful scrutiny for existence of casualty losses on the business schedule or among the itemized deductions, gains or losses on similar depreciable property arising from the distribution of partnership income and gains or losses from involuntary conversions. The Code relief provision requires consideration of these items in the aggregate, prior to classification between ordinary and capital gain. A thorough understanding of IRC 1231 is mandatory before any audit technique is useful.

(a) Often in the sale of depreciable assets or land, the agreement includes the sale of other items such as goodwill and inventories. These extraneous assets must be handled apart and the selling price allocated by using the fair market value of the actual assets sold. A thorough understanding of IRC 1245 (Gain from Disposition of Certain Depreciable Property) is necessary before any audit technique is useful.

738 *(8-30-76)* 4231

Annuities

(1) *General*—Other than the mechanical operations involved there are four points to the determination of the taxable portion of amounts received as a pension or annuity. They are as follows:

(a) the investment in the contract or the cost of the annuity,

(b) tax-free cost recovery in the past,

(c) the expected return, and

(d) payments received during the taxable year.

(2) *Employer-employee financed plans*—The Code distinguishes between employer-employee financed annuities, where the employee's cost will be recovered within three years, and between other so-called general rule annuities. The return does likewise. Examiners are cautioned that in the return schedule for general rule annuities, the investment in the contract—(1)(a) above—is the netted amount of the original cost less any tax-free recovery in the past. In the return schedule for employer-employee type annuities the equivalent amount is not netted, but is derived by subtracting line 2 from line 1 in the schedule itself.

(a) The cost of an annuity may be established by a statement from the employer or insurance company as the case may be. If there is no insurance company statement, it may be necessary to determine cost from the annuity contract. This contract should set forth the total consideration paid for the annuity whether as a lump sum or as periodic payments over a given period of time. Where employer annuities are involved, the statement from the employer, or the insurance company, should clearly indicate that portion of the cost which was contributed by the employee, as distinguished from the total cost including the employer's contribution.

(b) In checking an employer-employee type annuity the first thing an agent should do is determine whether the amounts received are reported in the correct part of the annuity schedule on the return. He/she should do this by determining the payments that will be received under the contract within the first three years. For instance, if payments are received monthly, multiplying their amount by 36 provides this information. If the resultant product exceeds the employee's cost, the payments within the taxable year are to be reported under the general rule: if it is less than the employee's cost, the payments are to be reported under the special rule. This three year provision applies even though payments began prior to 1954.

(3) *Purchased annuities*—Some purchased annuity contracts contain a life insurance feature. If the life insurance remains in effect after payments are receivable by the annuitant under the contract, that portion of the amount paid which is attributable to the insurance feature should be eliminated from the cost of the annuity. It may be necessary to secure this information from the insurance company.

(a) In any case where payments on an annuity began prior to 1954 there was a tax-free recovery of cost. This recovery should be computed as in the example below, assuming a calendar year taxpayer, investment in the annuity of $15,000.00, payments of $200.00 a month beginning on September 1, 1951.

Taxable year	Amount taxable	Received in year	Tax-free recovery
1951	$150.00 (1/3 Yr.)	$ 800.00	$ 650.00
1952	450.00	2,400.00	1,950.00
1953	450.00	2,400.00	1,950.00
			$4,550.00

(b) This type of tax-free recovery in the past, that is, pre-1954 recovery, is the only type that will occur in general rule annuity cases. It amy also occur in the employer-employee category for years up to and including 1956 but should not appear thereafter.

(c) The only other type of tax-free recovery in the past is the cumulative total of payments received under employer-employee type annuities which is not in excess of the cost of the annuity to the employee. Unless the starting date of such an annuity occurs in the taxable year under examination, such a recovery should always appear on returns for taxable years after 1954.

(d) There are two elements to the "expected return" from an annuity, the periodic payments and the term over which they are to be received. The annuity contract should be examined to determine these elements. For tax purposes the term commences with the annuity starting date, which is defined as the first day of the first period for which an annuity payment is to be received; except that if such date was prior to 1954, the annuity starting date shall be January 1, 1954. The term may end at either a fixed date or upon death of the annuitants.

(e) Where the duration of the term depends on the remaining life of one or more individuals it becomes necessary to consult the actuarial tables in the Regulations. These tables are based on the age and sex of the annuitants. The age to be used is the age on the birthday nearest the starting date of the annuity. The contract will usually specify the age at which payments are to begin. If the taxpayer claims that his/her age is different from the age shown in the contract, such a claim should be considered in the light of any evidence the taxpayer can produce. If the claim is backed up only by the taxpayer's oral assertions, the age shown in the contract should be used.

(f) While the contract frequently will specify the age at which payments are to begin, it is not necessarily the age which is to be applied in using the actuarial tables. The age to be used is the age on the birthday nearest the starting date of the annuity. Since the annuity starting date is the first day of the first period for which an amount is received, in those cases where the annuity payments are annual (or semi-annual in some cases), the age to be used in the actuarial table will be one year less than the age stated in the contract. For example, payments under an annuity are to be made annually, starting when the taxpayer becomes 65. His first payment is received on his 65th birthday, March 1, 1966. His annuity starting date is March 2, 1965, (the first day of the annual period) and his nearest birthday at that date would be his 64th birthday. Age 64 should be used in determining his expected return multiple from the actuarial tables.

(g) The provisions of the contract with respect to the amounts and duration of payments, and to whom they are to be paid, should be determined by an examination of the contract. Where the contract provides options for the manner of payment, the particular option elected is all that need be considered. Once the examiner has determined this information he/she is in a position to know which particular actuarial table should be used. A brief discussion follows concerning the annuity tables found in Reg. 1.72-9 which you may have an occasion to refer to:

1 Table I. Single annuitant type. One person until death.

2 Table II. Joint and survivor annuitants of the primary and secondary type. Uniform $100.00 to H or W until death of both. It is possible by combining the use of Tables I and II to handle a variable type of joint and survivor annity, where H receives $100.00 until his death and W $50.00 thereafter so long as she lives. The Regulations explain how this is to be done.

3 Table IIA. Joint and survivor annuitants, joint life type H or W $100.00 until death of either. Survivor $50.00 until death.

4 Table III. Refund or guarantee annuities. Annuitant or a named beneficiary guaranteed a certain amount, usually the amount paid in on the contract. For example, if the annuitant who had purchased an annuity for $8,000.00 died after receiving 42 monthly $100.00 payments, the contract might provide a beneficiary would get the $3,800.00 unrecovered cost.

5 Table III when necessary is always used in conjunction with the other actuarial tables. However it does not, as they do, affect the expected return under a contract. It reduces the investment in the contract.

(4) Verification of annuity payments received insofar as the amounts received by the taxpayer during the taxable year are concerned, if there is no Form 1099 from the insurance company, the amount can easily be determined from the contract.

(a) Some insurance companies furnish annuitants with a statement showing the exact amounts to be entered on Form 1040. The amounts are keyed directly to the annuity schedules on that form. Where taxpayer produces such a statement it may usually be accepted without further verification.

739 *(8-30-76)* 4231
Income from Rents

(1) The general provisions that apply to rental income, depreciation, repairs, etc., are discussed in Chapter 600. Specialized techniques for the small taxpayer are:

(a) *Applicable in all situations—*

1 Examine purchase contract to determine whether land is being depreciated. This erroneous practice is common in small taxpayer returns.

2 Proper application of the depreciation "allowed or allowable" rules is often not made in small taxpayer returns. To determine this it may be necessary in some cases to check retained copies of income tax returns for prior years.

3 Where the taxpayer presents a property management statement as support for the items reported, the underlying paid bills should be requested. Classification on such statements is often poor, particularly with respect to capital-repair items.

4 Property management fees in excess of 5% of the gross rentals should receive particular attention. That is the customary amount paid for such services to independent management concerns. Where this rate is exceeded, the possibility exists that the payment is other than a business expense. It might be a way of supporting an aged parent or of making a gift to a child or other relative.

5 The provisions of IRC 164(d) regarding real estate tax apportionment should be considered where the acquisition date per the return depreciation schedule indicates acquisition during the taxable year (or immediately preceding year in some States).

(b) *Applicable only where taxpayer occupies the property—*

1 Examiners should determine that expenses are properly grouped for tenant only, taxpayer only, and common to both. Depreciation on a refrigerator in the tenant's apartment should be allowed in full (subject to the depreciation rules) whereas depreciation on a refrigerator in the taxpayer's apartment would not be allowable. If only one furnace is used for central heating, only the proportionate part applicable to the tenant's apartment would be subject to depreciation. The taxpayer should not be permitted to include decoration of his/her own apartment.

2 Elimination of the portion attributable to the taxpayer's living quarters should be made in each of the three categories of depreciation, repairs, and other expenses. Taxpayers will at times eliminate the repairs or other expense element but neglect the depreciation element.

3 Real estate taxes and interest should be properly apportioned between itemized deductions and supplemental schedule of income on the return. The part applicable to the taxpayer's occupancy may only be claimed under itemized deductions.

4 Rental income may not include a theoretical rental charge for taxpayer's occupancy with all expenses deductible.

5 Allowance should be made for relative apartment sizes. Where there are, for instance, a three and a six room apartment in one house, apportionment should not be made on a 50-50 basis.

6 A net loss from rentals is sometimes attributable to property which is rented to a relative for an amount less than the rental value of the property. In such a case the loss is usually not deductible. Another type of loss is the rental of a vacation residence used part of the time by the taxpayer. The entire year's expenses are charged against the rental income from the property for that portion of the year when the house was not used by the taxpayer. The expenses should be allocated between personal and business use, preferably on a time basis.

73(10) *(11-2-78)* 4231
Other Income

(1) *Partnerships*—When partnership income is reported, inquiry should be made, whether a partnership return has been filed and whether the distributive share of the partnership income has been correctly reported. The retained copy of such a return may be inspected. If the examiner feels the best interests of the Service would be served by examining the partnership, and the partnership consists of no more than five partners, all of whom are individuals, the revenue agent should proceed with the related examination. If there are more than five partners or partners other than individuals, Form 5346, Examination Information Report, will be prepared and forwarded to the Returns Program Manager. An exception may be made with the approval of the group manager if there are more than five partners or nonindividual partners, provided that all partners are located within the partnership district, the related partners' returns are easily obtainable and controllable, and it would be mutually beneficial to the taxpayers and the Service to have the examinations conducted concurrently.

(2) *Estates or Trusts*—Distributable income should be verified from retained copies of fiduciary return. Secondary evidence that can be used is the letter or statement usually furnished beneficiaries by fiduciaries. If upon inspection of the copy of the fiduciary return it appears that the return should be examined, refer to Chapter 600 for guidelines for business returns and other parts of this chapter on nonbusiness returns.

(3) *Other sources*—Income reported in this category is often of a nonrecurring nature and therefore subject to a greater margin of error. The exact nature, source and method of arriving at the amount should be ascertained by questioning the taxpayer. If income from gambling is reported, the examiners should keep in mind that:

(a) Gambling losses are deductible only to the extent of gambling gains. If gambling does not constiute a principal business activity of the taxpayer then:

1 all gains are includible in gross income;

2 any substantiated gambling losses are deductible as itemized deductions on Form 1040 to arrive at taxable income.

(4) It appears appropriate at this time to divert from the nonbusiness taxpayer to the business taxpayer while discussing gambling income. If gambling constitutes a business of the taxpayer the substantiated losses are deductible in arriving at adjusted gross income. The key words "substantiated losses" require additional comment. For the gambler in business the payouts (gambling losses) would represent a business expense and should be accorded careful verification to insure the claimed losses are justified. Remember gambling payouts claimed as a deduction by one in the gambling business represent taxable income to the recipient. Examiners are encouraged to research court cases applicable to this taxable area to ascertain most recent positions.

(5) Various promotional contests are conducted by grocery stores, department stores and manufacturers. Prize lists are posted in various ways and newspapers generally carry stories and pictures of winners in the larger categories of prizes. Taxpayers may report the larger prizes because of publicity and reporting procedures carried out by the sponsor of the contest but may overlook smaller awards.

740 *(8-30-76)* 4231
Itemized Deductions

741 *(9-13-79)* 4231
Contributions

(1) Contributions claimed by individuals are divided into two classes; those fully substantiated by check and indicated as one amount on the return, and those paid in cash and listed individually on the return. Pledges are not allowable unless paid timely. Usually the agent will recognize the names of better known local or national organizations and know whether payments to them are deductible. Those not recognized should be checked against the List of Exempt Organizations, Publication No. 78. If Publication 78 does not contain the name(s) of the organization(s) in doubt, the examiner may informally contact the Exempt Organization Master File clerk in their EO key district, Employee Plans and Exempt Organizations Division, to verify the exempt status of those organizations in dobut, or the taxpayer may be requested to question the organization itself as to the deductibility of contributions to it.

(2) An individual may claim a charitable contribution deduction to a church that has not been recognized by the Service as tax exempt. Such deduction is not barred merely because the church has never applied for recognition of exempt status. Similarly, when an organization has applied but has not provided the Service with sufficient information upon which to make a favorable determination of exempt status, a charitable deduction is not automatically barred.

(a) If the question of the donee organization's exempt status is necassary to conclude an examination, a referral should be made to the appropriate EP/EO Division of Form 5346, Examination Information Report.

(b) When Form 5346 is prepared for referral to EP/EO Division, Items 1, 12, 13, 14, 15, 16, 17 and 22 should be completed. All other items should be blocked out to prevent subsequent use.

(3) The principal audit problem is the determination of amounts paid in cash and not substantiated. Is the total of contributions claimed reasonable in relation to the amount available out of which contributions could have been made? Such available cash must take into consideration gross income less the other deductions claimed on the return, personal living expenses, income taxes withheld and any estimated tax payments.

(4) Contributions to schools which taxpayer's dependents attend should be analyzed in order to determine whether the deduction claimed actually represents cost of tuition.

(5) It is the practice of many religious and other charitable organizations to conduct rummage or auction sales or to regularly offer for sale personal property that has been donated. As a result of these various fund raising activities, many valuable items, such as color televisions, jewelry, furs, etc. are disposed of at or near their fair market value. In many cases, the purchasers make their personal checks payable to the charitable organization in payment for the merchandise; therefore, examiners should be alert to the possibility that taxpayers are deducting such purchases as contributions to the organization concerned.

(6) See IRM 426(28) for additional information peculiar to mail order ministries, alleged churches and related individuals.

742 *(8-30-76)* 4231
Interest

Because of the situations that give rise to the payment of interest, documentary substantiation can be reasonably expected. The terms of the interest agreement should be examined, and payments should be analyzed to establish that principal payments have not been included as interest. Care should be exercised to distinguish between interest and discount since the Code provides different times for deduction by cash basis taxpayers. Eliminate life insurance premiums or other charges normally added to time payment contracts.

743 *(5-7-79)* 4231
Taxes

(1) Real estate taxes can be verified from actual receipts, or mortgagee statements when appropriate, which will reveal amounts paid as well as the name of the registered property owner. Prior taxes are deductible on the cash basis only if the taxpayer was the owner during the period.

(2) State gasoline taxes may be estimated from the local rate and mileage driven, taking into consideration the vehicle's rate of consumption. Agents should familiarize themselves with local office methods for approximating other local taxes for reasonableness.

(3) Federal excise taxes are not deductible.

(4) The Code requires proration of current real estate taxes in the year of purchase or sale. Therefore the examiner should determine in all cases when the property was acquired or sold.

(5) Also see text at 678:(2)(d) of this Handbook for method of deducting State income taxes.

744 *(8-30-76)* 4231
Medical Expenses

(1) The audit of medical expenses of a sizable amount usually does not present a problem since receipts and other records of payment can be secured for the larger doctor bills and hospital expenses. However, the examiner is cautioned against double deductions being claimed or against accepting unreceipted bills in general. For example, a hospital will present a taxpayer with a bill for $115.00 for a confinement. Because the taxpayer has a Blue Cross policy that provides $75.00 for confinements only $40.00 is paid the hospital. The taxpayer then has the $115.00 unreceipted bill and a $40.00 receipt. Only the latter is deductible.

(2) Deductions are sometimes claimed when the taxpayer actually pays the medical bill in total and subsequently receives an insurance settlement of all or part of the expenditure made.

(3) Problems also arise in connection with the audit of amounts claimed for drugs and prescriptions. If such amounts appear unreasonable an attempt should be made to tie them in with specific illnesses. Hospital bills usually describe the various charges. Pharmaceutical charges appearing on a hospital bill should be segregated and included in medicine and drugs for the purpose of applying the one percent limitation. Care should be exercised in the analysis of medicines and prescriptions in order to prevent the inclusion of various nondeductible expenses which are sometimes listed as medicine, such toothpaste, tooth brushes, and other toilet articles.

(4) Some types of insurance premiums constitute allowable medical expenses. If any are claimed, some consideration should be given to possible reimbursements of hospital and doctor bills.

(5) Premiums paid on a medical insurance policy which has elements of expense reimbursement as well as loss of earnings recovery are only partially deductible. Premiums paid on life insurance with incidental health insurance benefits are not deductible. Since various employers pay part of health insurance costs, the deduction claimed should be verified as paid by the taxpayer.

745 *(8-30-76)* 4231
Child Care Expenses

Child care expenses may be deducted by a widower or a woman who is gainfully employed, providing certain conditions are met. This deduction often presents an auditing problem because such payments are usually by cash. Aids in determining reasonableness of amounts paid are relationship of the payee, name and address, and whether multiple duties are being performed. The return of a taxpayer claiming expenses for child care should be checked to determine if the recipient is being claimed as a dependent. Form 2441 is a useful worksheet in computing the child care expense. A copy is provided as Exhibit 10.

746 *(8-30-76)* 4231
Casualty Losses

(1) *Fire, storm, or other casualty*—The amount deductible is the difference between the fair market value of the asset before and after the casualty, or the adjusted basis, whichever is less. (See IRC 1011 for adjusted basis.) From this amount must be deducted any insurance or other compensation received or recoverable.

(a) For example: A summer cottage which cost $3,600 was partially destroyed by fire in 1965. The value of the cottage immediately before the fire was $6,000, and the value immediately after the fire was $2,000; $3,000 was collected from the insurance company. The casualty loss from the fire is $500 computed in the following manner.

1 Value before fire	$6,000
2 Value after fire	2,000
3 Difference in value	$4,000
4 Cost or basis	3,600
5 Loss sustained (lesser of 3 or 4)	$3,600
6 Less insurance recovery	3,000
7 Casualty loss	$600
8 Less: $100 limitation	100
9 Casualty loss deduction allowable	$500

(b) In cases where the loss involves a minor portion of the asset, the cost of repairs or replacement may be used as a measure of the decrease in market value. If such a measure is used, care must be exercised to determine that the repair or replacement only restores the property to substantially the same condition as before the casualty. Any repair or replacement that results in improving the property beyond the condition that existed prior to the casualty would not be an acceptable measure.

(c) Casualty losses affecting items such as trees or shrubbery; incidental to real property, must be verified as a loss of a minor portion of the asset. The shrinkage in market value limited to adjusted basis, which forms the allowable deduction, must be determined by reference to the property as a whole, both as to FMV and adjusted basis.

(2) *Theft*—In the verification of the deductible loss resulting from theft the examiner should determine that a theft in fact did occur. Since it is common practice to report a theft to the police authorities the nonexistence of such a report could be material and might lead to the determination that the property was merely misplaced or lost and that, therefore, no deduction is allowable.

(3) *Insurance recovery*—In determining any allowable casualty loss the agent should fully explore the possibilities of insurance coverage and recovery thereon.

747 *(8-30-76)* 4231
Alimony and Separate Maintenance Payments

(1) Usually amounts paid for alimony can be verified from canceled checks or other evidence of payment. If the payments are for support, under a decree of a domestic relations court, they can sometimes be verified from court records, since in some localities it is the practice of this court to collect and transmit the payments.

(2) In any event, the agreement under which payments are made should be analyzed because of terms and dates that are material in determining deductibility under the Code. Payments for a combination of alimony and child support should be carefully analyzed, especially when they constitute arrearages.

748 *(8-30-76)* 4231
Educational Expenses

Deductions claimed for this type of expense can usually be verified without too much difficulty. In this particular area, the examiner is cautioned to see that the deductions are claimed in the proper year. He/she should also determine if the expenses were primarily incurred for the reasons set forth in the Code and Regulations. State and local laws governing certain professional educational requirements should be studied.

749 *(8-30-76)* 4231
Moving Expenses

Use Form 3903, Moving Expense Adjustment, (copy provided as Exhibit 12) as a guideline to determine correctness of deduction. Sometimes newspaper accounts point out some items involving personnel transfers that may affect tax liabilities such as disposition of residences through employers or related entities. Check closely to see if deduction is taken in the proper year.

750 *(8-30-76)* 4231

Decedent's Final Return

In general the audit of a decedent's final return would be made in the same manner as for any other return. The technique as described in 721 should be used to the extent necessary. It is also advisable to ascertain if the decedent left an estate. This can be done by questioning the representative about whether an estate tax return was filed under local or Federal law. If none was filed the representative will usually have all the facts. In either event, the inventory of assets the decedent owned should be analyzed to determine whether income is reported from those assets that are income producing. The net worth reflected in the inventory should also be compared with income reported to determine if the amount accumulated was reasonable. This might lead to a determination of net income under the net worth method as described in Chapter 900.

760 *(8-30-76)* 4231

Credits against the Tax

761 *(8-30-76)* 4231

Dividend Received Credit

Dividends received after December 31, 1964, do not qualify for any credit. However, taxpayers are entitled to the dividends received credit on qualifying dividends they received through a fiduciary or partnership on or before December 31, 1964. In addition, a fiscal year taxpayer may claim 2 percent credit for the amount of ordinary dividends received from qualifying corporations before January 1, 1965, and included in his/her 1964-1965 fiscal year returns.

762 *(8-30-76)* 4231

Retirement Income Credit

(1) There is little in the way of auditing technique for the retirement income credit. The computation is primarily mechanical.

(2) Rental income is to be included in full as retirement income without any deduction for repairs, depreciation, or other expenses.

(3) As to the 10 year, $600.00 earned income requirement, since even the years prior to 1913 may qualify a taxpayer, it will in most cases be unwise to go beyond taxpayer's assertion that he satisfied such requirements. It will be next to impossible to disprove such an assertion.

(4) Taxpayers should be specifically questioned about whether they are receiving Social Security, Railroad Retirement or other excludable pensions. They reduce retirement income.

770 *(8-30-76)* 4231

Partnerships and Fiduciaries

771 *(8-30-76)* 4231

General

The technique for partnership or fiduciary returns is the same as for determining income and deductions for any other entity. The following discussion relates only to the determination of distributable income.

772 *(8-30-76)* 4231

Partnerships

(1) The distribution of partnership income should be according to the partnership agreement, if any exists. In the absence of an agreement the distribution should be made according to the laws of the State in which the partnership is located. The principal problem is the computation of income to which the percentage applicable to each partner is applied. It does not necessarily follow that in a case of a 50-50 partnership the taxable net income will be divided equally. The applicable percentages should be applied after making specific allocations to each partner as provided in the agreement or as actually made if the agreement is silent. For example, a partnership provides that net profits are to be divided equally between two partners; there is no written agreement; capital accounts are not recorded on the books; and, the partners maintain that they are equal partners because each owns one half of all the business assets. In such a case it is necessary to determine actual withdrawals of each partner because even though they do not affect net income of the partnership, they do have a bearing on the distribution since the only amount which the partners share equally would be the amount not withdrawn from the business. It is also necessary to determine actual withdrawals in order to arrive at partner's basis in the business in case of liquidation.

(2) Since IRC 1231 applies to a taxable entity the distribution of transactions falling within that section should be made separately, so that when the gains or losses are included in the individual return, they will be grouped properly with the items reported thereon.

773 *(8-30-76)* 4231

Fiduciaries

(1) Copies of wills are filed with estate tax returns and copies of deeds of trust are usually filed with the first Form 1041 filed. These copies

should be referred to wherever possible. In those situations where it is necessary or more convenient to have recourse to taxpayer's copy, tact should be employed in requesting use of it and it should be returned so that the taxpayer is not faced with the necessity of supplying copies year after year.

(2) The distribution of net income should be made according to the trust instrument or will as the case may be, and in accordance with State law. In most States capital gains and losses are not distributable if the instrument makes no specific provision for distribution.

(3) The agent should scrutinize the trust instrument on trusts that are purportedly irrevocabie. Very often there are clauses in the instrument that could cause income, principal, or both, to revert to grantor resulting in a determination that the trust is revocable and all income taxable to the grantor.

Examination of Returns—Inadequate Records

910 *(8-30-76)* 4231
Introduction

(1) Taxpayers are required by law and regulations to maintain accounting records in such detail as to enable them to make a proper return of income. Because of the many professions and businesses, types and sources of income and deductions, it is obvious that a specific definition of what would be considered adequate records applicable in each case is not possible or practical. The factual determination of whether any particular taxpayer has maintained adequate records must necessarily be a matter of judgment in each case.

(2) If an agent determines that records are inadequate he/she should refer to 520 and IRM 4297. In addition, if there is a possible understatement of taxable income, he/she should consider use of the net worth method to reconstruct the correct income. This method, when properly applied and documented, has been upheld by the courts in many important fraud cases. It is one of the principal weapons of the government in its war against criminal tax evasion. In addition to the net worth method, this chapter includes other methods for verifying and determining the taxable income, such as application of funds, the bank deposit, and unit and volume methods.

920 *(8-30-76)* 4231
Approach

921 *(8-30-76)* 4231
Initial Interview

(1) One of the most important phases of any investigation is the initial interview with the taxpayer. This is especially true when the records are inadequate, nonexistent, or there is reason to believe that they are false. This first interview offers the examiner opportunities to obtain information which may not be forthcoming at a later date.

(2) This interview should be exploited to its utmost, for the information secured may save many days of work in the future. Encourage the taxpayer to discuss himself/herself, family, business hobbies, financial history, and his/her sources of income of himself/herself and other members of his/her family. The revenue agent, however, should not make the taxpayer feel subjected to a formal interrogation. He/she should try to make as many pertinent determinations as possible by guiding the interview rather than by direct questions.

(3) The revenue agent at this phase of the examination should attempt to secure from his/her conversation with the taxpayer sufficient facts to evaluate the overall financial picture of the taxpayer, his/her approximate mode of living, his/her life insurance program, investments, unusual expenditures, as well as gifts, loans, inheritances and other nontaxable receipts received by him/her. The examiner should then be in a position to see if the taxable income reported bears a plausible relationship to the taxpayer's net worth and manner of living.

(4) If the desired information cannot be secured from a casual interview with the taxpayer, the examiner should prepare a series of questions to ask. Except in unusual circumstances he/she should develop the case as much as possible from information and data furnished by the taxpayer rather than from an outside source, normally a much more time-consuming job.

(5) The following paragraphs contain some suggested approaches to use if there are inadequate records present, or if the taxpayer is uncooperative and there is reason to believe that fraud is involved.

(a) Secure information as to the taxpayer's dependents and family, and determine the status of the family as to age, degree of support and their names and addresses. This information will not only assist the examiner in the determination of the allowable exemptions and dependents in the computation of the tax, but will aid the agent in determining the cost of living of the taxpayer resulting from family size, dependents outside the household, unusual expenditures for children who may be in college, camp, etc.

(b) Secure information as to the taxpayer's bank accounts and those of his/her immediate family and, if possible, the ledger sheets and cancelled checks of all accounts. If the checks and ledger sheets are not available, the examiner should be sure to secure the locations and the names of these accounts. Particular emphasis should be placed on bank accounts which are not normally a part of the business records, since unreported receipts may have been deposited in the nonbusiness bank accounts. A more detailed discussion on the analysis of bank accounts appears at 940.

(c) Determine the taxpayer's security holdings including both stocks and bonds, taxable or nontaxable, governmental or commercial.

The agent should ascertain the dates acquired, dates sold, costs, selling price, where acquired, where sold. Such information may not only develop specific items of capital gains, interest and dividend income but may disclose cash purchases which are not accounted for by reported income and sales proceeds invested in previously undisclosed assets.

(d) Obtain a listing of the taxpayer's real estate holdings similar to the manner in (c) above from public records and escrow statements with the same purposes in mind. Also, questions about the taxpayer's personal residence may give indications that he/she is spending for this item more than could be justified by the size of the income reported.

(e) Determine the extent of the taxpayer's currency accumulations. Most taxpayers will not have a record of amounts as of particular dates. In many instances, the agent's entire case may hinge upon the correct determination of this one item alone. It is most important that the examiner word any questions in such a manner as to leave little doubt as to what was asked. If it appears that the examination will depend on this item, it may be necessary to secure an affidavit from the taxpayer or have a witness to corroborate the answer given. Some typical questions which may be asked about currency accumulations to develop this information are as follows:

1 Has it been your practice, or the practice of your spouse or children to accumulate cash on hand? This includes undeposited cash at all locations such as at your home, at your place of business, in a safety deposit box or in the possession of some third party. This does not include funds which are on deposit in a financial or savings and loan establishment, the amount of which is a matter of record.

2 Would you ever have had cash on hand to exceed $100.00? To exceed $500.00? To exceed $1,000.00? To exceed $5,000.00?

3 When?

4 For what purpose did you have that cash on hand?

5 How much cash on hand do you have at the present time? In this manner the desired information may be secured by indirect means rather than by a direct request as to what was on hand as of a particular date. In 932 a discussion is presented on methods of verification of taxpayer's contentions about cash on hand at the beginning of the period under examination.

(f) Secure information about the taxpayer's accounts, loans and notes receivable. This is especially significant when the taxpayer is required to report on the accrual basis. Since this information, in many instances, is most difficult and time consuming to secure from third parties, the examiner should secure for analysis any records, workpapers or other data which will assist in the determination of these items.

(g) Secure information on inventories, by whom they were prepared, the method used in the determination and any workpapers used in the computations.

(h) Obtain a list of the taxpayer's equipment, showing dates of acquisition and disposition, costs, selling prices, suppliers, purchasers, trade-ins, whether financed or paid for without borrowed funds.

(i) Make a list of other assets, both business and personal, securing dates of purchase, costs, dates of sale, selling prices, names of purchasers or suppliers.

(j) Secure information regarding bank loans, personal loans, accounts payable and other borrowed funds of the taxpayer. Information received may help to explain asset acquisitions or indicate undisclosed income being used to reduce the taxpayer's liabilities. In checking bank loans and other loans, ascertain if collateral is involved. This may lead to the discovery of hidden assets. The item of business accounts payable is especially significant when the taxpayer is required to report on the accrual basis and since this item may be difficult to secure from third parties, any records, workpapers or other data which will assist in this determination should be secured.

(k) Secure information regarding depreciation rates and methods of computation, and also develop facts as to depletion, if applicable. Since depreciation and depletion cause a reduction in taxable income without an outlay of cash, this should not be overlooked in the consideration of the taxpayer's overall financial picture.

(l) Obtain information about the taxpayer's living expenses. Many individual items may be included under this broad category. The example below will assist the agent in the determination of this item; however, at the initial interview it may be expedient to break down these expenditures on the basis of fixed and variable expenses. The fixed expenses which will normally repeat year to year without too much variance will include food, minimum clothing expense, rent or mortgage payments, life and other personal insurance payments and a certain amount of other living costs. The determination of the living expenses by this breakdown may disclose to the examining agent tax possibilities in other years besides the year or years assigned for examination. The example follows.

EXAMPLE

STATEMENT OF ANNUAL ESTIMATED PERSONAL AND FAMILY LIVING EXPENSES

of..........................for year ending......	Weekly	Monthly	Yearly
Food (groceries, etc.)			
Outside meals			
Clothing			
Medical expenses			
Rent or mortgage payments			
Repairs (home)			
Utilities (gas, electricity, fuel, etc.)			
Telephone—Telegraph			
Laundry—Dry cleaning			
Domestic help and FICA tax			
Home furnishings			
Auto expense			
Transportation (car fare)			
Recreation—Entertainment			
Vacation—Travel			
Education			
Magazines—Papers—Books			
Life Insurance			
Insurance (other)			
Dues (club, lodge, union)			
Personal tobacco, liquor, lunches, etc.)			
Beauty parlor, toiletries			
Jewelry, furs, etc.			
Gambling			
Taxes			
Federal			
State			
Local			
Contributions			
Gifts			
Unusual expenses			
Other			

922 *(8-30-76)* 4231
Bank Account Analysis

922.1 *(8-30-76)* 4231
Introduction

An important feature of any examination is the inspection or analysis of the taxpayer's bank records. The degree of the analysis will depend on the circumstances of the individual case. However, in the examination of an inadequate, nonexistent or possibly falsified set of records, the importance of this account should not be overlooked. Since usually a good portion of the taxpayer's receipts are represented by deposits and the use put to those receipts is reflected by checks, the analysis of the bank accounts is an invaluable source of leads to undisclosed income, investments and expenditures.

922.2 *(8-30-76)* 4231
Bank Deposits

(1) The purpose of the analysis of the bank deposits is self-evident. Where did the money come from? However, since a complete deposit analysis is time consuming and often unnecessary, the examiner must use judgment on the extent and degree of this analysis. He/she should consider, however, the following factors when the bank deposits are inspected.

(a) Are there any unusual or extraneous deposits which appear unlikely to result from sources of income reported? Such items are recognizable by:

1 *Size of deposit*—Due to expediency, the examiner may limit himself/herself to the examination of large deposits only. However, the identification of smaller deposits may be indicative of dividend, interest or other income, leading to a source of investment not previously known.

2 *Kind of deposit*—An item of deposit may be unusual due to the kind of deposit, check or cash, in its relationship to the taxpayer's business or source of income. An explanation may be required if a large cash deposit is made by a taxpayer whose receipts normally consist primarily of checks. Also a bank ledger card with only one or two large even dollar deposits, in lieu of the normal odd dollar and cents deposits, would be unusual and require explanation.

3 *Frequency of deposits*—Many taxpayers due to the nature of their business or the convenience of the depository will follow a set pattern in making deposits. Deviation from this pattern may bear questioning. Also, a bank ledger card or deposit slips which indicate repeat deposits of the same amount on a monthly, quarterly or semi-annual basis may indicate rental, dividend, interest or other income accruing to the taxpayer.

4 *Location of bank the check was drawn on*—The examination of deposit slips may indicate checks drawn on out-of-State banks. From the ABA identification number of the deposit slip the name and location of the bank can be readily determined by reference to a banker's guide. In all cases, if the location of the bank, on which the check for deposit has been drawn, bears little relation to the taxpayer's locality of business or source of income, it may bear further investigation.

(b) Are there any loans, repayment of loans, or extraneous items reflected in deposits? In the analysis of the bank deposits, the examiner should determine all items of this nature. This is a necessary step before comparing receipts with deposits.

(c) Are there transfers between bank accounts or redeposits? Before an agent can reach any conclusion on the relationship between deposits and reported receipts, he/she must eliminate transfers and redeposits. Thus, if a taxpayer in his/her business draws a check to cash for the purpose of cashing payroll checks and then redeposits the checks cashed, the agent would be incorrect to compare total deposits to receipts reported without this type of adjustments. The practice of "kiting" may sometimes be encountered and could mislead the examiner into faulty conclusions.

(d) Are there personal or nonbusiness bank accounts? The examiner should not overlook these accounts in his/her analysis. Many productive cases have developed from this alone. The examiner should ascertain whether the deposits as reflected in these accounts can be accounted for by withdrawals from business accounts or from other known sources of funds. In many instances, unreported income finds its way into the personal accounts, and if the agent limits himself/herself to an analysis or inspection of the business bank accounts only, this omitted income may not be discovered.

(e) Are the deposits, as adjusted, during short periods of time, accounted for by the records? It is not infrequent to find total deposits on a yearly basis tying in with the total receipts for the year. However, a closer examination on a weekly or monthly basis may indicate that these deposits are out of proportion with receipts reported during shorter periods of time. Many of the examining techniques of the revenue agent are also known by the taxpayer, therefore, reported receipts may not be deposited in the closing months of the year to balance out the excess of deposits and the understatement of receipts in the earlier months.

922.3 *(8-30-76)* 4231
Checks

(1) The purpose of the analysis of the taxpayer's check disbursements is not limited alone to the verification of the expenses and deductions claimed on the return, but is a source of information to determine the nondeductible expenditures which may give indications of the reliability or unreliability of the records under examination. The analysis of the checks is also a source of information to obtain leads about cash expenditures and investments acquired by cash or from sources of funds not previously known by the agent.

(2) Again, the extent of the check analysis will depend on each individual case and the possibility of its development by one of the methods to be described later in this chapter. On certain occasions all that may be required of the agent is a quick cursory examination of the checks or check stubs to see if the nondeductibles, such as checks for personal and investment purposes, are justified by the size of the income reported. On other occasions a more detailed analysis may be required.

(3) If a detailed analysis appears justified, due to the inadequacy of the records or to the possibility of omitted income, the following procedure is suggested.

(a) Total disbursements for the year should first be determined. This can be readily accomplished by adding the opening bank balance to the total deposits and subtracting the ending bank balance.

(b) The second phase of the analysis is to segregate business or deductible expenditures from nonbusiness or nondeductible expenditures. In the examination of an inadequate or possibly falsified set of records, time can usually be saved by listing only the nondeductible expenditures. The total business or deductible expenses are determined merely by the means of subtraction; however they should be compared to the items claimed on the return for any specific adjustment. The emphasis is on the nondeductible expenditures since these are the items which disclose where the taxpayer is spending his/her income or more than his/her reported income. It may be impossible by the analysis of the bank deposits to identify or segregate sources of funds; however, by the analysis of the nondeductibles, the agent will be able to establish how the taxpayer used these funds.

(c) In the detailed analysis of the nondeductibles, it is usually advisable that these checks be listed in chronological order and the amounts extended to columns indicating different categories of nondeductibility. These categories may consist of the following: food, clothing, life insurance payments, income tax, rent or mortgage payments, capital items, etc. By this type of breakdown the examiner will then be able to determine with more accuracy, those items which were paid by cash. If the analysis disclosed only minor food payments by check, the agent would know immediately that a cash determination must be made for this item. The same would be true if rent for only six months were disclosed by check payments or life insurance premiums which were paid by check in one year and did not appear in another.

(d) The third phase is the analysis of the cancelled checks as a source of leads to undisclosed income, investments or expenditures. First, the agent by knowing what was paid by check will get a good idea of what was paid by cash. Second, small insignificant payments may give leads to names or sources where large expenditures or investments were made. A dry cleaning or storage bill has on many occasions led to the discovery of the purchase of an expensive mink coat that would not otherwise be known. A safety deposit box rental payment may disclose a depository or aid in the disclosure of investments unknown beforehand.

(4) The examiner as he/she inspects or lists the checks, should glance at the endorsements, the clearing banks and bank markings. Checks to third parties endorsed by the taxpayer may mean a fictitious deduction, or endorsements not by firm stamps may indicate forgeries by the taxpayer. The location of the clearing bank may indicate to the agent, especially regarding checks to cash, the purpose of the check, such as for a vacation or for a transaction in another city. Bank markings, again, especially with respect to a check to cash or to a financial institution, may indicate that it was received by the loan department, bond department or another particular section of the bank. Occasionally a check which was not cancelled may be claimed as a deduction. The examiner should also look for the dates of clearances, especially on those checks written near the end of the year by cash basis taxpayers. Note the place of deposit of checks to third parties, and also indorsements. In some cases this may disclose bank accounts of taxpayers under fictitious names or fictitious purchases. This may also lead to disclosures that taxpayer's vendors are not reporting all sales and may form a basis for related examinations.

923 *(8-30-76)* 4231

Inspection of Safety Deposit Box

(1) If it becomes necessary from the above interrogation or for other reasons to examine the taxpayer's safety deposit box, permission should be sought from the taxpayer for this inspection. The appointment for this inspection should be arranged to ensure that neither the taxpayer nor others having access to the box enter it between the time of the request and the time of the actual inspection by the revenue agent. This can be accomplished by having the revenue agent go to the box immediately after the request or making the request after banking hours and arranging the appointment at the bank at the opening of the next banking day. After the box has been inventoried, the agent should enter a statement after the last item similar to the following:

The contents of Safe Deposit Box Number .... in the .... rented by ....
(Name of Bank and City) (Name of Taxpayer)
was inventoried by the undersigned on .... at
(Date)
...... and disclosed the above items, which have all
(Hour)
been restored to the box to be replaced in the vault.

....
(Signature of Taxpayer)

....
(Signature of Internal Revenue Agent)

Witnesses:

(2) The agent should provide the taxpayer with a carbon copy of the inventory if he/she so desires. The examiner should arrange for another agent to accompany him/her as a witness in the vault on occasions where it is felt the case may develop into fraud or the taxpayer's character or business make it advisable to have a witness to avoid embarrassment to the Government.

(3) In any event the agent should obtain from the bank the record of visits to the box. The dates of such visits may correspond with the dates of cash transactions or with the dates of regular deposits in the business bank account.

930 *(8-30-76)* 4231

Net Worth Method

931 *(8-30-76)* 4231

Introduction

(1) The net worth method of proving taxable income is based upon the theory that any increases or decreases in the taxpayer's net worth during a taxable period adjusted for nontaxable expenditures and nontaxable income must have been the result of taxable income. This system verifies the income statement through the approach of the balance sheet.

(2) In this type of an examination the taxpayer's net worth, that is, the difference between his/her assets and liabilities, is determined at a beginning date. The taxpayer's net worth is then established at the end of each succeeding year and the yearly increases and decreases are determined. Adjustments are made for nondeductible and nontaxable items.

(3) The net worth method is an excellent method to be employed when the accounts from which the income audit is to be made have been found to be false, incomplete or missing. Even when the net worth method is not used as

the eventual basis for computation, a preliminary net worth survey should indicate the correctness of the income audit.

(4) As was previously mentioned a set of records, which may appear to be adequate from observation, may be inadequate due to items of omission. Therefore, even though at the beginning of an examination the records may appear to be adequate, it may be advisable for the examiner to prepare a rough net worth analysis. In many instances, the inclusion in this rough net worth of years prior to the years assigned for examination may be advisable especially when those years were not previously examined.

(5) This rough net worth analysis may consist of only two balance sheets, one at the beginning and one at the end of the period, even though a number of years are involved. To illustrate this auditing procedure, the following example is given.

Reported net income from returns assigned and from retained copies	1960		$ 4,522.43
	1961		5,265.18
	1962		4,877.85
	1963		4,947.63
	1964		5,245.33
			$24,858.42
Depreciation expense as disclosed by returns or as corrected	1960		$ 305.10
	1961		455.44
	1962		722.19
	1963		865.83
	1964		1,008.50
			$ 3,357.06
Estimated net worth (not including accumulated depreciation)	12/31/64		$70,000.00
Estimated net worth (not including accumulated depreciation)	12/31/59		30,000.00
Increase for 5-year period			$40,000.00
Add:			
Income tax paid 1/1/60 to 12/31/64	$ 3,421.17		
Estimated living expenses 5 × $3,000.00	15,000.00		18,421.17
			$58,421.17
Deduct:			
Depreciation expense for 5 years	$ 3,357.06		
Nontaxable portion of capital gains—1962	1,210.50		4,567.56
Net income for 5-year period by rough net worth			$53,853.61
Net income as reported for 5-year period			24,858.42
Estimated understatement for 5 years			$28,995.10

(6) From the above example the overall survey indicates an understatement of approximately $29,000.00. The examiner is now in the position to know that the case is worth developing further, and should complete the net worth schedule by substituting accurate, verified figures on a year by year basis.

(7) A net worth statement prepared and submitted by the taxpayer, if one can be obtained, can save much of the agent's time. The statement should be checked carefully for inaccuracies and omissions. Such a net worth statement, as part of the file on the taxpayer, would always be available as a starting point for any future income verification.

(8) A study of the taxpayer's insurance coverage can suggest the extent of unreported income. Life insurance and annuities might be a good reflection of the taxpayer's own opinion of his/her earning power. Insurance on the stock of merchandise might give a clue to the true inventory value. Burglary and theft insurance could disclose the existence and the value of furs, jewelry, antiques and rare collections. However, some caution will be necessary before relying on these valuations; taxpayers may have had some reasons on their own for over insuring, or under insuring their assets.

(9) If the taxpayer is an alien or a naturalized citizen, the Immigration and Naturalization Service would have a sworn statement signed by the taxpayer as a declaration of the value of property brought into the country. This information may supply an excellent starting point in some cases.

932 *(8-30-76)* 4231

The Net Worth Computation

(1) The regular net worth computation consists of preparing balance sheets for the beginning and end of each year involved, including thereon reserves for depreciation and amortization computed on a statutory basis. Asset values should be listed at cost or at the taxpayer's basis in all cases. The accounting basis required by law or elected by the taxpayer should be followed in the balance sheet. If the taxpayer reports and is permitted by law to report on the cash basis, such items as business accounts receivable and business accounts payable should not be entered. On the other hand if the law requires that he/she report on the accrual basis, all accured assets and liabilities should be entered even though the return was filed on a cash basis. If the taxpayer is permitted and has elected to report on the installment basis, the element of unrealized gross profit should be set up in the liability of the balance sheet. Where returns are filed on a fiscal year basis, the balance sheet dates should conform thereto.

(2) After computing the net worth for each year, the increase or decrease in net worth is determined by comparing the net worth at the beginning and end of each year.

(3) After determining the increase or decrease in net worth it is necessary to make certain adjustments to account for any expenditures not included in the assets and liabilities as well as various nondeductible and nontaxable items. These adjustments are commonly referred to as below the line adjustments.

(a) The following are some examples of items which should be added to the increase or decrease in net worth:

1 personal living expenses;
2 income tax payments;
3 nondeductible portion of capital losses;
4 losses on sale of personal assets (if included as assets on the balance sheet);
5 gifts made.

(b) The following are some examples of items which should be subtracted from the increase or decrease in net worth:

1 nontaxable portions of capital gains;
2 tax-exempt interest;
3 nontaxable pensions;
4 nontaxable portion of proceeds from life insurance;
5 gifts received;
6 inheritances;
7 Veterans Benefits;
8 dividend exclusions;
9 excludable sick pay.

(4) The result of the adjustments to the increase or decrease in net worth is adjusted gross income as corrected.

(5) To arrive at the correct taxable income, the adjusted gross income figure is reduced by allowable itemized deductions (or standard deduction) plus the personal exemptions.

(6) Exhibit 13 contains an illustration of the net worth computation.

933 *(8-30-76)* 4231
Cash on Hand at the Beginning of the Period

933.1 *(8-30-76)* 4231
Introduction

One of the most important factors in a net worth computation is the establishment of a correct and "tight" opening net worth statement. This usually involves the sound determination of cash on hand in the opening net worth. In many cases the taxpayer, or his/her representative, will make claims of sizable cash accumulations at the beginning of the period in an attempt to counteract the increases determined by this method of computation. The examiner is faced with the difficult problem of verifying the truthfulness of the taxpayer's contention.

933.2 *(8-30-76)* 4231
Methods of Verifying Taxpayer's Statement of Cash Accumulation

(1) As was mentioned previously, the initial interview with the taxpayer can be, and usually is, the most important phase of an examination. At this time, the taxpayer may give accurate, dependable and useful information which he/she may be reluctant or unwilling to give at a later date. If the subject of cash on hand is approached with the emphasis placed on the taxpayer's present cash accumulations with inference to the past, the taxpayer may make statements which may solve this problem. If the taxpayer does make such a statement, the agent should be sure to make comprehensive notes in his/her workpapers as to the date of the statement and the information given. It even may be advisable at that time to prepare an affidavit to be signed by the taxpayer pertaining to this type of information.

(2) At the initial interview a casual discussion of the taxpayer's financial history may give the agent information which will disclose that the taxpayer had once been in some financial difficulty or even had been in bankruptcy or subject to a law suit where his/her assets and liabilities in the past were a matter of determination.

(3) In many instances the taxpayer may have filed balance sheets with financial or credit organizations. This may assist the examiner in the determination of the opening cash accumulations.

(4) On other occasions loans and chattel mortgages on automobiles, personal furniture and other equipment, especially if at a high interest rate, may be evidence that the taxpayer would not have any sizable cash accumulations during that period.

(5) Another consideration in the determination and allowance of cash on hand at the beginning of the period, is the taxpayer's filing history. An analysis of the income reported in prior years may indicate that cash accumulations claimed would be an impossibility when compared to the income previously reported.

934 *(8-30-76)* 4231
Application of Funds

(1) This method is a variation of the net worth method and is simply the comparison of all

known expenditures with all known receipts. The excess of expenditures, when reported adjusted gross income or net income is included among the sources, represents understated income. In this method only the increases and decreases in assets and liabilities are entered along with other nondeductible and nontaxable receipts.

(2) Where a quick preliminary survey is required or where only one or two years are under investigation, this method may be more expeditious than the net worth method. It assembles the increases in assets, decreases in liabilities, etc., directly without the need of subtracting opening from closing net worth. This method also eliminates the need for assembling those assets and liabilities which are on hand without change for both the beginning and ending of the year. Exhibit 14 contains an illustration of an "Application of Funds" and ties in with the net worth computation disclosed in Exhibit 13 for the year 1964.

(3) The same problem concerning cash on hand at the beginning of the period which was involved in net worth computation is also present in this method. The taxpayer may contend as an additional source, cash accumulations at the beginning of the year. This problem must be met in the same manner as previously explained.

940 *(8-30-76)* 4231
Bank Deposits Method

941 *(8-30-76)* 4231
Gross Receipts and Cash Expenditures

(1) The bank deposits method involved a determination of net profit by adding the taxpayer's cash disbursements to his/her net bank deposits and subtracting the business expenses claimed on the return. If an analysis indicates an understatement, it may be due either to unreported gross receipts or to the overstatement of cash expenses or a combination of both. Since, in most cases, the revenue agent is only interested in the net effect, the determination of the source of the adjustment need not be made.

(2) To demonstrate the computation, the following example is used. A, a cash basis taxpayer with no initial capital contribution, operates a business for one year with the following transactions.

Cash Receipts	$250,000
Business Expenses Paid by Check	136,000
Business Expenses Paid by Cash	2,000
Depreciation	6,000
Bank Loans	10,000
Personal Expenses Paid by Business Check	2,000
Returned Check Redeposited	500
Payment on Loan by Cash	1,000
Payment on Fixed Assets by Cash	1,000
Payment on Loan by Check	5,000
Payment on Fixed Assets by Check	5,000
Bank Deposits	257,500
Transfer from Personal Account	1,000

(3) A correct income summary statement for A is as follows:

Sales	$250,000
Business Expenses	144,000
Net Profit	$106,000

(4) Suppose when A files his income tax return for the year in question, he decides he is not going to pay taxes on all of his net income, so he inflates his expenses by $20,000. His income tax return will then show:

Sales	$250,000
Business Expenses	164,000
Net Profit	$ 86,000

(5) When A's income tax return is examined the revenue agent in our example decides to use the bank deposit's method. The agent, of course, does not know whether the return is correct as filed, sales are understated, or expenses overstated. He does know, however, that *there are two things which A cannot alter: The amount of his disbursements by check and the amount of his bank deposits.* The use of these figures will, in theory, adjust the income to the correct amount, regardless of where the distortion lies.

(6) The revenue agent makes the following analyses:

Analysis of Bank Deposits:		
Gross Deposits		$257,500
Less Deposits from Sources Other than Sales:		
Proceeds of loan—from bank	$10,000	
Returned check redeposited—bank debit slips	500	
Transfer from personal account—analysis of personal checks	1,000	
Total Deposits from Sources Other than Sales		11,500
Net Deposits from Sales		$246,000
Analysis of Business Checks:		
Disbursements by Check		$148,000
Less: Check Disbursements for Other than Business Expenses:		
1. Personal expenses by business check	$ 2,000	
2. Payment on loan by business check	5,000	
3. Payment on fixed assets by business check	5,000	12,000
Business Expenses by Check		$136,000
Business Expenses per Return		$164,000
Less: Expenses Included Not Involving Funds:		
1. Depreciation		6,000
Business Expenses per Return Involving Funds		$158,000
Business Expenses by Check—from Check Analysis		136,000
Business Expenses by Cash		$ 22,000
Add: Other Disbursements by Cash:		
Payment on note—from bank note ledger	$ 6,000	
Payment on note by check—from check analysis	5,000	
Payment on note by cash		1,000
Payment on fixed assets—from seller's records	$ 6,000	
Payment on fixed assets—from check analysis	5,000	
Payment on fixed assets by cash		1,000
Total Cash Disbursements		$ 24,000
Add: Net Bank Deposits		246,000
Gross Receipts Reconstructed		$270,000
Less: Business Expenses Claimed per return		164,000
Net Profit Corrected		$106,000

(7) The net result is that the inflated expense of $20,000 increases the sales by $20,000 and the net profit is corrected by subtracting an inflated expense figure from an inflated sales figure. This computation will work equally well in a situation where the taxpayer decides not to inflate his expenses but to understate his sales. Let us assume the same set of facts as was used in the foregoing illustration with the exception of assuming that the expenses were shown correctly on the return, but the sales were understated by $20,000. The income tax return will then show:

Sales	$230,000
Business Expenses	144,000
Net Profit	$ 86,000

(8) The revenue agent would follow the same procedure in either instance since, as was stated previously, he has no way of knowing what, if anything, is wrong with the reported income. His computation if sales were understated would be as follows:

Business Expenses as Shown per Return	$144,000
Less Expenses per Return Not Involving Cash—Depreciation	6,000
Business Expenses per Return Involving Funds	$138,000
Business Expenses by Check—from Check Analysis	136,000
Business Expenses by Cash	$ 2,000
Add: Other Disbursements by Cash:	
Payment on note by cash	1,000
Payment on fixed assets by cash	1,000
Total Cash Disbursements	$ 4,000
Add: Net Bank Deposits	246,000
Gross Receipts Reconstructed	$250,000
Less Expenses as Claimed per Return	144,000
Net Profit Corrected	$106,000

(9) It can readily be seen that in both instances the correct net profit was arrived at by the examiner without resorting to an analysis of individual expense deductions. In the illustrations given, it was assumed that there was no increase or decrease in the cash on hand (undeposited cash) during the year. Any change in the amount of cash on hand, however, will not alter the basic correctness of the computation, but an adjustment to the gross receipts should be made in instances where there is such a change. In arriving at the expenditures by cash in the illustration, add into the computation any personal living expenses by cash. This addition naturally serves to increase the gross receipts reconstructed.

(10) The bank deposits method can be used for accrual basis taxpayers by the adjustment of the receipts for any increase or decrease in accounts receivable and deferred items, and the adjustment of the expenses for any increase or decrease in accounts payable, or for items accrued during the taxable year.

(11) Particular attention should be given to redeposits, transfers of account, deposits from loans, deposits from sale of fixed or capital assets, deposits of nontaxable income, and deposits from any other source besides sales or gross receipts, all of which, if not properly excluded, will increase the net profit. Additionally, an effort should be made to determine checks included as business expenses, since an understatement of business expenses by check will increase the net profit correspondingly. In instances where inventories are used, care should be exercised to make sure that the business expenses per return include the purchase figure and not the cost of goods sold. If the cost of goods sold is used the computation will reflect the change in inventories.

(12) The bank deposits method, as well as the net worth method, is always open to the question of cash on hand at the beginning of the year under examination. Therefore, when using the bank deposits method the agent should obtain necessary evidence as to whether cash was available at the beginning of the year.

(13) An illustration of a formal bank deposits method is contained in Exhibit 15.

950 *(8-30-76)* 4231

Percentage Computation Method

951 *(8-30-76)* 4231

Introduction

(1) This method is a system of computation whereby determinations are made by the use of percentages or ratios considered typical to the business or item under examination. By reference to similar businesses or situations, percentage computations are secured to determine sales, cost of sales, gross profit or even net profit. Likewise by the use of some known base as the typical percentage applicable, individual items of income or expense may be determined. In this manner new elements of income and expenses may be disclosed.

(2) These percentages may be externally derived or they may in some instances be internally derived from the taxpayer's accounts for other periods or from an analysis of subsidiary records. Reference should be made to Chapter (21)00 for sources of typical percentages; however, many percentages may be secured from the examination of the taxpayer's records even though only partly available. Gross profit percentages may be determined by the analysis of purchase invoices to sales invoices, price lists and other similar data. Also other years not covered by the examination or portions of years under examination may indicate typical percentages applicable to the entire year or years under current investigation.

952 *(8-30-76)* 4231

Limitations

(1) Although the percentage method may be a useful method of determination or verification of taxable income, especially when the books and records are inadequate, judgment should be exercised by the examiner to make sure the comparisons are made to situations that are similar to those under examination. Some of the factors to be considered in the determination of a typical situation are as follows.

(2) *Type of merchandise handled*—In order that a proper comparison may be made, the business must be dealing in the same type of merchandise or service. For example, the comparison of the gross profit of a restaurant to that of a grocery store would be of little value and should not be used.

(3) *Size of operation*—In many instances gross profit, cost of doing business, and net profit percentage on sales will vary due to the size of a business. This is especially true for expense items and the net profit as compared to sales. The percentage of net profit to sales of a large department store would vary considerably from the small independently owned general store.

(4) *Locality*—This factor must be a consideration in the determination of a typical ratio to be used in this type of computation. Markups and costs of operations will normally vary to a certain degree by the size of the city or the location of the businesses in the locality. As an example, a small business in a community of 5,000 may use newspapers as a means of advertising, while a business doing the same volume in a city of 500,000 will normally find the cost prohibitive and confine advertising to some other medium.

(5) *Period covered*—Since gross profit ratios and expense ratios will tend to vary year by year due to economic conditions, the comparison should normally be made to similar periods covered by the examination.

(6) *General merchandising policy*—Care should be exercised in not making percentage comparisons between businesses having different merchandising policies. Some businesses may work on large volume with small markup, offering the customer little service; others may operate on the reverse policy. In situations of this kind, comparisons should be made only to those business having similar merchandising policies.

953 *(8-30-76)* 4231

Examples

The following examples illustrate the percentage method of computation. The percentages used are arbitrary and are not necessarily applicable to the businesses mentioned.

(a)

Gross Profit on Sales:	
Retail sporting goods store:	
Net sales (determined from books or by other means)	$50,000.00
Gross profit percentage	28.6%
Gross profit as computed	$14,300.00

(b)

Sales on Cost of Sales:	
Bar and tavern:	
Cost of liquor	$20,000.00
Cost of beer	15,000.00
Cost of food (determined from books or by other means)	5,000.00
	$40,000.00
Cost of sales—Liquor	33 1/3%
Costs of sales—Beer	66 2/3%
Cost of sales—Food	50%
Sale of liquor	$60,000.00
Sale of beer	22,500.00
Sale of food	10,000.00
Total sales as computed	$92,500.00

(c)

Net Profit on Sales:	
Filling station:	
Net sales (determined from books or by other means)	$30,000.00
Net profit percentage	8%
Net profit as computed	$2,400.00

(d)

Miscellaneous Ratios:	
Waitress:	
Sales by restaurant	$90,000.00
Number of waitresses employed	3
Average sales handled by waitress	30,000.00
Percentage of tips	15%
Income from tips as computed	$4,500.00

960 *(8-30-76)* 4231

Unit and Volume Method

(1) In some instances the determination or verification of gross receipts may be computed by applying price and profit figures to the known or ascertainable quantity of business done by the taxpayer. This method is feasible when the agent can ascertain the number of units handled by the taxpayer and also knows the price or profit charged per unit. The ascertainment of the number of units or quantity of business done by the taxpayer may be determined in certain instances from the taxpayer's books, as the records under the examination may be adequate as to cost of goods sold or as to expenses, but only inadequate as to sales. In other cases the determination of units or volume handled may require the agent to contact third party sources for this determination.

(2) The use of this method lends itself to those businesses in which only a few types of items are handled or there is little variation in the type of service performed, with the charges made by the taxpayer for the merchandise or services being relatively the same throughout the taxable period.

(3) The following examples illustrate the unit and volume method of computation.

(a) The gross income of a coin operated laundry might be determined from an analysis of the utility bills, the rate of consumption per appliance and the charge per load. The utilities consumed per load can be determined from the manufacturers of the appliances and the total number of loads of washing can be estimated by dividing gallons of water consumed by gallons per load. The rate charged per load of washing can then be applied to the total number of loads to arrive at an estimated gross income. The gross income of a gas dryer can be

similarly estimated by using total cubic feet of gas consumed, cubic feet used per load, and charge per load.

(b) The gross income of the operator of a cigarette vending machine business can often be made from an analysis of State cigarette tax stamp purchases in those States which have such a tax.

970 *(8-30-76)* 4231

Verification from Third Parties

(1) An important thing for an agent in any examination is to acquaint himself/herself with the activities of the taxpayer. If the major source of income of the taxpayer is from the operations of a business or profession, the examiner should be cognizant of the products or services offered, the market and customers for these products or services and the sources and manner of supply. This is especially true when the revenue agent encounters records which are inadequate.

(2) Many businesses whose scope of activities is limited to a few customers or a few suppliers lend themselves for verification through third parties. On these occasions a good portion of the taxpayer's income can be established through third party records which may disclose sales, purchases and other expenses attributable to the taxpayer. Thus, the examiner may be able to establish one portion of the profit and loss statement through third parties and, by the use of methods previously described, determine the remainder. The following examples will illustrate this auditing technique.

(a) A manufacturer of houseware items sold its entire output to three "chains." Sales were readily established from only three sources. The taxpayer, rather than the agent, is now confronted with the problem of verifying the deductions against these sales that have been established.

(b) A wholesale dealer in lubricants reported a gross profit on sales of only 6 percent. His records were inadequate and he was not cooperative. From a telephone directory the names of two competitors were obtained whose tax returns showing 14 and 17 percent gross profit were requisitioned for reference purposes. Discrete inquiries from these competitors revealed the general business methods of the industry and the names of the taxpayer's principal customers and suppliers. These customers and suppliers were contacted for a record of their transactions with the taxpayer. From the information obtained, a significant portion of the taxpayer's business transactions were determined and some valid conclusions were drawn about his true gross profit.

(3) While, as indicated by the above examples, the third party approach is best suited for taxpayers who have only a few customers or suppliers, it may be used, at least in part, in examining other types of businesses. Any determinations of unreported income or possible falsified expenses on a specific item basis will serve as a means for the use and support of the other methods shown in this chapter. The importance of this method is especially significant in fraud cases, since a pattern of specific omissions may indicate a willful attempt to defraud the Government.

Fraud

(10)10 *(8-30-76)* 4231
Introduction

(1) Fraud or indications of fraud are usually discovered by revenue agents during the course of an income tax examination. It is essential to understand the importance of detecting fraudulent schemes and devices, in order to be able to recognize indications of fraud, and promptly report these findings as required by the Internal Revenue Manual. See (10)92.

(2) Auditing returns and investigating taxpayers who attempt to evade payment of their taxes by fraudulent means is one of the most important phases in the enforcement of the internal revenue laws. The significance of this work can best be measured in terms of its effect on our voluntary assessment system. The lack of proper enforcement would result in a growing disrespect for our tax laws and, consequently, less compliance and loss of revenue.

(3) The recommendation for assertion of the fraud penalty is a very serious charge and should not be made lightly. The fraud penalty should be applied on a case-by-case basis giving consideration to all factors which indicate the existence of a fraudulent intent. Examiners should be diligent in developing the facts in any case in which there is an indication of fraud.

(4) The detection of most fraud cases is the result of alertness on the part of revenue agents in recognizing indications of fraud during their examinations. The successful development of a fraud case is an effective demonstration of an agent's professional skill. It requires a high degree of auditing ability and the use of appropriate investigative techniques as well as patience and perseverance. Furthermore, revenue agents are reminded that they have the duty and responsibility of reporting in writing fraud and other violations coming to their knowledge.

(5) Revenue agents are not expected to pursue every examination as a potential fraud case. However, they are expected to understand what fraud is, and to recognize indications of fraud where it exists.

(10)20 *(8-30-76)* 4231
Types of Violations

(10)21 *(8-30-76)* 4231
Introduction

The revenue agent is concerned primarily with determining the correct taxable income, and preparing reports setting forth the correct tax liability. In civil fraud cases, these reports serve as a basis for civil action in assessing the deficiencies and penalties. In criminal fraud cases, which are worked in cooperation with the Intelligence Division, revenue agents' reports are an important part of the material gathered to prove the taxpayer's guilt.

(10)22 *(8-30-76)* 4231
Civil and Criminal Cases Distinguished

(1) A civil fraud case is an examination or investigation to determine the taxpayer's tax liability as well as his/her liability for the 50 percent civil fraud penalty. Civil cases may be investigated jointly with the Intelligence Division or independently by the Audit Division. In a civil case, the evidence of intent must be clear and convincing to sustain the assertion of the 50 percent civil fraud penalty. Where such evidence is developed in a case, the normal three-year period of limitations does not apply and the tax and penalties may be assessed at any time without regard to the years involved. Civil penalties are assessed and collected administratively as part of the tax.

(2) A criminal fraud case is an investigation to determine if criminal prosecution should be undertaken. Criminal cases are usually investigated jointly by the Audit and Intelligence Divisions. In a criminal case, the evidence of intent must be shown beyond a reasonable doubt to sustain criminal prosecution. The statute of limitations for prosecution purposes generally expires six years from the time the offense was committed which is usually the due date of the return. Criminal penalties consist of fines and/or imprisonment and are assessed by the Federal Courts.

(3) If a taxpayer is proven guilty in a criminal case he/she is generally liable for the 50 percent civil fraud penalty in addition to any criminal penalties assessed by the courts. Because the requirements of proof differ, the income computations may also differ in a particular case for civil and criminal purposes. For instance, the evidence relating to a particular item of income may be sufficiently clear and convincing to prove civil fraud, but yet may not be provable beyond a reasonable doubt as required for criminal fraud. Thus, the item would be shown as income in the civil case but not included in the income computation in the criminal case.

(4) In a civil case, the liability is assessed against the taxpayer whose return is involved, except when transferee liability is recommended. In a criminal case, action may be taken

against all participants in the fraud, even though their own returns are not involved. A husband may be charged with evading his wife's taxes, or corporate officers may be charged with evading the corporation's taxes. An accountant or bookkeeper may be charged with evading his/her client's or employer's taxes when he/she aids or abets in the preparation of the false return. The civil assessment will be made against the estate of a deceased taxpayer whose return was found to be fraudulent. Criminal action cannot be taken against the estate of a deceased person for the acts of the deceased person in order to have a fine imposed against the estate. But, criminal action may be taken against any person who knowingly aided the decedent in preparing or filing the return or assisted in the preparation of the books or records.

(10)23 *(8-30-76)* 4231
Other Violations

(1) While most fraud situations will concern omissions and understatements of taxable income, there are other violations with which a revenue agent should be familiar. They are as follows:

(a) failure to file return;

(b) failure to collect and pay tax;

(c) failure to supply information;

(d) failure to pay tax;

(e) issuance of fraudulent withholding statements to employees, or failure to issue withholding statements;

(f) fraudulent withholding exemptions certificate submitted by employee (fictitious or nonallowable exemptions) or failure to supply information to employer;

(g) making and subscribing to a false and fraudulent return, document or other statement, or aiding and assisting such action;

(h) submission of false or fraudulent offers in compromise or closing agreement;

(i) failure to obey summons;

(j) attempts to interfere with administration of Internal Revenue Laws;

(k) filing of delinquent returns.

(2) These violations should be reported in the same manner as omissions and understatements of taxable income coming to the attention of the agent. See (10)90.

(10)24 *(8-30-76)* 4231
Other Taxes

Indications of fraud may develop from examinations of estate and gift tax, employment, and excise tax returns as well as income tax returns. Revenue agents who are regularly assigned such other tax returns are most likely to uncover such indications of fraud. But, income tax examiners should also be alert to discover and report any indications of fraud or underpayment of such other taxes.

(10)30 *(8-30-76)* 4231
Recognizing Fraud

(10)31 *(8-30-76)* 4231
Definition of Fraud

(1) Fraud is generally defined as deception brought about by misrepresentation of material facts, or silence when good faith requires expression, resulting in material damage to one who relies on it and has the right to do so. It may be defined more simply as deception with the object of gaining by another's loss.

(2) Fraud usually involves false documents, returns and or statements, and includes attempted evasion, conspiracy to defraud, aiding, abetting or counseling fraud and willful failure to file returns in income, estate, gift, and excise tax cases.

(10)32 *(8-30-76)* 4231
Avoidance Distinguished from Evasion

(1) The agent should not be misled into construing every attempt by a taxpayer to lessen his/her tax burden as a scheme to defraud. Every taxpayer has the right to reduce and minimize his/her tax liability by legitimate means, if in doing so he/she does not conceal or misrepresent the facts. A taxpayer may legitimately shape events and select methods of conducting his/her financial or business affairs with consideration to their ultimate tax effect. But once the events have occurred, he/she should fully report the transactions in his/her tax returns or reflect them in the books and records upon which his/her return is properly based. Such a taxpayer relies on interpretation of the law or competent advice and does not attempt to defraud by concealing or misrepresenting the facts.

(2) Tax evasion, on the other hand, involves deliberate concealment or misrepresentation of facts which result in a fraudulent understatement of tax liability. There may be a thin line of demarcation between avoidance and evasion; therefore, suspicious tax practices should be scrutinized to determine if any indications of fraud are present.

(10)40 *(8-30-76)* 4231
Basic Facts to be Proved to Establish Fraud

(10)41 *(8-30-76)* 4231
General

(1) Generally in order to establish fraud, the Government must show that:

(a) the tax liability reported was understated, and

(b) the understatement was the result of a willful intent to evade tax.

(10)42 *(8-30-76)* 4231
Understatement of Tax Liability

(1) The first basic fact to be proved is that the taxpayer failed to report his/her correct tax liability, i.e., there was taxable income which was understated, or the taxpayer had income subject to tax but failed to file a return and report this tax liability. Proof may be obtained by direct evidence of specific items not properly reported on the return or indirectly by use of circumstantial evidence to show that the tax on the return is an understatement of the correct tax liability.

(2) A tax return is a summary of the many transactions which the taxpayer engaged in during the year. This information is commonly gathered by the taxpayer from his/her books or records. In specific item cases, the agent will show that certain items were not completely or accurately reflected on the return resulting in an understatement of income. By contrast, the agent may resort to indirect measures to prove the inaccuracy of the return. He/she may make use of methods such as the net worth and expenditures method or bank deposit method. See Chapter 900. In using any of these methods the agent seeks to show that in its final result the return does not correctly reflect the taxpayer's income. The courts have approved the use of these methods in numerous civil and criminal fraud cases.

(3) Tax evasion schemes used by taxpayers to reduce their tax liability will fall into one of the following categories:

(a) understatement or omission of income;

(b) claiming fictitious or improper deductions;

(c) false allocation of income;

(d) improper claims for credit or exemption.

(4) There are numerous examples of tax evasion schemes and devices which will be presented under these categories later in the Chapter.

(10)43 *(8-30-76)* 4231
Willful Intent to Evade Tax

(10)43.1 *(8-30-76)* 4231
Introduction

(1) The Government must prove not only that the tax liability reported was understated, but that such understatement was the result of a deliberate or intentional design to knowingly evade tax. A willful intent to evade tax is evidenced by an understatement based on deceit, concealment, subterfuge, or attempt to color or obscure the true facts. An intent to evade tax usually cannot be inferred solely from the fact that income was understated, since proof that income was understated does not in itself establish that the omission was intentional. A failure to correctly report income may be due to mistake, inadvertence, reliance on technical advice, honest difference of opinion, negligence or carelessness, all of which may negate a willful intent to defraud.

(2) The problem of establishing intent when an agent finds a taxpayer has understated his/her income is basic. Intent to evade or defeat tax occurs when a taxpayer knows that he/she had deliberately misrepresented the facts. Intent is a state of mind. Hence, an agent working only with things done or said by the taxpayer, must determine the taxpayer's state of mind from such data, since the things done or said by a person are assumed to be the natural consequences of the person's intention. Intent, therefore, may be inferred from conduct of the taxpayer calculated to cheat, mislead, or conceal. The mere fact that a taxpayer files delinquent returns is not a sufficient basis to justify assertion of the civil fraud penalty. The circumstances surrounding the delinquent filings must strongly indicate an intent to evade tax.

(10)43.2 *(8-30-76)* 4231
Failure to File Cases

When examiners encounter cases in which the taxpayer failed to file required returns, a

determination must be made whether there is any indication of fraud. If so, the examiner should not solicit returns but should refer the case, through channels, to the Intelligence Division as provided in IRM 4562.3. (See also (10)91.) An indication of fraud exists when it is determined that the taxpayer knowingly failed to file a required return and that his/her failure to file was without reasonable cause. Thus, the examiner must determine that a return was due; that no return was filed; that the taxpayer knew he/she should have filed a return; and that there was no acceptable reason for his/her failure to file.

(10)44 *(8-30-76)* 4231
Indications of Fraud

(10)44.1 *(8-30-76)* 4231
Introduction

An indication of fraud is a fact or a set of facts, usually of an irregular nature, which in the light of all other known facts and circumstances may be reasonably interpreted as being part of a tax evasion scheme. There is no stereotyped tax evasion pattern which may be fitted to all particular situations to determine if an indication of fraud exists. Rather, the determination must be separately made in each case through application of the professional judgment of the examiner to the known facts and circumstances. Some of the most common indications of fraud which may point to a tax evasion scheme are indicated in the following subsections.

(10)44.2 *(8-30-76)* 4231
Understatement of Income

(1) An understatement of income attributable to specific transactions, and denial by the taxpayer of the receipt of the income or inability to provide satisfactory explanation for its omission.

(a) Omissions of specific items where similar items are included.

(b) Omissions of entire sources of income.

(2) An unexplained failure to report substantial amounts of income determined to have been received.

(a) Substantial unexplained increases in net worth, especially over a period of years.

(b) Substantial excess of personal expenditures over available resources.

(c) Bank deposits from unexplained sources substantially exceeding reported income.

(3) Concealment of bank accounts, brokerage accounts, and other property.

(a) Accounts in other cities.

(b) Using fictitious names, wife's maiden name, or names of relatives and other persons, without disclosing true ownership.

(c) Use of safe deposit box.

(4) Disguising income by false description of source of disclosed income.

(5) Inadequate explanation of large sums of currency, or the unexplained expenditure of currency.

(6) Failure to deposit receipts to business account, contrary to normal practices.

(10)44.3 *(8-30-76)* 4231
Claiming Fictitious or Improper Deductions

(1) Substantial overstatement of deductions, or substantial amount of personal expenditures charged to deductible business expenses.

(2) Inclusion of obviously unallowable items in unrelated accounts.

(3) Recurrence of improper and fictitious deductions.

(4) Claiming nonexistent, deceased, self-supporting, or nondependent exemptions.

(10)44.4 *(8-30-76)* 4231
Failure to File

(1) *Deliberate failure to file a required return*—Knowledge of the obligation to file should be assumed if the taxpayer is engaged in an occupation, the nature of which can be construed to be prima facie evidence of such knowledge. Examples below include the accounting and legal fields, real estate, insurance and stock brokers, teachers, and business executives.

(a) A taxpayer's refusal or apparent inability to explain the delinquency.

(b) Statements made by a taxpayer which are contrary to the facts known by the examiner.

(c) Repeated delinquencies in the past, especially when coupled with an apparent ability to pay.

(d) The taxpayer's failure to disclose assets, the transfer of his assets to others, or other acts to conceal assets.

(e) The payment of personal and business expenses in cash by taxpayers when such cash payments are not customary. Also, the cashing rather than the depositing of checks, representing business receipts.

(f) Taxpayer's belligerence, threats, and attempts to interfere with the examiner in the performance of his duties.

(10)44.5 *(8-30-76)* 4231
Accounting Irregularities

(1) Keeping a double set of books or failing to keep books.
(2) False entries or alterations made on the books and records, back-dated documents, false invoices or other false documents.
(3) Failure to keep adequate records, destruction of records, concealment of records, or refusal to make certain records available.
(4) Journalizing of questionable items out of correct account.
(5) Variance between treatment of questionable item on the return as compared with books.
(6) Unnumbered or irregularly numbered invoices.
(7) Understatement of both income and deductions.

(10)44.6 *(8-30-76)* 4231
Allocation of Income

(1) Distribution of profits to fictitious partners.
(2) Inclusion of income or deductions in books of related taxpayer, when difference in tax rates may be a factor.
(3) See Chapter 600, IRM 4(12)10, Tax Audit Guidelines—Individuals, Partnerships, Estates and Trusts, and Corporations (to be reissued as IRM 4233), for development of IRC 482 cases. Chapter 600 relates to International Enforcement Program; however, the material also applies to domestic cases.

(10)44.7 *(8-30-76)* 4231
Acts and Conduct of the Taxpayer

(1) False statements, especially if made under oath, about a material fact involved in the investigation.
(a) False affidavit.
(b) False net worth statement under oath.
(2) Attempts to hinder investigation.
(3) The bad reputation of the taxpayer and the doubtful character of his/her business dealings.
(4) The classification of the taxpayer in the "Racketeer" category.
(5) The taxpayer's knowledge of taxes and business practices where numerous questionable items are reflected on the return.
(6) Testimony of employees concerning irregular business practices by the taxpayer.

(10)44.8 *(8-30-76)* 4231
Other Items

(1) Pattern of consistent failure to fully report income over a period of years.
(2) Proof that the return was incorrect to such an extent and in respect to items of such character and magnitude as to compel the conclusion that the falsity was known and deliberate.

(10)44.9 *(8-30-76)* 4231
Summary

(1) In determining whether there is an intent to evade, the agent should review the information he/she has discovered in the light of the above "indicators" from which inferences of fraud may be drawn. However, the taxpayer should be given an opportunity to explain every questionable item and his/her explanation should be evaluated in the light of what a reasonable person would have done.
(2) In some cases, the presence of a substantial omission of income or unallowable deduction is quite often its own evidence of an intent to defraud. In other cases, the intent is not so obvious but must be determined according to the circumstances surrounding the case. For instance, such items as improper allocation of income or expenses between related businesses or improper original postings must be considered in relationship to the experience and skill of bookkeepers and accountants, directions given them by owners or officers, and the number of such transactions, etc. The explanation given by owners, officers and employees should be considered in arriving at a determination.

(10)50 *(8-30-76)* 4231
Requirements of Proof

(10)51 *(8-30-76)* 4231
Introduction

An understanding of the requirements of proof is essential in establishing fraud. It is necessary to prove actual fraud in a return in order to support the 50 percent civil penalty and in many cases to enable the assessment of a deficiency where such assessment would otherwise be barred by the statute of limitations.

(10)52 *(8-30-76)* 4231
Burden of Proof

As a general rule, the burden is on the taxpayer to overcome the presumption that the Commissioner's determination is correct. However, in a fraud case the burden is on the Government to prove the taxpayer intended to evade the tax.

(10)53 *(8-30-76)* 4231
Degree of Proof

(1) In a civil fraud case, simply amassing the evidence is not enough. Fraud is never presumed. It must be affirmatively established by clear and convincing evidence. The decisions of the courts are continually enunciating the need for "clear and convincing" evidence. It is not necessary to prove that the entire deficiency was based on fraud, but only that some part of the deficiency was due to fraud.
(2) In a criminal prosecution case, proof beyond a reasonable doubt is necessary for a

conviction. The special agent will be responsible for the sufficiency of the evidence in all joint investigation cases.

(10)60 *(10-29-79)* 4231
Tax Evasion Schemes

(1) Taxpayers use many schemes and devices to evade tax. What methods do they commonly use to evade taxes? What techniques can the agent employ to discover these schemes? What procedures should be followed after he/she has discovered an indication of fraud? These are some of the questions which will be answered in the succeeding sections.
(2) Tax evasion schemes fall into one or more of the categories enumerated in (10)42:(3). That is, the taxpayer will either fail to report all of his/her income, make false claims for deductions, credits or exemptions, or falsely represent his/her income as being another's, or belonging in other years. Some of the more common variations are shown below.
(3) Unreported incomes.
(a) Failure to record sales, fees, or commissions.
1 Cash receipts pocketed, or deposited in a personal bank account.
2 Check payment received, but check cashed or deposited in a hidden bank account.
3 Check payment deposited in regular bank account without posting to the cash receipts journal, with a check for the same amount drawn to cash (or taxpayer) also not entered in the cash disbursements journal.
4 Undertable payments by customers paying taxpayer's personal expenses, rendering personal services, or giving their own merchandise.
(b) Recording sales, fees, or commissions, but not including in income by offsetting false entries or falsifying records through erroneous postings.
1 Underfooting sales book, sales accounts, cash sale account, register tapes, etc.
2 A variation in the above would be erasing, crossing out, or altering amounts in the sales journal with compensating adjustments in the related accounts.
3 Overstatement of returned sales, sales allowances, and sales discounts.
4 Understatement of sales by fraudulent entries in a loan account, exchange account, reserve account, or capital account.

(c) Failure to record and report sales of scrap, by-products, or waste or other items not primarily held for sale or inventories regularly.
(d) Failure to record and report rents collected (with false representation that premises were vacant).
(e) Failure to report income from subrentals, concessions, or other similar miscellaneous income from business.
(f) Failure to record and report collections on accounts previously charged off as bad debts.
(g) Failure to report interest on loans, notes, bonds, bank accounts, or to report dividends received.
(h) Failure to report income from sales of securities, real estate or other assets.
(i) Failure to report income from insurance collected, insurance refunds, purchase discounts, advertising rebates, and other forms of refunds and rebates.
(j) Failure to report income from "kickbacks" by department store buyers, purchasing agents, retail store and restaurant managers, and other key employees in a position to place large orders.
(k) Failure by professional people to report referral fees received from specialists.
(4) Improper or false deductions.
(a) Overstatement by falsely charging purchases, travel and entertainment, or other expense accounts with cash paid to owners, partners, etc.
(b) Deliberate overstatement on return of expenditures allegedly made for business purposes.
(c) Overstatement by overfooting purchases account, other expense account, or cash disbursements book.
(d) Overstatement by charging purchases with checks issued to fictitious payees, or for false invoices, usually with the money eventually returning to the owners, partners, etc.
(e) Understatements or omissions of returned purchases, purchase allowances and purchase discounts.
(f) Duplication of merchandise costs under two headings, or on the books of two or more branches.
(g) Overstatement of opening inventory carried forward or deliberate understatement of closing inventory, often by actual concealment of goods or materials.
(h) Charging obviously personal living expenses, or obviously unallowable entertainment expenses, as business deductions.

(i) Padding payrolls by including persons no longer employed, fictitious names, personal servants and household help (as business expense), or by raising amounts of payroll vouchers.

(j) Kickback of portions of, or duplicate, salaries or wages by employees to their employers.

(k) Raising amounts on check stubs or cancelled checks after payment, and entering raised amounts in expense accounts, often issuing second check to cash for the difference in order to reconcile the checkbook with the bank statement.

(l) Fraudulent reduction of income by setting up improper accrued liability accounts.

(m) Charging gifts and contributions to relatives as salary or wages.

(n) Disguising graft payments or kickbacks as deductible expense.

(o) False accounts inserted in loose-leaf binder.

(p) Charging false interest expense, or other nonexistent expenses.

(q) Overstatement of allowable deductions on personal return.

1 Deliberate overestimate of contributions.

2 Excessive medical expenses.

3 False claims for casualty losses.

4 Nonreimbursed business expenses claimed by persons not incurring such expenses.

5 Fictitious miscellaneous deductions.

(5) False allocation of income.

(a) The claiming of a fictitious partnership, usually among related parties, for the purpose of escaping surtax.

(b) Two or more businesses owned by one person, but falsely represented as being owned by others. Profits after payment of taxes by nominee owner will be turned over to true owner.

(c) False payment or crediting of salaries or wages to wives, children, or relatives not actually working.

(d) Profitable brokerage accounts carried in the names of others.

(e) Purchase and sale of real estate in the names of other persons without adequate explanation.

(f) Reducing taxable income and shifting to other years by means of false inventory valuation.

(g) Losses claimed on transfers of assets between two persons, or between a corporation and stockholder, when the transaction is not made in good faith and no loss actually sustained.

(h) False gifts or assignments of income-producing property, or right to receive income from property such as real estate, stock, etc.

(i) Manipulation of income or expenses between related corporations, or individuals; or to other taxable periods.

(j) Use of fictitious related service company to reduce income.

(k) See Chapter 600, IRM 4233, Tax Audit Guidelines, Individuals, Partnerships, Estates and Trusts, and Corporations, for development of IRC 482 cases. Chapter 600 relates to International Enforcement Program; however, the material also applies to domestic cases.

(6) False claims for credits or exemptions.

(a) False statement regarding marital status.

(b) False statement with reference to the number of dependents.

(c) Filing joint returns without reporting incomes of spouse while latter files separate return, usually wife filing in maiden name.

(d) Fictitious or inflated prepayment credits.

(7) One specific scheme having possible tax consequences is arson-for-profit. The Service is not responsible for the enforcement of the crime of arson. However, the Service is committed to the enforcement of compliance with the tax laws to ensure that the proper tax is paid on income—whether legal or illegal.

(a) Indicators of possible arson schemes with potential tax consequences are:

1 Failure to report insurance proceeds which exceed the basis of the property destroyed by fire.

2 Failure to report the correct adjusted basis of the property destroyed.

3 Failure to reduce a large casualty loss claimed on a return by the insurance proceeds received.

4 Reducing insurance proceeds by payoffs to "torches"—individuals starting the fires.

5 Taxpayer concealing or burning business records after contact by IRS to make an examination of the tax return.

(b) Examiners should consider using in-depth examination techniques in cases where the taxpayer is suspected of being engaged in arson-for-profit activities.

(8) These schemes are representative only and are not intended to be a complete listing of all possible tax evasion schemes. Such schemes are limited only by the cunning and ingenuity of the dishonest taxpayer and the extent of his/her greed. They will vary from simple diverting of cash receipts, to falsification of complex accounting records. The size and type of business operations, the manner in which income is received, the extent of the records required, or other factors, all have a bearing on the extent of the manipulation followed in attempts to evade tax liability.

(10)70 *(10-29-79)* 4231
Techniques

(10)71 *(12-29-80)* 4231
Discovery and Development of Fraud Cases

(1) If, during the course of an examination, material discrepancies are discovered which may exist in prior and/or subsequent years, the examiner *may* expand the examination to include other year(s). A pattern of understated income or overstated expenses is one significant factor to consider in determining whether there are firm indications of fraud. If fraud is suspected, see (10)91 of this Handbook for further instructions.

(2) The discovery and development of fraud cases is a normal result of effective examinations. Auditing techniques employed by revenue agents, if they are to be effective, should be designed to disclose not only errors in accounting and application of tax law, but also irregularities that indicate the possibility of fraud. It is not suggested that an agent deliberately set out to make a fraud case of every return assigned to him/her. However, he/she should recognize indications of possible fraud when they exist.

(3) Fraud, as defined earlier, involves misrepresentation and concealment. Fraud, therefore, will not ordinarily be discovered when an agent readily accepts the completeness and accuracy of the records presented and the explanation offered by the taxpayer. The audit should not consist of a casual verification of a few of the items listed on the return. To discover fraud it is usually necessary to go behind the books and to probe beneath the surface. Just when an agent should use these techniques, how far he/she should follow them, and how far he/she should extend his/her examination will depend on the agent's judgment in a particular case. In a doubtful case he/she should always consult with his/her group manager.

(4) Many experienced agents attribute their ability to recognize a possible fraud case to "intuition." Closer analysis will reveal that it is not intuition but experience which enables them to recognize the signs, circumstances, and facts which are generally present in fraud cases. It is the unusual, the inconsistent, or the incongruous items which alert agents to the possibility of fraud, and the need for further investigation.

(5) See IRM 426(28) for additional fraudulent situations peculiar to alleged churches and related individuals.

(10)72 *(8-30-76)* 4231
Precontact Analysis of the Return

(10)72.1 *(8-30-76)* 4231
Introduction

By a careful scrutiny of the return, the agent will become familiar with its contents and this will enable him/her to note unusual items. The preliminary review of the return may be the first indication that the income is not being reported properly or that a more intensive examination may be required.

(10)72.2 *(8-30-76)* 4231
Source of Income

(1) At the outset, the source of the reported income should be studied. Some of the more common situations which should alert an agent to the likelihood of fraud are listed below.

(a) Some trades, businesses and professions may ordinarily enjoy high income possibilities. The agent should note the income reported to see if it is in keeping with the normal potential of the reported activity.

(b) Current economic conditions may enhance the earnings of some taxpayers. These "windfall" earnings may not be fully reported in order to avoid paying high taxes, or because they resulted from transactions in violation of the laws imposed by regulatory bodies.

(c) Trades and businesses which customarily do business with currency permit easy concealment and understatement of income. Their receipts may consist largely of currency or their expenditures may be required to be made with currency. In both instances the currency can easily be diverted to the principals, rather than correctly recorded and reported.

(d) Those taxpayers engaged in illegal activities or enterprises in which "shady" characters wield power should arouse the agent's suspicions.

(e) Taxpayers who are in sensitive or influential positions may be in a position to accept gratuities, bribes, or graft. The agent should proceed with his/her examination tactfully and cautiously lest he/she offend innocent parties.

(f) Small businesses and professions operated by individuals, partners, or closely held corporations, where both the receipts and records are controlled by the owner(s), present favorable opportunities to commit fraud. The agent should be alert in these situations.

(10)72.3 *(8-30-76)* 4231
Scrutiny of Return

See 231 of Law Enforcement Manual IV.

(10)72.4 *(8-30-76)* 4231
Case File

(1) Prior to contacting the taxpayer, an agent should review all the information available to him. Usually the available information will have already been associated with the case file, which should include the prior revenue agent's report. The reports and workpapers for prior years will contain valuable information regarding the taxpayer and his/her activities. The results of prior audits, including prior fraud investigations and possible suspicions from the findings of the preceding examiners will aid the revenue agent in making a current examination.

(2) The file may also contain information received through other channels, such as informant's communications, newspaper items, reports from financial institutions regarding unusual currency transactions, 1099's, revenue agent's information reports, reports from other government bodies or enforcement agencies, etc. These should be carefully scrutinized and compared with items on the return where practicable. At this point it is emphasized that information of this type is of a highly confidential nature. The agent is cautioned not to reveal to the taxpayer, his/her representative, or any other unauthorized person, that he/she has such other information. As a precaution it is advisable for the agent not to bring these documents with him/her to any meeting with the taxpayer or his/her representative. Instead, he/she should make notes in his/her workpapers of the items he/she wishes to verify or to search for in the taxpayer's records.

(3) If the taxpayer is engaged in a business with which the agent is not familiar he/she should consult with other agents who may have had experience with that type of business or refer to trade publications, e.g., Dun and Bradstreet, National Cash Register, etc., which report average mark-up and gross profit percentages. These publications will provide valuable information regarding ratios of expenses to sales and investment ratios to income. Although each type of business has its own peculiar trade practices, agents should be acquainted with the practices of the individual taxpayer, particularly those which are most likely to be utilized as a tax evasion device.

(10)73 *(8-30-76)* 4231
Initial Contact with Taxpayer

(1) At the time the agent contacts the taxpayer to arrange for an appointment, he/she should inform the taxpayer which records will be needed for the examination. The taxpayer should be requested to make available not only the summary accounting records, but also the supporting records, including bank statements, canceled checks, sales invoices, purchase bills, etc. Likewise, the taxpayer's personal financial records should be obtained. Personal records should be specified, particularly where the taxpayer has separate business records and might expect the agent to confine the examination to the business records. The taxpayer's personal bank account and other financial records are a primary source of information leading to unreported income; agents should always inspect them.

(2) The agent should take care not to request at the outset of the examination any particular records or documents relating specifically to transactions or sources of income on which he/she has information in addition to that reflected on the return. Usually, he/she would not be expected to have knowledge of such items with only the return assigned to him/her. Neither should he/she place undue emphasis on the request for records relating to items on the return which arouse his/her suspicions. A premature disclosure of the agent's suspicion or that he/her has additional information might cause the taxpayer to take steps to prevent the successful development of the examination.

(3) When examining a business or professional return, the agent should always try to make the examination at the taxpayer's office or place of business. In this way, underlying and supporting documents which may be needed as the examination progresses will be readily available. If it should be inconvenient to make the audit on the taxpayer's premises, the agent should consider making a personal visit at another time. At the place of business he/she will have an opportunity to observe the size and type of the business operation. The gross receipts reported on the return can be studied in relations to the nature of the business, the plant facilities, its location, the equipment, the number of employees, and the type of merchandise manufactured and sold. In the case of a professional person a similar comparison can be made with emphasis on the size and location of the office, its furnishings, the staff, the professional status of the taxpayer and the number of years in practice. If the examination is made at the taxpayer's home, the house and its furnishings can be evaluated in terms of reported income. On a farm, the acreage, the equipment, the barns and outbuildings may be indicators to the accuracy of the income. The agent will be able to gage the scope of the business operation and note any visible signs of unreported income.

(4) These observations should not be viewed as a venture in "spying." The agent is responsible for determining the taxpayer's correct taxable income. Hence, he/she should make use of all information obtainable consistent with good conduct and with regard for the rights of the taxpayer.

(5) At the start of the examination it is customary for agents to engage the taxpayer in conversation. In this way agents become acquainted with the nature of a taxpayer's business or other income-producing activities, the type of accounting records kept, who is responsible for them, who prepared the return, and in what capacity. The agent should also determine the manner in which the taxpayer accounts for his/her receipts. The development of this information will enable the agent to plan the audit accordingly. During this discussion taxpayers frequently disclose much information concerning themselves and their finances which will be useful to the agent in making the audit. The taxpayers may also inadvertently reveal information leading to unreported income. For a more complete discussion on the technique of interviewing the taxpayer, see 921.

(10)74 *(12-29-80)* 4231
Examination

(1) Usually the initial step in the audit is for the agent to compare the return with the records the taxpayer has made available to see if the return was prepared from these records. At the same time he/she will become familiar with the accounts and may note any unusual items which will require further analysis. At this time he/she should note any inadequacies in the books and records. The initial step is of particular importance if the return is later determined to be fraudulent, because to allege that the taxpayer has not reported certain income, it is first necessary to establish what income he/she has reported.

(2) During the examination, preferably in the early stages, the agent should review any statements, accountant's workpapers and audit reports, reports of examination by other Governmental agencies, copies of prior year tax returns and other papers furnished by the taxpayer. He/she should note any inconsistencies between the return and the data contained in these other documents. The accountant's audit report will indicate to what extent independent verification has been made of the entries in the taxpayer's books. The agent can take this factor into consideration in judging the reliability of the books and records. The reports of audits made by other agencies should be examined for their possible income tax effect.

(3) A comparison of returns for several years is an excellent method of obtaining valuable information. Changes in the taxpayer's financial position can be noted from the asset acquisitions over the years and the increasing or decreasing in liabilities and capital accounts. Changes in sources of income and deductions and their amounts may give leads to tax evasion practices. Any discrepancies in inventories or other balance sheet accounts carried forward in the current return can be discovered.

(4) Unless information on hand, or discovered, alerts the agent to the possibility of fraud, the examination contemplated by the agent will ordinarily not be of the same scope or intensity as in a fraud case. The extent of the examination will depend on the agent's judgment based on the facts in each case. Every examination should be thorough enough to explain any questionable items on the return and to adequately cover any information item associated with the return or which may have caused the examination. However, as the examination progresses, the scope or intensity of the examination may increase according to the agent's findings.

(5) If, during the course of an examination, material discrepancies are discovered which may exist in prior and/or subsequent years, the examiner may expand the examination to include other year(s). A pattern of understated income or overstated expenses is one significant factor to consider in determining whether there are firm indications of fraud. If fraud is suspected, see (10)91 of this Handbook for further instructions.

(10)75 *(8-30-76)* 4231
Attitude and Conduct of Taxpayer

(1) The first symptoms alerting the agent to the possibility of fraud will frequently be provided by the taxpayer. His/her conduct during the examination and his/her method of doing business may be symptomatic of improper returns being filed. The agent should look for the following regarding the possibility of fraud.

(a) Repeated procrastination on the part of the taxpayer in making and keeping appointments with the agent for the examination.

(b) Uncooperative attitude displayed by not complying with requests for records and not furnishing adequate explanations for discrepancies or questionable items.

(c) Failing to keep proper books and records in a business or profession, especially if previously advised to do so.

(d) Disregard for books and records.

(e) Destroying books and records without plausible explanation.

(f) Making false, misleading, and inconsistent statements.

(g) Submitting a false document or affidavit to substantiate items on return.

(h) Trying to conceal a pertinent fact on record.

(i) Altering records.

(j) Failing to deposit all receipts.

(k) Using currency instead of bank accounts.

(l) Extent of taxpayer's control of sales and receipts and his/her apparent unwillingness to delegate this function to his/her employees.

(m) Engaging in illegal activities.

(n) Hasty agreement to adjustments and undue concern about immediate closing of the case may indicate a more thorough examination is needed.

(10)76 *(8-30-76)* 4231
Audit of Books and Records

(1) In the examination of a return, either individual, partnership or corporation, the agent will usually find some records. In some cases because of the necessity of the taxpayer to maintain control over his/her business, these records will be complete, to the extent that all transactions will be recorded in them. In such cases, if the taxpayer seeks to understate his/her true income fraudulently, he/she may do so by concealing and disguising income through fictitious entries in the books or by improper allocation. Expenses and other deductions can be padded and overstated by similar manipulation. In other cases the books and records may appear to be complete, but may not be, as all transactions, particularly all income transactions, may not be entered.

(2) If the above is suspected and the books and records are available, a more comprehensive audit should be made. This should include comparison with the originating records, such as bank deposit slips, cancelled checks, sale and purchase invoices, expense vouchers and other pertinent supporting data. An agent should prepare complete workpapers, tying in items on the return with the books and records. He/she should properly identify his/her workpapers by describing the records from which they were prepared. The workpapers should be dated and initialed. If the books and records are found to be inadequate, in that they do not reflect income properly, or if the examiner suspects they are incomplete and that all income is not reported, the examination should be extended beyond the books.

(3) The agent is cautioned that he/she should not carry his/her investigation beyond the point where his/her suspicions concerning possible fraud are confirmed. He/she should proceed only to a point where he/she has developed a valid indication of fraud adequately supported by his/her workpapers. See (10)90.

(4) All agents should be familiar with the various tax evasion schemes listed in (10)60. In his/her examination, the agent should employ audit techniques designed to detect these schemes. For some of the techniques which have been found useful, see 232 of Law Enforcement Manual IV.

(10)80 *(8-30-76)* 4231
Information Affecting Other Taxpayers

(10)81 *(8-30-76)* 4231
General

(1) Revenue agents should also be alert to indications of fraud on the part of taxpayers other than those whose returns they have been assigned. Information affecting the tax liability of other taxpayers may be discovered in the course of their examinations, or at other times. It may be discovered in the audit of the taxpayer's records, in the records of others, or from other sources. It may affect a particular taxpayer or several taxpayers in a particular group or category.

(2) Information submitted by revenue agents is more reliable and generally more productive of revenue than information received from other sources. Agents are better qualified to judge the tax effect of information coming to their attention.

(10)82 *(8-30-76)* 4231
Information Developed During Examination

See 233 of Law Enforcement Manual IV.

(10)83 *(8-30-76)* 4231
Information Affecting Other Taxpayer Groups

(1) When an agent has successfully developed a tax evasion case he/she should consider the possibility that other taxpayers similarly situated might be using the same method or device to defraud the Government. If it appears that the use of the method is widespread or that particular areas of noncompliance can be identified, returns of other taxpayers can be selected for examinations. Examples of such returns are listed below.

(a) Returns filed by the same tax practitioner.

(b) Returns filed by taxpayers in the same business or profession.

(c) Returns filed by taxpayers in the same geographic locality because of conditions known to exist there.

(10)84 *(8-30-76)* 4231
Other Sources of Information

(1) Revenue agents, because of the nature of their duties, travel extensively within their district, meeting taxpayers and tax practitioners and inspecting public and private records. They have the opportunity to observe and receive information, sometimes inadvertently, relating to unusual business practices, expansion and growth of business organization, larger personal expenditures, high standards of living, and suspicious financial transactions. Information of this type frequently leads to the successful

development of tax fraud cases. Examples of such leads are listed below.

(a) Unusual or rapid expansion of a small or medium size business involving costly additions to business property.

(b) Purchase of a lavish home or substantial expenditures for additions and improvements.

(c) Substantial increases in standard of living.

(d) Public records. Large parcels of real property bought and sold. Mortgages acquired.

(e) Banks and brokerage houses. Bonds, cashiers checks, or securities purchased with currency. Checks cashed.

(f) Customers' and suppliers' books and records.

(g) Known transactions not properly recorded. Inadequate or no books and records.

(h) Boastful remarks regarding noncompliance with internal revenue laws.

(i) Advice to employees or business associates that indicate disregard of internal revenue laws.

(j) Newspaper articles indicating a violation of internal revenue laws.

(k) No returns filed.

(2) Information relating to the above or to any other suspicious financial transactions should be submitted in writing to the Chief, Audit Division.

(10)85 *(8-30-76)* 4231
Unethical Tax Advisors

(1) In many localities throughout the country, so-called "tax experts" prepare false returns for lower-bracket taxpayers (usually wage earners) which cause a serious loss in revenue. Returns prepared by these unethical individuals may contain fictitious and padded deductions resulting in excessive refunds of withholding tax and estimated tax credits. In many instances the taxpayer himself/herself may not know that his/her claimed deductions are false, or he/she may be persuaded that he/she should claim more because the "expert" assures him/her that such deductions are proper and allowable. The "expert" is usually motivated by a desire to build up a large clientele of satisfied customers or because his/her fees are based upon the size of the tax refund claimed.

(2) If any evidence is obtained indicating that a return containing any false or overstated deductions was prepared by or under the influence of such "tax expert," this information should be reported in the same manner as other fraud violations.

(3) The agent should keep in mind the possibility of the following when questioning a taxpayer.

(a) The taxpayer signed his/her return in blank and the "tax expert" entered false deductions.

(b) The taxpayer provided a listing of his/her income and the "expert" changed the amount listed or added other deductions not listed.

(c) The "expert" persuaded the taxpayer to claim deductions for expenditures not incurred with the assurance that he/she was entitled to the deductions.

(10)86 *(8-30-76)* 4231
Conduct of Revenue Agent

(1) When the revenue agent has been alerted to the possibility of fraud, he/she should be mindful that the work he/she is doing and the action he/she takes will play a vital part in the final outcome of any criminal case. Listed below are a few cautionary notes.

(a) When seeking additional information relating to possible understatement, the agent should not couch his/her request in language implying favored treatment if the requested information is furnished. He/she should avoid such expressions as: "It will be to your advantage . . ."; or "My office will appreciate it . . ."

(b) He/she should not place himself/herself in a position where he/she is under obligation to the taxpayer or his/her representative.

(c) He/she should not advise or counsel the taxpayer or his/her representative of possible defenses or explanations of understatements, acts of concealment, omissions or other possible acts of fraud.

(d) Statements, remarks or the commission of acts that are subject to misinterpretation should be avoided.

(e) Irregular arrangements for the examination of a taxpayer's books and records, which may lead the person under investigation to believe that prosecution is not contemplated, should be avoided.

(f) The revenue agent should not threaten to bring in the special agents if the requested information is not forthcoming.

(g) He/she should not say anything that could be construed as an offer of immunity or as a step toward settlement of the case on a civil basis.

(h) If the taxpayer or his/her representative questions why the return is being examined or the thoroughness of the audit, the revenue agent should not refer to the examination as "routine." He/she should state that under selection procedures it was selected for examination or that it is his/her responsibility to determine the accuracy of the return.

(i) He/she should make contemporaneous notes of all contacts and conversations with the taxpayer, his/her employees, or third parties, showing date, time of day, place, and exact words, if possible. He/she should make certain that his/her workpapers accurately and completely reflect the results of his/her investigation.

(j) The agent should not accuse the taxpayer of cheating or berate him/her for failing to comply with the income tax laws, nor should he/she indicate his/her conclusions about this during the audit.

(k) When he/she suspends his/her examination he/she should not do so in an abrupt manner so as to alarm or embarrass the taxpayer.

(l) The tax return should not be marked up or written upon in any fashion. The original tax return will be a principal exhibit in a prosecution case and should reflect only the taxpayer's entries and the official stamps and markings used in processing the return.

(m) He/she should never make any notations or marks in the taxpayer's records as they later could cause confusion as to who made them, and their meaning.

(n) A revenue agent should always be impartial in his/her official capacity. He/she must not be influenced by political, racial or religious considerations. He/she should avoid a mental attitude of attempting to "get" persons who are under investigation. He/she must so conduct himself/herself as to make it apparent to all persons connected with the case that his/her investigation is completely impartial.

(o) A revenue agent should be thorough in the conduct of all investigations. It is his/her duty to obtain all pertinent facts, both favorable and adverse, regardless of the conclusions that may later be formed from consideration of them. He/she should exercise initiative and zeal, but should avoid the appearance, in either action or speech, of being overzealous.

(p) A revenue agent should be tactful in his/her dealings with taxpayers. He/she should avoid making any remarks or acts during or following the investigations which are likely to be misinterpreted.

(q) A revenue agent should always be discreet. He/she should not make statements or ask questions that will divulge information which would tend to jeopardise the successful conclusion of the investigation. He/she must not unnecessarily injure the reputation of the person being investigated.

(10)90 *(8-30-76)* 4231
Procedure after Discovering Indications of Fraud

(10)91 *(9-2-80)* 4231
General

(1) IRM 4565.2 provides that if, during an examination, an examiner discovers a firm indication of fraud on the part of the taxpayer, the tax return preparer, or both, the examiner shall suspend his/her activities at the earliest opportunity without disclosing to the taxpayer, his/her representative or employees, the reason for such suspension. He/she will then prepare a report of his/her findings in writing as explained in (10)92. The purpose of the referral report is to enable the Criminal Investigation function to evaluate the criminal potential of the case and decide whether a joint investigation should be initiated. It is important, therefore, that the referral report contain sufficient information to enable the Criminal Investigation function, to make a proper evaluation.

(2) After an examiner discovers the possible existence of fraud he/she must decide when to suspend the examination and prepare a referral report. As stated above, "at the earliest opportunity" does not mean immediately. It means at the earliest point after discovering *firm* indications of fraud. This means more than suspicion. It means the agent has taken steps to perfect the indications of fraud and developed them to the degree necessary to form the basis for a sound referral. This must be done at the first instance while the books and records are available to the agent, because, later on, they may not be accessible and information contained therein may be impossible to obtain.

(3) On the other hand, if the agent extends his/her examination too far before submitting the referral report he/she may be doing unnecessary work. The special agent who will come into the case later may find it necessary to repeat some of the work previously done in order to document evidence required in a criminal case. Also, the over-extension of the examination may jeopardize criminal prosecution by giving the taxpayer a basis for claiming that the criminal case was substantially built by the examiner under the guise of making an audit for civil tax purposes.

(4) In some instances the presence of a substantial omission of income or unallowable deduction is its own evidence of intent. However,

unless the understatement speaks for itself, the taxpayer should be questioned concerning it and the reasons ascertained for treating the suspected items as he/she did. The examiner should ascertain and record the method used in understating the income, and weigh the adequacy and reasonableness of the taxpayer's explanation. These should be evaluated in terms of the nature of the understatement. In this respect (10)44 will be helpful since it contains many of the identifying earmarks from which intent to defraud can be inferred. At the same time the agent should bear in mind that he/she is not, at this point, building a fraud case against the taxpayer. The examiner should not make a detailed interrogation when questioning the taxpayer, nor should he/she argue about the answers. The examiner should delve into the intent element only as far as necessary to support a finding of an indication of fraud. If the explanations offered are considered inadequate or unreasonable, the agent may properly conclude that the understatement is probably due to fraud and a referral should then be made, and forwarded through proper channels as stated in (1) above.

(5) It is important that potential criminal cases be handled properly by the examiner. The examiner should not discuss the taxpayer's case with Criminal Investigation prior to submission of the referral report. After the referral report is submitted, there should be no further contact with the taxpayer until the referral is either accepted (in which case a special agent should be present) or declined. If contacted by the taxpayer or his/her representative, the examiner should be polite and tactful, without discussing the matter of referral with the taxpayer. The examiner should be sure to document any conversations, showing the date, time, and place.

(10)92 *(9-2-80)* 4231
Referral Report

(1) The referral report is to be prepared as provided in IRM 4565.2. This report is a summary of the agent's evaluation of the indications of fraud. It is used to enable Criminal Investigation Division to evaluate the criminal potential of a case and decide whether or not a joint investigation should be undertaken.

(2) The Form 2797, Referral Report for Potential Fraud Cases, is structured to allow an examiner to specifically identify cases that are being referred for Civil Fraud or Criminal Fraud. Cases may be suitable primarily for the possible assertion of the Civil Fraud Penalty due to mitigating factors. (See criteria in 565 of Law Enforcement Manual IV.) All facts should be carefully evaluated before designating the type of referral. If the facts in the referral satisfy the criteria, the referral will be designated "Civil Fraud"; otherwise, it will be designated "Criminal Fraud."

(3) Even if the information available when the report is prepared is insufficient to complete the requirements of Form 2797 in all respects, the agent will not delay preparing the report. He/she will complete his/her report to the extent possible, giving appropriate consideration to the information requested. Care should be taken in the preparation of this report so that it clearly states the indications of fraud which have been discovered. Particular attention should be given to the portions of the report wherein the agent should include information indicative of the taxpayer's intent to evade taxes, the manner in which the taxpayer understated his/her income, and any other significant facts not covered elsewhere in the referral report.

(4) Form 2797, is prepared in quintuplicate. One copy of the report is retained with the agent's case file. The original and three copies are forwarded through channels to the group manager and the Chief, Examination Division, for comments and signatures. The original and two copies are then immediately forwarded to the Chief, Criminal Investigation Division. The other copy is retained in the Examination Division's referral pending file. A copy of Form 2797 is provided as Exhibit 16.

(5) A separate Form 2797 is prepared for each person or legal entity involved, except that only one Form 2797 is prepared for a husband and wife who filed a joint return. For example, an alleged evasion of corporate income tax may result in a case against the corporation and one against the active officer. Thus, separate Forms 2797 are prepared even though the allegation against the officer may involve alleged evasion of both the corporate tax and his/her own individual income tax. Separate reports are not prepared for each different type of violation, but only for each separate classification; i.e., income tax fraud, other tax fraud, wagering excise, wagering occupational, and miscellaneous cases such as requests for penal action for failure to obey a summons, or attempts to inter-

fere with the administration of the internal revenue laws by assaulting an employee. Only one report is prepared covering an allegation of failure to comply with a notice issued as provided in IRC 7512, even though withheld income tax, social security tax, or collected excise taxes are involved.

(6) The agent is again reminded that although he/she should be certain that his/her suspicions concerning fraud are warranted, he/she should guard against proceeding too far in developing the fraud aspects of the case. Guidelines to assist the agent must necessarily be stated in general terms. There can be no absolute criterion established upon which to rely in making a decision when to suspend an investigation and refer a case to Criminal Investigation.

(7) The facts and circumstances in any particular case must be considered in the light of the foregoing. The agent should consult with his/her manager when in doubt as to how far to proceed.

(10)93 *(9-2-80)* 4231
Procedure after Referral to Criminal Investigation Division

(1) Where a referral has been declined by Criminal Investigation, returned due to lack of resources, or an investigation has been discontinued, and after screening for possible re-referrals by the examiner and his/her group manager, they will confer with the Civil Fraud (CF) Coordinator to receive advice and assistance concerning assertion of the Civil Fraud Penalty (CFP) unless one of the following conditions are present:

(a) cases where blatant evidence of fraud is present, where penalties will obviously be imposed but which are declined due to lack of resources, death of taxpayer, de minimis amount, etc.;

(b) cases returned for civil settlement where taxpayers have been prosecuted and found guilty under IRC 7201; and

(c) cases subjected to complete Criminal Investigation consideration where no evidence of fraud was found.

(2) The requirement to meet with the CF Coordinator is optional if one of the conditions outlined above is present. Group Managers will signify their approval that contact with the CF Coordinator is not required by initialing the case file and noting the reason.

(3) The CF Coordinator will meet with the referring examiner and group manager to outline how to document the fraud issues and if necessary make specific recommendations on how to obtain additional evidence of fraud for civil purposes. The CF Coordinator should, in particular, advise and assist the examiner in establishing and presenting evidence of willfulness. In selected cases, and upon request from the Examination Division, the CF Coordinator will participate in the civil examination by conducting interviews of the taxpayer or key witnesses, obtaining the documents, and taking other investigative steps necessary to establish and document the existence of fraud. However, his/her role is considered to be primarily advisory in nature with limited investigative involvement. The examiner retains full responsibility for the assertion of the CFP, subject to established review, and Appeals procedures. Participation by the CF Coordinator will ordinarily preclude any further criminal consideration. When the taxpayer is recontacted by Examination after Criminal Investigation has discontinued its investigation, the examiner will explain to the taxpayer the status of the criminal aspects of the case, and the administrative procedures that will be followed to conclude the examination. If the taxpayer refuses to produce the records for examination, a summons will immediately be issued after clearance through Counsel.

(4) Where a referral has been declined by Criminal Investigation, or an investigation has been discontinued, and the examiner does not recommend the CFP, he/she shall include a brief statement in the report supporting the determination that the penalty was inappropriate.

(10)94 *(5-27-77)* 4231
(Reserved)

(10)95 *(8-30-76)* 4231
Joint Investigations

(10)95.1 *(9-2-80)* 4231
General

(1) A joint investigation is a mutual undertaking by Examination and Criminal Investigation to establish all pertinent facts for determining the taxpayer's correct tax liability, his/her liability for civil penalties, and whether criminal prosecution should be initiated against him/her. Its success depends upon the close cooperation between the cooperating agent and the special agent.

(2) The overall management in a joint investigation rests with the group manager of the cooperating agent as well as the group manager of the special agent. The District Director has discretion to prescribe the use of work plans, investigation status reports and joint case review procedure in any joint investigation in his/her district. If the District Director does prescribe such plans, reports or reviews, he/she will also provide applicable detailed procedures.

(3) Since a joint investigation is a team effort, many of the duties and responsibilities of the revenue agent and the special agent will overlap. It is not possible to clearly define all of the Examination and Criminal Investigation Divisions' responsibilities in joint investigations. This is due to the many criminal charges that may be attached to taxpayers' actions involving Examination activities and the varying nature of criminal investigations made by Criminal Investigation in such matters. Because of the commingling of these features in joint investigation cases, only broad guidelines can be established.

(10)95.2 *(9-2-80)* 4231
Definition of Examination and Criminal Investigation Features

(1) The audit features of a joint investigation generally relate to the examination and verification of accounts in order to establish a firm basis for determining tax liabilities. These features include such items as reconciling taxpayer's records with tax returns, test-checking book entries, inspecting canceled checks, reconciling control accounts with subsidiary accounts transcribing such accounts or parts of accounts as necessary to disclose the basis for adjustments in tax liability, determining and substantiating tax and accounting adjustments having no significant effect on the criminal aspects of a case, and computation of the basis for tax and the tax liabilities, including such computations in those instances when the taxpayer has no books or records.

(2) In the earliest practicable stage of joint investigations, any original returns in the possession of the cooperating special agent should be transferred to the custody of the Examination Division for assignment to the internal revenue agent cooperating in the joint investigation.

(3) Intelligence features, on the other hand, usually include those activities of developing and presenting admissible evidence required to prove criminal violations and the ad valorem penalties for civil fraud, negligence and delinquency (except those concerning tax estimations) for all years involved in cases jointly investigated to completion. Such activities also include obtaining testimonies of witnesses, admissions of taxpayers, and proper documentation of pertinent records and transactions.

(4) Because of the importance of a criminal case from the deterrent standpoint in buttressing voluntary compliance, and the gravity of possible criminal punishment, the criminal aspect predominates in a joint investigation. The special agent is thus charged with responsibility for the method of procedure and conduct of such an investigation. Therefore, in order to protect the criminal features of a case, the special agent, unless and until he/she withdraws from the case, or until the criminal aspects of the case are concluded, will be responsible for the following determinations relating to the case:

(a) the method to be used for criminal purposes in determining the tax basis, such as the determination of income in an income tax case by the "net worth" or "specific item" method, or by a dual determination where it has a significant effect on the criminal case (the cooperating examiner in his/her report may, in addition to the computation for criminal purposes, present an alternative method for purposes of computation of the civil liability);

(b) the identification of those tax basis adjustments upon which a recommendation for criminal prosecution will rest and/or those which will constitute the basis for a recommendation for penalty additions to the tax;

(c) the preparation and issuance of Summons, Form 2039; and

(d) the timing and priority of investigative actions in the case.

(10)95.3 *(8-30-76)* 4231
General Responsibilities

(1) Determination as to whether the cooperating officer or the special agent should perform a specific task or part of a joint investigation, or whether they should perform it together, and the extent of participation of either officer therein must be decided on the basis of teamwork, mutual cooperation and the best interests of the Service in the light of the particular circumstances of the case. The following principles should be considered in making such a determination.

(a) The special agent should be sufficiently familiar with audit features of the case and the cooperating officer sufficiently familiar with its criminal features to corroborate or complement each other's testimony, if necessary.

(b) Accounting and tax features are usually the responsibility of the cooperating officer; developing and documenting evidence of intent is usually that of the special agent.

(c) Extensive documentation of adjustments required in a fraud case results in more detailed transcripts or extracts and more extended account verification than is required for the audit features in an ordinary case.

(d) Often it is less efficient to have the special agent and cooperating officer continually working together on tasks which are normally the responsibility of either one of the officers. To avoid duplication of effort, workpapers prepared by one agent should be made available to the other agent if needed. Such workpapers may be reproduced for that purpose, to the extent necessary.

(e) The special agent is responsible for conserving the cooperating officer's time on a joint investigation and should avoid calling upon him/her unnecessarily for other than normal audit functions. If, in making inquiries of third party witnesses, it is considered necessary to have two officers present the services of another special agent should be utilized whenever practical and the cooperating officers should not be requested to participate unless his/her presence is required. On the other hand, both officers, i.e., the cooperating officer and the special agent, should usually be present when the taxpayer is interviewed.

(f) The special agent should endeavor to plan a joint investigation with the cooperating officer in such a manner that the cooperating officer is engaged in a joint investigation during continuous periods of time without interruptions, as much as possible, rather than spasmodically. The cooperating officer should be informed as much in advance as possible of the plans for joint activities in the case and informed as soon as possible when his/her active participation is completed.

(10)95.4 *(8-30-76)* 4231
Intelligence Responsibilities

(1) Guided by the above, and to prevent duplication or overlapping effort in joint investigations, the special agent will determine the nature and extent of participation by the cooperating officer in the following activities:

(a) assistance in the interrogation of the principal and witnesses in the case;

(b) reconstruction of tax bases, including the determination of the starting point for a net worth computation in an income tax case, and third party inquiries, including cases where the taxpayer has no books of account;

(c) verification of the principal's records by comparison with records of other taxpayers;

(d) examination or transcription of records, accounts and relevant documents, including public records; and

(e) preparation of inventories of records and/or assets, such as listings of the principal's records or contents of a safe deposit box.

(10)96 *(8-30-76)* 4231
Separate Investigation

(1) Separate investigations will be made by the revenue agent in those cases in which the Intelligence Division has determined that there is no criminal potential in the case or for other reasons *does not* recommend a joint investigation. These cases will usually arise from three sources.

(a) Cases referred by a revenue agent as a result of his/her audit findings which are not accepted by the Chief, Intelligence Division, for joint investigation.

(b) Cases in which the special agent withdraws from the joint investigation because it was concluded there was no criminal potential.

(c) Cases which were the subject of a preliminary investigation originating in the Intelligence Division in which it was concluded that there was no criminal potential but the case was referred to the Audit Division because of a possible audit potential, including possible fraud or other appropriate civil penalties.

(2) In his/her examination of a case falling into one of the above categories, the revenue agent should develop all aspects of the case including the evidence to support the fraud penalty, if applicable. The revenue agent should bear in mind that the conclusions reached by the Intelligence Division concerning the sufficiency of the evidence and the credibility of the explanations of the taxpayer relate only to the criminal features of the case. Even though the evidence may be insufficient to support a criminal charge, it may be sufficient to sustain civil fraud. The evidence developed by the separate investigation must be documented sufficiently to enable the Government to carry its burden of proof. Of course, if the revenue agent in his/her subsequent investigation discovers additional facts indicative of fraud, he/she should refer the case again to the Intelligence Division.

(10)97 *(8-30-76)* 4231
Computation of Civil Fraud Penalty on Delinquent Returns

(1) Examiners should be informed of the manner in which the civil fraud penalty is computed in cases involving delinquent returns. IRC 6653(b) and (c)(1) provide that the addition to tax for fraud is computed upon the "total deficiency" which is the difference between the correct tax liability and the tax shown on the return if the return is timely filed and without regard to income taxes withheld. However, in the case of a delinquent return the additions to tax for fraud are properly imposed upon the correct tax liability without any deduction for either income taxes withheld or the amount of tax shown upon the delinquent return. It should also be kept in mind that if both the fraud and delinquency penalties are applicable, the fraud penalty only, rather than both penalties, should be asserted (IRC 6653(d)). The following examples illustrate the above provisions.

(a) Taxpayer's timely filed return showed a tax liability of $5,000, prepayment credits of $4,500 and a balance of tax due of $500. Upon examination it was determined that the correct liability was $15,000 and recommendation was made for assertion of the fraud penalty. The civil fraud penalty would be computed on the deficiency of $10,000 (the difference between the correct tax liability and the tax shown on the return).

(b) Assuming the same facts as in the above example with the exception that the return was delinquent, the penalty for fraud would be properly imposed upon $15,000 (the correct liability without any deduction for income taxes withheld or the amount of tax shown on the delinquent return).

(10)98 *(8-30-76)* 4231
Reference to Internal Revenue Manual

IRM 4560 should be consulted for a detailed discussion of procedures to be followed in handling a fraud case.

Professional Persons

(12)10 *(8-30-76)* 4231
Introduction

(1) Professional persons use many different systems of recording income and expense. Many professional persons practice their professions as sole proprietors, maintain single entry systems of accounting and use the cash basis method of reporting income on their returns. In other instances where partnerships, joint ventures, and associate arrangements exist, the systems usually tend to be more formal.

(2) The income of professional persons is derived from fees for personal services. This is important for the examiner to consider in planning his/her audit, since it will be incumbent on him/her to account for fee income and related professional expenses. Usually there are no inventories nor direct costs of sales involved in earning fees. Consequently, it is seldom that reliable ratios will be available as a rule-of-thumb test in estimating receipts.

(3) Generally, the professional person will employ one or two persons such as a secretary, receptionist or nurse. If one of these persons is related to the taxpayer, the revenue agent should be alert to the possibility of collusion since an internal control may not exist. In small offices where one person is responsible for the receipt and disbursement of funds, the revenue agent should be diligent in the application of auditing tests to assure himself/herself that adequate records are maintained and that income is properly reported. The revenue agent should be alert to the numerous ways in which fee income may be omitted from the records.

(4) Many cases of unreported income have been found by revenue agents involving highly regarded professional persons, who are active in civic and religious organizations. The revenue agent is counselled in regard to audits of this type only to point out that, regardless of the identity of the taxpayer, certain auditing techniques should be used. If the tests and analyses made indicate irregularities, ingenuity and judgment should be used to bring the examination to its proper conclusion. The utilization of information in Chapter (10)00 will be beneficial in this type of case.

(5) As a general rule it can be stated that the most important feature in the audit of a professional person's return is the auditing techniques used to test for omitted income. Of course, expenses should be given appropriate attention, considering the manner of payment and whether substantial in amount.

(6) Techniques suggested herein *are not intended to be all-inclusive,* but are mentioned to point out features which are found in most professions. It would be impractical to apply all techniques in each case. The facts and circumstances in each instance should guide the revenue agent.

(12)20 *(8-30-76)* 4231
Approach

(12)21 *(8-30-76)* 4231
Precontact Analysis of the Return

(1) An audit of a professional person's return requires precontact planning as in other examinations of business type returns. When possible, computations should be made by the revenue agent to determine significant financial information about investments, capital assets purchased, and the type and size of the taxpayer's practice. Experience has shown that a source and application of funds computation prepared from the return itself will frequently reveal beneficial information.

(2) See 233 and (10)72 for detailed information that can be secured from a thorough analysis of the return before contacting the taxpayer.

(12)22 *(8-30-76)* 4231
Initial Interview

(1) Contacting the taxpayer for an appointment and arranging for records to be made available for examination is covered in Chapter 400. A well-rehearsed technique of conducting an interview that will give it a spontaneous atmosphere can be of immense value to the revenue agent. Discussion of personal items usually elicits more forthright answers during the initial interview and should therefore be as all-inclusive as possible. The initial contact, whether by phone or mail, will be of the most value if the taxpayer fully understands the exact records he/she is to have available when the revenue agent arrives for his/her appointment. It is preferable that arrangements for the examination be made with the taxpayer and that the initial interview also be held with him/her.

(2) During the initial interview, the examiner should secure the following information.

(a) Explanation of the accounting system and manner of recording fee income.

(b) What records were used to account for income?

(c) What records were used, and by whom, to prepare the return?

(d) Who handles receipts in the office, who deposits them and are they all deposited?

(e) Length of time in practice, and specialty, if any.

(f) Did the taxpayer engage in teaching, writing, or lecturing?

(g) Number of offices, interoffices or chairs (dentists, podiatrists, urologists, etc.).

(h) Investment data.

(i) Names of all bank accounts and nature (business and personal).

(j) What method is used for billing delinquent accounts? If billings are made on a specific date during the month, some response in the form of collections should be apparent in the subsequent days.

(k) Are delinquent accounts turned over to collection agencies? If so, how are ultimate collections from this agency reported?

(l) Is the taxpayer associated with universities, governmental agencies, schools, industrial concerns, life insurance companies, etc.? If so, how is such income reported?

(m) Were any services rendered without cash remuneration but in exchange for some other asset or service performed by the patient or client?

(3) Securing the above information in the initial interview will usually save many hours of examination time. Experience has shown that this is the most opportune time to secure vital information. The lack of skill in conducting this interview can be injurious to the revenue agent's case in situations where the taxpayer later refuses to cooperate. See 921 and (10)73 for other information which may be secured in the first interview with the taxpayer.

(4) The remainder of this chapter is devoted to setting forth specific information dealing with certain professions, the type of records generally found in these professions, and audit techniques which can be effectively used to test these records and to verify the reported income.

(12)30 *(8-30-76)* 4231
Physicians

(12)31 *(8-30-76)* 4231
General

(1) In examining the returns of a physician (hereinafter referred to as a doctor) it is well to remember that, whereas he/she is highly trained in his/her profession, he/she is usually not trained or educated in the complications of accounting and taxes. Very often he/she will delegate the bookkeeping duties to an employee and depend on an accountant or attorney for tax advice. He/she is a busy person, with his/her time scheduled daily. The revenue agent, in requesting an appointment to audit his/her records, should be firm, as well as courteous.

(2) Attention is directed to the doctor who does not maintain adequate or complete records. It has also been found that doctors who have received notoriety for being involved in illegal abortions and narcotics generally maintain poor records. This should put the revenue agent on notice that other than usual auditing techniques may have to be applied. See Chapter 900.

(3) It is recognized that many doctors earn a very high income. Frequently they keep vital income records personally in order to avoid letting employees know about their business. Some have a constant turnover of clerical help to accomplish the same end. Many times fees are collected and, unknown to the employees, will be omitted from the records. The point for the revenue agent to bear in mind, regardless of the circumstances confronting him/her in each case, is how to test or audit vital parts of the records with the least amount of effort, in order to satisfy himself/herself that income has been properly reported.

(12)32 *(8-30-76)* 4231
Records

(12)32.1 *(8-30-76)* 4231
Introduction

(1) Many systems are in use by doctors to record their income and expenses, and the examiner should find in one form or another the following records:

(a) appointment book;

(b) daily log showing dates, names of patients and payments;

(c) receipt book;

(d) bank records;

(e) disbursement journal or ledger (active and inactive);

(f) recapitulation schedules or worksheets.

(12)32.2 *(8-30-76)* 4231

Appointment Book

The appointment book is not ordinarily used for the recording of bookkeeping entries, unless informal notations are made thereon. This record contains the listing in chronological order of appointments with patients whose names are recorded in advance, usually by the doctor's nurse or secretary. This book is the vital control of the doctor's time, and thus should indicate income activity. If a doctor states that this book has been lost or destroyed, it is very likely that the doctor does not wish to have his/her fee records probed into thoroughly. If this occurs, patient cards and other records for current and prior years should be analyzed carefully to detect errors or omissions in recording fees.

(12)32.3 *(8-30-76)* 4231

Daily Log

When the patient appears for his/her appointment, the visit may be recorded in a "Daily Log." A payment or charge may also be recorded after the visit. This log identifies the patient treated on the indicated date, and it is here that the charges for services are usually recorded. Receipts by mail are also usually recorded in the log.

(12)32.4 *(8-30-76)* 4231

Receipt Book

If a patient makes a payment in cash, a receipt is usually issued. If the receipts are serially numbered, they can easily be checked to the record containing cash payments received. If the receipts are not numbered, and this is common, it will be more difficult to establish that all receipts are recorded in income. If this situation exists, the revenue agent should make tests to satisfy himself/herself that all fees are consistently recorded as income.

(12)32.5 *(8-30-76)* 4231

Bank Records

(1) A vital part of the audit of a doctor's return is an analysis of the following records:

(a) check stubs and cancelled checks;

(b) bank statements—business and personal;

(c) deposit slips (or duplicates);

(d) deposit books (savings accounts).

(12)32.6 *(8-30-76)* 4231

Disbursement Journal or Ledger

This record may be in any form and, if disbursements are made by check, will not differ from other taxpayers' records. Expenses paid by cash should be given special attention.

(12)32.7 *(8-30-76)* 4231

Patients' Cards

It is customary to prepare a card for each patient. The information will vary, but essentially it will be used by the doctor for identification of the patient, and to record charges and payments (including those by mail). Sometimes the medical history will be a part of the card.

(12)32.8 *(8-30-76)* 4231

Recapitulation Schedules or Worksheets

(1) It is customary for doctors to prepare a schedule of fees received for each month. These schedules are then used at year's end to assist in preparing the return. The revenue agent is cautioned to make audit tests of the patient cards and daily log, rather than to rely on the monthly summary figures.

(2) Weekly or monthly totals are usually posted to a schedule to be used by the person making out the income tax return at the end of the year. If only the summaries are furnished during the audit, the revenue agent will make every effort to obtain the original records to determine that fee income has been reported correctly.

(12)33 *(8-30-76)* 4231

Determining Gross Income

(12)33.1 *(8-30-76)* 4231

Introduction

(1) When taxpayers in this category fail to keep complete records, it should alert the revenue agent that other than the usual audit procedures will apply.

(2) Many doctor's returns will show low gross receipts. This may be attributed to the taxpayer's recent start to practice, illness, or his/her aged or semi-retired condition. It also may be that the doctor simply is not capable, or does not have a profitable clientele. The correct reason should be determined as quickly as possible. However, it may be that a substantial portion of fees has been omitted from gross receipts. Whatever the reason, the revenue agent should attempt to establish the true facts before time-consuming audit procedures are undertaken.

(3) Usually medical practitioners earn more than dentists, and many surgeons and special-

ists earn higher fees than general practitioners. The revenue agent should consult with his/her supervisor or experienced agents about some of the facts found in their experience. This will assist the agent in utilizing his/her time in these examinations, particularly in those cases where some or all of the records are not available.

(12)33.2 *(8-30-76)* 4231

Fees

(1) Every doctor has a scale of fees. If possible, this should be determined during the initial interview with him/her. This information permits efficient tests for receipts, charges, and fee income reported. Fees may be received from regular or referred patients, drop-in or emergency patients, insurance companies, and health and accident companies.

(2) Inquiry can be made as to how payments from health insurance companies, such as Blue Cross, are recorded. If any doubts arise, the agent should utilize, if possible, the paying agencies to verify those receipts.

(3) It has been found that practitioners sometimes fail to report fees from after hours office or house calls. If the doctor's diary can be obtained for testing, any omissions can readily be determined.

(12)33.3 *(8-30-76)* 4231

Other Income

(1) Frequently it will be found that a doctor will teach or lecture at medical schools. Sometimes articles or books will be written, and some doctors do work as professional lecturers. Inquiry should be made into these features to ascertain if income from these activities has been reported.

(2) At times the doctor may be called in a professional capacity as an expert witness. Inquiry should be made about the procedure followed in recording this type of income.

(3) An important feature to keep in mind in the examination of doctors' returns is that they generally earn high income and therefore have a strong incentive to minimize their income taxes. Having substantial sums available, there is usually a strong desire to invest in securities, bonds, rental properties, oil properties, and real estate. This, in turn, creates a responsibility for the revenue agent not only to audit the professional records in an efficient manner, but also to investigate investment features in these returns.

(4) Doctors who enjoy a profitable practice, yet report little or no investment income, should be subject to close scrutiny by the revenue agent.

(5) Occasionally a doctor has income producing arrangements with other doctors or professional people. Some of these have been kickback arrangements with druggists on prescriptions, with opticians on prescriptions for glasses and frames, or with specialists on referrals. The examiner should be alert to indications that any of the above practices may exist. If the examiner has reason to doubt that these discounts or kickbacks have been properly recorded, inquiry should be made of the druggist, hospital, or specialist involved.

(12)34 *(8-30-76)* 4231

Verification of Income

(1) The verification of a doctor's income is a technique which calls for skill and judgment. The numerous cash transactions and the widespread absence of adequate accounting controls give rise to a possibility that a substantial portion of the income might be diverted to personal living expenses, investments or to hidden bank accounts without first being included in income. The verification of what is included in the records is a comparatively simple procedure. *It is the uncovering of what might not be in the records that tests the ingenuity and experience of the revenue agent.*

(2) In order to test the records the revenue agent should assemble the appointment book, patient cards, daily log, and deposit slips, if available, for a selected period. Some of the techniques would be:

(a) Test the footings in the daily log to the monthly recapitulation schedule, and then to the annual total gross receipts as reported on the return. Check receipts from Daily Log to deposit slips. Compare patient card financial records with Daily Log.

(b) In conjunction with the above records, effective results can also be obtained if the examiner will secure the names of several patients who have been treated for 1 to 2 years prior to the year under examination. The examiner should then secure the open and closed cards and compare them as to their completeness and for accuracy of the recording of the fees received for the entire period.

(c) Select patients' names by alphabet and taking those in one letter, test to the above records and the active and inactive patient cards.

(d) Analyze or reconcile the total deposits to gross funds available to the taxpayer. See Chapter 900 for techniques.

(e) If some of the records are not available or all receipts are not deposited, the examiner may wish to ascertain if there has been a substantial increase in net worth in the years under review. See 930 for techniques. Frequently an informed net worth computation will indicate an unexplained source of funds. If this occurs, the examiner should bring this to the attention of his/her supervisor since fraud may be involved.

(f) If the doctor permits the agent to review the record of individual patient's medical history, similar cross checks can be made to verify that either charges or collections are recorded when services are rendered. The doctor may neglect to record appointments for patients requiring treatment at regular intervals over a long period of time and instead rely on his/her memory.

(g) In the event some records are not available, the taxpayer is uncooperative, or the examiner wishes to test the accuracy of some of the records examined, the following sources may be of assistance.

1 *Local medical society records*—A file is maintained of all member physicians listing the hospital where each physician is associated.

2 *Hospitals*—Each hospital maintains a record of all admissions authorized by each physician. Another file is kept for all surgery performed or assisted by each physician.

3 *Public birth and death records*—These records usually indicate the name of the attending physician.

4 *Insurance company records*—(Life insurance, health and accident, hospitalization.)

5 *Pharmacies*—Druggists are required by law to keep a record of all prescriptions filled. Occasionally they also maintain a cross-index file by physician's name.

6 *Local telephone answering service.*

(12)35 *(8–30–76)* 4231
Expenses

(12)35.1 *(8–30–76)* 4231
Introduction

(1) A doctor is entitled to deduct from gross income, as ordinary and necessary business expenses, all amounts actually expended in carrying on his/her profession. Since most doctors are on the cash basis of accounting, the expenses must be paid to be deductible. Exceptions to this are depreciation, prepaid rent and insurance and other items of this type which should be deducted ratably as they expire.

(2) In the event the doctor has an office in his/her home, it will be necessary to apportion the personal and business expenses. The examiner must be alert to personal expenses claimed under the guise of business deductions.

(3) Although no specific comparison can be made between a physician's gross income and the amount of drugs and supplies he/she purchases, large expenditures for drugs and supplies would normally indicate either a large volume of business or that he/she is a combination physician-pharmacist who administers and sells preventive vaccines and drugs. However, a revenue agent should be aware that physicians do receive many free samples of drugs and supplies. Also, it is not unheard of for a medical supply house to stock personal items, such as, cameras, luggage or sports equipment. If these personal items are included in the drug expense, they should be disallowed.

(12)35.2 *(8–30–76)* 4231
Salaries and Wages

In some cases, a doctor will employ other doctors as assistants. Also, there may be a participation or bonus arrangement with them. In this event, the disbursement should be verified with the cash records. These persons are usually paid as independent contractors, not subject to withholding tax. The examiner should satisfy himself/herself that the amount received by the assistant was reported correctly. Referral fees or fee splitting payments are deductible when they are cutomary in the profession and in the community and are not prohibited by law.

(12)35.3 *(8–30–76)* 4231
Domestic Labor

The examiner should check the payroll records to determine the number of employees involved and inquire as to the duties of each, for the purpose of eliminating domestic help. Amounts paid to persons engaged in housework are not deductible. In the event the doctor maintains an office in his/her home, a proper apportionment of expenses must be made. Wages paid a chauffeur are rarely deductible.

(12)35.4 *(5–7–79)* 4231
Taxes

If the doctor owns any property, other than his/her home, and claims real estate taxes, the tax bills should be examined to eliminate any personal taxes from the business schedule. Also see text at 678:(2)(d) of this Handbook for method of deducting state income taxes.

(12)35.5 *(8–30–76)* 4231
Bad Debts

As has been stated, most doctors report on the cash basis, which usually precludes their claiming losses from bad debts. Occasionally a fee is paid by a check which later fails to be honored by the bank. If the check was reported when received, the taxpayer would then be entitled to a deduction when the check proves bad. If the doctor reports his/her gross fees as billed, he/she would be entitled to a bad-debt deduction for fees not actually received. If delinquent accounts are turned over to a collection agency, it should be determined how recoveries are handled.

(12)35.6 *(8–30–76)* 4231
Depreciation

(1) As a general rule, depreciation will not be a significant factor in examining the return of a doctor, since capital assets are not generally a substantial factor in producing his professional income. The year and manner of the acquisition of assets should be checked, noting the financial arrangements and whether the funds used came from a properly identified source.

(2) The agent should check for duplication of expense, such as depreciation of auto. It may also be claimed in auto upkeep.

(12)35.7 *(8–30–76)* 4231
Repairs

This is not usually a significant item in a doctor's return. However, if the amount is substantial, the canceled check should be examined in conjunction with the invoice to determine the nature of the expenditure as well as to verify the actual cost.

(12)35.8 *(8–30–76)* 4231
Insurance

(1) This deduction may include such nondeductible items as life insurance and insurance on personal dwelling. Care should be taken to exclude the personal portion of insurance on autos.

(2) Another reason this expense should be carefully scrutinized is that the doctors usually have no retirement plan to provide for necessities at an advanced age and consequently are often heavily insured. They may carry life insurance, hospitalization, health and accident, business interruption insurance and also may purchase annuities. The agent should assure himself/herself that these premiums are not being paid out of unreported income nor claimed as expense.

(12)35.9 *(8–30–76)* 4231
Travel and Entertainment

(1) Under present law, any deduction for travel and entertainment must meet the long-standing statutory test of ordinary and necessary as well as the requirements of IRC 274. The examiner should pay particular attention to those doctors' returns wherein amounts are claimed for entertainment and similar expense.

(2) Many abuses have been found in this area and the examiner should be thoroughly familiar with the requirements of IRC 274 before embarking upon an audit of travel and entertainment.

(12)35.10 *(8–30–76)* 4231
Dues

Dues for membership in professional associations and civic organizations are generally deductible as ordinary and necessary business expenses. The deductibility of dues for membership in any social, athletic, or sporting club or organization, however, is subject to the provisions of IRC 274; the agent, therefore, should be familiar with these requirements prior to the audit.

(12)35.11 *(8–30–76)* 4231
Automobile

Expenses for commuting between a doctor's residence and his/her office are nondeductible regardless of the distance. The examiner will usually have the problem of apportioning auto expense as to business and personal, and the facts in each case should govern.

(12)35.12 *(8–30–76)* 4231
Education

(1) The cost of a refresher course may be allowed only to the extent that it is necessary to keep the doctor advised on new developments in his/her field. The cost of instruction in a field in which he/she has not previously engaged is not allowable. Prolonged courses would indicate new skills were being acquired.

(2) Psychoanalysts and psychiatrists frequently incur expenses for personal analyses which may be required in their profession. Such expenses usually arise near the close of their training or just prior to the start of their practice. Such expenditures are not deductible as medical or business expenses. They may possibly be deductible as educational expenses, depending upon the facts of the particular case.

(12)36 *(8-30-76)* 4231
Physician and Patient—Privilege

The Federal courts have assumed the communications made by a patient to a physician, while seeking professional advice, are privileged.[1] This privilege has not been extended to financial matters, such as the amount of fees paid for professional services. The privilege has also been indirectly denied in connection with summonses issued by special agents for production of hospital records.[2] If the revenue agent is well informed on the subject of privileged matter in the doctor-patient relationship, an audit of the doctor's returns should pose no difficulty in obtaining the necessary information in regard to financial transactions of either party.

(12)40 *(8-30-76)* 4231
Dentists

(1) The accounting systems and records of dentists are very similar to that of other doctors. A dentist usually keeps an appointment and daily log book designed especially for dentists.

(2) In contrast to the examination of other doctors, the costs of supplies in a dentist's work will be higher, due to the use of gold, silver, etc.

(3) In determining the correct income, the revenue agent should verify that the sale of used precious metals has been included in gross income.

(4) Generally speaking, it will be difficult for a dentist to defend the need for extensive entertainment and travel expense and the revenue agent should be firm in his/her requests for substantiation of expense in this category.

(5) The procedures for verification of income of a doctor should be followed in the examination of a dentist's tax return.

(12)50 *(8-30-76)* 4231
Attorneys

(12)51 *(8-30-76)* 4231
Introduction

(1) It has often come to the attention of the Service, in examining the returns of attorneys, that there is a widespread practice of maintaining a minimum of accounting records. Very few attorneys keep a card index of clients; if they do, this index is rarely made available to agents in their audits. As a result of this, examiners are constantly pressed to use ingenuity in auditing available records in order to determine the accuracy of same and to evaluate the effort the taxpayer has made to correctly report his/her income. If is often necessary to resort to third-party records, such as the county court house, to determine if all fees on certain cases have been properly reported in income. In some instances it has been found that the attorney keeps a financial record of the case on the inside of the folder containing the case file. This may involve the important issue of "privileged communications" between an attorney and his/her clients, as related to an examination of an attorney's return. The revenue agent should understand this relationship in order to more successfully secure pertinent financial information when he/she is dealing with an attorney.

(2) There are certain special types of relationships in which information communicated by one person to the other is held confidential and privileged between them. In 8 Wigmore on Evidence (3d Ed.) 2285, it is stated there are four fundamental conditions that must exist:

(a) the communications must originate in a confidence that they will not be disclosed;

(b) the element of confidentialty must be essential to the full and satisfactory maintenance of the relationship between the parties;

(c) the relation must be one which in the opinion of the community ought to be sedulously fostered; and

(d) the injury that would inure to the relationship by the disclosure of the communications must be greater than the benefit thereby gained for the correct disposal of litigation.

(3) The mere relationship of attorney and client does not render confidential every communication made by the client to the attorney. If the attorney is just a conduit for handling funds, or the transaction involves a simple transfer of title to real estate, and there is no consultation for legal advice, communications made to him/her by the client are not privileged.[3]

(4) Communications made in the course of seeking business advice rather than legal advice are likewise not privileged.[4]

(5) It has been held that the privilege is inapplicable to communications made to a person

[1] *Mullen* v. *U.S.*, 263 F. 2d 275 (C.A., D.C.); *Totten* v. *U.S.*, 92 U.S., 105; *U.S.* v. *Kenney*, 111 F. Supp. 233 (D.C., D.C.), rev. on other grounds, 218 F. 2d 843 (C.A., D.C.)

[2] *Albert Lindley Lee Memorial Hospital*, 115 F. Supp. 643 (M.D., N.Y.) Aff'd 209 F. 2d 122 (CA-2), Cer. denied 347 U.S. 960; *Gretsky* v. *Basso*, 136 F. Supp. 640 (D.C., Mass.) 56-1 USTC 9148.

[3] *Pollock* v. *U.S.*, 202 F. 2d 281 (CA-5), 53-1 USTC 9229; *U.S.* v. *DeVasto*, 52 F. 2d 26 (C.A.-2); *McFee* v. *U.S.*, 206 F. 2d 872 (C.A.-9), 53-2 U.S.T.C. 9549; *Koerner* v. *Baird*, 59-2 USTC 9517 (S.D. California).

[4] *U.S.* v. *Vehicular Parking*, 52 F. Supp. 751 (D.C. Del.).

who is both an attorney and accountant, if they have been made solely to enable him/her to audit the client's books, prepare a federal income tax return, or otherwise act solely as an accountant.[5]

(6) As can be seen by the above court references, the protection accorded privileged communications between client and attorney does not extend to the financial transaction between them. The revenue agent should be able to secure from the attorney any records or information in his/her possession, except those containing the privileged communications, which will aid in his/her audit of the attorney's personal return. This will also be true in situations where the examiner seeks information from an attorney about some other taxpayer. It is well for the revenue agent to realize that a situation concerning privilege could be controversial, and the group manager should be consulted if a problem arises.

(12)52 *(8-30-76)* 4231
Records

(1) The records that a revenue agent can expect to find in the audit of an attorney's returns will vary. They usually depend on the business arrangement of those involved. In a partnership, or office where there is an associate arrangement, the examiner will usually find complete and adequate records. An attorney's records differ actually in one respect from others, and that is in the maintaining of an account identified as the client's trust fund or escrow account. There may be several accounts, or the attorney may handle all clients' funds through one account.

(2) The records will usually consist of:

(a) appointment book;

(b) client's card index;

(c) a daily log or receipts book;

(d) a disbursement book or ledger, showing breakdown of regular expenses paid, as well as disbursements made from trust funds;

(e) individual client's accounts showing description of service, charges and credits;

(f) case time record per client;

(g) register of cases in progress, by client's name;

(h) time report per attorney and per client, showing time, dates of work, and billings or charges.

(3) Contrary to a system of complete records maintained in the larger offices, the single attorney, practicing law under less formal office conditions, rarely keeps records in a manner satisfactory to an accountant. However, this does not mean that they are inaccurate or inadequate. They are usually sufficient to record the information that the attorney desires to know. The problem is how to test or audit the available records to determine the accuracy thereof, or to quickly find discrepancies that indicate that the records or manner of recording are inaccurate and necessitate further analysis. The records the examiner may find in this type of office may be:

(a) an appointment book;

(b) diary or day book;

(c) a recording of fees received (many times this is kept by the attorney himself/herself);

(d) a running account of expenses paid;

(e) costs relating to a case which may be maintained on the inside page of the folder containing the case file;

(f) single-entry disbursement book, ledger or sheet;

(g) monthly recapitulation schedule of fees and expenses;

(h) duplicate deposit slips, bank statements and cancelled checks.

(12)53 *(8-30-76)* 4231
Trust Fund or Escrow Account

(1) An accounting feature, peculiar to practicing attorneys, is the trust fund or escrow account. Some States prescribe responsibility for the accounting of client's funds, or funds held in suspense by the attorney. The Canons of Professional Ethics of the American Bar Association, Number 11, dealing with trust property, states: "The lawyer should refrain from any action whereby for his personal benefit or gain he abuses or takes advantage of the confidence reposed in him by his client. Money of the client or collected for the client or other trust property coming into the possession of the lawyer should be reported and accounted for promptly, and should not under any circumstances be commingled with his own or be used by him."

[5] *Olender* v. *US.*, 210 F. 2d 795 (C.A.-9), 54-1 U.S.T.C. 9254; *U.S.* v. *Chin Lim Mow*, 12 F.R.D. 433 (N.D., Calif.); *in re Fisher*, 51 F. 2d 424 (S.D., N.Y.).

(2) Usually the attorney will deposit into this account funds received from the client which will be subject to disbursement for various reasons. Some will apply to the attorney's fee, some will be disbursed to other attorneys, other parties to a suit, other parties to a transaction, and expenses. Good practice dictates that the attorney clearly withdraw funds for his/her fee, and record it in another part of his/her records, but this is not always done. The revenue agent must be alert and carefully analyze disbursements from the fund, and make an accurate accounting of the identity of the funds making up the balance of the account at the end of the period. It has been found that some attorneys misuse the trust fund account to the extent of holding portions of funds in the trust fund account which are actually earned fees or unexpended cost advances. This is difficult to detect, since it could well be that the attorney would be in a position to take alternative actions, or exercise options. Substantial amounts held for any length of time should be investigated to the extent that the examiner is satisfied that the fee income is reported, and in the proper year.

(3) By tracing the payment of funds to other attorneys out of the trust account, the examiner can verify the correctness of the disbursement and also verify that the payment was reported by the recipient.

(4) It is well to remember that attorneys' activities might encompass the whole field of business. He/she may be a specialist in any number of fields (corporation attorney, estates and trusts, criminal, general trial, income tax, grower associations). He/she may be an expert in real estate, giving legal advice in these transactions, and perhaps in some instances be a party to the transaction itself. If the attorney is engaged in investments or speculative transactions, as well as in a professional capacity, the revenue agent should probe the situation to be certain that the true tax liability for all parties concerned is accurately reported.

(5) The revenue agent should be alert to determine that the attorney has disclosed all special accounts, all accounts with associates, all trust fund accounts (since there may be more than one), and all partnership accounts.

(12)54 *(8-30-76)* 4231
Source of Fees

(1) A practicing attorney's principal source of income is from fees received for representing clients in any number of situations. Some sources of fees are from divorce actions, civil actions, trial work, probate work, estates, taxes, legal representation in negotiations for sale or purchase, referral from other attorneys, operation of collection agency or collector of accounts, fees from banks for servicing wills or other service, patents, admiralty law, and lobbyists' fees.

(2) Determining the value of promotional stock or other assets received by an attorney in lieu of a fee for services has always been a problem. The examiner should be aware that attorneys may receive such assets at the time of organizing a new corporation or negotiating a favorable situation.

(3) Sometimes an attorney will attempt to convey the impression that securities, bonds, or other assets, were received as gifts. It has been arranged, in some instances, that the attorney will be the residual beneficiary of an estate. The examiner should ask the taxpayer if any property has been or will be received. If the answer is in the affirmative, the examination should be pursued so that the true facts can be interpreted.

(4) In criminal cases fees are usually demanded in advance. In most cases, attorneys consider this to be the total fee. This is so, especially if the case is lost. Many attorneys maintain a folder for each case, not necessarily by client, so that one person could have several folders. This is well to remember when determining all fees paid by a particular client.

(5) In many areas, members of bar associations have established minimum fee schedules. The use of such a schedule, if available, would assist the examiner in testing the recorded fee income. Any income found by the agent to be inconsistent with the schedule will provide him/her with a good opportunity to discuss the reason for the variance with the attorney. Such a discussion may develop unreported cases and test the accuracy of the records.

(6) Types of fee arrangement include single retainer fees, annual retainer fees, contingent fees, and referral fees. The single retainer fee may be received in advance, in full or in part. The annual retainer fee may be received monthly or at other intervals. Contingent fees are based upon a percentage of amounts collected or recovered. Referral fees are received from other attorneys to whom clients are referred for services.

(7) In cases with inadequate records the following sources of information may be helpful in securing leads to names of clients an attorney may be representing. It would be necessary to

contact the client to determine the amount of fee paid. Local court dockets and legal newspapers contain names of attorneys representing clients before local courts. Certain administrative agencies, such as the Workmen's Compensation Commission, often maintain lists of the names of attorneys who have represented clients before their agencies. In insurance claim cases, regional index bureaus have information on attorneys which may be helpful. Any casualty insurance company can supply the name and address of the index bureau for the State of the taxpayer under examination. The amount of the information available will depend on the recordkeeping system of each index bureau.

(8) The examiner may occasionally find an attorney reporting a fee claimed to be earned over a 36-month period or more and coming under section 1301, as originally enacted. These original relief provisions apply to taxable years beginning before 1964 or, if elected by the taxpayer, to years beginning after 1963 provided "employment" began before February 6, 1963.

(9) With the exception of this election, for taxable years beginning after 1963, the income averaging provisions of IRC 1301-1305 would apply.

(10) In the event either situation exists, the examiner should determine whether the relief provisions are applicable.

(11) Practicing attorneys may also receive income from teaching and writing.

(12)55 *(8-30-76)* 4231
Expenses

(1) Many expenses of attorneys, such as rent and utilities, are similar to those of other professional persons. In addition to these similar expenses, an attorney often has expenses in behalf of a client.

(2) If the attorney's right to reimbursement is not contingent upon any event, though the timing of the reimbursement may be, then, as a general rule, the amounts expended on behalf of clients are not deductible in the year expended.

(3) If reimbursement is contingent upon successful completion of the case—a usual practice in personal injury actions—the amounts expended by the attorney would be deductible in the year expended provided they meet IRC 162's requirement of ordinary and necessary.

(4) If the amounts expended are for personal living expenses of the client and reimbursement is contingent upon successful completion of the case, there is authority for holding that the expenditures do not meet the requirements of ordinary and necessary under IRC 162 (W. Burnett, 356 F. 2d 755).

(5) The examiner should determine the proper treatment of expenses, advances and reimbursements in this area which will invariably require an analysis of the attorney's trust account.

(6) The examiner should satisfy himself/herself that any contributions to election campaigns of state, county and local officials have not been claimed as business expenses.

(12)60 *(8-30-76)* 4231
Engineers

(1) Engineers are usually subject to registration in the various States in order to operate on a professional basis. The work of the engineer is divided into several highly specialized fields and includes designing, estimating, supervising construction, and consulting, among other related activities. The major fields of specialization are civil, chemical, electrical, and mechanical engineering.

(2) Civil engineers make land surveys and maps, and generally plan and supervise heavy construction, such as buildings, roads, and bridges. Chemical engineers are called upon in the planning and operation of chemical plants.

(3) Electrical engineers are specialists in the electrical and electronic fields. Mechanical engineers design and supervise installation and operation of heavy machinery and heating plants.

(4) The income of professional engineers consists of fees which are usually received according to the terms of a contract. A written contract should exist between the engineer and his/her principal for each job undertaken. The contract should include a description of the services to be rendered, an estimate of the time required to perform the work, and the terms for the settlement of the fee.

(5) Fees may be received upon the completion of work or when it is delivered and accepted, or progressively as the work is completed. It is not unusual to find that the engineering services on long-term contracts are paid for according to the percentage of completion of the job, or in installments over the period of the project.

(6) Engineering firms may report income by the cash receipts and disbursements method, or by the accrual method, where they are engaged in an engineering capacity and are not functioning as the general contractors. In the latter case, the methods of accounting available to contractors would be available.

(7) Generally, the larger engineering firms report income by the accrual method. The accruals are usually computed by the percentage of completion method on long-term contracts or by the completed contract method.

(8) The examination of the accounts of an engineering firm presents no unusual problems. The contracts should be available for the verification of income, and the specific job costs can usually be related directly to the income items. Estimates of the percentage of completion of the jobs in progress at the end of the period are usually available for the verification of reportable income. In addition to the verification of income, there is one item which should be particularly investigated in the examination of an engineering firm. A reconciliation should be made of the amounts paid to engineer employees with the amounts reported on W-2 forms.

(12)70 *(8-30-76)* 4231
Architects

(1) The profession of the architect is in some respects similar to that of the engineer. The architect is employed to design buildings and to supervise their construction to see that it conforms to specifications. His/her income is derived from fees.

(2) The compensation of the architect is sometimes a fixed percentage of costs of construction. It is also based on direct labor costs plus an allowance for overhead, fees for consultants, etc. The compensation is usually paid in installments, the first payment being made when the contract is signed. Other installments may be received as the work progresses, with full settlement when the completed structure is accepted.

(3) There are occasions when the architect is issued stocks or securities in the corporation for which he/she has performed services. The examining agent should be aware of the possibility that this type of transaction has been negotiated.

(4) When contractors bid on the construction designed by the architect, they are usually required to deposit performance guarantees with the architect as security for the building plans and specifications used in making their estimates. The deposits are returnable to the contractor when the performance is completed. Until such time, the architect reports the deposit as a liability. The return of the deposit is not an expense.

(5) The architect may be called upon to make advances on behalf of his/her client, such as for the purchase of certain equipment which the client is obligated to furnish. This type of transaction is an account receivable until satisfied. It should not be charged as an expense.

(6) A large item of expenditure by architects is for blueprints and supplies. The costs of blueprints are usually charged to the cost of specific jobs.

(7) Usually contracts are signed with clients for the specific jobs, wherein the basis of compensation is defined. The examining agent should examine these contracts in connection with the verification of the fees recorded.

(8) Sources of information on the activity of architests include building permits issued, newspaper items on construction, and the examination of third parties.

(9) The accounts peculiar to architects are: Advances for clients, fees to engineers and consultants, and blueprints. These items are usually charged to the specific costs of jobs for which the expenditures were made or to accounts receivable.

(10) Income may be reported by the cash receipts and disbursements method or by the accrual method, in cases where the architect's income is purely from fees. Where the architect is also engaged in contracting, the methods available to contractors are available to him/her, i.e., the percentage of completion method, or the completed contract method.

(11) The examination of the return of an architect does not generally present any features not found in other types of business. The agent should be alert to any indication that reported income does not include all fees received. The examination of the expenses deducted follows the general procedures of other types of examination.

(12)80 *(8-30-76)* 4231
Funeral Directors

(1) In examining the income of funeral directors, public records are available in determining whether income from all funerals have been reported. Death certificates, executed by physicians or coroners, are filed with a Bureau of Vital Statistics or Public Health Department. Also permits for removal or burial of the bodies of deceased persons must be issued by public officials upon each death. Obituary news in local papers may state the name of the undertaker.

(2) The charges made by the undertaking establishment to the account of a funeral are for the following items:

(a) sale of caskets and vaults;
(b) sale of clothing;

(c) compensation for services rendered;
(d) reimbursement for cash outlay.

(3) One basis of charges is for specific items of service rendered, such as the price of the casket, the use of the chapel, limousines, casket bearers, etc. But a more prevalent basis of charges now in use is the setting of an all-inclusive price covering every essential detail, based on the cost of the selected casket plus other articles supplied and the value of various services rendered. The style of the casket is used as the basis for unit prices charged. The style and cost of a casket can be used as an indication of the amount being charged for the funeral services. The profit on the casket is the chief source of income, even though billing is usually made as a flat price for the complete service. Income may be received from the sale of the deceased person's clothing.

(4) Cash outlays are made for certain items, and are charged to the account receivable for reimbursement. Items such as newspaper advertising, cemetery fees, burial clothing, hiring of pallbearers, rental of vehicles, transportation of decedent by air or rail, and honorariums to ministers represent typical items for which cash outlays are made.

(5) Often the undertaking establishment is paid by the survivors of the deceased by tendering an insurance check for the proceeds of a life insurance policy. This may be in excess of the total funeral charges, and the excess is refunded to the beneficiary of the policy by the issue of a check by the undertaker. A test of the refunds should be made by the agent to verify that such check issued is not entered as a deduction. There have been instances where this has occurred. A reconciliation of cash receipts with bank deposits and with income recorded may reveal that cash receipts include the insurance checks, but the recorded income is not in balance with the receipts by the amount of the excess of the insurance checks over the funeral charges. Yet the refunds may be deducted as an expense item. This method results in an unallowable deduction of the amount refunded.

(6) The inventories of a funeral director include caskets, casket materials and supplies, embalming supplies, and miscellaneous supplies. The most significant item in the inventory is the caskets.

(7) In examining the returns of a funeral director, the revenue agent should be aware that there may be death certificates filed without corresponding burial permits, and vice versa. This comes about through deaths of visitors or of residents who are buried in other places than the city of the funeral director. Where items such as advertising, cemetery fees, pallbearers, etc., are being deducted as expenses of the undertaking establishment instead of being charged to accounts receivable, the examiner should make sufficient inquiry to determine that reimbursement was not made to the undertaker for those items in addition to the charges for services. Normally, such items are charged to accounts receivable and not to expense.

(8) Arranging for funeral services prior to death and the payment of so-called preneed funds to the funeral director is a growing practice. The examiner should determine that the funds received as well as income earned on the funds are properly handled for tax purposes.

(12)90 *(8-30-76)* 4231
Real Estate Brokers

(1) Real estate brokers engage in the management of properties for landlords and in the sales of real estate for owners. A percentage of the rents received or of the selling price of the property is received by the broker for his/her services. An agency relationship exists between the broker and his/her principal.

(2) Examiners should be aware that brokers often receive property other than money for their services, such as second deeds of trust. A determination should be made that such receipt is properly accounted for as well as any interest received on the other property.

(3) A real estate agency often is licensed by one or more insurance companies to write fire, automobile, and casualty insurance.

(4) Some real estate brokers, in addition to the above activities, buy real estate for resale on their own account or for investment purposes. Under these circumstances the examiner will often have to determine whether the real estate sold was purchased by the broker for resale, or whether it was originally purchased for investment. Where the sale is claimed as a capital transaction, the agent should require the submission of proof by the taxpayer that the property was not purchased primarily for resale. Very often the properties are purchased to be held until a satisfactory sale can be effected. In the meantime, the property is rented to a tenant and depreciation is claimed. It should be borne in mind that the deduction of depreciation is not determinative of intent.

(5) The agent should be alert to situations which would in fact be rentals with options to purchase. Examination of contracts will usually reveal the true intent of the parties. An examination of the broker's copies of sales agreements and settlement sheets will assist in determining when sales were consummated, thus indicating when commissions should be included in income.

(6) Sources of information on real estate dealer's transactions are records of deed transfers, mortgages, title company records, banks, mortgage companies, and savings and loan associations. Where a broker deals on his/her own account the financial establishments usually have statements of his/her net worth in their files. These statements may be useful in verifying that the broker's activities are properly reflected in his/her records.

(7) Where the broker also sells insurance, additional accounts will appear in his/her records reflecting accounts receivable from policy holders and accounts payable to insurance companies.

(8) The insurance companies require their agents to render monthly "Accounts Current" reflecting the issue and the cancellation of policies. The premium charged, commissions earned, cash received, and balance due are recorded for each policy issued. A carbon copy of the "Account Current" is retained by the broker, and is often referred to as the policy register. This register provides a means of verifying the insurance transactions. There should be a monthly policy register for each insurance company represented.

(9) Also see Techniques Handbook for Specialized Industries—Construction and Real Estate, IRM 4232.7.

(12)(10)0 *(10-30-79)* 4231
Income from Bartering

During every examination of an individual, partnership, corporation or other business entity, examiners should be alert to the possibility of "bartering" or "swapping" techniques or schemes. See text at 667 of this Handbook for areas of possible tax abuse.

Operating Ratios-Sole Proprietorships

(14)10 *(8-30-76)* 4231
Introduction

In screening and examining Form 1040 business returns the agent should have a knowledge of the operating ratios germane to specific businesses. To assist the agent operating ratios for a number of businesses are provided in exhibits at the end of this Handbook. The operating ratios set forth in the exhibits are to be used for information purposes only. *Under no circumstances should they be used as a basis for proposing adjustments or referred to in the examination report or referred to in discussions with a taxpayer.*

(14)20 *(8-30-76)* 4231
Use of Exhibits

(14)21 *(8-30-76)* 4231
Format

(1) The operating ratios for each year, beginning with 1967, are provided through the use of two exhibits. Exhibit 18 is an index by industry code of the various businesses for which operating ratios are included in Exhibit 19. Exhibit 19 contains all the operating ratios that are provided for a given year.

(2) The operating ratios for each business are shown on a separate page of an exhibit. To provide an easy means of identification, the first page of an exhibit is identified by the exhibit number only. Each succeeding page is identified by the exhibit number plus a continuation number. For example, Exhibit 19—Cont. (1) represents the second page in Exhibit 19; Exhibit 19—Cont. (2) represents the third page in Exhibit 19.

(3) All percentages are based on Gross Receipts which is expressed as the base (100%).

(4) A dash (—) in the exhibits indicates no entry on the tax returns sampled in the Gross Receipts class or that the amount expressed in dollars would be de minimis. No entries appear for samples of less than 600 businesses.

(14)22 *(8-30-76)* 4231
Explanation of Terms

(1) The following explanations of terms are designed to aid the user in interpreting the statistical content of the exhibits.

(a) *Gross Receipts*—Generally, these are reported net of return goods and allowances. Some taxpayers include sales and excise taxes collected in gross receipts and deduct the taxes as expenses, while others report their receipts after adjustments for any taxes. Included in gross receipts are incidental income items such as sale of scrap or cash rebates.

(b) *Professional Fees*—This deduction includes fees paid to attorneys, accountants and other professionals. Also included are amounts paid for subscriptions to professional publications and membership fees or dues to professional organizations.

(c) *Commissions*—This deduction includes payments to salesmen in lieu of salaries and wages and to brokers and agents for services connected with real estate, insurance, securities and other financial transactions. Forms 1099 are generally filed reporting these amounts.

(14)30 *(8-30-76)* 4231
Source of Information

(1) The source of the information contained in the exhibits is the Sole Proprietorship Tax Model as compiled by the Statistics Division from Federal Income Tax Returns filed.

(2) The operating ratios are pure mathematical averages based on the number of businesses shown in each category and the total dollar amounts reported by them.

(3) It is important to remember that these operating ratios may vary widely from operating ratios quoted in various other publications. These ratios are based on information on tax returns actually filed, and together with information on businesses from other sources may be helpful in gaining an insight on similar businesses examined.

(4) Due to changes in the grouping businesses, operating ratios for one year may not be comparable to ratios issued for another year.

(14)40 *(8-30-76)* 4231
Other Published Information

(1) Several publications containing information on operating ratios are published on a periodic basis which may be of value. Two of these publications are:

(a) *"Expenses in Retail Businesses,"* The National Cash Register Company, Dayton, Ohio 45409.

(b) *"Barometer of Small Business,"* Accounting Corporation of America, 1929 Fifth Avenue, San Diego, California 92112.

(3) Occasionally the agent may encounter a third party who is willing to furnish the desired information, but requests the issuance of a summons as a safeguard in order that he/she may not forfeit the business or friendship of the person under investigation. This frequently occurs when banks are requested to furnish information with respect to one of their customers. The agent should secure and issue the requested summons under what is generally referred to as a "friendly basis." The internal revenue agent is given authority to issue a summons in Reg. 301.7602-1. IRM 4022 sets forth the procedures for preparing, issuing and serving it.

(4) If the examiner encounters a third party or witness who is reluctant to furnish information or unwilling to testify, and the information is of sufficient importance in the investigation, and cannot be obtained by other means, the examiner should first discuss the problem with his/her group manager.

(5) Relating to caution to be exercised in the issuance of summonses, the examiner should carefully read IRM 4022.3 and 4022.4.

(21)90 *(8-30-76)* 4231
Available Records in Other Districts

(1) Occasionally an agent may need information which is located outside of his/her district or outside of his/her immediate examining area. If this is the case, the agent may obtain the desired information by requesting a collateral investigation from another district or by another revenue agent.

(2) The information requested in a collateral examination may include any number and kind of determinations needed by the agent. Requests may be made for the determination of the worthlessness of corporate securities, determinations and facts on specific transactions, interrogations of third parties and requests for the examination of related returns, such as partnership and fiduciary returns, which affect the taxpayer's distributive share of income.

(3) The examining agent should not hesitate to request a collateral investigation when the desired information is pertinent and cannot be secured by other means. The collateral investigation procedures are in IRM 4597.

(21)(10)0 *(8-30-76)* 4231
Referrals to Engineers

(1) In general the revenue agent is responsible for all features in the examination of a return. However, engineering personnel are available in the Internal Revenue Service to handle special features in cases involving engineering issues. The referral of these special engineering problems to engineers is covered in IRM 4216.12. Some of the engineering problems for which the revenue agent may deem it desirable to request the assistance of an engineer are:

(a) depletion deductions of $5,000 or more;

(b) depreciation deductions of $75,000 or more;

(c) gains or losses upon liquidation, sale or exchange or other disposition of property, including claims for loss of useful values (other than securities), having a claimed value of $50,000 or more;

(d) depreciation allowances in excess of normal depreciation based on plant activity, regardless of the amount of allowance claimed;

(e) valuation of properties denoted as war loss recoveries;

(f) extraordinary deductions for repairs which properly represent major capital expenditures;

(g) losses of $5,000 or more claimed as a result of worthlessness of mineral value; and

(h) exploration costs of $50,000 or more.

(2) Whenever engineering services are utilized, examiners and other Audit Division personnel are required to follow the recommendations with respect to engineering issues embodied in the report of an engineer unless:

(a) departure therefrom is authorized in writing (with reasons therefor) by the Chief, Field Audit Branch, or by the Chief, Audit Division, in those districts not having a Field Audit Branch organization, or

(b) the findings of the engineer are changed as a result of a district conference.

(3) The revenue agent may also request the services of an engineer agent where the taxpayer relies on the use of an engineer with respect to determinations or contentions in examinations and it appears especially appropriate that the services of an engineer in the Revenue Service be obtained to advise the agent with respect to such determinations or contentions.

(4) If a taxpayer in the course of an examination requests that the examiner refer engineering issues to engineering personnel in the Revenue Service, the Chief, Field Examination Branch, or Chief, Audit Division, may at his/her discretion comply with or disapprove the request and shall advise the taxpayer in writing of his/her action.

(21)(11)0 *(8-30-76)* 4231
Valuations

(21)(11)1 *(8-30-76)* 4231
Fair Market Value

(1) Numerous sections of the Internal Revenue Code make reference to the term "fair market value." Due to the significance of this term in the revenue agent's work and the frequent need by him/her to make valuation determinations, a basic understanding of both the meaning and methods by which fair market value determinations can be made is of considerable importance. In some district offices trained personnel have been assigned to handle the complicated valuation problems. In others, all valuation determinations are the responsibility of the agent to whom the return was assigned for examination. This section is intended to assist the revenue agent in the approach to solving a fair market value problem.

(2) The fair market value of property can be defined as the price at which the property would change hands between a willing buyer and a willing seller when the former is not under compulsion to buy and the latter is not under any compulsion to sell. Court decisions frequently state, in addition, that the hypothetical buyer and seller are assumed to be able, as well as willing, to trade and to be well informed about the property and the market for such property. The determination of the fair market value is a question of fact and will depend on the circumstances in each case. No formula can be devised that will be generally applicable to the many valuation issues that may arise. Often the examiner will find wide differences of opinion about the fair market value of a particular item. In resolving such differences the examiner should maintain a reasonable attitude in recognition of the fact that valuation is not an exact science. A sound valuation will be based upon all the relevant facts, but the element of common sense, informed judgment and reasonableness must enter into the process of weighing those facts and determining their aggregate significance.

(21)(11)2 *(8-30-76)* 4231
Real Estate

(1) The valuation to be recommended for real estate is that shown by the weight of competent evidence. This does not mean, for example, what the property would bring at a forced sale or the price for which it is sold when the vendor is in need of money or the vendee has some motive in acquiring the property which would induce him to pay a price in excess of what he would pay, under normal circumstances, for similar property. The test in all cases is the price at which the property would change hands between a willing buyer and a willing seller, neither being under any compulsion to buy or sell. In the absence of actual sales in the ordinary course of business, the matter of valuation is largely one of opinion, and for this reason the examiner must exercise sound judgment.

(2) In making inquiries relative to the valuation of real estate, the revenue agent should consider the following.

(a) Sales of comparable property which conclusively establish the value of the property under examination.

(b) The local tax assessment records, as well as the method of assessment. This is a frequent procedure to use in the allocation of price between land and building (a common depreciation problem).

(c) The opinion of competent, disinterested real estate people who are familiar with the property at the valuation date.

(d) One indication of fair market value may be the assessed value adjusted by use of equalization rates. The examining agent may secure such rates from Equalization Boards maintained by some counties, cities and towns. These Boards determine the ratio of assessed valuation of local assessors to market value.

(e) The valuation of real estate may often be related to rental rates. In many localities annual rental for residential and some commercial property would be expected to be about 10% of purchase price or value of real property. As an example, the annual rental of property with a cost of $12,000.00 would be $1,200.00. Conversely, where the rental rate is known, one indication of fair market value of the property would be an amount equal to 10 times the annual rental. Sources of information in addition to local real estate brokers and banks, particularly in case of manufacturing facilities would be the local Chamber of Commerce, which may keep current lists of available space with the related rental rate. Information which helps to determine a fair rental may be particularly useful in cases where the lessor and lessee are related parties. Also, when property used for personal purposes is converted to rental or business use, rental rates may be helpful in determining fair market value at time of conversion, which value if less than cost would be the basis for depreciation and would limit loss on sale.

(21)(11)3 *(8-30-76)* 4231
Stocks and Bonds

(1) There are three different classes of stocks and bonds for which it may be necessary to determine fair market value, namely:

(a) *Listed stocks and bonds*—The fair market value of a listed stock or bond at a particular date can be determined from the quoted prices as ascertained from the stock exchanges. The mean between the high and low sales price on the valuation date can be taken as the fair market value. If there were no sales on the valuation date, the value should be determined by prorating the difference between the mean of sales on the nearest dates before and after the valuation date.

(b) *Unlisted, but active securities*—Stocks and bonds which are listed, but are dealt in through brokers or have an over-the-counter market, should be valued as in the case of listed securities if there were sales on or within a reasonable period before or after the valuation date. If there were no actual sales the value should be determined by taking the mean between bona fide bid and ask prices on or within a reasonable period before or after the valuation date.

(c) *Securities of a closed corporation*—In the valuation of a security of a closely held corporation or one where the market quotations are either lacking or too scarce to be recognized, all available financial data, as well as all relevant factors affecting the fair market value, should be considered. The following factors, although not all-inclusive, are fundamental and require careful analysis in each case:

1 the nature of the business and the history of the enterprise, including the date of incorporation;

2 the economic outlook in general and the condition and outlook of the specific industry in particular;

3 the book value of the stock and the financial condition of the business;

4 the market value of the assets;

5 the earning capacity of the company;

6 the dividend-paying capacity;

7 goodwill;

8 sale of the security and the size of the block of security to be valued; and

9 the market price of securities of corporations engaged in the same or a similar line of business which are listed on an exchange.

(d) *Open-end Investment Companies (a type of "mutual fund")*—The rules for valuation of such shares for Estate and Gift Tax purposes are provided in Rev. Proc. 64-18, 1964-1 C.B. 681. Such value becomes or affects the basis for determining gain or loss on later disposition. Beginning with October 11, 1963, the fair market value of a share in an open-end investment company is the public offering price of a share, adjusted for any reduction in price available to the public. Valuation of shares prior to October 11, 1963, on basis of redemption value or the means between redemption value and public offering price will not be disturbed, provided that in Estate Tax cases if requested by the District Director of Internal Revenue, a collateral agreement is furnished by all interested parties that the value so determined will be treated by the executor and all distributees as the tax basis of any shares so valued.

(21)(11)4 *(8-30-76)* 4231
Works of Art

(1) There has been a trend among taxpayers to purchase works of art with the intention of immediately contributing them to charitable institutions. Deductions are then taken on tax returns for an amount based on an appraised value which is far in excess of the cost to the taxpayers. Upon the examination of a tax return with a deduction for a contribution for a work of art too much emphasis can be placed on the fact that an expert appraisal was submitted to substantiate the deduction and not enough consideration given to the evidence surrounding the history of the asset.

(2) If a contribution is made in property other than money, the amount of the deduction is determined by the fair market value of the property at the time of the contribution. The fair market value is the price at which the property would change hands between a willing buyer and a willing seller, neither under any compulsion to buy or sell and both having reasonable knowledge of relevant facts. However, the fact that an appraisal has been submitted does not necessarily mean that it is synonymous with the fair market value. In making an appraisal, an appraiser may take into consideration the purpose of the appraisal and this purpose may be reflected in the appraised value. An appraisal is no more than the appraiser's opinion or estimate of value which may be used when value cannot be determined by more exact means. Of course, such evidence is useful information; but should not be followed blindly, and should be weighed in the light of other facts developed in the case. The taxpayer has the burden of showing that the appraisal is reasonable.

(3) An example of this tax avoidance scheme follows: A gallery sold a painting to B gallery for $8,000; B gallery sold it to Mr. Art Dealer for $9,500; Mr. Art Dealer sold it to the taxpayer for $49,000; and the taxpayer contributed the painting to a museum and deducted $95,000 on his return as a contribution. All four of these transactions took place within 30 days.

(4) The taxpayer would have to show how the valuation could have increased from $9,500 to $49,000 and then to $95,000 in less than a month, and also show that the transaction was at arm's length. Normally, this would not be a reasonable rise. In a rare case where there has been a true rise in value there would be a definite identifiable event which would account for the rise, such as the discovery that a so-called copy is in reality an original; the removal of a veneer reveals that a masterpiece has been discovered; or the death of a contemporary artist. Unless there is a definite identifiable event, an increase in value would take place gradually over a period of years.

(5) In the example, the $49,000 could be the price paid, not only for the painting, but also for an excessive appraisal fee and perhaps a fee for initiating the tax avoidance scheme. Therefore, this would not be the fair market value of the painting by itself. The sales at $8,000 and $9,500 were sales between experts and would more closely fit the actual fair market value. The best measurement of fair market value is an actual sale at arm's length reasonably close in time to the date of valuation.

(6) Prior history of the asset should be checked when substantial deductions are claimed for contributions of property other than money to qualified organizations. Although the nearest arm's length sale within a reasonable period of time to the date of donation is generally the best evidence of the fair market value, all available evidence should be considered. Unless there is strong evidence to the contrary, the nearest arm's length sale within a reasonable period of time will be presumed to be the fair market value. If available evidence shows that the taxpayer's purchase of the asset was at arm's length, the deduction would be limited to the taxpayer's cost. In the example, this would be $49,000. If available evidence shows that this was not at arm's length, it would be necessary to go back to the next prior sale, if within a reasonable period of time, which may limit the deduction to less than the taxpayer's cost. In the example, this would be $9,500.

(7) There are publications which list the results of auction sales of works of art. One may not find in these publications a sale listed for the exact work of art under consideration, but it is possible these publications may show a sale of an artist's work that closely matches the donated work. These publications may be referred to in libraries, museums, and offices of art dealers. Two of these publications are *Art Prices Current*, printed by Loxley Brothers Limited, Sheffield and London; and *World Collectors Annuary*, printed in the Netherlands.

(8) IRM 4216.3 contains procedures for securing assistance in valuing works of art in significant cases involving indicated tax abuse or wide divergence of opinion as to fair market values.

(21)(11)5 *(8-30-76)* 4231
Other Types of Property

The determination of the fair market value of other types of property which may include partnerships, sole proprietorships, business interests, royalty interests, patents, leaseholds, notes and mortgages will depend on the facts and circumstances in each case. The factors to be considered will vary depending on the type of asset involved. For example, many of the factors as listed under closely held corporations will be applicable to the determination of other types of business interests. The useful life and expected return will be prime considerations in valuing royalty interests, patents and leaseholds. The value of notes and mortgages will normally be worth the unpaid amounts at the valuation date unless evidence to the contrary is established by the taxpayer. Since no general formula can be devised, the examining agent should develop all relevant facts to meet the particular determination of the case under examination.